SCHOOL CHOICE

SCHOOL CHOICE

THE MORAL DEBATE

Edited by Alan Wolfe

PRINCETON UNIVERSITY PRESS   PRINCETON AND OXFORD

KH

Library of Congress Cataloging-in-Publication Data

School choice : the moral debate / edited by Alan Wolfe.
p. cm.
Includes bibliographical references and index.
ISBN: 0-691-09660-0 (alk. paper)—0-691-09661-9 (pbk. : alk. paper)
1. School choice—Social aspects—United States. 2. School choice—
Law and legislation—United States. 3. Educational equalization—
United States. 4. Politics and education—United States.
I. Wolfe, Alan, 1942–
LB1027.9.S336 2003
379.1′11—dc21   2002074904

British Library Cataloging-in-Publication Data is available.

This book has been composed in Palatino

Printed on acid-free paper.∞

www.pupress.princeton.edu

Printed in the United States of America

10 9 8 7 6 5 4 3 2 1

11/22/04

Contents

SCHOOL CHOICE AND SOCIAL ECOLOGY

SCHOOL CHOICE AND THE LAW

Acknowledgments ────────────────

Mark Steinmeyer of the Smith Richardson Foundation immediately saw the value of a series of discussions devoted to the moral and normative aspects of school choice. His support, and the resulting support of his organization, made possible the conference at which drafts of the essays contained in this volume were first discussed. I thank him for that support.

Two graduate students—Kim Kosman of Boston College and Thornton Lockwood of Boston University—were instrumental in seeing the project through to completion. Kim's help with the original proposal, and her passsion for the ideas involved in the school-choice debate, started the whole process. And when she moved on to other, and more important work, Thornton took over and made the whole thing possible. I was lucky to have them with me.

The staff at the Boisi Center for Religion and American Public Life, especially Susan Richard and Patricia Chang, were helpful in so many ways that I long ago lost track. And I thank the support of Boston College for hosting the conference and, indeed, for hosting me.

Alan Wolfe
Chestnut Hill, Massachusetts
November 2001

SCHOOL CHOICE

Introduction _____

ALAN WOLFE

I

After a long period during which the minds of most Americans turned to other matters, questions of education are now very much a central concern to them, both as parents and as citizens. Many of the issues that have begun to dominate the news and the speeches of political candidates have a long history behind them, such as school discipline, testing, character education, and issues of income and racial inequality. Accompanying them, however, has been a concern with school choice that suggests a departure from previous debates. Whether hailed as a needed kick in the pants or condemned as a radical attack on public schooling, school choice is a new terrain involving new ideas, new figures, new alignments, and new solutions.

Because it is so controversial an idea, school choice has generated an impassioned debate. A good deal of that debate involves questions of effectiveness. Scholars on different sides of the issue challenge one another's methodologies, findings, and, alas, motives. That is, except perhaps for motives, as it should be. Eventually the dust will settle, the statistical evidence will point one way or another, or perhaps both, and minds will (or will not) be made up. But it is also important to remember that questions of effectiveness are not the only questions raised by a greater emphasis on parental choice. Ideas about choice, like ideas about education throughout all of American history, touch on fundamental questions of our public philosophy: the kind of people we want to be, the requirements for economic and racial equality, the nature of the institutions we wish to see flourish, and our ideas about private and public character.

The essays assembled in this volume explore those aspects of the school choice controversy that touch on these essential moral, normative, philosophical, and religious concerns. This book seeks to broaden public attention and to further the public debate by addressing questions such as School choice for what? and School choice for whom? Both advocates and opponents of school choice at times get so involved in their criticisms of each other that they tend to neglect the fact that school choice, like all kinds of schooling, is intimately connected to issues involving the nature of the person, citizenship, and the purposes of political life. Although school choice remains a "new" issue, many of the voices in the debate, on all sides, have become predictable, suggesting that is perhaps time to hear from even newer participants. In particular, we need to look to moral philosophers, theologians, and historians—even those who have not written on school choice before but whose concern with issues of equality, pluralism, and fairness has been long established—to offer guidance on an issue as contentious as school choice. School choice is too important an issue to be left solely to economics and educators.

II

To provide a better grasp on the moral and normative dimensions of school choice, this volume is broken into four sections. One deals with issues of equality; a second with issues of pluralism; a third with the relationship between schools and other institutions that constitute the "social ecology" of society, such as families, churches, and neighborhoods; and a fourth with legal issues, especially, but not exclusively, with the relationship between school choice and First Amendment issues of religious establishment and religious freedom.

School Choice and Equality

Whether public or private, religious or secular, elementary or secondary, schools in America have understood their mission less as the transmission of timeless wisdom and more as the means by which those lacking economic advantages could raise themselves up, through schooling, in ways that would enable them to pass on those advantages to their children. To be sure, not all American educators were in agreement on these goals; as Diane Ravitch's book *Left Behind* shows, there long existed in America a group of educators who emphasized the need for schools to introduce students to the life of the mind. But such critics, Ravich also demonstrates, have became forgotten voices as a consensus formed among professional educators to stress the role that schools ought to play in helping pupils adjust to the practical circumstances of everyday life.

So strong is this consensus that most critics of schooling these days, especially those on the left end of spectrum, do not object—however problematic they may find other aspects of schooling—to the tendency of schools in America to promote practical advantages over intellectual discipline. Their point, rather, is that schools too often fail to achieve the objective of promoting equality that they say constitutes their primary justification, but reinforce instead the inequalities of capitalism. The same could be said of those who have criticized schools for the persistence of racial segregation within them. The essence of their criticism is usually not that segregation per se is bad, for under some circumstances they would defend the advantages of all-minority education; it is instead that segregated schools condemn those who attend stigmatized schools to greater risk of failure in a market-driven economic system.

When the idea of school choice was first introduced, questions of equality did not play much of a role among advocates, but they did among critics. Those who believed that the introduction of marketlike mechanisms into schooling was a bad idea often emphasized that vouchers would result in lower levels of public support for already underfunded inner-city schools and in that sense would harm the opportunities of the poor pupils who attended them. Carrying forward the consensus around the notion that the purpose of education ought to be one of furthering the goal of equality, they concluded that vouchers represented one mechanism among many that middle-class Americans often use to avoid their obligations to the poor. In this phase of the debate over school choice, the usual political terms held: the "right" was in favor of the market, while the "left" emphasized the importance of the state. No one who would have predicted at the time that eventually arguments for equality would become the major arguments in favor of school choice would have been taken seriously.

In his book *Choosing Equality*, as well as in his chapter in this volume, Joseph Viteritti asks the question of how we can justify allowing middle- and upper-class parents to choose schooling for their children without extending the same right to those who lack economic means. He also asks the same question with respect to choices involving religion, insisting that it is wrong for society to prevent parents from choosing a religious education for their children solely on the grounds that they cannot afford the cost. The debate over school choice, Viteritti believes, has shifted from one stressing freedom to one emphasizing equality. If he is right, a new set of issues are raised that require careful attention.

Those questions have already begun to be asked. Will school choice result in "skimming"? Should poor urban children be given vouchers while vouchers are withheld from their lower-middle-class peers? Should suburban parents be excluded from school choice on the grounds that they have mobility? Does the egalitarian defense of choice turn the property-tax-financing system of schools into an open question? Will the future politics around school choice change as the issue moves from one emphasizing freedom to one stressing racial equality? What do debates about school choice teach us about the American preference for freedom over equality? Joseph Viteritti, Stephen Macedo, and I all try to address questions like these in our essays; we do so in different ways and come down on different sides of the debate. But what unites all three essays is the sense that school choice has entered a new terrain in which questions of justice and fairness will dominate the discussion.

School Choice and Pluralism

The debate over school choice cannot be separated from larger questions of the appropriate role that schools should play in sustaining common ideas about national cohesion. America became the first country in the world to create a comprehensive system of public schools, at least in part because the American nation, unlike the French or British nation, was so young and composed of people of so many different nationalities. Without cohesion fashioned through an established church, without the grandeur of a literature that could extend back in time to Shakespeare or Milton, without a monarchy and its royal patronage, Americans created their nation consciousness through more modern means, including the use of schools to insist upon what were, despite the lack of an established church, essentially Protestant moral ideals.

From the first moment of substantial non-Protestant immigration to the United States, the question of whether schools should insist on commonality or encourage pluralism and diversity has been repeatedly posed—and never satisfactorily answered. Meeting hostility toward their religion and way of life, Catholics eventually opted to create a system of parochial schools. Jews, by contrast, resisted, until very recent times, a similar move and became enthusiasts for public education. When issues of racial equality came to America, they came in controversies over schooling; *Brown v. Board of Education*, in insisting on the unconstitutionality of segregated schooling, adopted the ideal of common values, but in more recent times the popularity of Afrocentric curricula suggests a move in the other direction. Americans are strongly committed to the integrationist and assimilationist nature of public schools, but also do not object if distinct religious or ethnic communities want to form their own schools and programs, so long as they do not, in the process, undermine generally consensual ideals.

Unexplored in these debates over pluralism is the question of school choice. If America moves in the direction of greater choice, including vouchers, will the result be greater respect for diversity? Or, in fact, will it be the opposite, greater public regulation of private schooling?

Aside from the important question of what might happen, there is also the question of what ought to happen. Should we encourage school choice because we want to encourage diversity? Or if we are truly committed to diversity, ought we to resist school choice? The essays in this volume by Meira and Sanford Levinson, Amy Gutmann, and Nancy Rosenblum address these questions. They do so, moreover, by concentrating not so much on ethnic or racial identity, but on religious pluralism, appropriately so because religious differences have, throughout the course of American history, been our most conflictual.

One does not have to agree fully with Louis Hartz to conclude that America was fashioned in the image of Lockean liberalism. The idea of individual rights, although it does not place emphasis on the priority of government over the individual, is crucial to the way Americans define their common ideals. Amy Gutmann and Nancy Rosenblum find the concept of school vouchers problematic to the degree that vouchers would enable parents or religious communities to impose their authority over the authority of the rights of individual members or those of the future citizens their children will someday be. Gutmann reminds us that pluralism, in and of itself, ought not to be the first virtue of schooling; a liberal-democratic society can insist on the importance that schools attach to liberal-democratic values. In her writings, especially in *Membership and Morals*, Nancy Rosenblum is a strong advocate for pluralism; in her essay for this volume, however, she argues that school choice and pluralism are not the same thing and that, indeed, children who attend schools chosen by their parents, especially if those schools are committed to only one way to the truth, may not be introduced to pluralistic ideals at all. Finally, Levinson and Levinson argue for the educational benefits that flow from the presence of a more diverse study body, an argument that leads them to conclude, against Gutmann and Rosenblum, that religious schools may be more deserving of vouchers than nonreligious schools are.

School Choice and Social Ecology

Schools are one of many institutions, including churches, families, unions, and business corporations, in our society. One of John Dewey's contributions to education was to emphasize the institutional character of schools. Yet Dewey was somewhat tone deaf to real-life institutions, preferring to think of schools—or churches, for that matter—in ideal terms. It is preferable, in thinking through the implications of school choice, to focus on actual institutions, for it has become clear to thinkers from all over the political spectrum that the institutions which exist in "civil society" are being transformed under pressures from both the market and the state.

While there has been a discussion of the effects that school choice might have on the institutional character of schools, there has not been sufficient attention to what might be called the "ecology" of institutions throughout American society. All schools, in a sense, including public schools, are part of civil society, for although public schools receive funding from the government, they also rely on voluntary associations like PTAs and PTOs. (Indeed, the question of whether such organizations are in decline has been a central element in the debate over civil society). In that sense, schools are like families, neighborhood institutions, and churches. If they flourish, so does society. If they atrophy, civil society is indeed in trouble.

We know very little about the effects that a greater emphasis on school choice would have on the voluntary character of American society. On the one hand, if school choice, by moving away from top-heavy public bureaucracies such as school systems in favor of charter schools or independent schools, would seem to promote those institutions that lie between the market and the state, in that sense it would have positive consequences for civil society. On the other hand, vouchers have often been linked to the market so completely that the emphasis on free choice they promote could undermine civil society by encouraging a kind of selfish egoism that disregards the needs of others. Choice, after all, is not necessarily a good in and of itself. We may believe that parents ought to be as free as possible in choosing schools for their children. Marital choice is another term for divorce. It is perfectly plausible to argue in favor of school choice because it will help children but against marital choice because it will harm them. But that is just another way of saying that because choice may be good in one area of life does not mean that it is good in all.

As with pluralism, religious institutions play a particularly important role when we think about the institutions that constitute our social ecology. In Europe, each country has usually established one religion as its official faith; America, no doubt due to its Protestant character, has placed a much stronger emphasis on the voluntary nature of church and sect. We have usually believed that religious institutions flourish best when left to the individuals who build their churches, collect the funds, publish the newsletters, and attend the Bible study groups. Since the question of school vouchers is so often linked to the question of whether religious schools will and should receive public funds, it is impossible to discuss the issue without considering whether vouchers would strengthen or weaken the voluntary character of America's religious institutions. Arguments can be made on either side. Would an infusion of public funds into Catholic and evangelical schools restrict their freedom to teach the very religious principles they believe essential to education? Or are they so vital to the country that they ought not be punished by being denied the public support given to just about every other kind of voluntary association in America?

Charles Glenn has been one of America's leading commentators on this issue. In his chapter for this volume, he turns to the experiences of other countries to show that their religious institutions have not been corrupted by the receipt of public funds. The Dutch experience is in many ways the most relevant here, for Holland has been the leading Western country to finance its welfare-state activities through public support for voluntary organizations. Richard Mouw knows the Dutch situation at first hand and presents his view of the lessons it contains for Americans in his contribution. Finally Joseph O'Keefe, S.J., turns to the United States and the specific question of how and in what ways Catholic schools would and should benefit from the introduction of vouchers. While there is no particular agreed-upon point of view uniting these three authors, their conclusions tend to be more sympathetic to the idea that school choice would strengthen the social ecology of American life than those in the contributions of Rosenblum and Gutmann.

School Choice and Law

As Tocqueville noted long ago, America's political questions eventually become legal ones. So do America's moral questions. And, if one can even presume to bring Tocqueville up to date, all moral and legal questions in America eventually seem to involve children and the schools they attend. If any of the issues that are addressed in this volume are ever to be resolved, it is likely to be the courts that resolve them in the context of decisions about what students ought to learn and who should have the authority to teach them. In the meantime, some of the most serious thinking about America's moral, religious, and normative concerns is done by legal scholars in the form of legal questions.

The reason that legal questions are so central to the debate over school choice is that schools have always played such an important role in the promotion of common values. In the absence of a strong state, schools became the public institution par excellence in America, and since the function of the law is to lay down rules by which public institutions will be guided, the schools, for all their voluntary character, especially in the twentieth century, have had their decisions reviewed by courts. Can states compel all students to attend public schools? Should schools teach morality and, if so, whose morality should they teach? Can they require students to say prayers just as they say the pledge of allegiance? If so, should those prayers be to a specific god or to a generalized one? How should religion be taught in schools? Should it be taught after school or incorporated into the curriculum? Should those activities deemed too religious to take place during school hours be allowed to take place in school by after hours? At football games? At graduation ceremonies? Are schools under an obligation to respect the religious rights of non-Christians? Of nonbelievers? Since children are too young to make their own choices, should their parents choose for them? If they do, can they violate the rights those children would have as adults? The range of legal questions the courts have had to address involving the schools has been truly astonishing.

When the issue of school choice is overlaid on an already complicated—and often contradictory—jurisprudence, the difficulty of drawing firm guidelines increases. A number of advocates for school choice believe that choice without the ability to choose religious schools would hardly be a choice at all. (This explains why choice advocates in places like Milwaukee have relied on private sources of funds, thereby avoiding constitutional issues.) Were the U.S. Supreme Court, when it finally enters the area of school choice, to rule definitely against any voucher proposals that enabled parents to use public funds to send their children to religious schools, whatever remaining voucher proposals existed would attract neither many applicants nor much intellectual excitement.

The chapters by Martha Minow, Rosemary Salamone, and Michael Perry make clear that while religious issues are central to the legal debates over school choice, they are not the only constitutional issues that will need to be considered by the courts as they enter this thicket. Salamone reminds us that the notion of choice gives preference to private actions, but the question of what is actually private is a complicated one that affects many areas of constitutional inquiry. On the other hand, school choice is also, as Minow and Perry show, intimately connected with the Fourteenth Amendment's commitment to equality before the law. These three authors raise a series of at least crucial questions: Should the principle of choice be overridden if the consequence is racial segregation? Should the commitment to public schooling be overridden if the consequence is a violation of an individual's right to decide with dignity how best to live? Because these questions have no easy answers, we can be sure of one thing: Should school choice ever gain greater public support and be widely adopted as a public policy in America, the constitutional and legal questions it will raise have only just begun to be addressed.

III

On September 25, 2001, the Supreme Court granted certiorari and consolidated three cases (*Zelman v. Simmons-Harris; Hanna Perkins School et al. v. Simmons-Harris et al.*; and *Taylor, Senel, et al. v. Simmons-Harris et al.*) arising from the establishment of the Ohio Pilot Project Scholarship program in 1995 in Cleveland. The scholarship program provided tuition vouchers (paying up to $2,250) to the parents of students in Kindergarten through eighth grade for use at participating schools, whether public or private. No public schools elected to participate in the program, and of the fifty-six private schools that participated in 1999–2000, forty-six were church affiliated. On February 20, 2002, with advocates on both sides of the question peacefully demonstrating outside its chambers, the U.S. Supreme Court heard oral argument in the consolidated Cleveland school voucher case. On June 27, 2002, the court ruled that the voucher program in Cleveland was constitutional.

As this case suggests, no one expects the issue of school choice to disappear from American politics any time soon. To be sure, school choice turned out not to have the irresistible force that many of its critics assumed it would have; in their view, America's commitment to capitalism was so strong that people would rush out to embrace choice in schools, an event that never happened. The 2002 U.S. Supreme Court decision, however, has given the pro-voucher forces new momentum. Indeed, it is likely that just at the moment when conservatives find themselves unable to build support for the idea, African American support for that decision will give the issue new life.

Focusing on the moral and normative aspects of school choice will not result in any immediate consensus; after all, disagreements about constitutional issues are as deep as those over pedagogy and economic methodology. That is why this book seeks no such premature closure over the questions it asks; its contributors range the gamut in religious views from evangelical Protestant to Catholic, Jewish to atheist, and they come as well from all points on the political spectrum. Authors were invited to state their positions with both passion and clarity. In addition to the essays that were commissioned for the volume, four commentators, with backgrounds in philosophy, legal theory, and theology, were asked to focus on the implications of the issues raised in each of the book's sections. The objective has been to to get behind the headlines over school choice. It is important not to forget that never-ending debates take place in American education because we have always made schools so central to the question of the kind of society to which we aspire.

SCHOOL CHOICE AND EQUALITY

One

Defining Equity: Politics, Markets, and Public Policy

JOSEPH P. VITERITTI

WE ARE NOW IN THE SECOND GENERATION of debate on school choice. During the first generation, discussion focused on the economic goal of market efficiency. Proponents of the market approach have a dismal outlook on the condition of education. They place primary blame on a monopolistic system that limits government support to public schools, where 90 percent of our students are enrolled. They advocate a radical restructuring of education so that parents would be able to send their children to nonpublic schools at government expense. They believe that market competition would result in a better quality of education for all students, winnowing out low-performing institutions as parents are able to select from a wider array of offerings.[1]

The second generation of discussion has focused on an opportunity model. Advocates of this approach define the problem in education more sharply, and see choice as a mechanism for improving educational opportunities for underserved communities, primarily low-income racial minorities whose children attend failing schools. Rather than make government supported choice available to all, proponents of the opportunity model—now more popular among reformers—would target vouchers to disadvantaged children.[2]

There is empirical support for both perspectives. Although education spending in the United States has risen by more than 60 percent in real dollars since 1970, student performance on national exams in reading has remained stagnant and math scores have improved only slightly.[3] The results of tests administered by the National Assessment of Educational Progress indicate that 60 percent of our twelfth graders are below proficiency in reading. This suggests that our system of schooling is not only inefficient, but also ineffective. Some scholars claim that standardized tests of this sort are not a fair measure of how our schools are doing,[4] but the statistics are difficult to ignore.

Even more difficult to ignore are disparities in educational achievement between the races. The learning gap between black and white students has been a matter of public record for several decades.[5] Although there were encouraging signs that this gap was closing during the 1980s, a report released by the U.S. Department of Education last year showed that the disparity was growing again in the 1990s.[6] Today the average black twelfth grader reads with the same proficiency as the average white eighth grader; there are similar gaps in math, science, and other subjects.

These racial disparities paint a different picture of American education. Instead of whole-scale breakdown we see a system of education that is serving some students and not others, or perhaps two systems— one that works fairly well and another that does not seem to work at all. The dichotomy is defined not only by race and class, but also by place. A national survey conducted by *Education Week* shows that nearly two-thirds of the students in suburban and rural public schools meet or exceed standards on national exams in reading, math, and science, compared to 40 percent of their peers in urban schools.[7] Education failure in the United States is largely, though not entirely, an urban phenomenon.

The gap is not just a matter of efficiency and effectiveness. It also has normative implications for our ideals as a democratic nation. So long as black and white children enjoy dramatically different levels of educational achievement, there can be no real hope of attaining social, economic, or political equality between the races. Education is correlated with nearly every positive social attribute imaginable, from economic security, to civic participation, to a healthy family life.[8]

As a result of their more focused attention on disadvantaged populations, advocates of the opportunity model have laid claim to the high moral ground of the choice debate. There is validity to their claim, but it is overstated. Liberal social scientists are apt to draw cartoonlike caricatures of market schemes, exaggerating less-attractive features while understating more-positive attributes. These pictures entertain sympathetic colleagues, but confuse the uninformed.[9] Conservative social thinkers have contributed to the negative images with theoretical tracts that attempt to treat greed as an enlightened virtue.[10] There is no virtue in greed, but the market has intrinsic and extrinsic merits worthy of attention. For one, the opportunity model could not work effectively without relying on the market.

There are different ways to define equity when designing choice programs, and each has unique consequences in determining who gets rewarded. What is apparent under the present arrangement is that some parents enjoy the opportunity to choose the schools their children attend, and some children get assigned to schools whether or not their parents want them there. It is also clear that the difference between those who have choice and those who do not is associated with race and class. Choice is not just a question of who can afford tuition for a private school. The matter is more subtle, also determined by residential mobility that allows the better off to select a home in a community with decent public schools.[11]

It is difficult to believe that the great numbers of African American and Hispanic children who attend failing inner-city public schools are there because their mothers and fathers want them there. They are there because they have no choice. For reasons that go beyond considerations of test scores, their predicament is fundamentally unjust. In this sense it may seem that any form of choice is better than no form of choice. But based on what we already know from ongoing choice experiments, that assumption is open to dispute. My objective in this chapter is to explore a variety of approaches to school choice and explain why I believe some are more compelling than others.

The Market Model

Most social scientists trace the market model to an essay written by Milton Friedman in 1955. The Nobel Prize–winning economist laid out a far-reaching voucher plan designed to replace the public education system with one characterized by universal choice.[12] Friedman predicted that competition would lead to the elimination of failing public schools, and that the availability of public dollars for private institutions would increase the supply of new schools.

Foreseeing charter schools that would come thirty-five years later, Friedman contemplated nonprofit institutions like the YMCA and the Boy Scouts (not controversial then) running schools alongside for-profit companies (still controversial now). While he welcomed the involvement of public schools in the competitive stakes, he seemed to have little doubt about the eventual outcome of the contest. Friedman's ultimate vision of education in America was to supplant the existing school system with a marketplace of schools that were publicly financed and privately run. Others would see his vision as a plan for the demise of public education.

Friedman explicated his thinking in a book brought out in 1980, that was more moderate in tone and political in content.[13] In it the disciple of Adam Smith develops a normative argument that is informed by Jefferson's notion of human equality, Tocqueville's appreciation for the tension between liberty and equality, and the classical liberalism of John Stuart Mill. The highest value in Friedman's regime is that of individual freedom. It flows from a conception of equity defined as equality of opportunity, or what political theorists refer to as *une carriere ouverte aux les talents*, rejecting a more positive government role associated with the modern liberal state in achieving equality of results.

By today's nomenclature Friedman's conception of the proper balance between liberty and equality is a conservative one, but contrary to the image projected by some opponents, it is not simply a mechanistic system devoid of humanistic values. George W. Bush would probably call it "compassionate conservatism"—an intriguing term not just for its attempt to recast the political right, but also for the reaction it gets from those on the left, who like to believe that compassion is theirs alone.

Friedman focuses attention on educational disparities inherent in the status quo; he explains the superiority of suburban schools over urban, and the failure of public education to meet the needs of racial minorities. He predicts that his universal voucher scheme will have differential effects, benefiting the rich hardly at all, the middle class moderately, and the poor enormously. Thus, for Friedman, getting rid of the educational monopoly not only promotes economic efficiency, but it has social consequences. The perpetuation of the bureaucratic monopoly is portrayed as a political problem. The argument is best illustrated with a direct quote from his book:

> What is most important to understanding the ability of the educational establishment to resist change is the fact that public school systems are protected public monopolies with only minimal competition from private and parochial schools. Few critics of American urban education . . . dare to question the givens of the present organization of public education . . . or the relevance of all (this) to the objectives of public education—to produce literate and informed citizens to carry out the business of democracy.
>
> A monopoly need not genuinely concern itself with these matters. As long as local school systems can be assured of state aid and increasing federal aid without the accountability that inevitably comes with aggressive competition, it would be sentimental, wishful thinking to expect any significant increase in the efficiency of our public schools.[14]

These are not Friedman's words. Nor are they borrowed from Adam Smith. They are quoted by Friedman from an article that appeared in the 1968 edition of the *Harvard Educational Review*. The author was Dr. Kenneth Clark, the psychologist whose persuasive testimony before the U.S. Supreme Court in *Brown v. Board of Education* moved the nation to outlaw racial segregation in the nation's public schools.

In 1990 two political scientists took up the charge, challenging the institutional structure of American education. John Chubb and Terry Moe's *Politics, Markets, and American Schools* was a significant contribution to the debate for several reasons.[15] First of all, the Chubb and Moe book furnished empirical support for several of the premises inherent in Friedman's model: the academic superiority of private schools over public schools, the detrimental effects of bureaucratic organization on school performance, and the incorrigibility of the monopolistic system. Chubb and Moe's book also drove the choice issue into the mainstream of the national policy debate on education. However, as an item on the reform agenda in 1990, choice failed to garner significant political support beyond the Republican Party and those identified with the conservative cause.

In some ways Chubb and Moe's proposal was more modest than Friedman's. They envisioned not a fully privatized system of education, but one in which private schools would compete with public schools for students who were given publicly supported "scholarships." While endorsing a universal system of choice, they recommended that scholarship amounts be higher for poor and at-risk students. Anticipating the charter-school concept first enacted into law in Minnesota a year after the publication of their book, Chubb and Moe recommended that the public education system should be restructured in order to maximize managerial autonomy at the school level. In a concession to constitutional arguments, they suggested that each state should set its own policy regarding the eligibility of religious schools to participate until the question was settled by the federal courts.

Even though Chubb and Moe's plan was designed to be more politically acceptable than Friedman's, it would stir more controversy. Part of the problem was their language. Although they consciously avoided the "voucher" word, Chubb and Moe cast their argument as a choice between democracy and the market. They asserted that "democratic control threatens to generate a vicious circle of problems and ineffectiveness."[16] This wording fed allegations by critics that the market approach was not just amoral but also antidemocratic.[17] A more careful reading of the book shows that it was not democracy per se that the two political scientists were bothered by, but rather the way the democratic process had been dominated by organized interests. They explained the problem as a dichotomy between "constituents and consumers," meaning that decision making was controlled by groups that did not represent the best interests of students.[18] The "interest group" paradigm had been a prevalent influence in the political science discipline for decades. Chubb and Moe were the first to suggest (at least in the education arena) that the ugly sores it exposed in the democratic process could be healed by the market.

It did not take a great leap of imagination for critics to conclude that Chubb, Moe, and their market approach were antigovernment, confirming fears that the net result of their plan would be the elimination of public schools.[19] Ironically, the "evacuation thesis" purported by choice opponents gave credence to the idea that more democratic decision making was anathema to the institutional framework of public education. It was these critics, after all, who alleged that if families were allowed to abandon the public schools, they would, in large numbers. Conversely, one had to conclude that the sole reason why students remain in public schools is a lack of choice. Public education may be the only sector of the economy in which the providers' lack of confidence in their own product is used as an argument against offering an alternative.

A second argument put forward by market antagonists is more persuasive. Here the argument, in contradiction to Friedman's claims, is that a universal system of choice would have differential effects that penalize disadvantaged populations.[20] There is solid evidence from public choice and magnet programs to support the thesis. It shows that middle-class parents are generally more informed, more aggressive, and more capable in securing the best placements for their children, and that poor children are left behind. Although valid, these claims are somewhat exaggerated in the present context. Choice opponents fail to recognize that the same competitive social advantages are operable in public schools without choice, exacerbated by the fact that the better off have the private means to opt out of the local system when it no longer suits their needs. Nonetheless, what is often referred to as the "skimming" or "creaming" thesis has merit. We will return to it later.

The Opportunity Model

The most fully developed of the early equity-based proposals was that put forward by John Coons and Stephen Sugarman in 1978.[21] The two law professors from the University of California brought different credentials to the choice debate—not because of their legal training, but for the paramount role they had previously played in the fight for educational equity. Their seminal scholarship on spending disparities between rich and poor school districts was responsible for launching school-finance-reform efforts in California that led the way for similar campaigns across the country.[22] One possible way of dealing with spending and educational inequity, they suggested, was to provide poor parents with funds to send their children to private schools. It was not market efficiency that inspired Coons and Sugarman, but the pursuit of social justice. Given their previous writing and advocacy on behalf of poor parents, it was difficult for choice opponents on the left to impeach their motives. Most instead ignored their proposal.

Although Coons and Sugarman originally (1970) conceived of choice as a mechanism to promote equality, their fuller treatment of the subject (1978) explained how equity would advance freedom. Understanding the central role that schools play conveying social values and the ideological diversity among schools, they saw choice as a way to assure parents that their children were educated according to their own values. Thus as market advocates perceived equality and liberty to be in tension, those who adopted an opportunity approach to choice saw the two values as complementary. Where the former embraced choice as a form of economic empowerment, the latter embraced it as a form of political empowerment.

Although they addressed parental philosophy as a relevant aspect of the choice debate, Coons and Sugarman devoted little attention to the matter of religion. It is one thing to select a school because you are attracted by the thinking of Maria Montessori or E. D. Hirsch, quite another to pick a school because it reflects your religious values. Religious values are more fundamental. Public schools cannot accommodate religious values very well. At times public schools have been insensitive or even hostile to the beliefs of devout observers.[23] For many devout observers who regard education as an instrument for instilling faith-based values, a public education is either irrelevant or counterproductive. Despite the recent ruling of the Supreme Court approving vouchers, there remain deeply debated constitutional issues associated with providing aid for children to attend religious schools. These questions cannot be addressed in the present essay.[24] It is important to note, however, regardless of constitutional constraints, that without vouchers only those with private means can acquire a religious education for their children. In this way, choice can be more broadly conceived as an issue of religious liberty.

Coons and Sugarman's book did not offer specific policy recommendations. Instead it laid out several options that might be the basis for social experiments.[25] The authors did, however, take specific exception to a feature in the Friedman plan that would allow parents to supplement public vouchers with private payments for higher tuition at some private schools. This offended the sense of equity that animated their earlier school finance initiatives. They warned that Friedman's proposal would frustrate the goal of modifying the connection between private wealth and educational quality, in the end supplementing the economic privileges of the wealthy with public subsidies in the form of vouchers. Coons and Sugarman also rejected Friedman's idea of a voucher that would pay less than the full cost of private school tuition. Their position remains consistent: Last year again they campaigned against a California voucher initiative on the grounds that the amount of the voucher under consideration was too small to accommodate those families most in need.[26]

Coons and Sugarman were among many choice supporters on the left, including the Catholic bishops of California, who regarded the statewide initiative as retrograde, especially in light of more progressive plans that had been enacted in Wisconsin, Ohio, and Florida.[27] The Wisconsin program, first adopted in 1990, then revised in 1993 to include religious schools, was specifically designed to target low-income students in Milwaukee. One of the more remarkable aspects of the Wisconsin episode was the unusual blend of the political alliances that converted the bill into a law. The coalition included African American activists, business leaders, free-market advocates, a Republican governor, and a Democratic mayor.

The passage of Wisconsin's innovative law was living proof that the political constituency for vouchers was growing. In practical terms, choice was no longer the sole province of the political right. Similar coalitions were responsible for the passage of the voucher bills in Ohio and Florida. The Ohio plan, available to a wider population of students in Cleveland, gave priority to low-income families. The Florida program, implemented statewide, targeted its vouchers to children who were attending chronically failing schools.

In many ways the Florida plan served a similar population as the two that preceded it, since there is much overlap among race, income, and educational achievement. The distinct approaches, however, have varying implications regarding the equity question, which we will take up shortly. At this point there is a more significant observation to be made about what the various targeted programs have in common and how they differ from the market model. Although never explicitly described as such by it their proponents, targeted voucher programs are a form of redistributive public policy that has historically been identified with the modern liberal state. In order to achieve a common public good in the name of equality, targeted vouchers provide disadvantaged people with public resources so that they can acquire essential private goods that are usually available only to the more advantaged.

In a lesser sense, it could be argued that universal market programs are also redistributive. Even though such plans provide vouchers to everyone, they do succeed in giving poor families access to private markets who before did not have access. Of course, as Coons and Sugarman explained, the level of access is determined by the size and nature of the voucher. And again, it is arguable whether any form of voucher is better than no form of voucher.

Also striking is the common ground shared by the two camps in the way they view education. That the left views educational opportunity as fundamental to a free and equal society has been apparent at least since the U.S. Supreme Court decided *Brown v. Board of Education* in 1954. That the right views education similarly is less apparent—partly because the left is loath to admit it, partly because the right is disinclined to do the same. At times the two camps seem to be in collusion in presuming that moral high ground is naturally located on the left side of the political terrain. Since Wisconsin, the right has gotten better about this. I want to make the point more explicitly.

Even as free-market advocates call for a diminished governmental role in promoting social equality—challenging the welfare state and a redistributive social agenda—there is little dissension within their ranks regarding the need to provide everyone with a decent education at public expense. What is sometimes referred to as privatization is usually a process of contracting out public services to private providers, paid for by and accountable to a public authority.[28] True privatization would limit government actors to a much-reduced regulatory function, as is the case in the automobile or airline industry. It is not the suppression of public schools by private schools that is at stake in the choice debate. It is rather a redefinition of what is meant by a public education.

Although market advocates like to pretend that it is competition that empowers poor people, it is really the redistribution of public resources by the government that empowers the poor by allowing them to participate in the market. Left to its own devices, the market is not a friend to the poor. Anyone who has driven through a depressed inner-city neighborhood dotted with boarded-up storefronts knows that. And the poor know it better than anyone. Simply stated, the market responds to money and people who have it.

The ongoing public controversy about vouchers must seem surreal from the perspective of our least-fortunate citizens. On one side there are political leaders and public intellectuals from the right promising that educational salvation can be found in the market. On the other, their antagonists from the left preach that poor children should remain in public schools, as if they were defending a higher public good. All the while, many of the preachers (elected officials included) send their own children to private schools, or live in communities where the public schools bear little resemblance to the urban public schools they demand for others.[29]

What We Know

In addition to the publicly supported voucher programs operating in Milwaukee, Cleveland, and Florida, there are numerous private scholarship initiatives designed to provide choice for children whose parents cannot afford tuition payments in nonpublic schools. Thirty-six states and the District of Columbia also have charter school laws that expand the range of public school alternatives. One by-product of all this experimentation is a substantial body of empirical research documenting how choice works under differing circumstances.[30] In only the last five years the choice debate has been transformed from a conversation about abstract policy models to a discussion of the evidence. As with all policy debates, there has been a tendency on both sides to read the findings to suit their respective agendas. Still we know a great deal more now than we did before.

First, we know that there is a significant unmet demand for expanded public and private school choice. The demand is evident from the long waiting lists associated with most public voucher, private scholarship, and charter school programs. Most of the demand is prompted by parents' motivation to flee failing schools and find more desirable educational opportunities for their children. A smaller part reflects the inclination of some parents to have their children educated in schools with a religious orientation. Sometimes the religious motivation is specific to a particular faith, sometimes not. It may be that some parents believe there is a connection between the strong value-structure found in parochial schools and their higher level of academic achievement. Coleman had asserted this more than twenty years ago.[31] I think many poor parents agree, but I cannot prove it.

Public opinion polls consistently show that there is strong support for vouchers and other forms of choice in African American and Hispanic communities. This is fairly easy to understand. It is minority children who routinely get assigned to failing schools, and most do not have the means to exercise choice on their own. Less appreciated by social scientists is the attraction that religious institutions have for many African American and Hispanic parents.

Support for choice among the general public is more evenly divided. Many middle-class parents, especially those in the suburbs, are content with their public schools and view choice as a potential threat to public education.[32] If we are to take these parents at their word, there does not seem to be an immediate risk of mass evacuation from public schools, although the response in urban areas is likely to be more dramatic. In 1999, when the Children's Scholarship Fund, a private foundation, announced that it would make 40,000 partial scholarships available to low-income students, it received 1 million applications. In New York City, nearly one-third of those eligible applied. It is quite telling that so many poor families were ready to abandon a free education in their local public schools and assume responsibility for up to half the cost of private-school tuition.

The evidence on the so-called skimming problem is encouraging but mixed. Designing programs targeted at disadvantaged students goes a long way toward eliminating a racial or class bias among the beneficiaries. Research from private voucher programs shows, however, that when parents are expected to assume part of the responsibility for tuition, the poorest of the poor are excluded from participation. Also, those poor parents who exercise choice tend to be slightly better educated than those who do not. Research from public charter schools that take students either on a first-come, first-served basis or by lottery shows that their students are generally representative of the population in their districts. In those cases where a racial disparity exists, it is usually weighted toward minority students. The latter pattern is consistent with the higher demand for educational alternatives from minority communities.

The waiting lists associated with public voucher and charter programs are also a function of public policy. Most publicly supported choice programs, whether they be vouchers or charters, limit the number of schools and students that can participate. (The Florida voucher plan is a notable exception.) These limitations make it nearly impossible to truly assess the impact that market competition could have on public school performance. At the behest of powerful choice opponents, most of these laws have been written to constrain competition. The constraints are also apparent in the funding provisions of laws. The average charter school receives 80 percent of the per capita government funding that a regular public school in the same district would receive. Funding disparities can be greater for voucher recipients.

Cleveland is a notable case in point. Per-capita annual spending for children who attend regular public schools in that city is $7,746; children who attend charter schools there get $4,519; voucher recipients get $2,250. Public discussion around these disparities is distorted and confusing. Voucher opponents have argued in federal court that the low voucher amount provides students with an incentive to attend religious schools with low tuition costs. The same groups do not always acknowledge that it was they who lobbied the legislature to minimize the amount of the voucher. Market purists have claimed bragging rights that parochial schools can educate kids at "a fraction of the price," as if less spending on education is inherently commendable. School finance reformers who have taken the state to court for more modest disparities in interdistrict spending remained silent, suggesting that they place a higher priority on district equity than equity for students. The net result of these policies is to underfund programs that are designed to help those students who are most at risk.

This is the stuff of political compromise, imposing an opportunity cost on poor parents who dare to act in the interest of their children. The policy in effect undermines both efficiency and equity. Even with the artificial controls imposed on the market, there is evidence that competition has provided public schools in some jurisdictions with an incentive to improve,[33] but the evidence remains inconclusive. We will not know the full impact of market competition until it is allowed to function in a less encumbered fashion.

Lots of ink has been spilled on the battlefields of educational research over whether disadvantaged children derive academic benefits from the exercise of choice. The evidence from charter schools is quite mixed. The most encouraging reports from the public and private voucher programs indicate modest academic gains over short periods of time. Less-positive reports say there is no significant difference in the academic performance of "choosers" and their public school peers. Given the level of funding invested in these programs and the uncertainty imposed by constant litigation, it is quite an accomplishment for their students to do as well as their public school peers. It is not good enough, however, if choice is to help close the achievement gap between the races.

Surveys of parents whose children participate in public voucher, private scholarship, and charter programs indicate high levels of satisfaction. Parents are consistent in their responses about what they find and what they like in comparing the choice schools with their former public schools. They point to the higher expectations held for their children, the more rigorous academic standards, the more orderly environment, and the greater sense of safety. Many of those with children in religious schools claim that the religious values conveyed are a positive attribute.

There has long been speculation about whether poor parents are capable of making intelligent decisions on behalf of their children. The research evidence suggests that, while poor parents do not have the same advantages as their middle-class counterparts, they are sufficiently informed to make decisions that reflect the aspirations they have.[34] This suggests that low-income parents are more limited by the range of educational options made available to them than by their own ability to take advantage of new opportunities made possible by a robust agenda for school choice.

Policy Priorities:
Who, What, Why, When, How Much?

From what we know about the operation of choice programs thus far, there are three basic rules that apply for designing an equitable program: (1) target new opportunities to disadvantaged students; (2) assure that the amount of the voucher covers the full cost of tuition at nonpublic schools; (3) maximize the options so that competition is rigorous and families have a full range of public, private, parochial, and charter schools from which to choose. This being said, filling in the details of a program involves conscious decisions with important consequences.

The strongest argument for targeted choice over universal choice is that it helps counter class, racial, and educational biases in determining who benefits. Whether universal choice is preferable to no choice at all—or, more precisely, the status quo situation in which only the more advantaged have choice—is more complicated. Certainly universal choice improves the options for a large population of parents whose children are stuck in awful schools. And universal choice becomes more appealing when parents are guaranteed that publicly financed vouchers cover the full cost of tuition.

The real problem in implementing universal choice now is one of capacity. Even if the legislative constraints were removed regarding the number of children or schools that could participate, there would be an insufficient supply of seats available in private and parochial schools to meet the demand. This disparity between supply and demand raises the probability of disparate outcomes that can be addressed only through policy design. With equity as the goal, it is preferable to target benefits than to leave the distributive outcome to a system of "natural selection," in which some start out with certain advantages over others. In the end this kind of arrangement sets off competition between families rather than schools, and the least advantaged fare the worst.

Assuming that it is preferable under the current circumstances to target benefits to the disadvantaged, we next need to define what we mean by the disadvantaged. There are two models in operation. The Milwaukee and (to a large extent) Cleveland programs define need by income. The Florida program targets children who attend failing schools. As discussed earlier, there is an overlap in the populations that fall into these two categories. Nonetheless, they are not the same. Some low-income children are fortunate to find themselves in well-functioning public schools, and some middle-class (more probably, lower-middle-class) students end up in failing schools. The equity implications from the different models are even more significant than they first appear, for they are premised (consciously or not) on different concepts of educational opportunity.

The objective of the Florida model is to give every child a decent education measured in terms of traditional academic standards. The Milwaukee model is designed to equalize opportunity by income (and implicitly race) so that the poor are empowered to make a wider range of choices for their children than is usually possible. Admittedly the bulk of these educational decisions are motivated by academic considerations, but the plan also allows poor families to make educational decisions based on philosophical or religious considerations, as the middle class typically does. It grants poor parents a wider scope of both equality and freedom. For this reason the latter seems preferable, but again the outcome and its determination must turn on circumstances.

If adequate space were available to accommodate all poor children who wanted to opt out of the public schools, for whatever reason they wanted to do so, the Milwaukee model would go farther in assuring that poor families enjoy opportunities similar to the middle class. If, however, space were available to accommodate only part of the demand, then preference should be given to those poor students who attend failing schools. The premise here is that a sound education is so essential to living a good life in today's world that the state has a positive obligation to make one available to every child.[35] Indeed, all students need a sound education to enjoy the full benefits of a free society and any aspiration to economic, social, and political equality. On this there appears to be a consensus among partisans on all sides of the choice debate.

Even so, we must note, the immediate outcome of this distributive arrangement is not altogether satisfactory. There are still likely to be some less-privileged (lower-middle-class) children left attending low-performing schools who do not qualify for a voucher based on income. Unfortunately, the high incidence of failure in some school districts requires us to make such arbitrary determinations. But this alternative is preferable to a system that leaves so many more in failing schools as we do now.

Guaranteeing that no participant in a voucher program would be obliged to pay tuition at a private school will not resolve all the funding questions. Many parochial schools subsidize the costs of educating disadvantaged students with voluntary contributions, which keeps tuition artificially deflated. Some private independent schools have such high costs that their tuition far exceeds the average cost of educating a child in public school. Then there are the bulk of nonpublic schools in which the costs lie somewhere between those of inner-city parochial schools and public schools. Should financially stressed private and parochial schools be expected to assume part of the fiscal burden for educating society's disadvantaged children where public schools have failed? Should the state assume responsibility for sending poor students to extraordinarily expensive private schools?

Similar questions have arisen in debates over school finance reform. Residents of wealthy suburbs have been willing and able to pay exorbitant property taxes to give their children an expensive education, while those who live in "property poor" districts struggle to provide an ample one. The courts have generally backed away from equal funding remedies in favor of an adequacy standard. The adequacy standard has not been without problems, but it appears reasonable in light of the goal to provide every child with at least a decent education. That children who attend charter schools should receive the same level of funding as children who attend regular public schools is incontestable by most reasonable standards. Funding for private school vouchers is a slightly more challenging but not unresolvable puzzle.

Assuming that the per-capita expenditure for public school children is sufficient to provide an adequate education, as it should be, no private school should receive public funding in excess of that amount in a given district. The amount of a voucher, however, should be capped at the cost, not the tuition, of a particular nonpublic school. Relieving economically burdened nonpublic schools of the responsibility to make up the difference between operating and tuition costs should allow these financially strapped schools to better serve more children. The availability of public funding in excess of their present expenditures might encourage some of these schools to reexamine their cost structure to invest more resources for upgrading dilapidated physical plants, modernizing instructional equipment, and making teacher salaries more competitive. Public school advocates might be appalled by such a prospect; people who put the interests of children before those of any particular system of schools should be cheered. Elite private schools that already provide financial aid for disadvantaged students should be able to increase the number of scholarships they offer.

Redefining Public Education

What might the future hold under this roughly designed plan for educational equity? At minimum it would encompass a renewed public commitment to provide each child with a publicly supported education of choice, hopefully resulting in a better quality of education for all children. Such a system is preferable to one that provides only some with choice and far too few with a decent education. But there are still children who need to be accounted for in this plan. There are the children whose parents are not sufficiently motivated or informed to exercise choice on their behalf. There are also those lower-middle-class children in low-performing public schools who do not meet the income standard to qualify for a voucher. How will they be served?

The deus ex machina at this late stage of the story is a familiar if surprising one. It is the market. If competition is allowed to surge unfettered by politically imposed constraints on costs, price, and supply, three positive outcomes might be anticipated: Low-performing schools (public and private) will close, better schools will open, and government-run schools will improve. We do not have the evidence we would like to support these predictions because revolutionary competition has not been tried for elementary and secondary schools in the United States. The claim is an act of faith encouraged by miraculous signs of an afterlife in American education, if not the hard evidence that evolutionary social scientists would need to join the congregation. It is a faith not only in the market, but in public education—a belief that public schools can and will improve when given the proper incentives (and organizational models) to do so.

This is a sound basis on which to proceed, much more hopeful than the skimming scenario. The skimming thesis starts with the presumption that failing schools will be permitted to subsist and that somebody's children will be forced to remain in them. A story that begins on such a horrible premise is not heading for a happy conclusion. A more effective way to address the burden of an inferior education is to guarantee that failing schools will be closed. Therefore, as George Bush likes to say, "no child gets left behind."

This is a big promise, though. Here certainly our god is in the details. The obstacles to winning are so powerful that even the divine forces of the market are not quite up to the task. Their unlikely, but inevitable, ally is also a familiar player in the drama of educational reform. It is the state. In the tough world of education policy, market purity must be compromised. The state must set minimum academic standards for all schools that either directly or indirectly accept public funds—public, private, and parochial. Those which do not meet standards should lose their funding.

Such accountability should not be misconstrued as an invitation to impose the strangling form of regulation that currently characterizes public education. The appropriate model for the relationship between the state and the schools is a good charter school law that exchanges

autonomy for accountability: ensuring high academic standards, protecting the civil rights, health, and safety of all people within the school
community—children and parents, teachers and administrators. At the
same time this arrangement should allow religious schools to thrive as
vibrant faith-based institutions—unencumbered by the secular dispositions of those who would not choose them—so that they are a real
and distinct choice for families who want a religious education for
their children.

It is difficult to imagine what the marketplace of education will
eventually look like. While those schools within the nonpublic sphere
probably will grow from their current 10 percent market share, how
much depends on the response of government-run schools to the new
system. Hopefully, with proper support, a larger proportion of public
schools will be charter schools. As the system reshapes itself, it may
become more difficult to distinguish between public and private
schools except for those of the latter which are religious. Both spheres
would include a larger number of institutions run by nonprofit and
for-profit organizations.

With new options appearing, it is likely that a certain number of
families who previously resorted to religious schools—the ones with
an academic rather than religious motivation—will turn to other
places. There are already indications that charter schools are taking
students from Catholic schools in urban communities. The percentage
of schools run by religious congregations could possibly shrink. Or it
might not. The assortment of religious schools, however, is likely to
become more diverse and less Catholic (which schools now comprise
50 percent of the private schools, and 77 percent of the sectarian). We
can expect to see more Islamic schools in the city, and many black
Christian churches will be encouraged to start new schools or expand
existing ones—not to mention the likely appearance of an array of secular private schools formed around competing educational approaches
and philosophies.

The prospects are exciting. If properly designed and implemented,
school choice could offer more opportunities to more people without
penalizing anyone for exercising their options or compromising the
quality of the education they deserve. We are a long way, however,
from the promise of educational equality.

The definitive chapter in the story will be a political one. If the second generation of the choice debate is characterized by a policy agenda
designed to benefit the least advantaged members of society, perhaps
it is time to advance to the next stage, where a political consensus is
forged to do so. Although the political constituency for choice has ex-

panded over the last decade, its boldest support remains concentrated in our weakest communities. As with most issues of social justice, real movement on the political front will require a broader coalition of advocates that share a sense of outrage with an education system that offers different opportunities to different people and consigns poor children to failing schools. Right now some of the staunchest opposition to an equitable system of school choice comes from partisans who claim to have an affinity with the poor. That needs to change.

Two

The Irony of School Choice: Liberals, Conservatives, and the New Politics of Race

ALAN WOLFE

Freedom, Equality, and School Choice

Two different kinds of arguments have been advanced in favor of school choice. One, associated with those whom Joseph Viteritti calls the "first generation" of school choice advocates, speaks primarily about the economic advantages that accrue as schools become more responsive to the freedoms associated with the market.[1] "The interjection of competition would do much to promote a healthy variety of schools," wrote Milton Friedman in his famous 1955 essay on school vouchers. "It would do much, also, to introduce flexibility into school systems. Not least of its benefits would be to make the salaries of school teachers responsive to market forces."[2] Along similar lines, John Chubb and Terry Moe argue that governmental monopolies encourage teachers' unions, principals, and other agents of the institutional structure of school systems to engage in self-maximizing behavior to the detriment of parents as consumers of educational products. Like Friedman, Chubb and Moe emphasize the importance of freedom. "Choice," they write, "is a self-contained reform with its own rationale and justification. It has the capacity *all by itself* to bring about the kind of transformation that, for years, reformers have been seeking to engineer in myriad other ways."[3]

In the past decade or so, much of the discussion around school choice has shifted to arguments about equality. The problem with the public-school monopoly, from this "second-generation" point of view, is not economic inefficiency but social injustice. Once we recognize that middle-class Americans who use private schools or who move to the suburbs are essentially buying access to good public schools and paying the cost through taxes, so the arguments run, just about any standard of fairness demands equivalent choices for inner-city residents. What makes choice valuable is not freedom per se; it is instead a principle of justice which holds that no one should be deprived of an advantage available to others for arbitrary reasons. Second-generation arguments for school choice target underperforming schools for special public assistance; even if that assistance comes in the form of vouchers, it often resembles the redistributive policies favored by the left more than the self-interested policies often adopted by the right.

Given that the disproportionate number of those who lack the choices possessed by middle-class Americans are members of racial minorities, moreover, equality-based arguments on behalf of school choice, which are arguments for social justice in general, become arguments for racial justice in particular. The failure to make school choice more widely available constitutes an unacceptable double standard, it has been argued, in which those who already have choice are primarily white and those who lack it are primarily black, and one consequence of this injustice is a crisis in the schools borne disproportionately by members of one race.[4] As Felicia Wong has emphasized, there are two different moral discourses involved in school choice controversies, and the one utilized by African Americans and their supporters emphasizes such values as solidarity, duty, and caring as opposed to choice, opportunity, and rights.[5]

Americans, we have been told since at least the time of Louis Hartz[6]—who published his classic book on the subject in the same year that Milton Friedman made the first case for vouchers—value liberty above all other political goods. Except for the 1950s and its organization-man conformity, Americans have traditionally been viewed as individualistic, socially and geographically mobile, and entrepreneurial in spirit. This tendency to put freedom first, often lauded as a positive aspect of the American character, can also be portrayed in negative terms; in recent years, Americans have been described as distrustful of institutions and unwilling to recognize the requirements of community.[7] However expressed, the American commitment to freedom has implications for issues involving schooling; indeed, the extent of membership decline in those voluntary associations that grew up around schools—such as parent-teacher associations—has become a major chapter in the story of how Americans can take individualism too far.[8] Those data are subject to many and varied interpretations, yet few doubt that when it comes to fundamental values, Americans make freedom of choice one of their guiding principles. As Lipset writes, "Americans remain much more individualistic, meritocratic-oriented, and anti-statist than peoples elsewhere."[9]

Just as Americans are routinely described as individualistic and freedom loving, their commitment to equality has traditionally been viewed as more tenuous. To be sure, Tocqueville emphasized the American love of equality—and worried that it might result in a substantial diminution of liberty. Ever since, the American commitment to equality has often been viewed as more rhetorical than real. According to one study, for example, 71 percent of Americans in 1990 favored personal liberty as a value, compared to 24 percent who favored class equality, significantly different figures when compared to the attitudes of Western Europeans or the Japanese.[10] To the degree to which Americans appreciate equality, furthermore, they often mean equality of opportunity, a formulation that brings it more in line with individualism than equality of results, which could be viewed as antithetical to individual liberty.

When racial justice is added to issues involving social justice, the American reluctance to put equality first becomes that much more pronounced. Although there is a debate over how much progress has been made in race relations in the United States since the days of legalized segregation, there is little doubt that some forms of racial inequality, especially in wealth, and some forms of discrimination, particularly in housing, still exist.[11] Whatever the extent of those inequalities, it is also the case that blacks and whites differ on the question of what remedies ought to be pursued.[12] The most widely discussed example of these differences is the persistent opposition of whites to affirmative action, when compared to its support by blacks.[13] Those who believe that the United States has not made sufficient progress on these issues interpret such opposition as revealing "a growing willingness to move away from racial equality in the post–Cold War environment."[14] Americans, they conclude, profess to value social justice and equality, but they shy away from those concrete actions government can take to insure greater amounts of it in real-world institutions. Those concrete actions, furthermore, invariably involve educational institutions, which have become the focus for most of the litigation over affirmative action. Weakly committed to equality, when committed at all, white Americans, from this point of view, will be unresponsive to efforts to equalize opportunity through schooling, especially when they perceive those efforts as detrimental to the future chances of their own children.

If it is true that Americans prefer freedom to equality, two conclusions with respect to school choice ought to follow. One is that the public would, as a matter of course, support attempts to introduce the principle of school choice into the ways they think about education. The other is that to the degree they the public may still need to be persuaded that school choice is a good idea, arguments on behalf of freedom ought to be more attractive to them than arguments about equality or social justice. Yet the first of these propositions is, at least until this point, not true at all; the public has neither supported school choice when it has been on the ballot nor rushed with enthusiasm to endorse the idea in surveys. And the second of these propositions, as

I will argue in this chapter, also has little support; if anything, school choice, which has little appeal in the United States, is more attractive when the arguments on its behalf are framed by concepts of social justice and less so when they are framed by appeals to freedom.

School choice, in other words, provides a window for an exploration of American public values. Three implications follow from the way public attitudes toward school choice have developed. First, we may need to revisit the near-automatic assumption that Americans prize freedom over all other values, including equality; that formulation may hold in the economic sphere, but it does not necessarily apply in all spheres, including education. Second, the transition from first-generation arguments over school choice rooted in freedom to second-generation arguments rooted in equality suggests that despite public skepticism about the idea of school choice, the issue is unlikely to go away so long as racial minorities view school choice as a strategy to achieve greater racial justice. Third, school choice emerged from the right end of the political spectrum, not the left; should its identification with a politics of equality continue, it foreshadows a "new politics of race" that rearranges existing bundles of ideological concepts and the political coalitions that go along with them.

The Changing Politics of School Choice

School choice is a broad term that includes many ideas, such as magnet schools or inner-district choice, that are not especially controversial. But when school choice is meant in a narrower sense to include vouchers and, to a lesser degree, charter schools, it has never been popular in the sense that large majorities support the idea in surveys.[15] One of the reasons is that however important vouchers and similar policies are to their supporters and opponents, most Americans do not follow the controversies over them.[16] According to a study done by Public Agenda, for example, 63 percent of Americans know little or nothing about vouchers and 81 percent know little or nothing about charter schools.[17] Even in those states which have taken the lead in experimenting with school choice, such as Wisconsin and Arizona, Public Agenda found similarly low levels of knowledge about the idea.

This lack of knowledge about vouchers is itself an interesting finding that has received too little commentary. It is widely agreed that Americans do not follow the specific details of politics and policies.[18] Still, school choice ought not to be just an issue that concentrates the minds of policy wonks; it concerns children, and parents tend to profess deep concern for and interest in their children. If Americans are as freedom loving as they are generally portrayed, they ought to be in favor of doing everything in their power to advance the educational prospects for their children. To some degree they are; if the idea of school choice is considered capaciously to include private schools and residential preferences, it has been estimated that roughly 60 percent of American school children go to schools that were chosen by their parents.[19] Yet such concern with the prospects for one's own child does not translate into support for radically new public policies; when it comes to schooling, there seems to be an almost ingrained conservatism, understood as resistance to change, in the way Americans respond. Large majorities, for example, favor reforming existing schools compared to finding alternatives.[20] And when the idea of vouchers is explained to people, they respond favorably, but without any distinct zeal or enthusiasm.[21]

Vouchers, which represent freedom of choice in its purest form, remain preferred by only a minority of Americans. Polling data on vouchers, notoriously dependent upon how questions are worded, show a general lack of enthusiasm, as the relatively broad question asked by the Phi Delta Kappa/Gallup surveys demonstrates. "Do you favor or oppose allowing students and parents to choose a private school to attend at public expense?" the question reads. In 2000, 56 percent were opposed and 39 percent were in favor.[22] Other polls show different results, and some even show modest support for vouchers. A perceptible increase in support for the idea has taken place over the past few years; in 1993, 74 percent were opposed in the Phi Delta Kappa/Gallup survey and 24 percent were in favor. One advocate for vouchers, Terry Moe, contends, based on a 1995 telephone survey, that when people are given appropriate information about vouchers, support increases.[23] But there is also evidence that support peaked in 1999 and is now abating.[24] However the data are interpreted, there seems to be no powerful public demand behind the idea that government should provide funds to help parents choose schools for their children.

Part of the reason why vouchers are not all that popular may overlap with concerns about church-state separation. In response to President George W. Bush's creation of a government office on faith-based initiatives, the Pew Research Center for the People and the Press surveyed public attitudes toward church-state issues and discovered considerable concern about too close a connection between religion and politics: 68 percent worried that the president's plans might result in too much government involvement in religion; 60 percent thought that it might force people to take part in religious activities against their will; and 52 percent expressed the view that the plan would interfere with church-state separation.[25] These responses suggest that some of the opposition to vouchers, at least on the part of those who know some of the details of the issue, may involve concerns about public money going to religious schools that can be viewed as sectarian. To be sure, when it comes to school vouchers specifically, people say that they are more likely to support them when the wording of the question specifies religious schools as one of the options.[26] Yet only a minority of Americans (17 percent) would choose to send their own children to a religious school if they had public support.[27] There are few consistent patterns here, other than to say that Americans respect religion and would like to see it encouraged but worry that encouraging it, even indirectly, through government may be the wrong way to do it. What is certain is that courts, especially in Maine and Vermont, often express concerns about church-state issues, even when they have little problem with intrasystem choice.

Because charter schools rely less on the market—they are held to degrees of public accountability—they are usually understood as a less-radical alternative than vouchers.[28] Yet the distinct lack of enthusiasm in the public for vouchers extends to charter schools. As is the case with vouchers, Americans do not know that much about the issue; a slightly higher number of Americans say that they have not read about charter schools compared to those who say they have. When the principles of charter schools are explained to them, 47 percent remain opposed, compared to 42 percent who say they are in favor. Innately conservative, Americans resist freeing charter schools from state requirements for curriculum, although they are more in favor of allowing charter schools to experiment with the length of the school day and year. And 79 percent would insist that charter schools be accountable to the state the same way public schools are.[29]

As the data on charter schools indicate, parents generally know what they want from schools: high-quality teaching ranks the first (98 percent), followed by student discipline (89 percent), a good curriculum (89 percent), and decent class size (75 percent). Furthermore, when asked to rank in importance the purposes of public schools, Americans rate a decidedly individualistic objective—"to enhance people's happiness and enrich their lives"—lower than they do the distinctly communitarian objective, "to prepare people to become responsible citizens."[30] Americans, it would seem, continue to view schools as a public good more than as a private asset. By large margins, Americans believe that the purpose of schooling should be to provide a good education for students and good citizenship for the country. So long as those purposes are served, choice is not a high priority. And to the degree that it becomes a high priority, it is because choice is viewed as helping to bring about good education and good citizenship.

African Americans and other racial minorities share this same understanding of education as a means rather than an end, except their view leads to support for school choice, since the ends—effective schools, small classes, citizenship training—seem so unlikely to be achieved in currently existing inner-city public schools that radical means become necessary. This helps explain why African Americans and other minorities express higher degrees of support for school choice than do whites; typical of this pattern is a survey by Public Agenda, which showed that 46 percent of African Americans and 41 percent of Hispanics strongly support school choice, compared to 29 percent of the general public.[31] Furthermore, racial minorities are more likely actually to utilize school choice options such as vouchers when they are made available.[32] This is especially true of those African American parents who hold strong views about achievement and pass those views on to their children.[33]

Because minority support for choice is viewed as a means, it can be understood as tentative; were inner-city public schools to show dramatic improvements, support for vouchers would likely decrease.[34] Yet since inner-city public schools are unlikely to improve in the near future, the support for school choice by racial minorities stands out as the major exception to the general indifference to vouchers by the general population. Two aspects of this support are worth emphasizing. The first is that it has emerged spontaneously and, to some degree, against the leadership of civil rights organizations, which remain hostile to the idea. Public support for choice in minority communities may be even stronger than it appears; in other words, it takes some knowledge of the issue and some political independence to favor it. Second, strong public support for school choice among minorities means less support among majorities; the already relatively weak backing of school choice in the electorate in general would be even weaker if only whites were counted. Add considerations of equality to those of freedom, and support for choice, while not overwhelming, goes up.

Evidence for the proposition that it is not freedom, and freedom alone, that constitutes the appeal of school choice comes from two additional sources. One is the widespread lack of support for the single most individualistic form that school choice can take: home schooling. When asked whether home schoolers ought to have services made available to them that are already available to school children, most Americans, reflecting a sense of fairness, say yes. But it is also clear that a majority of Americans find something problematic in the idea that students should be encouraged not to interact with other children in public settings. Although questions are not routinely asked by polling organizations on the issue, a 1997 Gallup Survey indicated that 57 percent of parents thought that home schooling was a bad thing for the nation, a drop from 73 percent in 1985, but still a majority sentiment.[35]

A second source of evidence against the idea that freedom of choice trumps all other values when it comes to education comes from the ballot box. By one estimate, vouchers were put on the ballot twenty-two times between 1966 and 1999 and defeated on all but one of those occasions.[36] Indicative of the kind of hostile reaction school choice can face from voters was Proposition 38 in California, placed on the ballot in the election of 2000. Fashioned in a way to be as simple as possible, Proposition 38 offered a $4,000 voucher for every school child in California to attend a private or religious school. The amount, while barely sufficient to pay full tuition at the least-expensive schools, was none-theless more generous than were many other school choice plans. No income levels, moreover, were placed into the proposition that might have created administrative complications. In theory, Proposition 38 seemed designed to appeal to self-interest, since anyone, even those living in affluent areas, could have benefited from its provisions. Yet in practice, the initiative failed overwhelmingly, as 70.6 percent of the voters were in opposition, compared to 29.4 percent who were in favor. Moreover, Proposition 38 failed across the board. According to a *Los Angeles Times* exit poll, every single category of voter was against Proposition 38, including conservatives (51 percent), Republicans (53 percent), Blacks (68 percent), Catholics (69 percent), Latinos (77 percent), Jews (83 percent), and Democrats (85 percent).[37]

Many advocates of school choice, upset with the unrestricted wording of Proposition 38, did not support it, thereby contributing to its defeat. But that in itself indicates the ways in which Proposition 38 marked a transition from first-generation arguments over school choice to second-generation ones. As the *Los Angeles Times* analysis of the polls suggest, many Californians opposed the measure on the grounds that it was unfair and wasteful to give already wealthy parents an additional break they did not need.[38] This does not mean that the measure would have fared better had it targeted vouchers specifically for parents who could not afford private schools. In Michigan, a proposal put on the fall 2000 ballot targeted underperforming schools; in districts where two-thirds of the students failed to graduate, students would be eligible for scholarships worth approximately $3,300 to be used for private schools of their parents' choice. While not specifically targeted to poor communities, the proposal would, in effect, have eliminated the possibility of vouchers for suburban parents, since suburban schools generally graduate students on time. Yet Michigan's school choice proposal also failed to pass, this time by a margin of 31 percent to 69 percent. Vouchers, when put to the test of the ballot box, simply cannot command significant majorities, or, more frequently, any majority at all.

The conclusion to be drawn from both surveys and recent electoral results is that vouchers are unlikely at any time to win substantial public support. Proposition 38 in California in particular seems to suggest that appeals to self-interest—which, given the generally accepted American preference for freedom, ought to generate widespread support for school choice—do not, in fact, work. Is there more support for vouchers when equality arguments take precedence over freedom arguments? Despite the Michigan vote, which suggests that reframing school choice to downplay pure market considerations does not increase levels of support, there is nonetheless reason to conclude that the issue fares somewhat better as an issue when framed in terms of racial justice than when framed in terms of choice. The reality is that those voucher experiments which do exist—and which furnish the bulk of the empirical material for arguments about whether they work—can be found in urban districts such as Milwaukee and Cleveland and are the result of activism on the part of minority advocates.[39] If vouchers have any future in America, it will be because of support from inner-city parents and community activists, not from suburbanites, who tend to be fairly satisfied with their schools.

Whatever its future as a viable political issue, then, the political arguments that surround vouchers are unlikely to return to a first-generation emphasis upon pure freedom of choice; as Viteritti summarizes the point, Friedman-like arguments "have become outmoded" because school-choice advocates must recognize the need "to improve the lot of the poor so that their level of opportunity more closely resembles that which is available to the middle class."[40] The rhetoric around school choice has changed; Bulman and Kirp correctly characterize this change: "The growing importance of choice in educational policy is partly explained by the way advocates have been able to characterize their ideas, creating a more sympathetic picture by shifting the conversation away from an emphasis on market-based choice and toward an emphasis on equity-based choice."[41]

There is good news and bad news in these developments, both for advocates and opponents of school choice. Conservative advocates, unable to win widespread support for the idea on libertarian principles, may find that the only way to keep the idea alive is to adopt the themes of social justice and racial equality, which the American right has generally not emphasized. Liberal opponents of school choice, on the other hand, may find themselves in the position of achieving a significant social reform that would advance the interests of racial minorities, but only by moving away from a language that assumes an active government to one that accords greater respect to marketlike notions of individualism. But the most interesting aspect of the emergence of second-generation arguments over school choice is their potential to alter America's politics of race, and thereby to shed light on the degree to which support for (and opposition to) historic measures designed to achieve racial justice has been motivated by primarily racial or primarily political considerations.

The New Politics of Race

Historically, concerns with racial justice have emerged from the left end of the political spectrum and have been resisted from the right. There were good reasons why this was the case. Especially in the South, racial segregation was official policy enforced by state and local government.[42] But with the collapse of Jim Crow and the movement of so many African Americans to the North, discrimination came to be viewed as a result of private decisions that, to be effectively controlled, required active governmental involvement and enforcement. Certain that a Democratic Party whose electoral strength lay in Northern cities would protect their interests more than a Republican Party that increasingly appealed to voters in the West and the South, African Americans became the most reliable liberal supporters of Democratic administrations.[43] Minority voters wanted Democrats to support new governmental programs such as the war on poverty or federal assistance for housing issues, and as such programs were created, they strengthened the support Democrats received from minority voters. At the same time, Republicans who opposed such programs, even when they did so on fiscal grounds, lost support among minority voters; even when they made conscious efforts to reach out to minorities, they found themselves unable to overcome minority voters' strong preferences toward the Democrats.

To some extent, the historic pattern of racial politics in America remains very much alive; George W. Bush was able to win very few votes among African Americans in 2000 and did not do as well among other racial minorities as he may have hoped. At the same time, however, there is also clearly emerging a "new politics of race" that breaks with historic patterns. Unwilling to continue to write off minority voters, some Republicans and conservatives are seeking ways to appeal to them that are more consistent with their traditional conservative resistance to new government programs. One such effort, ironically, involves affirmative action, which began with initiatives taken by the Nixon administration.[44] Since that time, however, affirmative action has fallen back into the "old" politics of race, as liberals, who once had questions about preferences, began to support it and conservatives, who once opposed the Civil Rights Act of 1964, now cite that act in opposition to affirmative action. Yet affirmative action is not the only example of a new racial politics originated from the right. Charitable choice and the proposal to create a government office to support faith-based initiatives are others. And to that list, now that it has become primarily an issue about equal opportunity for inner-city parents, must be added the issue of school choice. "Despite the rhetoric of choice supporters that the movement for vouchers is a bipartisan issue," writes John Witte, "generally the evidence indicates that it is not—Republicans support vouchers, Democrats by and large do not."[45] Yet if Republican support for vouchers remains strong, the reasons are changing; conservatives have found new life in the school choice issue through an alliance with inner-city politicians, and part of the reason for their concern with the issue is an effort to woo more members of racial minority groups to their side. Although President Bush dropped his own support for vouchers in his education reform proposals in the first year of his presidency, vouchers remains an appealing issue to those Republicans who continue to see possible political opportunities among minority voters.

Because it involves questions of how a public good such as schooling should be financed, school choice offers a particularly appropriate comparison between the "old" and the "new" politics of race. Since at least *Brown v. Board of Education* (1954), schooling has been at the center of the way Americans think about racial equality. *Brown* itself—or, more specifically, its follow-up decision on implementation a year later—Gary Orfield writes, established the fundamental pattern when it called for "all deliberate speed" in efforts to bring about integrated education, signaling an understanding that when it came to their children, whites would be likely to resist too rapid a course toward integration.[46] There has been no lack of such resistance. Many whites chose to flee to the suburbs rather than remain in the city and contribute their share of the taxes for already strapped urban schools. Advocates for racial integration responded by trying to join urban and suburban districts together in order to promote greater racial integration within both, but when the U.S. Supreme Court in *Milliken v. Bradley* (1974) stopped those efforts, the courts began to rule that, in the words of one decision, public officials "have no affirmative fourteenth amendment duty to respond to the private actions of those who vote with their feet."[47] Meanwhile, many whites who remained in the cities, and who were therefore more likely to find their children being bused to achieve improved levels of racial integration, resisted, sometimes violently.[48]

Brown may have insisted that segregated schools were inherently unequal, but integrated schools were not about to become the norm in
American public education, as residential preferences reinforced
nearly all-minority schools in the cities and nearly all-white ones in
the suburbs.

Once in the suburbs, whites did not end their resistance to equality
in schooling. Because schools are financed through property taxes,
wealthy districts have more funds available than do poor districts and
are therefore likely to offer better schools to their residents. Although
the U.S. Supreme Court in *Rodriguez v. San Antonio Independent School
District* (411 U.S. 1, 1973) held that the federal Constitution does not
provide remedies against such unequal school financing, the way was
cleared for state action. Many states responded. One of the most highly
publicized was New Jersey, where, on the basis of the state constitution; successful challenges were brought against school financing inequities. As a result of extended litigation, the courts asked that funding
between districts be equalized and that poorer districts be given additional funds to meet the more expensive needs of teaching children
from deprived economic backgrounds.[49] Those decisions were, to say
the least, not very popular; the defeat of New Jersey governor Jim Flo-
rio in 1993 is generally attributed to his willingness to raise taxes to
meet the equality standards set by the New Jersey Supreme Court in
Abbott v. Burke (1985).[50] Like busing, efforts to bring about greater
equality in schooling through court orders often led to a politics of
backlash and resentment.[51]

When the effects of white flight, opposition to busing, and an unwill-
ingness to combine districts or redistribute property tax revenues are
added together, the result is the persistence of considerable inequality
in American schooling—an inequality, moreover, that clearly has a racial component. If equality means that the quality of schools and the
opportunities they provide should be roughly the same irrespective of
the racial composition of the school's student body, America has not
achieved racial equality in schooling. As Berne and Stiefel summarize
the situation, "Wide differences in property bases still persist and often
lead to inequities in finance; educational outputs and lifetime outcomes are still highly related to socioeconomic status, race, ethnicity,
and gender; and inequality in income and wealth continues at high
levels."[52]

This failure of American schooling to achieve greater equality of educational opportunity strengthens the position of those who argue that
Americans see a trade-off between freedom and equality and who believe that, when faced with such a trade-off, Americans will nearly always choose freedom. Orfield's words are harsh, but they are also rep-

resentative of those who believe that a reluctance to support principles of racial equality stains the American character:

> Racial segregation and unequal education have been the norm, combined with rhetoric about equal opportunity for all Americans to develop their educational potential. The commitment to equal education is used, in turn, to justify the industrial world's most limited system of social welfare and the largest criminal justice system, since education is said to offer everyone a full and fair chance to make it in the free market, and this equal opportunity makes it just to expect equal performance with minimal public help.[53]

For Orfield, it is axiomatic that racial equality will be associated with active welfare-state programs. And he is not alone. "The reality," write Klinkner and Smith along similar lines, "is that government aid programs, governmental antidiscrimination efforts, subsequent affirmative action initiatives, and public sector employment generally have been crucial to modern black economic progress."[54] Both of these accounts can be taken as illustrative of what I have been calling the "old politics of race." According to that interpretation, those who oppose an active role for government, including those who seek greater reliance on the market, are, whether intentionally or not, standing in the way of racial justice. It follows, then, that Republican efforts to pursue a "new politics of race" do not represent genuine efforts to bring about racial equality but instead suggest an opportunistic strategy that may result in significant setbacks. Klinkner and Smith, for example, suggest that efforts to promote vouchers and other school-choice plans, despite the support they may have from African Americans in surveys or among some African American activists, are "not aimed at providing integrated education for all and are more likely to carry de facto segregation even further."[55]

The argument that the politics of race continues to be shaped by liberal support for governmental activism and conservative resistance to it has a substantial basis in reality. Despite the fact that roughly two-thirds of Americans indicate that they would be willing to pay more taxes to improve inner-city schools, such sentiments rarely are translated into policy.[56] When racial equality is sought through direct means, and when those means involve active governmental programs and an increased tax burden, many white Americans refuse to go along. At the same time, however, because we can never be sure why white Americans resist such direct means, there are also significant shortcomings in the analysis that lies behind the old politics of race; each leg of the argument that Americans will resist efforts to achieve greater racial equality is capable of alternative explanations that rely little on racial motivations.

White flight from the cities, for example, does exist, and efforts to escape from inferior schools often drives it. But the expansion of the black middle class has led to much the same phenomenon, suggesting that the desire to improve schooling for one's children may not be completely, or even primarily, racially motivated.[57] Along similar lines, busing to achieve racial integration, it is now widely recognized, was not much of a panacea for racial segregation; many parents had solid, nonracial reasons for wanting their children nearby when they attended school; blacks were anything but unified in their own support for busing or, for that matter, integration; and numerous white liberals who advocated busing could never overcome the seeming hypocrisy involved in sending their own children to private or suburban schools. Even resistance to property tax equalization can have nonracial roots; Proposition 13 in California suggested pent-up resentment against rising property taxes in general, and many suburbanites feel, not without reason, that directing more money to inner-city schools without reforming them would be wasteful.

The suggestion that Americans whose conservative views lead them to question new government programs are therefore expressing a form of racial prejudice is particularly controversial. On the one hand, an issue such as opposition to welfare can, some scholars argue, mask not very deeply hidden racial stereotypes. Gilens, for example, has shown that "the perception that blacks are lazy emerged as the strongest determinant of white's beliefs about welfare recipients, and it was a powerful influence on their preferences with regard to welfare spending."[58] On this ground, there is reason, he believes, to conclude that opposition to welfare, which is formally a race-neutral policy, is motivated to some extent by prejudiced attitudes toward African Americans. Yet other scholars, most notably Sniderman and his colleagues, argue that white opposition to programs that blacks often view as central to their quest for equality—such as affirmative action or busing—is in large part a product of a general skepticism about government or a commitment to a principle such as reward on the basis of merit.[59]

It is beyond the scope of this chapter to settle the issue of whether the oft-noted fiscal conservatism of Americans constitutes an effort to stand in the way of racial equality. But it is within this chapter's purview to point out that "the new politics of race," especially in the area of school choice, opens up questions involving freedom, equality, and the way Americans rank order both. And those new ways offer the possibility of disentangling views on the question of whether the government or the market ought to be the proper instrument of social policy from the question of whether Americans are supporters or opponents of the idea of greater racial equality.

The most obvious point to emphasize in this regard is that when it comes to education, the traditional American skepticism toward government usually moderates. It has been said that although the United States was the last Western society to create an extensive welfare state, it was the first to create a system of public schools.[60] Despite tax revolts and the emergence of a strong conservative movement in the United States, public support for public schools has not appreciably diminished. The interesting question in this regard is not why vouchers have become an issue in American politics; given the American preference for freedom, the real questions are why it took so long and why—despite evidence of the less-than-stellar performance of America's schools—vouchers still cannot assemble majority support in surveys. However strong the American commitment to freedom may be, it should not be understood as an automatic vote for independence and an automatic vote against communal values and public institutions.

Second, critics of school choice worry that the attractions of freedom in America, and the consequent skepticism toward equality, means that once vouchers have been adopted in some places, they will spread to all places. Too great a reliance on the market, Jeffrey Henig writes, runs "the risk that the market rationale associated with educational-choice proposals will undermine the social and political institutions that are prerequisites to achieving genuine reform."[61] Along similar lines, Peter Cookson attributes the popularity of school choice to the power of a conservative ideology that, under the presidency of Ronald Reagan, showed renewed vitality in American life. For Cookson, the dangers of extending freedom of choice into education are also self-evident: "Market solutions to educational problems will not lead to educational wonderlands, but could possibly lead to educational wastelands."[62]

The problem with this point of view is that vouchers have been adopted in some places, especially in Cleveland and Milwaukee, and they have not spread to all places. This is clearly due to the second-generation character of America's already existing voucher schemes; vouchers are more politically acceptable when they are viewed as possible correctives to what are widely regarded to be poor-performing inner-city schools. While both Henig and Cookson recognize that there are arguments to be made for school choice on grounds other than freedom of choice, neither anticipated the rapidity with which those arguments would displace freedom of choice in the rhetoric around school choice. Henig acknowledges that school choice is not overly popular according to surveys, but he fails to recognize the degree to which the enthusiasm for market models of education advocated by those who are pro-voucher is not shared by the general public; if anything, advocates for vouchers have to work so hard to make their ideas persuasive precisely because there is little support for extending the market into the realm of education. Had conservatives remain committed to the marketlike principles that Henig and Cookson assumed to be so powerful, school choice would likely have become far more marginalized an issue than it already is.

Thirdly, once school choice does emerge as an issue, the extent to which arguments on its behalf eventually shift to arguments about equality is worth noting. The transformation of school choice into an issue identified with African Americans and their quest for greater equality has not, contrary to many expectations, doomed the issue politically, but has given it a second life. There is something in the intellectual atmosphere of the United States that renders arguments based on the primacy of self-interest generally unattractive and unpersuasive and that makes arguments favoring equality, if fashioned in a certain way, surprisingly attractive. Americans may not like welfare, but that does not mean they are opposed to the principles that underlie welfare, especially principles that recognize that sometimes people need help in order to be as self-reliant as American ideology often suggests they ought to be.[63] The fact that Americans rank equality second to freedom in their hierarchy of values, in other words, should not be taken to mean that they do not value equality at all. The reason school choice advocates have not stuck to the script written by Milton Friedman is that most Americans would find something wrong with a pure-market view of the world—and what they would find wrong is the market's unforgiving face toward those who lack opportunity or are down on their luck.

It is therefore somewhat surprising that more liberals have not rallied to the cause of vouchers as the issue has become more identified with African Americans. Part of the reason lies in the quite legitimate fear that vouchers would "skim off" the best and the brightest among racial minority groups, leaving the rest worse off. And part of the reason may also lie in the concern that vouchers will encourage greater reliance on religious schools. For some liberals, this is reason enough to distrust them; children ought not to be held hostage to the choices of their parents, particularly those parents who belong to religious traditions that do not believe in the principles of autonomy and self-development so central to liberalism.[64] Others worry not about conservative religion per se, but about public support for any form of religion, which would violate the First Amendment. This too is a legitimate concern, but it also stands in sharp contrast to the tendency of liberals to bend their adherence to principle in order to support racial equality. Affirmative action is the clearest example. Although affirmative action seems to violate liberal principles of meritocratic achievement, many liberals defend preferences on the grounds that African Americans view them as central to their quest for equality. At the same time, however, even though many African Americans see vouchers as crucial to ensuring a better future for their children, not as many liberals conclude on that basis that they are therefore best off suspending their concerns about church-state separation.

Fourth, there is reason to believe that the support for equality that does exist in the United States tends to evaporate when people believe equality is being brought about by artificial or coercive means. Harold Wilensky once wrote that tax revolts against the welfare state were more common when the taxes that paid for governmental services were more visible than when they were more hidden.[65] Much the same could be said about efforts to bring about equality through governmental programs. Since few forms of taxation are more visible than property tax, a program that raises the taxes of some in order to support educational equality for others is almost bound to be unpopular.

But there are other ways to equalize spending between school districts. In 1994, voters in Michigan approved Proposition A. Instead of funding education through property taxes, the state would instead rely directly on state appropriations and would apportion spending depending upon the number of pupils enrolled in a particular district.[66] Public controversy around the change centered on the fact that because students could essentially take their dollars with them, the new Michigan system created a basis for school-choice opportunities. (Those opportunities, especially opportunities for charter schools, remained in place after the 2000 referendum, while opportunities for vouchers constricted greatly.) Lost to some degree in the controversy was the fact that delinking school finance from property taxes makes greater equity possible by rendering transfers of funds more "invisible" than they would be with direct property-tax increases, with the consequence that Proposition A, which did bring about greater equality between school districts, remains politically popular. One of the lessons of the Michigan experience is that opponents of school choice can, if they wish, find other arguments to support the principle of equal opportunity in schooling without resorting to increases in taxation or highly visible redistributive policies that are often political suicide.

Finally, and most importantly, the new politics of race surrounding school choice raises the possibility of a kind of natural experiment that permits additional light to be shed on the question of whether those who oppose more-active government programs are also necessarily expressing resistance to greater racial justice. Sniderman and his colleagues argue that one can properly differentiate opposition to active government from opposition to racism. This point of view has been criticized on the grounds that the agreement between blacks and whites on broad egalitarian goals breaks down when specific policies are introduced; "white public opinion," write Klinkner and Smith "has rarely shown strong support for any reform designed to promote racial equality until after its enactment, and on many issues support has remained weak even then."[67] When it comes to public programs with real potential for bringing about effective steps toward racial equality—here affirmative action becomes paradigmatic—white resistance inevitably asserts itself.

School choice raises the question of what happens when the proposed means for achieving greater equality shift from reliance on government to reliance on marketlike mechanisms. The obvious answer to the question at this time is that we do not know: school choice experiments have not been in existence long enough nor are social science methods definitive enough to permit a consensus to emerge on their effectiveness, both in this country and abroad.[68] But much the same could be said for affirmative-action programs; despite efforts to demonstrate their effectiveness, the social-science jury is still out.[69] In the absence of compelling data on either state-based or market-based methods of achieving greater racial equality, the wise course would be one that resisted the temptation to insist that those who question either method are acting in bad faith. Second-generation advocates of school choice would be wrong to conclude that those who have questions about the appropriateness of vouchers must be opponents of racial equality. But those who support affirmative action or question welfare reform should resist concluding that opponents of the former and supporters of the latter are motivated primarily, or even secondarily, by hostility to the legitimate demands of racial minorities. It is possible to reject active government and not be racist for the same reasons it is possible to reject market alternatives and not be racist.

Conclusion

The commonly accepted notion that Americans value freedom more than they do equality—and, consequently, that they will choose the former whenever it comes into conflict with the latter—suggests that the most effective way to build consensus around schooling would be to appeal to the market, for that is presumably the most commonly held value in the United States. If so, then the shift to second-generation debates over equality ought to be far more contentious, for equality is the far more contentious ideal. Yet this is not how the politics of school choice has worked itself out. It was under first-generation arguments about freedom that school choice appeared as a deeply ideological issue pitting Republican-leaning politicians against Democratic-leaning schoolteachers. And the more school choice progresses as a policy under equality arguments than under freedom arguments, the greater the common recognition that the ends of education ought to receive much more attention than the means selected to achieve them.

Those ends, moreover, usually involve equality issues. As Richard Kahlenberg reminds, us, Horace Mann, the founder of the American common school, viewed education as "the great equalizer."[70] Mann meant this in a particularly nineteenth-century way; it was not the purpose of public schools to make sure that everyone was equal, but instead to offer everyone the opportunity to make him- or herself equal. That view of education as an avenue of social mobility is still widely shared in the United States; according to a Phi Delta Kappa/Gallup poll, Americans do not rank dispelling inequities among schools and groups very high among the purposes of education, but they do consider schools to be very important in helping people to become economically self-sufficient.[71] In the realm of Americans values, schooling can be understood as the one area in which Americans unambiguously support the principle that government ought to help promote a fairer and more equal society, so long as government is understood to be primarily about education and equality is understood to be primarily about opportunity.

Once this recognition of the role that equality arguments play in debates over schooling is appreciated, the issue of vouchers and other versions of school choice take their place among two increasingly shared conclusions about the relationship between education and equality. One is that a traditional reliance on property taxes to finance education, which in turn makes educational inequalities a function of residence, has created inequalities in opportunity that deserve correction. The other is that redistributing property taxes between wealthier and poorer districts may not be the best way to correct the problem, if for no other reason than the resistance it generates. Out of these two conclusions have emerged a gamut of possibilities. They range from increased federal aid to education to correct imbalances between states that redistribution within states does not touch, to, on the other side of the government/market divide, experiments with charter schools, vouchers, and every combination in between.[72]

If it were the case that reliance on market-driven mechanisms, once introduced, had a tendency to drive all other mechanisms out of business, reliance on vouchers might well undermine the emerging consensus about spreading the benefits of economic opportunity. But be-

Three

Equity and School Choice: How Can We Bridge the Gap between Ideals and Realities?

STEPHEN MACEDO

THIS CHAPTER FOCUSES ON equality-based arguments about school choice. Equality (or, as I prefer, equity) is indeed a crucial standard for assessing school choice proposals. But equity is interpreted in various ways. The best arguments for school choice invoke equity, but so do the least-defensible arguments and the least-attractive forms of school choice. It all depends on what we mean by equity.

The strongest arguments for school choice are based on improving the education of the most-deprived children in the worst-performing urban schools. That millions of children fail to receive a good education in the United States of America is shameful. However, much weaker arguments for publicly funded school choice argue on the basis of fairness or equity among parents with differing religious and cultural values. Focusing on the wrong sorts of equity will lead us astray. Focusing on the right sorts of equity will at least encourage us to ask the right questions, but it will not yield easy answers.

Limited school choice experiments, and the more extensive school choice plans advanced by scholars, have been *designed* to promote greater equality of educational opportunity. The important question remains, especially with respect to extensive school choice plans on the drawing board: Can the political will be mustered in practice to preserve the equity-enhancing features of choice? We cannot affirm this with confidence. The practical consequences of taking school choice seriously will be complex and difficult to predict. We should proceed cautiously, and make sure that we hold school choice up to the right sorts of public standards. We should also consider the possibility that the most urgently needed educational reforms have little to do with school choice.

How Not to Argue for School Choice, Part I: Is "Paying Twice for Education" Unfair?

One very broad, equity-based argument for publicly funded school choice rests on pointing out that some people pay school taxes but choose to send their children to private schools. *It is unfair that people should pay twice for education.* It would be fairer if they were given a share of public funds to subsidize their preferred nonpublic educational option. This argument is not totally crazy, because publicly regulated private schools do typically provide children with what we publicly require that all children should learn. Private schools are not just providers of private goods; they are one way that we allow parents to fulfill their public obligation to educate their children. And when parents decide to avail themselves of private schools, they reduce the cost of providing a public education. The degree of public oversight and regulation of private schooling varies from state to state and may tend to be inadequate, but any private school that fails to provide children with what we as a society regard as educationally essential should not be allowed to fulfill the public educational requirement (at least as a matter of principle; in practice the costs of forcibly removing children from private schools and requiring them to attend other schools may be prohibitively high).[1] It is permissible for public policy to permit and subsidize these educational options in various ways, at least insofar as private schools do prepare children to be free and equal persons and citizens. This already occurs: bus transportation, schoolbooks, tax exemptions for nonprofit schools and for churches, and various forms of broad-based tax credits for school-related expenses are among the ways in which public institutions in many places choose to subsidize the choice of parents to send their children to private schools.

The argument that the public is *obliged* to subsidize the choice of families to avail themselves of a private education is not totally crazy, but it unconvincing. Many public goods are publicly funded and made available to everyone at no additional cost even though some taxpayers choose not to take advantage of them. There are all sorts of variations, moreover, in the extent to which people take advantage of free public schooling, and so the "no one should pay twice for education" argument leads to some bizarre results. Some people forgo this benefit of mere legal residence by sending their children to an accredited private school, others by choosing not to have children. If we have an obligation of fairness to subsidize those who choose private schools, what about those who choose not to have children? What about parents with large families or parents of children with special and expensive educational needs? Do they owe money to everyone else, including private school choosers, the childless, and families with fewer children in public school? The logic of this position suggests governments are required to fund public education via "user fees," but what is the principled basis for this assertion? It might be legitimate (if foolish) for governments to consider that funding option, but I cannot see why they should be required to do so. Underlying the "no one should pay twice" argument, it appears, is the conviction that education is a merely private good, to be paid for by those who use it. This position was rejected at the outset of the common school movement in America. The confusion implicit in this argument—the refusal to recognize distinctively *public* educational aims—runs through many arguments for school reform.

The education provided by private schools is not obviously in the fullest sense a public education. Public schools and private schools are not perfect substitutes for each other when it comes to providing all the public goods embodied in the enterprise of common schooling. The model of common schooling—geographically based public schools that all of the children in a jurisdiction could attend for free—was chosen not accidentally but deliberately in the second third of the nineteenth century and for a variety of public-regarding reasons. Common schools open to all children without regard to class or religious denomination were believed to be a way to help break down class distinctions and to provide all children with an equal opportunity to develop their talents and capacities. Common schooling was also favored as a way of helping to bridge ethnic and religious divisions, divisions that provoked keen anxieties in this new republic teeming with immigrants. Parents were left free to send their children to private academies or religious schools, but from the inception of the movement toward common schooling in the 1830s and 1840s the prevailing opinion was that these private options should not be subsidized because private schools could not be reliably counted upon to represent public educational values. From the beginning, therefore, common schools were considered the preferred instrument for advancing specifically public educational values, which included not only reading, writing, arithmetic, and the like, but also equal freedom and civic friendship among citizens of all classes and ethnic and religious groups. Less admirable motives also played an important role: xenophobia and indeed racism toward foreigners, including the Irish and later southern and eastern Europeans, and intense anti-Catholicism. The historical role of these motives should not be discounted, but neither should it be seen as all-important.[2]

Of course, public schools often fail to be all that we would like them to be. Bureaucratic failure and mismanagement play their part, but so do underfunding and a great deal of white and middle-class flight to the suburbs in order to avoid race and class integration. Parents who can afford it are able to pack up and move for any reasons they would like to. Nevertheless, the common school ideal retains a great deal of attractiveness and appropriateness. It is reasonable and legitimate for governments to decide that they wish to continue to favor the distinctive values of common schooling by concentrating public funds in public schools and leaving parents who want a private education for their children to pay for it themselves. For all these reasons, the "no one should pay twice" argument for school choice not only fails to be convincing, it seems to miss the whole point of a *public* educational policy.

How Not to Argue for School Choice, Part II: Religious Pluralism and Equal Freedom

In spite of its difficulties, the notion that fairness requires us to subsidize the choice of parents to send their children to private schools continues to be advanced in various guises. It is given a First Amendment twist by Michael W. McConnell and others. In place of an educational system that is "democratic and collective," we should adopt one that is "private and pluralistic," argues McConnell. Given the range of reasonable disagreement in our society about the moral and religious viewpoints relevant to education, "it is time to discard the notion that democratic control over education is *in principle* the form best suited to a liberal, pluralistic society. The opposite is true." McConnell argues that public schools have always sought to assimilate children to a preferred religious view or a close equivalent to a religious view: in the nineteenth century the favored values were broadly Protestant; nowadays they are more like "secular self-actualization." Now, as before, dissenters from the official educational orthodoxy are treated as second-class citizens. Imposing one official educational vision on all is akin to maintaining an established church: the current system of public schooling is inconsistent with the "disestablishmentarian" values of the First Amendment. A system of publicly subsidized parental choice among schools (all of which would have to satisfy minimal civic standards) would be fairer to parents who disagree with the substantive values of public schools, or who want their children to learn in a school environment informed by a particular religious or philosophical framework, or who simply disagree with the educational ideals of public schools.[3]

In the current system, public funds are concentrated in common schools, while parents are allowed to send their children to private schools, including religious schools, *if* they can afford to pay or can secure scholarships. Concentrating public funds in common schools means that poorer religious parents do not have the same ability as wealthier religious parents to send their children to religious schools. Thus, a system of public funding of private educational choices would provide more "equitably" for the freedom of poorer parents who disagree with the values of public schools (on religious or other grounds), and who wish to be empowered—as their wealthier fellow citizens are—to choose the school that reflects their particular religious or philosophical values. As Joseph Viteritti puts it in his contribution to this volume, "Without vouchers, only those with private means can acquire a religious education for their children. In this way, choice can be more broadly conceived as an issue of religious liberty."[4] Religious freedom, social pluralism, and equity seem increasingly to march together in school reform debates. Publicly funded educational choice can, accordingly, promote substantive equality of religious liberty.

There are different ways to interpret objections to common schooling that wed pluralism and equity. One could say that publicly subsidized educational choice would be fairer to all the *worldviews* that compete in society, in which case the focus would be on fairness or neutrality among competing intellectual or normative worldviews, including religious systems. Or one could emphasize fairness to poorer *families* who object to the values embodied in public schools, in which case the emphasis would be on fairer or more equal treatment of poorer parents who wish to have the same ability as their wealthier fellow citizens to make educational choices for their children. Either way, this is not a promising line of argument.

The proposition that public schools or other public institutions need to strive to be fair or neutral among worldviews is a nonstarter. The values taught in public schools will often be controversial, and sometimes at odds with some people's religious views. There is no getting around that. It is important that the values taught in public schools should be publicly defensible; it is impossible that they should be equally attractive to the different worldviews and religious views that people espouse in America. That some people object—even on religious grounds—to what is taught in public schools does not necessarily give rise to fundamental objections based on fairness or equity (and it should not be thought that religion furnishes the only grounds for disagreement here).[5]

The equity argument may seem more powerful when it focuses on empowering poorer parents, as opposed to trying to establish a public environment that is neutral in its effects on worldviews. But we need to recall that there are all sorts of things that the rich are able to afford that the poor cannot on account of the fact that the rich (or better off) do not count on public support. Our public obligation to the less well off is not to give them what they want above all, nor is it to provide "equitably" for the satisfaction of people's deepest desires or beliefs. Our public obligation is rather to provide people with a fair measure of basic goods that can be justified from a public point of view. Many people will not believe that the forms of public support provided by a liberal-democratic state represent the most important things in life. That is not, however, the point. The point is rather that these are goods that we share as a *political* society: goods that we have chosen to embody in public schools after due deliberation. As a political community, we educate children with an eye toward a variety of public values: literacy, numeracy, knowledge of history, of the natural world, and of social and political relations; and we seek to promote children's equal freedom, to prepare them for their status as future citizens, help them develop their capacity to lead a good life as we publicly understand this, and discover the wide range of values and virtues relevant to these. We educate this way in public institutions not because we disvalue other nonpublic interests and aspirations, but because it would be inappropriate to pursue these nonpublic values and aspirations in public institutions that *we support and share as fellow citizens.* Insofar as people regard nonpublic goods as more important, they are free to pursue those goods.

A wealthy society such as ours has a moral obligation to try to make sure that all children receive a good education. Whatever we think of the responsibilities of poorer adults, children are certainly not responsible for being born into disadvantaged circumstances. It goes too far to say that we owe all children an equal education, but we are wealthy enough as a society to try to insure that all children receive a good education.[6] Some parents may understand "good education" to mean an education in which the study of reading, history, science, and other subjects are explicitly approached from a religious point of view.[7] We are not obligated as a political society to adopt these parents' views of a good education. We fulfill our public obligations as a political society when strive to furnish all children with a good education as we can best understand what that means from a public point of view. Of course, there are various legitimate ways for a democratic society to decide to fulfill this obligation: providing certain forms of aid to parents who chose appropriate private schools including religious schools may be permissible, but it is not required as a matter of basic principle.

No doubt the children of poorer parents will have fewer options with respect to schooling, as well as to everything else. This may be an argument for the redistribution of income. I do not think it is a particularly urgent reason for publicly subsidizing the desire of poor parents to send their children to religious schools: with respect to school funding choices, our basic obligation is to somehow provide all children with what we publicly understand to be a good education. If certain forms of school choice improve the education of disadvantaged and poorly educated children, that is the beginning at least of a good equity-based argument for choice. But satisfying poor parents' desire to secure a religious education for their children is not only *not a good argument*, it is *not even a legitimate argument* for allocating public monies to school choice plans. The reform of public educational policy should focus on securing all children a better education as we publicly understand that. Public subsidies for tuition at a religious school should be based on the more-effective pursuit of public educational ends, not on parents' religious interests.[8] Poorer parents who, based on their religious beliefs and interests, want to secure a religious education for their children should appeal to wealthier co-religionists.

It should not be thought, moreover, that wealthy parents have an untrammeled right to educate their children with an eye toward their own values and beliefs. All schools, including religious schools, should be required to comply with various public educational requirements: richer religious parents do not have an untrammeled right to choose the sort of religious education they want for their children.

Public support for primary and secondary education has centered on common schooling and the values associated with it. Devoting public monies to educating children together in a common school has been thought to be a way of trying to overcome class divisions and to break down other barriers between citizens (of ethnicity, race, and religion). It has been believed that public schools more reliably stand for *public* educational values: they are directly and fully answerable in public forums in a way that private schools are not. In addition, we simply do not trust parents with full responsibility for their children's educational needs: our interest in promoting the freedom and equality of children may require helping children to get some distance on the values and interests of their parents.

Obviously, the foregoing is a quite partial way of looking at the debate over school choice. Many or even most of the parents who press for greater school choice, including publicly funded vouchers that can be used in religious schools, are not arguing for this based solely on their desire to give their children a more religious education. Far more typically (I am prepared to accept) those parents—especially those disadvantaged parents in inner cities—are convinced that public schools as currently organized and funded are failing to give their children a good education, as we would understand that from a public point of view. Many are desperate to get a decent education for their children, and they want help to pay for a religious education for their children because those institutions are thought to provide a superior education, a safer environment, and a more coherent moral framework that will better promote the public virtues and values needed by young adults and future citizens nowadays.

It is important to sort out the more- and less-urgent public reasons for favoring education reforms emphasizing school choice, because the values that lead us to embrace school choice will also shape the way school choice is structured and regulated in public policy. It is important to fix on the right sort of equity-based argument. The most urgent and weighty arguments for school choice are not based on social, intellectual, or religious pluralism; they are based rather on the equitable provision of a good public education for all.[9]

How to Argue for School Choice

I do not want to belabor the connection between equity and pluralism. More urgent arguments for school choice are based on improving the education of the most-disadvantaged students in the worst-performing school districts. There is plausible, if still sketchy and far from definitive, evidence that giving poorer families greater educational choice—with public funds—will improve education as we publicly understand it.

I am going to accept the plausibility of the public-good justification for choice for the sake of argument, and consider next the objections based on equality of educational opportunity for all children irrespective of accidents of birth. Is moving in the direction of school choice likely to exacerbate an admittedly lousy situation in this country with respect to the equal access of all children to a good education? How will the least-well-off children fare? Can school choice be fashioned as a way of pursuing educational equity?

It is often charged that school choice will make a bad situation worse. This is most especially likely to be the case with respect to very broad-based and unfocused voucher plans such as the one proposed and defeated recently in California. Under that plan, California would have provided $4,000 for any child attending private school or even being home schooled. This plan was defeated in a referendum, and that appears due in important part to concerns about equity. Evidence cited by Robert C. Bulman and David L. Kirp indicate that voter rejection followed in part from three objections: first, that the primary benefits of the plan would flow to better-off parents with kids already in private schools; second, that the plan would drain funds from the public school system; and third, that regulation was inadequate to prevent public funds flowing to outrageous schools, such as a witches' coven school that gained some notoriety in the public debates.[10] The plan was defeated overwhelmingly, and the good news here is that apparently equity-based considerations do matter to the voters, at least in California.

Even when school choice measures focus on disadvantaged kids in underperforming schools, equity based worries come into play. This is true even as concerns expanded choice within the public system, such as the option of public charter schools. All forms of choice give rise to worries about "creaming." The children who can take advantage of choice may benefit, but when parents can choose better schools, the least-capable children and the least-engaged families will tend to be left behind, and those children will be even worse off. The families most likely to take advantage of vouchers or to seek and gain admission to the best charter schools will be those children of parents who are better educated (even if disadvantaged) and most attentive to and engaged with the education of their children. The loss of these children and the engagement of these parents will be keenly felt. Moreover, schools that can and must compete for applicants have an incentive to discourage troublesome applicants, and may find informal ways of doing so even when they must be formally open (they may require parent-teacher conferences at awkward times or find other ways of putting off undesirable applicants). The least-capable and most-troublesome students, and those whose parents are least involved with and supportive of their education, will be left worse off in residual public schools.

This sort of dire scenario cannot be altogether discounted. Important worries about creaming apply to virtually every choice plan.[11] Nevertheless, they are not automatically fatal. There may still be gains to the least-well-off children: from the demonstration effects of good charter and private schools, and the more competitive atmosphere in education generally.

If we take these equity-based worries seriously, as we should, the crucial questions are: Can choice plans be designed so as not to exacerbate social inequalities, but indeed rather to promote greater equity? Insofar as equity-enhancing choice plans can be designed, what are the prospects that political institutions in practice will muster the political will to implement and sustain the choice plans' equity-enhancing features?

So far as the first question is concerned, there is no question that school reforms can be designed to promote equity, and sometimes their implementation promotes equity. Limited voucher experiments have been designed and implemented that are targeted at disadvantaged children and poorly performing schools. More extensive choice-based school systems have been designed to make choice an engine of greater equality. The problem is that the equity-enhancing features of the most-ambitious school choice plans are politically unsustainable. So the second question, concerning whether the equity-enhancing features of school choice can be preserved in practice, is extremely difficult to answer. The political dynamics unleashed by choice are hard to predict, and well-meaning reforms could lead to a more divided and unequal society.

Choice and Equity

Choice has long been advanced as a means of advancing equity. Magnet schools within the public system were designed as a way of promoting voluntary racial integration. Charter schools have been advanced as a way of providing the benefits of smaller and more-focused schools within an overall public system. Even the voucher experiments underway in Milwaukee and Cleveland and the one that was terminated in Florida have or had strikingly egalitarian elements. I will focus here on the voucher plans because they are the most controversial.

In Florida, the statewide voucher experiment, which was struck down by state courts, confined eligibility to children in schools that had failed to meet minimum overall state standards for two years running. The voucher experiments underway in Cleveland and Milwaukee concentrate on poorly performing school districts attended by children who are overwhelmingly poor, disadvantaged, and minority.

School reform in Cleveland was ordered by courts after a long history of abysmal school performance.[12] In both Cleveland and Milwaukee eligibility for participation in the voucher program depended on means tests (in Cleveland, the highest tuition benefits went to children from families with incomes of no more than double the federal poverty level; in Milwaukee, school vouchers were limited to no more than 15 percent of public school students, and to those families earning no more than 1.75 times the poverty level).

The Milwaukee and Cleveland voucher experiments had other valuable features that help insure that public purposes were served. In Cleveland, private schools could decide whether and how many students with vouchers they wish to take, but if those schools were oversubscribed, they could not pick and choose among students on religious grounds. (They were allowed to prefer students enrolled the previous year, siblings of students enrolled the previous year, and children from the school's neighborhood; the Ohio Supreme Court struck down a provision that would have allowed schools to preferentially admit students with vouchers whose parents "are affiliated with any organization that provides financial support to the school.")[13] The Milwaukee choice plan similarly disallowed participating schools to favor co-religionists when choosing among children with vouchers. In addition, the Wisconsin legislature added a provision requiring that children with vouchers should be able to opt out of any religious activity that they or their parents would find objectionable. This rule goes a step beyond Cleveland's program in helping to insure that public funds are not paying for religious coercion, and that schools participating in publicly funded voucher programs really are open to all of the children in the political community on a fair basis.[14]

The details of these limited voucher programs matter. The design of admissions procedures and opt-out provisions can help insure that schools receiving public monies are relatively open on a nondiscriminatory basis to all children. Of course, these provisions are not simply regulations about administrative details; they have the effect of reconstituting private institutions in ways that make them more internally diverse and more conformable with public values. They seem likely to alter the nature of many religious schools that receive vouchers, perhaps dampening diversity: these conditions at least inhibit the imposition of a pervasive religious atmosphere in those schools that choose to receive children with publicly funded vouchers. And if the nature of religious schooling is altered, pressure may be exerted on the larger religious community as well. But the purpose and effect of these sorts of restrictions is to help insure that schools participating in these public programs are fairly open to all of the children in the community who might wish to attend. If the schools find that these restrictions are an encumbrance on their religious autonomy and integrity, they have an effective way to guard those values: they can avoid becoming conduits for the delivery of public educational services.

The Cleveland school-voucher plan had an additional valuable feature that was never realized in practice, and this contributed to its temporary undoing in the courts (it was saved by the U.S. Supreme Court). Participation was open not only to private schools within the city of Cleveland, but to public schools in districts bordering on the city of Cleveland: all of these schools were invited to accept children with vouchers to fill empty seats. Fifty-six private schools within Cleveland registered to participate in the program, and court records as of 1995 indicate that sectarian schools comprised 80 percent of participating schools and enrolled 85 percent of the program's students.[15] Public schools in districts adjacent to the city of Cleveland could register to receive voucher program students, but none opted to participate. The plan was struck down in part because the nonparticipation of schools from neighboring suburban public school districts meant that the effective choice available to students was to remain in failing public schools or to attend a religious school. A federal court found that because of

this, the program was excessively biased toward religious-school attendance, but the U.S. Supreme Court reversed it.

It is open to the state of Ohio to require suburban-school-district participation. Doing so would make the Cleveland voucher plan a better,
more-equitable program: it would help break down the class and race
barriers that separate city and suburb, making the overall school system more inclusive in spite of residential segregation. Unfortunately,
the Ohio legislature is not eager to revise the plan to require suburban
participation.

The programs in Cleveland and Milwaukee are designed to make a
decent education available to a relatively small number of disadvantaged students who would otherwise have an inadequate education.
Mayor John Norquist has emphasized that expanding school choice
could help keep middle-class families with children from moving to
the suburbs, thus enlisting school policy as an engine of residential
integration as opposed to segregation.[16]

Voucher experiments designed to address the educational needs of
disadvantaged students in poorly performing school districts ought to
be welcomed when the programs are designed and implemented to
pursue public educational aims as a whole more effectively. The most
defensible voucher plans are designed and implemented with public
purposes in view; they enlist private providers on behalf of public educational aims, rather than sacrificing public educational aims to private
choices. The right sorts of voucher plans ought to be welcomed, at least
in the absence of preferable and politically feasible alternatives.

But these are, of course, small experiments targeted at populations
that are especially badly served by public schooling: populations left
behind by the flight of middle-class city dwellers to the suburbs. It is
difficult to say how easy it will be to keep the focus on helping the
disadvantaged if the voucher plans are expanded or if choice becomes
not a supplement to but a substitute for common schooling. We do not
appear to be in any headlong rush to do away with common schooling,
but it is worth considering how the concern with equity may be built
into larger-scale voucher reforms.

Vouchers on a Larger Scale

The current voucher experiments target particular populations of disadvantaged parents in poor school systems. But what can be done to
address the needs of larger numbers of children? Can choice-based reforms be counted upon to systematically favor educational improvement for the less well off? Or do worries about creaming, and perhaps

other worries, mean that choice-based reforms must be carefully regulated and controlled to insure that public purposes are served?

There is one great attraction of school vouchers from an egalitarian perspective: If designed properly, they can help sever the link between education and local tax bases. As things stand, school districts differ enormously in their ability to fund education. These vast inequalities arise from the dependence on property taxes. Older cities often have a very weak property-tax base, while suburban districts have very strong tax bases and can provide far more generous support for their school systems. School voucher proposals generally issue from state governments and are funded out of general state revenues. School vouchers might contribute to the more equitable distribution of public educational resources in direct and obvious ways: state-financed school vouchers could give each child in the state, irrespective of place of residence, an equal sum of money to be used to pay for schooling. To truly promote educational equity, the vouchers would have to be adjusted upward for children with special educational needs. Shifting education funding upward toward the states via vouchers could help equalize education funding.

Sweeping voucher proposals have been designed to promote greater equality in education. Herbert Gintis, Harry Brighouse, and James Dwyer have all proposed equality-based voucher schemes. Brighouse has recently followed Gintis in proposing a publicly funded voucher scheme available to all children, but with the following crucial feature: parents would not be allowed to "top-up," or add onto the amount of the voucher. If parents want a better (or at least costlier) education for their children, they will have to push for a better education for all children, for all schools would have to rely for tuition on publicly funded vouchers only. Along with this, Brighouse and Dwyer argue that private schools should be regulated far more extensively than they are now. These scholars are particularly concerned that private schools may indoctrinate children into particular ethical frameworks in a way that inhibits their individual autonomy. But the larger point is that all schools should be held up to rigorous and rigorously enforced public standards with respect to the content of education. Choice can promote equality if educational content is more thoroughly regulated across schools and if expenditures on education are equalized according to students' particular needs.[17]

Voucher schemes so designed could enhance equity. But what are the chances of schemes such as these being designed and implemented in the United States? It is quite difficult to generalize based on the very limited experiments, targeted at poor and disadvantaged families. Voucher plans will bring greater regulation of private schooling, as we have already seen, though we should not minimize the difficulties attending efforts to regulate the internal workings of private schools, including religious schools. Limited voucher experiments, such as that in Milwaukee, do prohibit schools that opt to receive children with vouchers from requiring additional tuition payments over and above the voucher's value. And indeed, the prohibition on "top-ups" is another way of making private schools that receive public monies for educating children a bit more like public schools. If a child with a voucher wants to attend a certain school that has decided to receive children with vouchers, the child should not be barred because his or her parents cannot afford to pay some additional sum of tuition money. If a school wants to open its doors to children attending with public monies, it should not be allowed to discriminate on grounds of religion, class, race, or other factors. In the Milwaukee choice plan, schools are allowed to charge parents an additional fee only in order for children to participate in certain extracurricular activities.[18] If voucher plans became widely available to more than the poorest parents, it could become difficult to prohibit top-ups by parents, but the rationale for them is reasonable.

The merits of prohibiting top-ups might well be contested. The really pernicious problem in our society, some would argue, is not that some children (thanks in part to the generosity of their parents) receive an excellent education; it is rather that some other children receive a miserable education. Educational inequality should not be the focus of public policy. The focus should rather be on providing a good education for all. Our aim should be to lift up those children at the bottom, not to hold back the children of better-off parents or of parents of limited means who care a great deal about education for their children. It would be perverse and deeply divisive to prevent parents from seeking to do all they can to help their children. Our duty as citizens is not to hold back the advantaged, but to boost the disadvantaged.

Moreover, it could be argued that the attractiveness of prohibiting top-ups rests on viewing the quest for improved education as a zero-sum game, according to which excellence for some is a loss for others. To the contrary, however, the entire society benefits when some children have the very best opportunities to develop their talents and capacities. (Of course, there are broader social reasons to want to equalize wealth across generations via estate taxes and other measures.) Top-ups are not invidious so long as every child has access to a good education, which the public can and should provide for in any case. If the public concentrates on providing a good education for all, it should do nothing more to inhibit additional educational expenditures by parents or others.

How should we assess these arguments for allowing parents to top-up state-provided vouchers? It is doubtful that the prohibition on top-ups is required in all circumstances for vouchers to be permissible, but it is an effective and reasonable way of insuring that public support is not being used to subsidize class exclusion. If it seems right that schools that decide to take children with publicly funded vouchers should not be allowed to exclude children on religious grounds, then too it also seems to me appropriate to disallow schools admitting children with vouchers to exclude children who cannot pay additional fees. Targeting vouchers at disadvantaged children and failing school systems may help promote greater educational equality. If vouchers are going to be made more widely available to children—as Brighouse and others propose—then the prohibition on top-ups helps insure that public funds are not subsidizing class-based exclusion.[19]

Choice and Equality

The most-attractive voucher schemes, or so I have tried to suggest, are those targeted at improving the education of disadvantaged children. Insofar as vouchers are not tied to student disadvantage or school failure, they probably should contain safeguards to insure that public funds are not being used to subsidize unfair forms of exclusion. If the most urgent underlying aim is to improve failing schools, are vouchers and various forms of school choice really the most promising means? Would it be better simply to attack unequal school funding directly? The current system of school funding is highly inequitable: expenditures vary greatly from one school district to another. Can school choice of various sorts help address these inequalities, or would it be more effective to attack inequality directly without all the fuss about school choice? In many states, as we shall see, inadequate school funding is being challenged directly in state courts.

Comparing spending levels across districts does not begin to measure inequalities in the provision of educational services. Inequalities are greatly exacerbated by the fact that children from disadvantaged backgrounds are much more expensive to educate: children from immigrant backgrounds need bilingual education classes, and children from economically and culturally impoverished backgrounds have special needs of all kinds. Giving all children a decent education will require greater resources in districts composed of large numbers of disadvantaged children: equity requires special expenditures for children whose special needs make them expensive to educate. Unfortunately, the poorest school districts tend to have the largest numbers of special-needs students. There are vast inequalities across and within neighboring school districts.

Against this background, Stephen D. Sugarman has recently argued that a wide variety of choice-based educational reforms—not just vouchers, but charter schools, and even simply transfers across public school districts—can be expected to create pressures toward more equitable funding within the public school system. Parental choice and student mobility have the effect of increasing the information that people in poorer school districts—parents, principals, and school administrators—have about the relative advantages enjoyed by wealthier and better-off districts. Choice should bring home to disadvantaged districts the facts of inequity, and give them a greater incentive to lobby for greater equity. It will also help people see that there are important disparities of spending and quality in different schools *within* school districts.[20]

This argument (and I should emphasize that this is only one of Sugarman's arguments for school choice) puts a great deal of trust in the efficacy of certain mechanisms. Subsidizing movements of students across district boundaries will, he supposes, transfer information about inequities to poorer districts and foment pressure for greater equity; in that way, many forms of school choice will create political pressures for greater equalization of school spending and quality. But will this happen? The awful state of inner-city schools in New York City, for example, is very well known. Parents and administrators know full well that the students suffer great disadvantages: not simply because absolute levels of spending per pupil are lower, but because the school-age population in New York City is especially disadvantaged and therefore expensive to educate; everything is more expensive in New York City, including the living expenses of teachers who reside in the city (the city has to pay more to keep good teachers than do cities with lower costs of living). The problem in New York City and other cities is not information so much as politics: how to get state and local governments and citizens across the state to support more adequate school funding. The expected political pressures for greater equalization may not appear as a consequence of choice, especially if choice has the effect of creaming students whose parents are relatively engaged and active. Within many big school districts, moreover, teachers with seniority can transfer to the schools they prefer; instead of working to improve lousy schools, teachers upset about poor conditions can bide their time until they can move to better schools.

There are many good arguments for altering the spending formula for schools in a state like New York, in order to weaken the linkage between local tax bases and educational expenditures. But the argument just surveyed does not give enough weight to the complex politics of school reform, and so it is excessively hopeful. It is far from obvious that school choice is the most effective way to address the disparities in public-education funding.

Equity before Choice: State Courts to the Rescue?

In spite of the dependence of education funding on local taxes, some equalization is fostered by the federal government (which subsidizes particular programs for the needy) and especially by state governments, many of whose constitutions have provisions mandating the provision of a decent education for all. Some argue, therefore, that New York City is already treated generously by the state of New York. The city receives $4,500 per pupil in state aid annually, whereas Westchester receives only $2,000 per pupil. Nevertheless, the city's funding levels—at $9,000 per pupil—are well below those of wealthy Westchester County, which spends $13,000 per pupil. This discrepancy is greatly exacerbated by the fact that New York City has a vastly higher proportion of students from deprived backgrounds and with special educational needs: New York City must provide vastly more expensive bilingual and remedial education to large numbers of students.

Fully 60 percent of the state's poor children reside in New York City. In the 1998–99 school year, 40 percent of the total attendance at New York City schools—or 442,000 out of one million children in this school system—were children from families receiving Aid to Families with Dependent Children. As Christopher Jencks and Meredith Phillips have put it, children with severe academic and behavioral problems, who are disproportionately poor and black,

> consume many times more resources than the average child. To begin with they are often assigned to very small classes. . . . Schools where many children have serious academic, emotional, or disciplinary problems need more reading specialists, more psychologists, and more security guards. That leaves less money for regular teachers. Finally, children with serious problems consume a disproportionate share of the teachers' time when they are in regular classes, leaving less time for other students.

Disadvantaged students are disproportionately black, so, as Jencks and Philips put it,

> the net result is that while predominantly black schools spend about as much per pupil as predominantly white schools, ordinary black children without special problems are likely to be in large classes, get less attention, and have less academically skilled teachers than similar white children.[21]

Differences in per-pupil expenditures hardly begin to calibrate the real inequalities in educational opportunities available to poorer children in New York City and to children in the better-off suburbs. The average city teacher attended a less-competitive college than did teachers elsewhere in the state, and neighboring suburbs can lure the best teachers by paying them 20–36 percent more than the city does. In the 1997–98 school year, 13.7 percent of city's teachers were not qualified to teach in any of the subjects they taught, compared with just 3.3 percent statewide. In that same year, 31 percent of the city's teachers failed the Liberal Arts and Science Test on their first try, compared with just 4.7 percent statewide.[22]

All of these facts were cited by Justice Leland DeGrasse of the New York State Supreme Court in an opinion striking down what he called the "unnecessarily complex and opaque" state education funding system. The state must do more, he insisted, to "align funding with need." The education system of New York fails to fulfill the state constitution's guarantee of a "sound basic education" for all children. Providing at-risk kids with a sound basic education requires greater levels of education spending than the state is now providing.[23]

Not only in New York but in other states as diverse as North Carolina and Arkansas, state courts are striking down state educational funding systems on the grounds that the education provided is inadequate and inequitable. On May 25, 2001, a state judge in a chancery court of Pulaski County declared that "the school funding system now in place in the State of Arkansas is inequitable and inadequate under . . . the Arkansas Constitution." The state must provide sufficient funding for an "adequate educational system" for all of Arkansas's children. The court specifically noted that "the Little Rock Public Schools cannot meet the needs of their children with the money it has and yet it has more money per student and in total than any other school district in Arkansas."[24]

Conclusion

Providing at least an "adequate" or a good education for all children ought to be the central touchstone when it comes to assessing school reform proposals. The failure of this country to provide an adequate education to disadvantaged youngsters—who are disproportionately black and Hispanic—is a national shame that calls out for redress. Is choice the most effective way of addressing these needs? Limited school choice experiments targeted at disadvantaged youngsters and at failing school systems provide some welcome relief for a few.

Larger-scale voucher reforms might be designed to equalize educational expenditures. It is by no means obvious that the equity-enhancing potential of some voucher plans will be sustained as reform plays out in the political process.

There are equity-based concerns with every form of school choice, and even if we focus on what seem to me the right sorts of equity concerns, public charter schools may make some of the advantages of private schools available within the public sector, and yet they may also have the effect of "creaming" the best students off public schools (they may thus promote more equal opportunities for some public school children while leaving others worse off, at least in the short run).[25] The actual consequences of every form of school choice are going to be extremely difficult to sort out. In addition, the introduction of any form of school reform is liable to change the nature of the public argument over education in ways that could be hard to anticipate.

At least as hopeful as the halting progress of school vouchers are the dramatic decisions being handed down in state courts, decisions that (according to a preliminary study by Douglas Reed) may really be having the effect of increasing education expenditures for poorly performing school districts serving disadvantaged children.[26] We can proceed to expand school choice with confidence only if courts and other political bodies insist that the pursuit of greater equity—properly understood—is a nonnegotiable touchstone for improved public-education policy. States should be understood to have a positive duty to see to it that every child has access to a good education. School choice should be welcomed when it advances this goal.

Response

PAUL WEITHMAN

THE QUESTION OF WHETHER school choice should be publicly subsidized is of obvious interest and importance. Just as interesting and important are two other questions closely connected with it: (i) Which arguments for subsidizing school choice are morally compelling? and (ii) Which arguments for subsidizing school choice are politically successful? Question (i) matters because if school choice is to be publicly subsidized, it should be subsidized for good reasons. Answering (i) helps us locate those reasons. Question (ii) matters because of what answers to it show about the American electorate. The arguments that enjoy political success enjoy it because they appeal to what voters care about. One way to find out about what Americans value is to look at which arguments for school choice they accept. We also learn something about Americans, and about the possibilities and limits of American politics, by considering (i) and (ii) together. If American voters are moved by considerations that are in fact morally compelling, we have some grounds for optimism about American politics. On the other hand, if arguments that are morally compelling are not successful—if American voters are not responsive to considerations that ought to move them—we need to ask why.

The most natural defense of subsidized choice might seem to be a line of thought we can call "the free-choice argument." This argument seizes on the morally significant gains that would be realized when parents and students have choices among educational options that are unconstrained because each of the options can be exercised at no cost. To see what those gains would be, note first that public subsidies which would cover the costs of educating all children at any school of their or their parents' choice would break the near monopoly now enjoyed by American public schools. Alternatives to public schools would proliferate, increasing parental and student liberty by increasing the range of affordable options. Once parents and students were free to choose among the expanded educational options, schools would try to secure market niches by differentiating themselves philosophically and by offering better educations than their competitors. The results, according to the free-choice argument, would be desirable on two counts. First, parents and students could choose schools that suited their own educational philosophies. This would be fairer to parents and students who dissent from the philosophy that now animates American public education. Second, good schools would drive bad ones from the market. The desirability of these two results is supposed to be sufficient to justify subsidizing school choice. If it does, then the free-choice argument is the answer to (i). Furthermore, since Americans are said to attach such a high value to liberty, the free-choice argument seems destined for political success. It can therefore be expected to be the answer to (ii).

Stephen Macedo argues, in effect, that the free-choice argument is not as compelling as it initially seems. He does so by challenging two of the assumptions on which it rests. One is that a free educational market financed by universal subsidies is the best way to solve the problem posed by poor schools. The other is that a fair educational system is one which results from the choices parents and students make when they are free to act on their educational preferences. The second assumption is mistaken, Macedo thinks, because not all the preferences consumers would bring to the educational market have an equal claim to satisfaction. Indeed, Macedo would insist, a much weaker assumption is also mistaken: the assumption that one educational scheme is fairer than another if it better satisfies preferences founded on fundamental interests, such as an interest in the free exercise of religion. There are, Macedo maintains, legitimate public purposes to education. Dissent from the educational philosophy underlying those purposes does not give parents or students a claim to relief, even if their dissent is religiously based. Thus the American educational system is not unfair because it fails to satisfy the preferences, even the religious preferences, students and parents happen to have. If it is unfair, it is unfair because some students but not others have no choice but to attend schools that are not serving the legitimate public purpose of providing them a good education. The best argument for school choice, Macedo thinks, is that it would provide *these* students relief. Since schools that fail to satisfy this public purpose are disproportionately attended by certain segments of the population, relief does not require universal subsidies. It requires targeted subsidies, aimed at producing a more equitable distribution of educational benefits. An equity argument for targeted subsidies, not a free-choice argument for universal ones, is Macedo's answer to (i).

In their chapters, Alan Wolfe and Joseph Viteritti document a generational shift in arguments for subsidized school choice toward exactly the sort of argument Macedo claims is most morally compelling. What Wolfe and Viteritti call "first-generation" arguments for vouchers and other subsidies were free-choice arguments for an unfettered, publicly subsidized educational market. These arguments failed to secure significant public backing for the measures they supported. They failed because most Americans, Wolfe says, want schools to teach well and to prepare students for citizenship. Parents are largely satisfied with the education provided by schools in their districts because they believe schools meet these standards. Free-choice arguments are widely accepted only among segments of the voting-age population whose children have no choice at all but to attend failing public schools. This suggests that the political success or failure of the free-choice argument depends not upon a desire for the individual satisfaction the free choice argument promises, but upon whether the currently available educational options are adequate to advance what Macedo would identify as legitimate public purposes.

Because of the political failure of free-choice arguments, the first generation of arguments for subsidized universal choice has given way to a second. Arguments of the newer generation are mustered to defend not subsidized universal choice, but subsidies directed to parents whose children attend failing public schools. Arguments of the second generation, unlike those of the first, do not ultimately depend upon the appeal of freedom. They are premised instead on the moral imperative of providing alternatives for students in poor schools. That imperative, in turn, is premised on the moral imperative to distribute an important public good—publicly subsidized education—more equitably.

These arguments, unlike free-choice arguments, secure some support for subsidies even among voters who would not receive them. As Viteritti shows, subsidized school-choice programs were passed in Wisconsin, Ohio, and Florida with the support of broad-based and nontraditional political coalitions. Wolfe argues that these broad-based coalitions illustrate a "new politics of race" in which smaller-government, market-friendly conservatives form political alliances with minorities who have traditionally supported liberal candidates and policies. He also argues that the failure of free-choice arguments and the moderate political success of equity-based arguments shows something interesting and important about the temper of the American electorate: Americans are less individualistic, and less willing to give overriding importance to freedom of choice, than they are often said to be.

This section thus juxtaposes two chapters that answer (ii) with a chapter that answers (i). Taken together, the essays suggest some happy coincidences. The arguments for subsidized choice to which

Wolfe and Viteritti say Americans are most responsive are also those which Macedo says are the most compelling. Furthermore, Wolfe and Viteritti show that support for subsidized choice is far from whole-hearted. Those who oppose subsidized choice do so because, among other reasons, they worry that nonpublic schools would skim the best students from public schools and that subsidizing religious schools would threaten the separation of church and state. These are just the grounds on which Macedo thinks equity-based arguments for subsidized school choice are most vulnerable. The three chapters of this section therefore suggest that the American electorate as a whole is appropriately responsive to, and appropriately tentative in its acceptance of, the strongest arguments for subsidized choice. Macedo, Wolfe, and Viteritti all recognize that Americans are only partway through a long national debate and that a settled solution to it is far in the future. But if the arguments of all three chapters are sound, then we have grounds to hope that the measures we eventually adopt will enjoy political support for the right reasons and that the degree of support will be proportional to their merits.

I want to suggest that we should not be as sanguine about either the school-choice debate or the wisdom of the American electorate as the conjunction of essays in this section suggests. To begin to see why, note first that the equity arguments discussed in the chapters in this section are unclear on the crucial point of just what good is supposed to be distributed equitably, or more equitably, by measures that subsidize school choice. The most defensible answer to the question "Equity of what?" I shall suggest, points to a good the equitable distribution of which is very unlikely to be the subject of American political debate. It is unlikely to be the subject of debate both because of the complexity of the questions equitable distribution would raise and because taking equitable distribution seriously as a public responsibility would require the American electorate to challenge assumptions many of us are reluctant to rethink. Thus the conclusions initially suggested in this section need to be qualified. The qualifications tell us as much about the American electorate as they do about the conclusions they hedge in.

The problem with equity arguments is that once we get beyond very abstract talk about the equitable distribution of educational benefits or educational goods, it is not clear exactly *what* is supposed to be equitably distributed and why. Consider the various kinds of equity or equality that are mentioned as prima facie grounds for subsidized school choice in the chapters here. Proponents of subsidized school choice say it promises to:

- address inequities or inequalities in the per-child expenditure of public school funds
- equalize or make more nearly equal the range of options open to well-off and less-well-off parents
- equalize test scores across racial divides
- promote racial equality
- promote equality of opportunity to attain the goods with which education is correlated
- equalize opportunities for educational attainment by equally able and motivated students

Which of these are the benefits we want to distribute? Equalizing per-child expenditure is not an end in itself. Rather, it is a *means* to the equitable distribution of the educational benefits money can buy. Equalizing the range of options open to parents is also a means. Equal test scores across significant lines is an imperfect *indicator* that a school system is distributing educational benefits equitably. Racial equality in society might be the *result* of equitable distribution. It *is* important to equalize opportunities to attain goods with which education is correlated later in life. But if we think of these opportunities as the primary benefits conferred by education, we lapse into instrumentalism. We thereby risk misrepresenting the value of many of the benefits education should confer, benefits like the appreciation of literature, painting, and music; acquaintance with one's own and other cultures; knowledge of history and philosophy. Expenditures, options, test scores, opportunities for later success—none takes us any closer to identifying the benefits that we are most interested in distributing equitably.

A more plausible answer to the question Equity of what? is that equity demands providing equally talented and motivated students the opportunity for equal educational attainment. Thus the benefit to be distributed is the opportunity for educational attainment; equitable distribution of this benefit consists in providing it equally to students with the same abilities and initiative. Unfortunately this answer, though attractive, is at best misleading and perhaps mistaken. This is because the answer suggests that we can identify motivated students— as we try to identify talented ones—apart from seeing what stock of educational benefits they enjoy. It therefore suggests that motivation is exogenous to education, that it is something students bring to school. In fact, one of an educator's most important tasks is eliciting the motivation to learn. Motivation is not, therefore, an independent variable according to which the intended recipients of educational benefits can be ranked. It is among the benefits schools distribute. Once we see this, we see just how difficult the problem of equitably distributing educational benefits is. It is in part the problem of how equitably to create incentives the effective operation of which brings other benefits into being. Better, it is in part the problem of equitably providing one educational benefit—motivation—that induces students to realize other educational benefits by acting on it, benefits like their own knowledge and wisdom, as well as the skills needed for meaningful work.

Americans are, I believe, unlikely to demand that the education system distribute this benefit equitably. They are therefore unlikely to debate the question of whether subsidized choice is necessary to satisfy this standard of equity. One reason we are unlikely to hold the education system to this standard of equity—rather than one according to which we should equitably distribute opportunity for attainment to students who are equally talented—is that it is far more difficult to measure and compare students' motivation than it is to measure and compare their talent or their attainment. Unfortunately, standards of success that are easily quantified and applied drive out standards that are more difficult to operationalize but that would, if formulated, tell us what we really want to know. Another reason we are unlikely to hold the education system to this standard of equity is that it would be very difficult for schools to know what steps they could take to meet it. The problem of eliciting and sustaining students' motivation is extraordinarily difficult. The motivation to learn depends upon curiosity and desire for the joy of discovery. It depends upon self-esteem, faith that one's efforts will be rewarded, hope that the rewards are worth the effort, and the conviction that expending the effort it takes to learn is not a fool's game. We are very far from understanding the motivation to persevere and succeed in school. And we are very far from understanding how differences in economic opportunity, social location, family structure, parental or adult solicitude, and gender can affect it.

Our refusal to debate these matters is hardly cost-free. We are most likely to gain insight into them by conducting educational experiments—experiments like single-sex academies for at-risk youth. These experiments, conducted to see how educational benefits can be made available more *equitably* across divisions of race and class, may violate canons of *equal* access to benefits. A girls-only public school in Harlem has been challenged by civil liberties groups. Officials in the Clinton education department declined to respond to the challenge.[1] But in 1991 a U.S. district judge enjoined the Detroit school board from opening three inner-city male-only academies on the grounds that single-sex academies would violate, among other things, the equal protection clause of the Constitution.[2] It seems that experiments in single-sex education will most safely be conducted in the private educational sector. I want to suggest that those experiments should be publicly subsidized. What grounds the argument for a subsidy is not the proven value of the schools' educational methods. It is the importance of finding out whether promising methods can serve equity by delivering educational benefits—including self-esteem, hope, and curiosity—to those most at risk. Until complicated motivational questions are seriously debated, such experiments are unlikely to be performed and subsidized as widely as they need to be for us to learn from their outcomes.

Educators are not alone in being vexed by the question of how to elicit and sustain motivation. Questions about human motivation are among the hardest in psychology and moral philosophy. But if the only reasons Americans are unlikely to debate how the education system could satisfy the standard of equity I have suggested were the inherent difficulty of the issue, the absence of debate would be troubling enough. Many of the problems facing us in the twenty-first century are problems of enormous complexity. We will not solve them by ignoring their difficulty or wishing it away.

More troubling is the fear that Americans will not debate difficult motivational questions because too many of us think that the desire to succeed is an instinctual or natural response to poor circumstances. It is the absence rather than the presence of motivation that, we think, needs to be explained. As a result, Americans are uncomfortable with the thought that the willingness to try might be stifled rather than elicited by the crushing circumstances and dim life prospects of many students who attend the worst schools. Asking how to motivate these students would eventually require us to ask more probing questions about how their social, economic, and political circumstances dampen their hopes. These are questions—like questions about how school choice can promote equity as measured by the most defensible standards—that we are unlikely to debate any time soon. We should take heart, as Wolfe suggests, from the fact that Americans care about equality as well as liberty and that we are somewhat willing to promote equality of opportunity through educational policy. But we should be disappointed that we are unwilling to challenge cherished assumptions about the preconditions for taking advantage of opportunities when they are provided.

SCHOOL CHOICE AND PLURALISM

Four

Separating the Siamese Twins, "Pluralism" and "School Choice"

NANCY L. ROSENBLUM

DISCUSSIONS OF PLURALISM and school choice assume that the two go together. Arguments rely on their inseparability, their implied identity. The promise of vouchers and tax credits, charter schools, and non-zoned schools within the public system is parental choice, and the assumption is opportunities for choice among schools that differ across dimensions that matter. Advocates are not always explicit about what pluralist dimensions we can expect to find in education—supporters are encouraged to fill in their own aspirations. In these discussions the twins are symbiotic; each reinforces the positive aspects of the other. Choice is supposed to increase pluralism, and pluralism is supposed to be generally accessible, with opportunities for choice.

My thesis is that pluralism and school choice have no inherent connection and that attempts to link them reflect a degree of careless presumption or bad faith. Looked at carefully, arguments for choice are not pluralist, and pluralist arguments do not assign special value to choice. Moreover, under present conditions in the United States, the implication that school choice means effective choice among imagined pluralist alternatives in practice is misleading, is wrong as a likely consequence of policy changes, and is vulnerable even as an aspiration. My purpose is to be alert and skeptical of their assumed connection as a matter of theoretical argument, advocacy, and practice. I will separate the Siamese twins and show that when that operation is performed, both are weak survivors.

I want to emphasize at the outset that for my purposes, *pluralism* means more than educational diversity. Diversity exists today among independent schools, within and among public school systems, and from school to school and classroom to classroom. There are roughly 90,000 public schools in the United States, 15,000 school districts, and 1,700 charter schools; there are roughly 27,400 private schools, 30 percent of them Catholic, 48 percent other sectarian, and fewer than a quarter nonsectarian.[1] In public education, the fluctuating tug of war between federal and state, and state and local "control" (itself an abstraction that must be broken down into an array of legal requirements, funding schemes, curricular decisions, classroom organization, standards and assessment, and so on) is part of a larger field of competing authorities. Active on the field are professional educators' groups, teachers' unions, textbook publishers, advocacy groups, and parents (organized and disorganized). Arrangements for student opt-outs, parental vetoes over aspects of the curriculum, charter schools, and so on further dilute unitary government control. Many so-called monopolistic and hierarchic public school systems have instituted reforms that produce a degree of educational diversity and choice.

And this is to say nothing of the fact that the substantive content of education is a moving target. "Not every generation but every few years the content of American history books changes appreciably"; the same generation of children in the same school district will have been exposed to vastly different narratives and pictures of national identity.[2] To take celebrated examples from education of what Alan Wolfe has called "moral federalism": Kansas recently eliminated evolution from the required curriculum; Utah prohibits sex education in birth-control methods other than abstinence; at least six urban school systems have instituted Afrocentric curricula; Philadelphia permits single-sex public schools.

The forces of standardization will always fail, for unintended reasons and because they are deliberately (and often justifiably) subverted. That said, diversity is not pluralism. Pluralism refers to schools designed in accord with a particular group or community's values and goals, most often schools organized around culture, language, or religion. In a multicultural society, strong pluralist advocates and their arguments deserve our attention. Attention is diverted if we confound pluralism with just any difference in pedagogy and curriculum.

Pluralism Eclipsed, Choice Ascendant

Advocates of school choice propose a "new *Pierce* compromise." In 1925 the Supreme Court in *Pierce v. Society of Sisters* paired state responsibility for inculcating "the fundamental values necessary to the maintenance of a democratic political system" with individual freedom to exit public schools for reasons related to "the private beliefs of the student and his or her family." It ruled criminal penalties for those who elect private schooling unconstitutional, while upholding compulsory school attendance and "reasonable" government regulation of all schools, including curriculum content standards.[3] School-choice advocates would refashion the compromise by providing public funding to parents who elect private education.[4] "School choice" refers also to options offered by public school systems: charter and magnet schools, "schools within schools," examination schools, special non-zoned schools within or across residence-based public school districts, and so on.

The arguments in support of school choice employed most often by academics, advocates, politicians, and the media have nothing to do with pluralism. Recent shifts in the terms of discussion of public support for private schooling reflect this. One shift goes from subsidizing schools to subsidizing children—that is, "true private-choice programs,"[5] another shift goes from subsidizing children generally to compensating some students for failing public schools, in order to provide the educationally worst off with an educational minimum.[6] Whether choice refers to grants or tuition tax benefits to families who send their children to private schools or to publicly or privately run charter schools, pluralism is not a principal justification. Pluralism is present in the background of these arguments as an implicit adjunct of choice. But pluralism is not the reason for choice schemes. Instead, we find three main lines of argument.

The dominant justification for choice appeals to the quality of education, to *performance* and outcomes. One argument sees choice as compensatory for unacceptable school performance; in these cases choice is restricted to educationally disadvantaged students who qualify because they attend inadequate public schools.[7] President George W. Bush alludes to the inner-city population targeted by this sort of plan by calling literacy "the new civil right." The Cleveland voucher program, a legislative response to the district court ruling that placed the Cleveland School District under receivership "due to mismanagement by the local school board" was designed to provide financial help to allow poverty-level students "to escape the devastating consequences of attending Cleveland's demonstrably failed public schools."[8] In addition to vouchers to attend private schools, the program provided options for special tutoring in the public schools. (Notice that the stratification that counts for purposes of choice in the United States is the educational bottom; there is no parallel movement advocating public funding for eligible students to attend elite private schools.)

Alternatively, universal choice is justified as the principal instrument for creating "effective schools" broadly, rather than as correctives for the most egregious deficiencies.[9] This justification for choice is also contingent; it rests on the perception that public education overall is in need of substantial improvement, fast, as well as on the judgment that alternative mechanisms for improvement are inadequate.[10]

Periods of educational innovation have all been marked by pronouncements of American "declinism."[11] Whether they are promoted
by progressives or conservatives and whatever the form—school-to-
work plans, computer-based learning, school-based budgeting, multiculturalism, content standards, testing, merit pay, more homework,
less homework, site-based management, or choice—reforms are represented as cures for "crisis".[12] The term is distorted and overused; nothing is as normal as invoking "crisis" to spur fast action to reverse decline. Ironically, an early tuition-reimbursement program struck down
by the Supreme Court as a violation of the establishment clause in
Committee for Public Education v. Nyquist in 1973 was designed to subsidize private, mostly Catholic schools for the purpose of preventing an
influx of students into the already overburdened New York City school
system. In short, the program was justified as an effort to hold off a
fiscal crisis in the state's public schools.[13] Educational reform in this
country is a crusade. The emphasis is parceled out in shifting fashion
among concern for democratic values and "civic literacy," for an educated workforce and enhanced "human capital" with a view to economic competition and productivity, and for national security.[14] We can
add to this list diffuse moral declinism—vice, crime, or baleful egotism
corrigible with the rehabilitative programs demanded by "vir-
tuecrats."[15] The contemporary alliance of state governors and corporate
executives trumpeting technology invokes a new economic definition
of national security ("We have, in effect, been committing an act of
unthinking, unilateral educational disarmament.")[16]

That choice proponents should draw on these grim assessments of
the state of education is not surprising. Neither is the criticism that the
alleged school-quality "crisis" is manufactured by one or another faction to undermine confidence in public schools. Still, we recognize the
inherent optimism of choice proposals. They insist that all children are
capable of the sort of achievement historically reserved for a few. They
put the onus for disappointing achievement on schools and not on students' background characteristics or abilities. State-imposed standardized testing (along with attention to attendance, dropout rates, promotion rates, and so on) is principally a way of holding schools
accountable.[17] Choice emphasizes the independent power of educational reform to set and enforce academic standards.[18]

The most comprehensive framework for choice on performance
grounds has it that some form of public funding for private schools or
charter schools or both is justified because competition and *only* competition improves education. And because the motor of competition is
consumer choice, the demand side, as well as the supply side, of education must be liberated from political control. Fifty years ago Milton

Friedman attributed educational mediocrity to state monopoly and bureaucratic inertia, proposing market competition as the necessary condition for reform. Chubb and Moe continue in this vein, insisting that
"the schools cannot be reformed without making more basic changes
in the educational system that governs them, since the system is the
source of their ineffectiveness."[19] So long as democratic control of
schools is preserved, bureaucratization and hierarchy will be irremedi-
able, public schools will continue to be "incompatible with effective
education," and reforms will be destined to fail.[20]

Integral to this argument are two assumptions. One is that the exercise of consumer power presents rational incentives to schools "whose
primary concern is to please their clients." Giving this dynamic its
force is the further assumption that choice is guided by the demand for
quality rather than a school's convenience and proximity; or religious
instruction; or a particular social, racial, or cultural makeup; or a simple refuge from an unsafe neighborhood. Choice's importance in increasing the power of parents and students relative to school boards,
administrators, and other interest groups (beneficiaries of patronage
appointments in urban schools, for example) depends on academic excellence being the goal. That is what allows Chubb and Moe to characterize choice as a "self-contained reform" that "has the capacity *all by
itself* to bring about the kind of transformation" reformers have tried
to engineer in other ways.[21]

For my purposes, the important point is that in this argumentative
framework, pluralism is eclipsed. Chubb and Moe say nothing about
religious schools, for example. Their goal is institutional change for effective education. Schools "whose primary concern is to please their
clients," the kinds of schools they say people want, means quality on
their view, not distinctiveness.[22] The leading choice argument does not
link choice to pluralism.

Competition need not be market competition and choice need not
be a stalking horse for privatization. Advocates of public school reform
see movement away from zoned neighborhood schools to a parallel or
alternative system of competing public schools as an efficient tool for
change.[23] For Chubb and Moe, market competition in the private sector
is a practical necessity, given what they see as the fatal inhibitions democratic politics places on competition. But they insist that private
schools are not inherently better than public schools, and that with the
right governing institutions, public schools could develop the same effective organizations.[24]

In fact, the competition thesis can be dropped altogether from justifications for choice based on performance. What remains is the more
modest proposition that choice per se, whether the selected school is

public or private, increases the "social capital" invested in education: PTA membership, parent volunteerism, trust in teachers, and so on.[25] Nor is competition integral to the proposition that in practice private schools just do produce measurably superior educational outcomes.[26] The reasons offered are legion. They range from internal governance practices to discipline, from loosening the constraints of teacher tenure and union contracts to more cooperative unions between family and school. Or perhaps it is just that private schools "find it easier . . . to place a high priority on excellence and to choose a set of goals that is clear and consistent, whatever those goals may be."[27] So facilitating access to private schools would improve education for more children.[28] Of course, the same argument is available to advocates of public school reform; insofar as measurable academic improvement can be traced to systematic changes like class size or academic expectations, the comparative advantage of private over public schools is diminished.

Often, choice proponents add that private schools do not present the dangers to democratic education opponents warn against. Given state regulation regarding what schools must or may not teach, and voluntary congruence between most private education and democratic values, private education serves public purposes well. Private education is not just compatible with the values attributed to public education, but is as good or better than public establishment for education in democratic values and practices. Consider some of the leading propositions in this vein:

- When it comes to inculcating substantive values, private schools provide the basic requirements of a civic curriculum—and do a better job of it insofar as they do a better job of teaching generally.
- Pedagogy is as important for instilling democratic values and practices as curriculum, and private schools are as likely as public schools to implement participatory activities that foster cooperation over competition, deliberation, and so on.[29]
- In cultivating democratic dispositions—from tolerance generally to comfort with racial integration specifically—private education is better and would be better still if economic barriers were reduced so that student populations were more diverse.[30]
- Overall, private school populations are more diverse than the populations in most suburban schools.
- Christopher Jencks and Meredith Phillips argue that reducing the black-white test-score gap "is probably both necessary and sufficient for substantially reducing racial inequality in educational attainment and earnings . . . which would in turn help reduce racial differences in crime, health, and family structure.[31]

As if to deemphasize pluralism and the link between education and faith or particular cultural values, advocates often deny that choice proposals amount to privatization. *Public* is redefined to include "any school that serves the public interest and is ultimately accountable to public authorities."[32] For some, the ideal is to see every school as a charter school, part of a system of national public education. The performance justification for choice is a public-good argument, after all. And critics of choice confirm the public interest in policy decisions about choice: "Our political fortunes, retirement benefits, and tax dollars are at stake."[33]

A principal weakness of performance arguments is that choice per se is no guarantee of quality education or even of adequate education, of course; public schools have no monopoly on low expectations. There are daunting inhibitions on the creation of good schools, quite apart from the political obstacles stressed by choice theorists. Even as regards minimal public standards like attendance requirements or teacher qualification and certification, experience with *Pierce*-mandated government oversight of private schools shows radical variation among states and lax implementation.[34] Critics challenge both the relative performance claims of choice proponents and the benign picture of private schools as compatible with the goals of public education.[35]

For some critics, many private institutions and fundamentalist Christian schools in particular have identifiably harmful effects and are a threat to students' well-being. These schools inculcate a worldview that involves "racism, antifeminism, anti-intellectualism, and plutocratic politics." They "infringe children's basic liberties by imposing excessive restrictions on students' intellectual and physical freedom and fostering excessive repression of desires and inclinations." They "actively discourage children's development of the generalized capacity for independent and informed critical thinking." "They foster . . . dogmatic, inflexible modes of thought and expression" and intolerance. They have "adverse psychological effects for many students, including diminished self-esteem, extreme anxiety, and pronounced and sometimes lifelong anger and resentment." It follows that government should not tolerate, much less fund, the educational deprivation of millions of children.[36]

In short, for the dominant group of supporters of choice the justification and goal is "neutral" academic performance. Arguments do not focus on pluralism—on schools geared to the interests and needs of particularist groups and communities. Quality is key, and choice is instrumental.

There are two other frameworks of argument besides performance used to justify school choice. One appeals to the general principle of liberty.[37] Here too pluralism is an assumed accompaniment of choice but not the justification for choice. That similarity aside, the performance and liberty frameworks are analytically separable. Nothing in educational liberty insures or even speaks to choice among quality alternatives. And here, choice is not an instrument of school reform, but the sole end.

Liberty arguments switch the ground from public schooling as an inefficient monopoly to public schooling as despotism. Terms like *establishment* and *empire, compulsory* and *coercive indoctrination* are staples of this literature. Libertarian critics represent compulsory education as "conscription." "Comrade John Dewey" is a particular target; his stress on the need for children to get along in groups is cast as preparation for socialism.[38] While some would end compulsory schooling altogether and others would settle for curricular opt-outs for dissenters or curricular opt-ins requiring parental permission, the dominant position is choice.

An appeal to liberty is the heart of Michael McConnell's argument for public funding for secular and sectarian private schooling in "Educational Disestablishment: Why Democratic Values Are Ill-Served by Democratic Control of Schooling." He refers to "government" in the singular: should "*the* government itself" control "the development and propagation of ideas, information, opinions, and culture," for example, and asserts that government imposes "one conception of 'common democratic values' *by force*" (italics added). Though his essay is a brief for government financing of private schooling, the state is portrayed as overbearing sovereign, not as patron.

McConnell's specific claim is that the "public school establishment" is inconsistent with disestablishmentarian liberal values because public education imposes a "civic religion" of "secular humanism." As sheer description, the "antiestablishment" portrait is vulnerable on one side from those with even an iota of comparative historical perspective, who have in mind, for example, the French public system with its history of severe anticlericalism; from this standpoint, talk of an American "civic religion" is a wild exaggeration. The antiestablishment case is vulnerable on the other side from those who would enforce a much more robust and uniform civic education. In any case, McConnell's antiestablishment argument makes common cause with poststructuralist and multiculturalist reports of disciplinary techniques and with the insidious ideological hegemony of liberal democracy. A distinguished First Amendment scholar, McConnell knows that there is no political establishment clause. There is no gag rule on democratic authority when it comes to ideology.[39] Government is constrained as coercive sovereign from censoring or chilling private speech, but not when it acts in its capacity as patron or educator. There is no prohibition on conditioning public funding on recipients' willingness to deliver government's message, either, even if this quid pro quo is characterized as professing "civic religion."

A much more specific variation on the liberty theme is Stephen Arons's attack on the "education empire" established by the Goals 2000 Education Act of 1994.[40] On Arons's reading, the act establishes government intervention in virtually every aspect of public schooling by means of national goals, planning and implementation of national or state content standards, assessments of student competency, and application of standards for promotion and graduation. It uses content standards as the basis for teacher training, certification, and assessment, for textbook publishing, for education research, and for employability certification. The act standardizes schooling and enforces politicized "official knowledge." It ignores the "essential principle" that for self-government to work, "freedom of belief, intellect, and expression must be protected from majority control."[41]

Liberty arguments for school choice join a broader debate in moral and political philosophy about whether government has plenary power over all schools, consistent with constitutional values. And, what can justify imposing *any* requirements on *any* schools, particularly some sort of "political education" thought to undergird liberal democracy?[42] Most advocates of choice in terms of educational liberty concede that *some* content standards are justifiably enforced on all schools—either things that must be taught or cannot be taught (McConnell supports some compulsory "civic minimum"), as well as some inspection, supervision, and regulation.[43] The acceptable range spans virtually the entire spectrum, from regulations and compliance mechanisms so comprehensive as to effectively eradicate the distinction between public and private education (teacher-certification requirements, state accreditation standards, approved textbooks, prescribed courses, and so on), to some sort of vague and middling measure of "substantially equivalent instruction" and standard of "teacher competence," to latitudinarian requirements like maintaining attendance and immunization records as well as health and safety rules.[44]

As McConnell's subtitle, "Why Democratic Values Are Ill-Served by Democratic Control of Schooling," suggests, opponents of "government controlled education" on liberty grounds engage in a family quarrel with their opponents over the contours of democratic education. They are not engaged in the graver and theoretically more challenging clash between democracy and a regime of pluralism.[45] I turn to that clash in the next section. The concessions these choice advocates make to both the public functions of education and the supervisory role for political authorities leave room for democratic decision making. So long as education is publicly funded, the kind and degree of democratic control will be decided politically.

Which is why for some, the only assurance of liberty is to separate public funding from public regulation altogether. Arons proposes a constitutional amendment that would add freedom of education to the list of fundamental rights protected against all levels of government. He would guarantee the right to public funding to every child to attend any school in the state; equal grants to every school-age child regardless of income, wealth, or local tax base; and the independence of every teacher and school from government regulation of the content of education.

Liberty arguments imply the existence of educational pluralism, of course. But pluralism is not the justification for liberty, and these discussions do not focus on the character or quality or range of the educational alternatives. Liberty arguments for choice are propelled by political theory, not educational theory, and not by considerations of religious or cultural pluralism. The energy here is negative—a thrust against coercion and the "bootcamps" that are public schools.

The *egalitarian* framework for justifying school choice looks to redistribute opportunities for students to attend private schools, and here too we find inattention to pluralism. The radical idea behind this case for choice is that equality requires not just formal rights of exit from assigned public schools, but also power to exercise choice effectively. Without public support for choice, there is an unfair distribution of educational resources, intergenerational transfer of advantages (and of disadvantages), and a compounding of the educational inequalities built into public education assigned by districting and residential neighborhoods.

In fact, few choice proposals are strictly egalitarian. Some focus on tax credits; others put no ceilings on the private contributions affluent parents can make to supplement vouchers, for example.[46]—to say nothing of the fact that they do not propose giving poor families the means to live in suburban areas with high-quality public schools. Still, tax-credit plans can be designed to support low-income families' tuitions. Voucher plans can be designed to reduce inequality of educational opportunity by giving priority to low-income students, building in ceilings, varying grants according to income, or requiring participating schools to accept voucher amounts as full tuition. In any case, "if those who are the primary, though not the only, victims of unequal access to school choice are members of minority racial, ethnic, and linguistic

groups, then these victims of discrimination will be the primary beneficiaries of a properly designed restoration of choice."[47]

The most common argument appeals to fairness and not to educational equality. It favors removing the unequal burden imposed on
those who choose private schools but must continue to pay taxes to
support public schools.[48] A more forceful version moves from the pre-
sumptive unfairness of "double taxation" to "double taxation" as a
violation of the constitutional right to equal protection of the laws.
Instead of seeing public support for private education as a discretionary subsidy, on this view we should see denial of public support as
a penalty—an unconstitutional condition or burden imposed on the
exercise of a constitutional right. In effect, government coerces people
to relinquish their rights through "double taxation."[49] What rights?
Typically the right at stake is religious free exercise, but theorists of
fairness sometimes propose the existence of a general right to private
schooling not only as against criminal penalties but as against financial pressures.

Egalitarian justifications for choice multiply. Another focuses on diversity. Advocates of school choice are determined to answer critics
who see choice as a way to subvert the legally mandated egalitarian
gains of the last thirty years in matters of race, gender, and disability.
Because state tuition-grant programs originated as a reaction against
school desegregation, and given the rise of private institutions in
places like Little Rock and Memphis after 1957, many voucher proponents try to deflect suspicion that choice intentionally or unintention-
ally works against progressive social objectives.[50] Toward this end they
may accede to constitutionalizing private schools in antidiscrimination
matters, using IRS withholding of tax-exempt status to insure compliance with regulations concerning admissions policy and hiring practices as a condition for public support.[51] Proposals may require participating schools to admit a certain percentage of students at random by
lottery, as charter schools often do. "Controlled choice" public programs give weight to race. Public school choice proposals may prohibit
participating schools from rejecting students on the basis of academic
achievement, athletic or extracurricular interest, handicapping condition, English-language deficiency, or disciplinary history.[52]

Egalitarian arguments aimed at deflecting the charge that *choice* is
code for whites escaping racial integration receive added force from
the presence of legal and political constraints on public school desegregation. These arguments include: centralized public school assignments have not always served equality; courts uphold remedies only
in the face of discriminatory purpose, not effect, thus immunizing racial segregation; political resistance bars metropolitan interdistrict rem-

edies; deference to local zoning laws and housing patterns fixes segregated neighborhoods; and amendments to Goals 2000 eliminated the requirement that states provide all schools with the resources necessary for students to meet the competency bars, a provision that would have made the act's content standards a basis for litigation. All of these confer at least rhetorical plausibility on the notion of "educational choice as a civil rights strategy."

Finally, egalitarian choice arguments may focus on *political equality* in decision making about schools. From the point of view of religionists, the values taught in public schools are the product of collective decisions to which they are not equal parties, since their beliefs are constitutionally excluded at the outset.[53] Comprehensive choice would correct this inequality. And on the positive side, the argument goes, the muted political voice of parents without the financial means to exit the public system would be enhanced. "Consumer sovereignty" is cast as the ally, not the alternative, to democratic equality. Some advocates of vouchers for African Americans emphasize community empowerment. For one choice proponent, "the principle is simple. If individuals do not have a community rooted in personal relations within which to test ideas and develop political skills, involvement in public life will decline," and schools are cast as the principal participatory institutions.[54]

In none of the three frameworks of justification for choice I have surveyed—performance, liberty, and equality—does pluralism serve as justification or goal.[55] Indeed, it is worth noting that an added impetus to each of these lines of arguments, perhaps *the* impetus behind vouchers, has little to do with *either* pluralism *or* choice: it is frustration with public institutions generally and schools specifically. That many Americans contending with inflexible public schools are prepared to place their confidence in sectarian groups or educational entrepreneurs is understandable. They may be open to literally any proposed solution, however faddish and unproved, from "teacher-proof" instructional methods to top-down standardization. Frustration fires the home-schooling movement, whose growth is no longer propelled exclusively by religious concerns.

We do not know how much opposition to public schools reflects deeper, more-virulent antigovernmentalism. Antigovernmentalism certainly fuels preferences for market solutions, but its foundation is resentment at lack of democratic control over alien institutions. Voters' withdrawal of support from public schools by way of statewide tax revolts or local votes to reject school-bond issues are dramatic but purely negative actions. No constructive measures follow; neither choice nor pluralism directly benefits from this virulent political pose.

Pluralism Ascendant:
  ## Choice Eclipsed

What about twin pluralism? The push for publicly supported pluralist education comes mainly from religious groups. Some proponents extend support for religious pluralism in education ecumenically; "partnering" is the official policy of alliances practiced by the Catholic Church, for example. Some include in the orbit of educational pluralism secular communities based on culture, ethnicity, or language—at least as a matter of consistency or political strategy.[56] Others argue for pluralist education for their own group, making common cause with others in a limited fashion at best. (Though every group is inhibited from publicly invoking the historic dissenters' claim for religious liberty: as second best to establishment, liberty only for themselves, and solely on grounds that they are right.) Advocates of Afrocentric schools, Asian-heritage schools, Hispanic culture–bilingual schools rarely join forces. Some advocates of all-black education mobilize to combat white-dominated alliances; if black social capital and empowerment have been associated with community control of urban schools, proposed educational alternatives are likely to be resisted. Many evangelicals are uneasy about coalitions and ecumenical arguments for educational pluralism because their first principle is refusal to tolerate regulatory constraints on sectarian schools that other religious groups are willing to abide.[57]

In any case, pluralists invert the question at the heart of the choice debate, from How unlike public schools *can* private schools be? to How unlike public schools *must* private schools be to serve pluralist goals? And neither of the principal frameworks for pluralist education puts an emphasis on choice.

One line of argument invokes secular democratic principles to justify educational pluralism. In "Believers as Equal Citizens," Michael McConnell observes that religious believers are accountable to a sovereign higher than democratic government. Demands of faith transcend obligations of citizenship, even if these obligations are the result of legitimate democratic decisions and within constitutional limits. "The first freedom," he asserts, is the ability to act according to conscience. Because of the tension between citizenship and faith, the *Pierce* compromise, which privatizes faith, is untenable. The only way to make believers feel that they are full members of the political community is to reduce the potential for conflict. In the case of Christian schools, for example, faith has led to defiance of state laws requiring licensing or teacher certification, credit hours, and testing.[58]

A key element of this argument for pluralism as a condition of equal citizenship is the judgment that standard judicial measures to ensure free exercise and legislative measures to accommodate believers are inadequate. The escape to private schooling provided by *Pierce*, accommodations like *Yoder*, or opt-outs from specific classes or assignments do not suffice. Nor would McConnell be satisfied to restrict vouchers to "legitimate values dissenters."[59] The whole point is to avoid singling groups out as dissenters. That is to stigmatize them as second-class citizens. "Accommodation" is not full inclusion.[60]

McConnell calls instead for a "regime of pluralism." This regime prescribes entitlements for communities of conscience as well as exemptions and accommodations. In this respect it goes beyond the terms of the failed Religious Freedom Restoration Bill, which would have extended the terms of the free exercise clause by insuring religious institutions and individual believers exemption from a wide range of neutral government regulations and obligations. The pluralist argument would also undo the constitutional disabilities imposed by the establishment clause, rejecting severe separationism. On McConnell's interpretation, an act of government amounts to unconstitutional establishment only if it has the purpose or effect of increasing religious uniformity (reducing "product differentiation" in religion).[61] Provision for religious flourishing is not just permitted, but required; support is an entitlement.[62]

McConnell acknowledges that a "regime of pluralism" might dilute the concept of citizen. But that result is unregrettable if it corrects the injustice of second-class citizenship. He does not concede that educational pluralism poses the danger of civic fragmentation.[63] On the contrary, refusing accommodation "would make out-groups more antagonistic toward the mainstream," and public support for pluralist education would encourage the perception of stakeholding.[64] Plainly, the equal-citizenship case for a regime of educational pluralism is magnified if it is applied to groups with strongly held secular ideologies, counterparts of religious faith who also experience tension between the obligations of citizenship and demands of deep personal commitment. (Pluralism is magnified immeasurably if it extends to pluralist schools based on "values" or "culture" or "identity" broadly.)

In the case for pluralist education as a condition of equal citizenship, choice is eclipsed. For one thing, claims of conscience and community are not elective but categorical. There is every reason to retreat from voluntarism as part of the justification for public funding. "Conscience"—judgments that "connect to ultimate concerns"—attributes depth and comprehensiveness to the demand for pluralist schemes of education. It makes the terminology of "choice" and market analogies applied to schooling seem like a trivialization of what is at stake. For every academic subject to be "bathed in scripture" and spiritual warfare to permeate schooling as life, for example, has nothing to do with choice, and neither does the imperative to seek out religious schooling wherever possible. (Recall papal encyclicals warning parents of their responsibility to resist "godless" public schools and insisting that the only "true education" was Catholic, which were tempered only in the 1950s.) Thus supporters of Christian schools may not welcome parents who turn to their schools out of dissatisfaction with public education; absence of compelling faith is disqualifying.[65]

Of course, insofar as voucher plans are the preferred route to pluralist education, choice is implied. But it is not an explicit value. In fact, the logical policy implication of pluralism is direct aid to religious schools (or more broadly to schools organized around language heritage or culture) on some sort of proportional or per-capita basis. In a regime of pluralism, "communities of conscience" are the first homes of McConnell's unequal citizens. It goes without saying that their schools cannot be inclusive and admission is not purely elective; the whole point is to attract a specific type of family to participate on the basis of some deep commitment or identification. Insofar as a significant proportion of students are not co-religionists, pluralism is diluted.

Because the claims of conscience are tied to equal citizenship, McConnell must concede *something* to the democratic purposes of education as a condition of support. Once democratic constraints on education enter at all, however, if only as some elusive "civic minimum," the particularist purposes of pluralist schooling are potentially diluted or subverted—which is why to his strong pluralist critics McConnell's position is unstable and promises only an "illusory pluralism."[66]

Hence the second argument for educational pluralism does not appeal to the democratic principle of equal citizenship. Pluralism per se (or some defined set of communities) is the foundational value. The idea is to recognize and support particularist differences, again with an emphasis on communities of faith, and to create the conditions for communities to effectively resist unwanted assimilation or "Americanism." Here too, opt-outs or vouchers limited to sincere dissenters are inadequate, but for reasons other than the stigma of second-class citizenship. The goal is to sustain comprehensive, flourishing educational settings for cultivating conscience. Exemption does not insure community building. Public recognition and school funding do.

The model of education invoked here is schooling provided by formal, publicly recognized communities in which membership is ascriptive or legally determined by a domain of personal law. Thus Graham Walker points to state support for religious education in Israel to illustrate his "more plural version of pluralism." Walker would permit official religious establishment so long as other faiths retain authority over laws of personal status and funding for their schools.

A cursory survey of comparative educational systems in Western democracies cautions us that the pluralist case for public funding of private schools is context based. The United States comprises wildly diverse religious, racial, ethnic, and cultural groups. But society is not segmented, and membership in particularist communities is neither legally nor practically ascriptive. Moreover, groups and communities and their authoritative spokespersons are internally divided on the subject of education.[67] There are exceptions to this picture, of course: separatist and geographically defined enclaves like the Old World Amish or New York's Satmar Hasidim (which successfully petitioned to form their own village of Kiryas Joel, defined by the property owned and occupied exclusively by Satmars).[68] Because these are small minority communities, because their survival is said to be at issue, and because they are sometimes economically disadvantaged, pluralists may argue for special privileges or protections. But this familiar version of multiculturalism does not advance the general case for educational pluralism, much less choice. I do not want to pass over regional ethnic concentrations in the United States like Cubans in Miami, which account for the fact that some public schools assume the character of particularist pluralism[69]—to say nothing of the enthusiasm with which local school boards exercise their "unfettered discretion to transmit community values" and exploit their constitutional permission to advance the "legitimate and substantial community interest in promoting respect for authority and traditional values be they social, moral, or political."[70]

That said, the United States is plainly unsuited to the sort of pluralist accommodations that are standard in educational systems abroad. Historically, churches fighting for recognition alongside national establishments and cultural communities fighting for recognition in multiethnic societies have won public support for their schools. Educational pluralism there reflected deep cultural and social cleavages.[71] In fact, the contest against secular public education (and the anticlericalism that sometimes accompanied it) and for government support for religious and ethnic schools was a chief impetus to the rise of religious political parties in Europe.[72] These pluralist systems were organized to be restrictive, not inclusive. The recipients of funding were known and fixed: "pillars." Whether pluralism was more a matter of modus vivendi than principled politics does not matter here. My point is that strong pluralist education has been tied to public recognition and support for distinct, stable communities. Aid goes directly to these groups or to their schools; it is not infinitely dispersed. Dutch education is said to be "dominated by large cartels."[73] In short, a specific set of religious or ethnic groups is defined as constituting the state—at best, they are formally acknowledged as elements of an overarching national identity.

Small wonder determining the groups that receive government support is more than just a matter of limited resources. And not surprisingly, it has been difficult for new groups to win the same entitlements. Immigration, programs of multiculturalism, and antigovernmentalism have contributed to the push for neutral government funding of all religious schools or even all independent schools. Everywhere, the extension of educational pluralism, and in some cases evolution from pluralism to an open-ended system of school choice, has been difficult. Pillarization and other forms of pluralism were rooted in opposition to individualist, voluntarist choice. Extension has also been difficult for familiar political reasons. Consider the long-standing British privileging of Anglican schools, the incorporation of Christian denominational schools in the public system, and later of Jewish schools; extension of aid to evangelical Christian and Muslim schools is belated and contentious. Or the complex adjustment for language schooling in Belgium, now challenged by immigration and demands by Turks and others for support for instruction in a wider range of languages along with demands for government support for Koran schools. Or the Dutch accommodation upset by recent resistance to broadening the range of ethnic and linguistic pluralism.

In the United States, the number and kind of religious and cultural groups with a distinct identity arguably relevant for educational pluralism is enormous and fluid. There are no "pillars." Only if pluralists concede the open and basically elective nature of membership in groups and subcommunities with standing to claim public support for their schools do we find an explicit connection between pluralism and choice. For reasons I have discussed, pluralists are reluctant to detach government support from communities of value and comprehensive commitment. There are several steps along this route, several stopping points at which pluralists can take their stand on the way from community-sensitive educational pluralism to pluralism that is elective and self-created—*a product, not just an object, of choice.* Consider the steps in this unraveling spiral.

At the first stopping point the pluralist case broadens beyond the exemplary community of faith. Communities of conscience lose their exclusive claim on public support. Beyond that, the locus of pluralism shifts away from established communities of any kind, including those defined by tradition, language, and culture. Labile communities of value or belief, including new and fragile commitments, are entitled to support. This step is propelled by the chaotic nature of pluralism in the United States; here, schism and religious invention are commonplace. It is not misleading to think of religious schools less in terms of stable communities of faith than as a springboard for small groups to arise in the first place. Lutheran schools sometimes preceded the formation of congregations, for example, and there are vivid instances of sects without institutions of any kind except for a basement school. At this point the universe of commitments is relentlessly expanding, but pluralism nonetheless retains its presumption connection with groups organized around deep and comprehensive commitments.

It is another step to the view that "real community building must be voluntary."[74] This position entails a willingness to stop privileging communities of faith, tradition, or comprehensive commitment altogether. The pluralist case for schools embodying some distinct collective identity opens out to industry- or union-sponsored schools or political-party schools. From this pluralist perspective, communities and their schools are indistinguishable from voluntary associations subsidized by the state.

At the third step, "community" is loosed from its anchor in pluralist groups altogether. It refers more broadly to groups organized around educational goals independent of any other shared social identity. (Distinctive schools that "specialize" in apathetic and unmotivated students who do not have strong interests or academic abilities, is one curious example.)[75] We know that advocates of religious education do not always, or only instrumentally, focus on doctrine or faith; as is often noted, Catholic schools today educate more non-Catholics than faithful.[76] The key elements of educational pluralism for many parents and educators are authority and pedagogy, not faith or community. Still, to retain its pluralist character, an education-based community cannot refer to just any difference between schools with distinct constituencies. Curricular and pedagogical diversity per se are not weighty enough. Thus the designation "educational community" would not extend to the East Harlem junior high schools organized around subject matter: environmental science, "creative learning," a maritime school, a school for health and biomedical studies, for performing arts, for math and science, for communications arts and computer science, and for bilingualism.[77]

Finally, pluralism is eclipsed and we come full circle to choice ascendant, with the emphasis again on performance. The case for particularist education is no longer that it sustains community but that *some* community, any "chosen community," is a condition for effective education.

Not until the logic of pluralism is extended beyond the point its proponents intend and logic permits—beyond public solicitude and support for the particularist goals of organized groups and communities—do we find a strong nexus between pluralism and choice. At precisely that instant the conjoined twins are separated. Pluralism dissolves into public support for any school any parent prefers—portable among schools at will—into unalloyed choice. Choice is dictated by any number of considerations, not only instrinsic educational considerations such as commitment to the reproduction of pluralist community value or commitment to some pedagogical idea, but extrinsic practical concerns. School choice is consistent with educational "grazing," and pluralism falls away.

Separating the Siamese Twins: From Justification to Practice

In theoretical and political arguments for choice, pluralism does not function as justification. But it looms large as a background assumption, and the vigor of choice arguments derives in part from exciting pluralist expectations. Arguments for educational pluralism do not have choice as justification or goal; the individualist and performance implications of choice are antithetical to pluralist objectives. The analytic separation I have performed illuminates the fissure at the foundational level. It also suggests the contingency and potential instability of political alliances. It indicates that the practical obstacles to both pluralism and choice have roots deeper than limited resources, inertia, and political opposition. Finally, I mean to suggest that once the twins are separated, both are weak and neither is likely to survive or thrive.

When we look beyond theory to policy, then, nothing in proposals for school choice, public or private, speaks to the kind or degree of pluralism likely to result in practice. It is an empirical question whether direct public funding of private schools or vouchers, charters, or nonzoned public schools would increase the actual range of educational choices, or for whom, or for how much. This is not to deny that a well-funded universal voucher plan would increase pluralism across some dimensions—mostly serving religion. But short of the most radical reforms, skepticism about the ability of choice to produce access to the desired range of pluralist alternatives is warranted. Diversity exists today among independent schools, within and among public school systems, and from classroom to classroom. But these differences mostly arise de facto and with haphazard consequences for both pluralism and choice. Rationalized pluralism and choice are elusive.

McConnell is optimistic that "families with determination and organization can find or organize schools that address their pedagogical, methodological, and substantive concerns." Pluralism depends, then, on who has the resources of money, leadership, organizational skill, and motivation to create alternative schools, and how accessible they are to populations in different areas. In practice, decisions about what the range of available schools will be are widely dispersed. The range itself is not amenable to easy voluntarist institution building or to democratic decision making.

Pluralism also depends on whether educational entrepreneurs (both literal private investors and educational founders) reflect or create the market for alternative educational forms and goals. Pluralism depends on the possibility of matching the goals of founders with the availability of appropriate teachers. Of course, the degree of autonomy permitted by public funding would also affect pluralism—everything from the content and enforceability of curricular goals to hiring practices.

Consider a short list of factors limiting both the capacity to exercise choice and the number, kind, and durability of pluralist alternatives. This expandable list suggests some of the concrete grounds for skepticism about the implicit promise that pluralism and choice would increase, together, through public policy. The list gives the lie to the avowal, clearly intended to be inspirational, that "most individual families could have genuine choices wherever they lived."[78] It lends credence to the judge on the Sixth Circuit Court, who said of the Cleveland voucher plan, "The alleged choice . . . is illusory."[79]

- Difficulty of setting up and maintaining *any school*: private, charter, or nonzoned public. Experiments are often short-lived. Financial and management crises and school failures are not the prerogatives of public schools only.
- Dependence of charter and magnet schools on corporations, foundations, and political entrepreneurs.
- Community resistance to private management and school autonomy; fear of "disempowerment" and loss of jobs and patronage.
- Dependence of schools on charismatic founders who effect change through force of personality. Successful schools are not easily sustained or replicated.
- The rarity of visionary educators who also have the skills to institute educational plans.
- The disinclination of private, especially sectarian, schools to go beyond primary and middle school and to deal with the costs and difficulties associated with the higher grades.
- Constraints on the number of teachers suited for particular schools.

- An energetic recruitment of public school teachers that thins the ranks of teachers available for private schools.
- The relatively few families who receive resources for choice where choice depends on grants or subsidies, reimbursements, or tax deductions. Universal choice is not on the horizon.
- The ability of schools to set their own tuition rates. Low-level grants means that subsidized sectarian schools are the ones most likely to accept the tuition restrictions imposed by programs. In part because of fees, independent private schools and neighboring public school systems decline to participate in voucher programs.[80]
- Schools' idiosyncratic admission decisions. Whether private or charter, they are not open to all comers. Even if the method of selection in the case of alternative public schools were by lottery, selection, not election, determines admission.[81]
- The particular exclusions produced by highly selective "creaming" on academic grounds as well as exclusion of truants, dropouts, discipline problems, apathetic and disinterested students, or those disabled by severe physical, cognitive, or emotional problems.
- Local program design and control over the schools to which students can apply.[82]
- The paucity of interdistrict choice.
- Geographic and demographic constraints—rural areas, sparsely populated areas, and areas with homogeneous populations do not afford the critical mass of choosers to support alternative schools.
- Resources that constrain family choices—the cost of transportation as well as flexibility to adapt daily family life to the obligations of sometimes distant schools.
- Limitations of parents' information and motivation, which results in various forms of resegregation.
- Lack of opportunities for parental involvement, much less control.

Conclusion:
Surviving Separation

The twin most likely to survive and benefit from policy changes is choice, not pluralism. Despite the independent justifications offered for educational pluralism, for many parents (including those opting for sectarian schools) the principal goal is to expose their children to a certain form of authority and pedagogy rather than a particular value perspective or community. In fact, alternative modes of authority and pedagogy are the first and most direct beneficiaries of increased autonomy for public as well as private schools. The reason is that authority and pedagogy are the elements decided and given effect by faculty and school leaders. And autonomy to determine these matters is perhaps the one educational reform that enjoys virtual consensus. Chubb and Moe conclude that school autonomy is the single most important factor in school organizations that provide effective education[83]—that is, schools "with control over a sufficient number of parameters that count": budget and use of resources, staffing, scheduling and organization of time, counseling, and the specifics of curriculum and assessment.[84] It follows that choice is more important for faculty and staff than for parents. They should be the chief beneficiaries of policy change.

Principals or teacher teams must have greater freedom to recruit colleagues, and teachers to elect schools. Professionalism is only in part formalized credentials and licensing standards; it is mainly the exercise of discretion and decision making. The expression of professionalism is the desire to liberate energy from "negotiating with school officials over what [seem] like nonsense requests" in order to apply it to pedagogy. "One of the unverbalized assumptions undergirding the organization and thrust of our schools is that the conditions that make schools interesting places for children can be created and sustained by teachers for whom these conditions exist minimally at best."[85]

Coherent organization produces effective education, Chubb and Moe argue, and organization "seems to capture the essential features of what people normally mean by a team—principals and teachers working together, cooperatively and informally, in pursuit of a common mission."[86] So choice arguments and advocacy are important mainly as one vehicle among others for promoting school autonomy.

Relatively autonomous public schools will not produce strong pluralism, but they will produce a degree of planned rather than de facto educational diversity. This change may also open the way to parental choice, though that is an open question that will be decided politically. The choice most likely to become available, in short, is choice among relatively independent public schools.

What is left for twin pluralism? Only the sternest civic educationalists argue that *Pierce* was wrongly decided. There is widespread public support for private educational pluralism, for release-time arrangements in public schools, and for a degree of material public support for private, including sectarian, schools. The Supreme Court has upheld public subsidies or loans across an array of goods and services: transportation, textbooks, special education and remedial education services, testing and diagnostic services, and other materials that can be reviewed for bias and insured not to promote religious beliefs. Only the most anxious separationists would urge the courts to continue to be restrictive in defining permissible "secular, neutral, and nonideological services, materials, and equipment" to exclude televisions, video recorders, and library books (loans for computers are now allowed).[87]

That is the pretty clear limit of public support for pluralist education. There are two reasons beyond the familiar ones alluded to above to withhold approval from comprehensive public-funding schemes aimed at particularist pluralism, and to breathe life instead into choice among public schools.

One reason emerges if we consider the strangest proposition advanced by pluralists to sustain their claims: that public support for strong pluralism would temper political disagreement. Pluralism is irreducible in practice, the argument goes. Compulsory education, districtwide textbook adoptions, and other elements of public education that make it difficult or impossible to be responsive to the diversity of groups and beliefs positively provoke battles for control in divisive "school wars." The Lake County, Florida, school-board fight with the state over "Americanism," for example: Should schools teach that American values are superior to all others, or should they teach understanding and respect for other cultures and values? The conflict went on for years in the state legislature, state Department of Education, public school-board meetings, the circuit court, and election campaigns.[88] By removing the object of contestation—control of schools—pluralists argue, education would be depoliticized and peace restored.

In fact, the opposite outcome is predictable: educational pluralism would produce more profound divisions. Comprehensive public funding arrangements may require only government "acknowledgment," not "endorsement," of these schools (to borrow Justice Sandra Day O'Connor's establishment clause terminology), especially if the funding is indirect via vouchers and parental choice. But it is not likely to be perceived that way, and in this context, that is what counts. Rather, state funding, even if it is impartial among public and private schools, and even if it is doled out to parents, is ultimately inseparable from endorsement of the value, if not the truth, of religious tenets and practices, secular ideologies, and cultures. If publicly supported private or public schools "serve the tribal agendas of well-off white parents, faithful home schoolers, la Raza devotees, even Mormons and Muslims, then why should society continue to support the public purposes that hold together public education?"[89] Indeed, why should religious groups? Predictably, ecumenical cooperation gives way to sectarian division among the roughly two thousand denominations in the United States today. Tolerance of alien faiths does not extend to subsidizing the educational missions of strange and despised sects: an expansive network of Muslim schools, or establishments run by the Nation of

Islam or the Church of Scientology or Wiccans. Policy proposals for "charitable choice" have provoked criticism from the likely beneficiaries: conservative evangelicals are "appalled" at the thought of government partnerships with non-Western religions and new religious movements; Lutheran Services and Catholic Charities attack policies that would permit religious discrimination in hiring.

The reason for keeping choice alive at the expense of twin pluralism is tied to more than the educational business of schools. It points to a deeper reason for withholding public support from pluralist education: the symbolic significance of the public purposes of public schools in the United States. What would it mean to say that it makes no difference if we support private schools so long as they are universally accessible and conform to a minimal set of standards? In some profound way, it would be interpreted by many as an abandonment of public institutions, bordering on a wholesale disavowal of the capacity of government for positive good.

I say this because for better or worse, disagreement about the relation between government and schooling is our form of collective self-exploration. It is the occasion for the dialogues (civil and uncivil), political battles, election campaigns, federal and state legislation, and litigation by which we construct and deconstruct our civic identity and our particular, pluralist identities—deciding what the essential elements are that must be reproduced. It is where we are most engaged—most passionate and most participatory—in "revising America." The ritualistic way we engage in collective self-definition in the context of public schools has becoming a defining characteristic of American political culture.

Most democracies do distribute government funds to support pluralist education. But public institutions have expressive as well as instrumental functions, and in the United States this is particularly true of public schools. To say that it is irrational to restrict public funding to public schools even if the evidence were that private ones do the job as well or better is a slur against prejudice, which is not always irrational or self-serving. Our emotions are informed by reasons, including reasons for seeing a major shift of commitment and resources as abandonment of *the* public institution most closely identified with American democracy and progressive hopes.[90] There may be alternative means of democratic education, and good reasons not to put the whole burden on schools when we consider democratic education. But there is no alternative institutional repository of these aspirations.[91] Pluralism threatens to undermine this civic remainder; choice does not.

I have characterized pluralism and school choice as Siamese twins and not as Hippocrates' twins who smile (and frown) together.[92] Pluralism and choice live in unhealthy connection with each other. Their conjunction is a mistake, and even successful surgery does not hold out much hope that either will flourish. Twin choice is stronger, though, for the reasons I have advanced, and will survive.

Five

"Getting Religion": Religion, Diversity, and Community in Public and Private Schools

MEIRA LEVINSON AND SANFORD LEVINSON

THERE ARE MANY ARGUMENTS for and against school vouchers or—should *vouchers* be too politically loaded or descriptively restrictive a term—for the use of public funds, either directly or indirectly, to support private (including religious) schools. Some of these arguments are explicitly constitutional, based on one or another reading of the establishment and free exercise clauses of the First Amendment. Although one of us is a constitutional lawyer, we emphasize at the outset that this essay is not in any way an analysis of the validity of such legal arguments, even if we make occasional descriptive reference to them. Here we are interested in the more general normative and empirical debates surrounding such aid. If it is a good idea, then the possibility that it is unconstitutional counts against the Constitution (or judicial doctrine), not against the proposal, and we might then turn our attention to the best ways of changing constitutional understanding, whether through the appointment of different judges or formal amendment of the Constitution. Concomitantly, if such aid is a bad idea, then it is irrelevant that it might be constitutional. The terms "constitutional/unconstitutional" are not at all necessarily synonymous with "meritorious/unmeritorious," and it is the latter that is exclusively our focus.

There are, of course, many normative questions raised by proposals for aid to religious schools. We focus on one particularly common—and, for many, especially potent—normative argument against vouchers and other such aid. This involves the ostensible tension between such programs and the achievement of a desirable degree of diversity within the aided schools themselves. That is, heterogeneous schools are deemed by many contemporary liberals (and, no doubt, others as well) to be better than homogeneous ones, and the dispersion of public funds to private schools, whatever the process by which this is done, is viewed as encouraging homogeneity and therefore as generating public harm rather than benefit. Thus, for example, it is often suggested that school vouchers will result in some students going to private schools that by design are segregated along one or more axes. This book focuses on one such axis—religion—but, obviously, many others deserve attention as well; these include, but are not limited to, nonreligious belief systems, race or ethnicity, achievement, gender, sexual orientation, raw intelligence as ostensibly measured by aptitude or similar tests, and socioeconomic status. The assumption is that in the absence of movement to ideologically compatible private schools, these students would remain in public schools, and that their very presence would promote the kinds of diversity that are desirable.

Why is diversity so desirable? Although we will offer a more elaborate answer to this question later, we can offer in outline form two especially common defenses of diversity. First, a diverse student body can help to develop the toleration of others—perhaps we should refer to "Others"—that is functional to developing the liberal-democratic civic project that relies on mutual respect and tolerance. This view is articulated by former university presidents William Bowen and Derek Bok in their highly influential defense of affirmative action at the university level, but the argument holds for primary and secondary education as well: Diverse student bodies help to produce "greater 'cultural awareness across racial lines' and stronger commitments to improving racial understandings."[1] One can substitute practically any term for "racial" and the argument still works. This is the "civic education" or "civic toleration" justification.

A second, quite different, argument emphasizes the relevance of a diverse student body to enabling students to develop better their own autonomy by interacting with people who hold beliefs and lead lives that are different from their own. This argument can be traced back at least to John Stuart Mill, who in *On Liberty* defended the importance of tolerating experiments in living not only because of the beneficial effects of learning to accept the existence of different approaches to life, but also because confrontation with such experiments would possibly lead the observer to evaluate one's own values and conduct and, perhaps, to change the direction taken in one's life in quite dramatic ways. Even if no change takes place, a person forced to confront significantly different ways of life would have a far sharper sense of why she remained committed to her own views. It is no coincidence that another university president, Harvard's Neil Rudenstine, when presenting his own reflections (and defenses) about this issue in his article "The Uses of Diversity," quoted Mill's insistence that a person "must be able to hear [diverse opinions] from persons who actually believe them; who defend them in earnest, and do their very utmost for them. He must ... feel the whole force of the difficulty which the true view of the subject has to encounter and dispose of."[2] Presumably, if the person challenged cannot "dispose of" the difficulties presented to her own views, then she will change them and, as a result, partake in a very different form of life than might otherwise have been the case. This is the "autonomy promotion" justification, and taken together, these are, albeit very sketchily, the "diversity arguments."

The relationship between vouchers (or other relevant forms of aid) and the diversity arguments is fairly straightforward. First, as mentioned above, opponents often focus on the homogeneity of the schools strengthened as the result of such aid.[3] That is, parents are assumed to want to send their children to schools whose student body will be very similar along a given metric. (Were there no such parental preferences, then one can assume that little or no advantage would be taken of policies that would allow greater homogeneity along the particular metric.) Second, they also assert that by enabling such parents, whether smart/committed/active/religious/white, and so forth, to take their involvement and their children to private schools, vouchers leave public schools and the students stuck in them worse off than before. This latter argument is usually made from an egalitarian perspective, as treated in other chapters in this book, where the focus is the harm done to public schools by losing involved parents. But the "cream-off effect" argument also can derive strength from the diversity argument, insofar as the disappearance of religious, white, lower-middle class, or other groups of students from the public schools leaves the public schools less diverse along that axis, and therefore (drawing on the diversity argument) harms the civic education or autonomy development or both of public school students left behind.

Our aim in this essay is not to rehash the pros and cons of these quite well known arguments in the course of justifying or discrediting them. Instead, we are interested in examining the normative consequences of applying them to a question that seems to have been incongruously (and remarkably) overlooked in the general debates regarding "diversity," which have focused almost exclusively on race and ethnicity. The question is this: Does the liberal-democratic state and/ or do children have a compelling interest in children's going to school in a diverse *religious* setting? Positive (and negative) answers abound to the racial version of this question; the importance of "mingling" is the foundation of most defenses of so-called diversity admissions policies by universities;[4] and it (along with important egalitarian considerations) also undergirds the attempt by many public school systems to preserve "racial balancing" policies against the recent antibusing and antidesegregation backlash.[5] Interestingly, however, the religious version of this question has gone virtually unconsidered except to the extent that it applies to the autonomy-development and civic-membership interests specifically of children of religious parents who want to remove them from public education entirely.

The best-known case regarding the education of religious children, *Wisconsin v. Yoder*,[6] is discussed in terms of whether the state can force Amish children to attend schools until at least through the tenth grade or whether, on the contrary, the parents of these children can terminate their formal schooling after eight years in order to further their socialization into the Amish community itself. (Interestingly enough, *Yoder* did not involve either the presence of alternative Amish schools or "home schooling" by Amish parents.) In both the majority and minority opinions, careful attention was paid to the implications for maintaining civic order and for maintaining the Amish community, and for the Amish youth themselves. But although Justice William O. Douglas, dissenting, issued a strong objection to the Court's seeming willingness to ignore the particular autonomy interests of the affected Yoder children, he wrote nary a word about any losses to the potential classmates of the Amish children whose absence from the public schools was upheld.

The same is true with regard to the much-discussed case of *Mozert v. Hawkins*,[7] which involves a clash between fundamentalist religious parents and a local school board with regard to the necessity that each and every child be exposed to the particular reading program offered by the school system, one of whose aims is precisely to expose children to different viewpoints and to teach them critical thinking skills. Much has been written about the loss (or gain) to the particular children of Vicki Frost if they cannot continue to attend public schools or "opt out" of having to confront the reading program chosen by the school board. Almost nothing has been written about the losses suffered by other children if the plaintiffs' children retreat from the public schools. Finally, there are, most recently, the so-called Yale Five, who objected to having to live in Yale student dormitories that they claimed violated certain rules and behaviors attached to Orthodox Judaism. Yale defended its requirement on the ground that the Orthodox Jewish students would greatly benefit from living in dormitories consisting of diverse students. Less was said about the benefits to other students of having to live with—and to some degree accommodate themselves to—the Orthodox Jews.

Even when compromises are suggested, such as allowing students to opt out of reading programs or residence requirements, they most often are defended by statements to the effect that "these very specific, named, children will be better off and will be exposed to a wider range of opinions if they stay in the public schools (or live in the Yale dorms), and, therefore, we must accept these compromises as unfortunate but necessary costs of allowing them to achieve such benefits." This is thought preferable to having the students withdraw, though the metric of evaluation is entirely in terms of those specific students' own interests. This assessment, of course, may be correct. Yet it is worth noting how rarely consideration is given to the consequences for *nonfundamentalist* children or *non-Orthodox* students who, by stipulation, face the possibility of remaining in public schools (or private universities) now lacking the diversity provided by their former classmates.

A similar point can be made with regard to the design of assignment zones or what the British call "catchment areas" for public schools. Despite the vast amount of literature arguing in favor of diverse public schools and, concomitantly, the conscious use of demographic materials relating to race or ethnicity when constructing school boundaries (or deciding on the use of busing to achieve certain kinds of demographic balance), we know of no serious consideration that has ever been given to whether public schools might alter their catchment areas to achieve "religious balancing," or less drastically and therefore potentially more intriguingly, offer incentives (e.g., a kosher or halal cafeteria, or an adjusted school schedule, including, say, no athletic events on Friday and Saturday) to attract religious-minority families to a school located in an otherwise all-Christian area of town. Thus our title—"Getting Religion"—which is intended, among other things, to suggest the possibility that it is a positive good if schools get those with religious views (and behaviors) among their student bodies and, therefore, that educational policy ought consciously be designed with a view to maximizing that possibility.

It is possible, of course, that the reason for such an absence of much discussion of this question is legal; many lawyers would no doubt say that it would be unconstitutional for such factors to play a part in designing public school boundaries in the United States. As indicated earlier, even if this is so, we are still entitled to ask if this is a cost, rather than a benefit, of current constitutional norms. If it is viewed as a cost, of course, then that would be a good reason for supporting changes in the interpretation of these norms.

There are many attributes beyond the religious, of course, that lend themselves to a "diversity" analysis. So a second focus of this essay is how religious-diversity interests balance against other types of diversity. For example, even if the answer to the question posed above is yes—it is a compelling interest of either the state and/or children for students to be educated with other students whose religious sensibilities are significantly different from their own—it is possible that a school that is not religiously diverse (e.g., a private Baptist academy or a Jewish yeshiva) will be more racially or socioeconomically diverse than other private or public schools. Indeed, as one of us has recently argued, one reality (and, perhaps, significant weakness) attached to invocations of the diversity argument is precisely that diversity, if taken seriously, is truly without limit insofar as there are almost literally an infinite number of ways that sets of humans can be described as interestingly different (and thus diverse) from one another.[8] Or, as Judge Weiner put it by way of chastising the University of Texas Law School with regard to its own diversity defense of a program that was in fact limited to African and Mexican Americans: "Blacks and Mexican Americans are but two among any number of racial or ethnic groups that could and presumably should contribute to genuine diversity."[9] Surely he is correct; moreover, as already suggested, there is no good reason to think only in terms of racial or ethnic groups when imagining desirable forms of diversity.[10]

One might well believe that any given diversity is beneficial to all concerned. Catholic schools, for example, are notable for drawing families across many racial and socioeconomic lines. It seems quite probable that the widespread availability of vouchers or other programs of public aid would allow many other denominationally identified religious schools to draw from a much wider socioeconomic range than would a typical prep school—even one that courted diversity—or a neighborhood public school. After all, the continued (renewed?) segregation of students in public schools—whether it be all lower-income blacks in urban Atlanta or Detroit, or mostly middle- and upper-income whites in Scarsdale—has been well documented.[11] Furthermore, as we will discuss below, certain nonreligious but otherwise "special emphasis" private schools (e.g., military academies, Waldorf schools, "free" schools, mountain/wilderness academies, etc.)[12] are for a variety of reasons far less diverse along most axes than are many religious schools. Even self-consciously "progressive" schools, both public and private, have a hard time attracting families that are nonwhite and non–middle class; even when access to them is easy and free, black, Hispanic, and lower-income parents all typically favor traditional "three R's" schools. To the extent that voucher programs must satisfy diversity claims, therefore, it could be that vouchers should arguably be provided for some religious schools but not for these other private schools. This, obviously, would be a highly unexpected twist for the application of diversity considerations to religious schools, since usually proponents of diversity (for either civic-toleration-building or autonomy-promoting reasons) come down squarely against the use of vouchers for religious schools precisely on the grounds that they inappropriately segregate students.

We should note one significant variation of a diversity argument, which focuses more on the overall distribution of institutional possibilities than on the demography of any particular institution. Thus, the argument might go, society in general benefits from the presence of a continuing Amish (or Seventh-Day Adventist, or hippies, etc.) community, and the only way to assure the maintenance of such communities is to allow (and perhaps even encourage through public subsidy) homogeneous schools that will minimize the likelihood that the young will be tempted to leave these communities. This is, of course, the classic argument linked with pluralism or multiculturalism, which, in some variants, has a distinctly separatist tilt. Although much more could be said about the costs or benefits of a widespread pluralism within a liberal political order—and it is possible that the coauthors would disagree about the assessment of such costs or benefits—we are interested far more in the state's and children's interest in encouraging a less-separatist form of education by maximizing the presence of diversity within any given educational institution. Moreover, we note Nancy Rosenblum's important insight in her own contribution to this volume that remarkably few partisans of educational vouchers defend their position by offering forthright advocacy of separatist pluralism or multiculturalism. Instead, the primary defenses appear to emphasize less overtly controversial criteria of "achievement" and "educational quality." And, as already noted, at least some notions of "educational quality" include reference to the importance of demographic diversity.[13] We thus return to the basic arguments for diversity and attempt to spell out their implications more fully in the sections below.

The Diversity Argument Elaborated: The Importance of "Mingling"

Since their founding in America, "public" or "common" schools (as they were originally designated) have been justified by reference to the social goods that were and are thought to be produced by the process of bringing together children of different backgrounds in a single setting. As Horace Bushnell wrote in 1853 of the "great institution . . . of common schools," "There needs to be some place where, in early childhood, [individuals] may be brought together and made acquainted with each other; thus to wear away the sense of distance, otherwise certain to become an established animosity of orders; to form friendships; to be exercised together on a common footing of ingenuous rivalry. . . . Without this he can never be a fully qualified citizen, or pre-

pared to act his part wisely as a citizen."[14] Similarly, Theodore
Roosevelt commented some half-century later, "We stand unalterably
in favor of the public school system in its entirety," because when
"Americans of every origin and faith [are] brought up in them," they
"inevitably in after-life have kindlier feelings toward their old school-
fellows of different creeds, and look at them with a wiser and manlier
charity, than could possibly be the case had they never had the chance
to mingle together in their youth."[15] These high ideals carry into contemporary times. As Stephen Macedo has recently written, "The whole
point of the common school is to be a primary arena where children
from the different normative perspectives that compose our polity encounter one another in a respectful setting, learn about one another,
and discover that their differences do not preclude cooperation and
mutual respect as participants in a shared political order."[16] One might
be tempted to ask, with a suitably rhetorical flourish: If "common"
does not mean this, then what *does* it mean?

All three of these men agree that a diverse student body is essential
for educating citizens. It is generally agreed that citizenship in a liberal
democracy requires that one tolerate and even respect people who are
different from oneself, who hold different beliefs, and engage in actions
or life practices that are unfamiliar, discomfiting, or even repugnant.
The reason is eminently practical: In a contemporary society consisting
of many different groups with quite conflicting ways of understanding
the world, a Hobbesian world of endless conflict can be avoided only
if individual citizens develop at least enough respect for one another to
resist the temptation to suppress those they disagree with or, equally
important, to escape the constant anxiety that one will herself be the
target of suppression if other groups come to power. (The existence of
legal "parchment barriers" against such suppression will scarcely suffice to control the manifold forms of hostility or oppression that can
result from antagonistic views of the Other.) In order for people to come
to tolerate and respect others, it is generally thought that they need to
interact with these "others" in close, meaningful ways that enable them
to see the commonalities among them (that are therefore respectwor-
thy) and at least to understand the reasons for the differences that remain between them.[17] It is also useful if these interactions occur at an
early age, before prejudices have the chance to harden and block the
development of mutual understanding. Schools are thus seen as being
essential, possibly unique, institutions for bringing diverse individuals
together under these conditions. As a result, diverse schools are lauded
for their service in promoting toleration and civic virtue.

This is no small point. Both of us attribute great—and positive—significance to our experiences growing up in Southern communities with

a group of close friends drawn from a variety of Christian religious denominations, ranging from Roman Catholic to Southern Baptist.[18] Not only did we (separately) spend a lot of time discussing and debating fundamental questions of religion, but we also learned to tolerate the different answers that were given. Sanford Levinson has written about his experiences in Hendersonville, North Carolina, and the importance of ensuing friendships: "We too often automatically sneer at the phrase 'some of my best friends are Jewish (or any other religion or race),' but, surely, it would be a profound social good if all of us could in fact say, with conviction, that some of our best friends are from groups other than those with which we most centrally identify."[19] It is hard to believe that societies as heterogeneous as our own can flourish (or perhaps even survive) if the particular intimacies of friendship are limited to those who are exactly like oneself.[20]

We see this same process playing out in schools today. In the eighth-grade Boston classroom where Meira Levinson teaches, it has been striking to observe how the presence of even one student from a minority group can over time alter other students' attitudes toward that group. In one notable discussion, students' diatribes against the house calls made by Jehovah's Witnesses were brought to a screeching halt when they discovered that one of the most popular boys in the class is a Jehovah's Witness. Although the initial change in the tenor of the discussion was undoubtedly due to students' feeling the need to *show* respect rather than their actually *feeling* more respect, students also then started paying attention to an explanation about *why* Jehovah's Witnesses proselytized door-to-door—an explanation which they had totally ignored (although it had been brought up by the teacher) earlier in the conversation. Increases in mutual respect have also been brought about by critical confrontation in the classroom. For example, in another class, a Haitian student commented that the Chinese ate rats,[21] and turned to the sole Asian student in the classroom for confirmation. When informed that she was Vietnamese, not Chinese, he responded, "Vietnamese, Chinese, whatever"—but was none too pleased a second later to hear the teacher comment, "Yeah, Dominican, Haitian, Puerto Rican, whatever." This led to a series of discussions about history (Asian, American, Caribbean, Latin American), stereotypes, prejudice, cultural differences, and (of course) eating habits, among other topics, and noticeably increased some students' toleration of and understanding of each other, although there is still a long way to go. Furthermore, it has been blindingly clear that this author's students in a highly integrated Boston middle school are much more worldly and tolerant than her students were in an all–African American middle school in Atlanta, largely because of the relative limitedness of the latter's experience with Others.

Such anecdotal offerings are bolstered by some social scientists, such as those relied on by both the University of Michigan, and in turn the federal district court that ruled in favor of the university, when they defended the university's racial- and ethnic-preference programs against Fourteenth Amendment attack. Patricia Y. Gurin, a professor of psychology at the university, prepared a report that found that "students . . . are better prepared to become active participants in our pluralistic, democratic society once they leave" what the court described as "a racially and ethnically diverse student body."[22] The judge also quoted Professor Gurin's finding that such students were also "better able to appreciate the common values and integrative forces that harness differences in pursuit of common ground."[23]

In addition to diversity's civic accomplishments, student (and sometimes teacher) diversity is also lauded for enabling individual students to develop their capacities for autonomy. This is an educational goal distinct from students' development of civic toleration and respect—although as many people have pointed out (including each of us in other contexts), probably not a distinct pedagogical process; while the goals may be logically separable, their achievement or failure seem not to be separable in practice.[24] The aim of helping students develop their autonomy, however, is a distinct justification for maintaining diverse, "common" schools. As children encounter peers and teachers who do and believe different things from what they do and believe, and as they discuss, compare, and debate their own ways of life with others, children necessarily move from accepting their lives simply as unexamined givens to some version of an examined life. Indeed, in explaining his own intellectual development (including developing into a highly self-conscious intellectual), Sanford Levinson gives far greater weight to his friends and their intense discussions than to the formal courses he took at Hendersonville High School. And this is not meant as a particular knock at that particular high school; one suspects that many persons could offer similar autobiographical anecdotes even if they attended far more urbane institutions of secondary education.

The material offered by Professor Gurin (and the University of Michigan) is relevant to this strand of the argument as well. She reports that multiple sources of data demonstrate that "students who experienced the most racial and ethnic diversity in classroom settings and in informal interactions with peers showed the greatest engagement in active thinking processes, growth in intellectual engagement and motivation, and growth in intellectual and academic skills." They are also described as especially able to "understand and consider multiple perspectives [and] deal with the conflicts that different perspectives sometimes create."[25] Diversity thus seems an altogether winning policy, insofar as it led Gurin to conclude that "on average, students who attend more diverse institutions" exhibit a greater "intellectual engagement and motivation index" and a greater "citizenship engagement index."[26] In addition, an amicus brief by the United States cited "a study by Alexander Astin, Director of the Higher Education Research Institute at the University of California, in which Astin associates diversity with increased satisfaction in most areas of the college experience and an increased commitment to promoting racial understanding and participation in cultural activities, leadership, and citizenship."[27] There are, no doubt, many empirical studies of primary and secondary schools that reach similar conclusions, though, equally without doubt, one could raise all sorts of methodological questions about the ways that one could actually test with confidence for the qualities allegedly causally linked with diversity.

In sum, diversity in schools is thought (and was historically thought) to be both civic promoting and autonomy promoting. Schools with diverse student bodies serve both the community, by promoting the civic virtues of toleration and respect for others, and the individual, by enabling students' development of autonomy through interaction with students who are different. As a result, for both toleration-promoting (civic) and autonomy-promoting (individualistic) reasons, "common schools" with diverse student bodies should be maintained, protected, and further developed, and school diversity should be taken into consideration when examining and evaluating school voucher programs or other school-assignment options.

To say that diversity matters, of course, is to leave many questions unanswered. The most obvious is, what kinds of diversity matter? The importance of racial and ethnic diversity is what is defended in the Michigan (and earlier University of Texas Law School) case, just as gender diversity is assumed insofar as in America (although, notably, not in Great Britain and many other countries), virtually all public schools are coeducational. For both civic- and autonomy-promoting reasons, however, it would seem that religious diversity would be at least as highly desirable. In the next section, therefore, we will examine two questions: (1) Should our measurement of diversity include religious diversity, and if so, what are the implications for both public and private schools? (2) Do diversity arguments support or undermine vouchers for religious schools?

"Getting Religion"

Should our measurement of student diversity include religious diversity? On civic-toleration grounds, the answer *must* be yes. In the United States, there is considerable mutual suspicion between and among conservative Christians, secularist cosmopolitans, liberal and Orthodox Jews,[28] atheists, Muslims, Mormons, Wiccans, members of the Nation of Islam, and Scientologists, to name only a few of the relevant groups. Whether or not it is accurate to describe Americans as involved in a "culture war,"[29] it is hard to believe that sustained, respectful interaction among members of different religious groups would not be beneficial to American society. In order to promote the development of a mutually tolerant and respectful civil society, therefore, it would seem that schools should have a student body that is religiously diverse (as well as diverse along other dimensions). Indeed, immediately after university presidents Bowen and Bok speak of the importance of "greater 'cultural awareness across racial lines . . .' and stronger commitments to improving racial understandings," they go on to write as well of the "importance of differences in religion."[30] If schools are successful in their efforts to "get religion" in the sense of encouraging attendance by religious students, then their classmates might be considerably more likely to "get religion" at least in the sense of realizing that people holding even exceedingly odd religious views are nonetheless members of the same overarching community.

On autonomy-promoting grounds, it would also seem obvious that children would be well served by going to school with other children from a variety of religious backgrounds and genuinely engaging with them in respectful discussion about the ways and reasons their lives are different. Although cultural-coherence arguments have some play here—we should not rock a child's foundations before those foundations are even in place—certainly by middle school students should be exposed to practitioners of a variety of religious beliefs if the aim is to help them both to recognize the reasonableness of other beliefs and ways of life and to critically examine their own beliefs and practices in service of developing their autonomy. This seems to be especially true for religious diversity, because religion is explicitly about belief (at least for most religions), unlike race, social class, gender, and the like. While racial diversity, for example, clearly serves civic-toleration ends, it less obviously directly promotes autonomy, insofar as white students cannot chose to become black, for example; even the questioning of one's assumptions, which is the hallmark of autonomy, would depend in this case on the questionable assumption itself that racial diversity necessarily implies belief diversity. Religious diversity thus not only promotes children's development of autonomy, but may be superior to other types of diversity in doing so.

This assumption that students' interaction with others will lead to engagement with others (and Otherness) is buttressed in a recent article by University of Chicago law professor Emily Buss. As she notes (and as any parent or, indeed, middle-school teacher knows without needing to read academic tomes), adolescents often withdraw in one measure or another from the intensity of the domestic setting and develop close friendships with peers, who are often those they meet at school. Citing a great deal of evidence from the literature of child development, Buss views such relationships as central to the formation by adolescents of what will, in time, become their mature adult identity. "It is largely through these relationships that [adolescents] pursue the difficult and important task of identity formation—the sorting and selecting of values, beliefs, and tastes that will define their adult selves. Who those peers are and, particularly, the diversity of their convictions and attitudes, will have a significant effect on the course of that development."[31]

As a practical matter, this means that some religious children will be likely to be lured away from "home truths" because of the impact of their more secular classmates; it also means, though, that the opposite may occur as well, that a Jewish child will in fact be persuaded that salvation requires acceptance of Jesus as her Savior or simply that a secular child raised in a relentlessly rationalistic household will develop a more "spiritual" posture toward the world than the parents might prefer. So what? It is hard to see how a liberal society can prefer, as an abstract matter, a shift from religious to secular identities, whatever might be the preferences of most people who call themselves liberals. And the fact that the various parents of the respective children might be unhappy about their "straying" from the parents' preferences is not an interest that a liberal society can regard as particularly significant. The primary goals of any such society are the reproduction of its basic commitments (i.e., to a defensible form of liberalism) in future generations and, at the same time, production of the conditions by which students can themselves become autonomous selves and not the mere reflections of their parents' desires as to how they should live their lives.[32]

If religious diversity in schools is important for promoting both civic virtue and individual autonomy, then adherents of either goal (liberal civic education or the development of an autonomous self) would have a strong incentive to oppose public vouchers for religious schools if it is true that they would serve both to increase the number of homogeneous schools and at the same time decrease the amount of religious diversity in public schools. (Indeed, strong proponents of these goals should also oppose even private financing of religious schools, as one of us has demonstrated elsewhere,[33] but this is obviously a very controversial position. And, thanks to *Pierce v. Society of Sisters*,[34] it would also certainly violate currently accepted constitutional norms. In any event, our focus here is only on the advisability of religious-school vouchers and similar aid, and not on the legitimacy of religious schools themselves.)

It is to be expected that most religious schools explicitly promote religious segregation. To take the easiest case, a Seventh-Day Adventist or fundamentalist school that is run by and uses curricula supplied by the parent church or like-minded co-religionists is unlikely, as an empirical matter, to attract students from different religious backgrounds, even assuming that the schools in fact have space remaining after serving their primary constituency of fellow members of the given church. The same is true for a yeshiva or, indeed, a Jewish Day School. We are aware of a very prominent legal academic, an evangelical Christian, who, having sent his child to a Jewish Day School because he admired its pedagogy and emphasis on values, was told that the child would not be welcome to continue his education there because it was, after all, a *Jewish* Day school and the child was obviously not Jewish. (One does not know if the school was a bit worried that the child, as an evangelical, would engage in a witnessing of the Good News of Jesus' Messiahship, though we have never detected a propensity on the part of the father to try to convert his Jewish friends, of whom one of us is one.) Catholic schools, interestingly enough, seem quite receptive to non-Catholic students, though it would also be surprising if there were no significant selection biases with regard to parents who choose to send their children to such schools. (How often do atheist or even agnostic parents choose a Catholic education for their children?)

In addition to religiously segregating students who choose to attend such a school, religious schools also function to promote religious segregation in the public and nonsectarian private schools they leave behind. This is because of the "cream-off effect" mentioned at the opening of this chapter. As religious students make use of school vouchers to attend religious schools, fewer religious students will remain back in the public schools, thus reducing religious diversity in these public schools. (Presumably some students using already-available vouchers at nonsectarian private schools would also choose to switch to religious schools once vouchers became available, so the argument would apply to some extent to private schools as well.) This assumes, of course, that a greater proportion of religious students than nonreligious students would choose to avail themselves of vouchers to attend religious schools, but this assumption does not seem unreasonable. This is therefore an additional diversity-based (and ultimately civic- and autonomy-based) argument against religious-school vouchers.

The same grounds that initially seem to mandate against religious-school vouchers, however, also mandate in favor of new, positive, religious-diversity-promotion policies in the public schools. Religious diversity should be taken into account along with racial, ethnic, socioeconomic, and gender diversity. A heavy-handed program would be to assign students to schools in a way that promotes religious diversity, via altering catchment areas and bus routes.[35] But a less heavy-handed and more realistic policy could establish schools that act as religious "magnets" to draw religious minorities voluntarily into otherwise religiously homogeneous schools. One "magnet" draw could be an adjusted school schedule that satisfies local board requirements but has longer days on Mondays through Thursdays and halfdays on Fridays, or plays only Thursday-night football games, or takes off Rosh Hashanah, Eid Fitr, Epiphany, and Chinese New Year as official school holidays in exchange for extending the term slightly longer into the summer. Another approach would be to have a vegetarian cafeteria that is compliant with Jewish, Muslim, Buddhist, Jain, or Hindu dietary practices. Both of these strategies are entirely structural and would have no appreciable effect on the curriculum, but could significantly increase the religious diversity of the student body. This could be true as well of a third accommodation, which would be to allow "moments of silent reflection" or the installation of chapels into which, for example, Muslim students could go to say those of their five daily prayers which occur during school hours.[36] These would, presumably, alleviate at least some expressed concerns that schools are hostile to even the most minimal expression of religious commitments.[37]

A fourth strategy that does have curricular implications, but ones that seem quite minor, would be to broaden or change foreign-language offerings at the middle- or high-school level to include Hebrew, Arabic, Japanese, or Hindi, and the like, depending on the local population. This approach again might attract a number of families who would otherwise either stay in a neighborhood school within a minority-religious enclave or seek out private religious schools for their children. All of these strategies would have the instrumental goal of encouraging religious diversity on the grounds that it is at least as valuable in pursuing traditional liberal goals as racial and ethnic diversity, at least insofar as the grounds for that pursuit rest on civic-education or individual-autonomy justifications. (If they rely on rectification of past injustices, then the argument takes a decidedly different form, which, interestingly enough, has almost nothing to do with the merits of diversity per se.)

Balancing Diversities

The last section concluded that religious diversity matters and is desirable, and that educational policies, including those affecting the public schools, should be designed in order to promote religious diversity. Public schools should innovate in ways to attract minority religious families, but private religious schools should not be aided in attracting those or other religious families to them, as vouchers would presumably do. The normative—even if not the constitutional—policy implications seem pretty clear. But of course, nothing about public education policies is ever quick or easy, especially when it comes to student assignments. There were (at least) two glaring omissions in the previous section that we need now to include in our analysis. First, religious diversity is not the only desirable kind of diversity to pursue and achieve in a school community. And second, as was implied in the first section, diversity is only a means, and not even a sufficient means, to two ends: children's development of civic virtue and of autonomy. What are the implications of these points in practice? We will take these objections in reverse order, beginning with the recognition that diversity is not and should not be treated as an end in itself.

An extremely diverse school may, whether because its academic programs are substandard, its school culture mean-spirited, or its discipline lousy, get nowhere in promoting the development of mutual civic respect or autonomy among its students. A mostly homogeneous school, on the other hand, may successfully promote both goals because its academic programs are strong, discipline problems do not interfere with student learning, and it promotes a school culture that encourages mutual respect, critical thinking, and interaction with a diverse range of people via community service learning projects, field trips, after-school programs, or Internet projects. If two of the central goals of public education, therefore, are promoting students' development of civic virtue and autonomy, then more than the potential for diversity must be taken into account when evaluating types of schools for inclusion in voucher programs. If private religious schools have better discipline and academics than public schools in the same area, then a well-designed voucher program that includes religious as well as nonsectarian private schools might be desirable.

This is especially true considering that nonsectarian schools comprise only 22 percent of the private schools in the United States.[38] To restrict school vouchers to nonsectarian schools, therefore, is automatically to exclude *78 percent* of private schools in the United States. If there is any reason to favor school vouchers, this should give us pause; no matter whether vouchers are desirable for egalitarian, libertarian, pro-competitive, "antimonopolistic," academic, or civic reasons, the automatic exclusion of over three-quarters of American private schools without regard to their curriculum, student body, aims and objectives, academic quality, or level of innovation ought to raise eyebrows. This gains further purchase when one considers the practical implementation of vouchers. With approximately 27,400 private schools serving almost six million students,[39] as compared to approximately 90,000 public schools serving over 47 million students, the private sector is already too small to absorb students participating in a large-scale voucher program. To limit vouchers to the 6,025 nonsectarian private schools that existed in 1997–98,[40] plus those that would spring up in response to demand—and how academically, pedagogically, and civically sound could we trust them to be in their first few years of existence, when schools are always struggling to define and establish themselves?—would be to invalidate before we even started the effectiveness of vouchers in providing a real range of worthwhile choices for parents.

It is also worth noting that neither Friends schools nor Episcopal schools generally even take religious affiliation into account in their student-selection process, and also do not rate it as their most important goal. In 1993–94, *zero* percent of Friends elementary schools and 2.6 percent of Episcopal elementary schools (compared with 5 and 1.9 percent of Friends and Episcopal high schools, respectively) included religious affiliation as an admission requirement at all. Reflecting this apparent lack of religious focus, only 1.6 percent of Episcopal schools and 11.6 percent of Friends schools rated "religious development" as their most important educational goal, and well under half of these schools rated it as even one of their three most important educational goals.[41] Given that most of these schools thus neither select students according to religious affiliation nor emphasize religious belief within the curriculum, it would be fair to surmise that many Friends and Episcopal religious schools, at least, might exhibit significant religious diversity.

Even among more religiously oriented and restrictive religious schools, though, religious diversity may be the only type of diversity that is reliably lower in religious schools than in other private or public schools. Let us examine, for example, racial diversity. In terms of raw percentages, Catholic and nonsectarian schools have virtually identical racial minority enrollment—23.4 percent and 23.3 percent, respectively—based on data from the 1997–98 school year. Only 18.8 percent of students in other religious schools (conservative Christian, affiliated, and unaffiliated) are minorities, but it is worth noting that only 19.9 percent of students in regular-education nonsectarian schools are minorities; it is only because 27.1 percent of students in special-education schools and a whopping 38.3 percent of students in nonsectarian special-education schools are minorities that nonsectarian schools as a whole achieve the 23.3 percent minority enrollment mark.[42] By way of comparison, in 1997–98, the public school system, nationally, was 36.5 percent minority.[43]

This is, of course, an almost meaningless data point given the vast demographic differences not only among given school districts but also at times within a given school system itself. Almost a half-century after *Brown v. Board of Education,* many school systems continue to look like checkerboards with identifiably "white" and "minority" schools,[44] underscoring the point that many researchers have made that more important than raw demographic percentages is the actual distribution of different groups within a system or a school.[45] If we compare the percentage of Catholic, other religious, and regular nonsectarian schools (which seems the most appropriate comparison, since almost all religious schools offer a regular-education program) in which minority students make up 10–49 percent of the student body, therefore, we find that 27.7 percent of Catholic schools, 26 percent of other religious schools, and 44.9 percent of regular nonsectarian private schools are racially integrated by this measure. By comparison, 33.4 percent of public schools in 1993–94 were similarly racially integrated (11–50 percent minority).[46] Thus, nonsectarian private schools are far ahead of public schools in promoting racial diversity, and religious private schools are not too far behind.

These statistics are inevitably fairly crude, and many religious schools will predictably not satisfy these criteria for racial diversity. In 1993–94, Jewish schools were 98 percent white overall, and fully 78 percent of Hebrew Day Schools had *no* minority enrollment. (Solomon Schechter schools were better, insofar as only 41.5 percent had no minority enrollment, but 95 percent had less than 10 percent minority enrollment, as did 90 percent of other Jewish schools.) Other religious schools are also likely to be less diverse than the above statistics suggest: AME schools are likely all black, and nearly half of Evangelical Lutheran schools are more than 50 percent minority. Non–Evangelical Lutheran schools, too, are overall at least 85–95 percent white.[47] In addition, some types of religious schools are likely to be socioeconomically homogeneous: Episcopal schools are likely, save for relatively few scholarship students, to be predominantly middle-, if not indeed upper-middle, class; and many small, nonmainstream Protestant schools may be working class.

It should be obvious, though, that this latter concern about demographic segregation is scarcely limited to private-sector schools or even to religious schools within the private sector. Military schools are, we suspect, quite unlikely to draw many poor students, and, almost by definition, they draw only such students whose parents believe in the virtues of military discipline. The same, of course, could be said of "progressive" schools. Not only do schools like Dalton in New York or Shady Hill in Cambridge cost far, far more than most non-well-off families could possibly afford; they also tempt only parents who in fact agree with the particular pedagogic (and ideological) doctrines linked with them. This means that the extent of actual "mingling" may be quite limited.[48] Although most self-styled progressive schools, no doubt, explicitly set themselves up to foster and respond to diversity, there is no reason to believe that they attract a particularly diverse clientele. If actually having "representatives" of diverse groups in the classroom is as important as suggested by, say, the University of Michigan, as distinguished from presenting materials *about* such groups, then we suspect that most progressive schools are little better than, say, a Southern Baptist religious academy. There is no evidence, for example, that racial minorities (or the poor more generally) are eager to place their children in progressive schools as against schools that emphasize traditional programs, including emphasis on the the three 'Rs' and discipline. Moreover, one doubts that many parents with strong religious viewpoints are particularly attracted to schools that are likely dominated by teachers and parents—and by verbally skilled children of these parents—with far more secular identities and viewpoints.

Many of these points could and should be made, of course, with regard to public schools as well. "Public" is not synonymous with "common." The first refers only to funding and, possibly, to overt state sponsorship; the second, on the other hand, directs our attention to a host of demographic issues having little direct connection to the source of funds. It is obvious that "neighborhood schools" have all sorts of selection biases insofar as American neighborhoods tend to discourage, as a practical matter, the maximalist "mingling" of populations. Most American neighborhoods are segregated at least by race and class, and neighborhood schools tend to reflect this segregation. Furthermore, to the extent that school districts have attempted to overcome residential segregation's affect on schools through busing, they often simply end up segregating the entire district from others, as the phenomenon of "white flight"—or its cousin, "middle-class flight"—contributes to furthering the homogenization of the relevant school districts.

In recognition of this effect, and as a way of responding to increasing "market" pressures, many school districts have tried to make schools more diverse and attract families through voluntary mechanisms. Even these nonneighborhood schools may be little better, however, if they are organized along ideological or pedagogical lines that have predictable selection biases, which is true of many of these "magnet," "theme," "specialization," or "school-to-career-oriented" schools. To take one example, we mentioned private-market progressive schools a moment ago. Some public school systems, including Cambridge, Massachusetts, have taken to offering similarly progressive schools as an alternative, presumably, to more traditionally organized institutions. (One hesitates to call them "unprogressive.") White, upper-middle class, academically oriented parents, many of them Cantabridgians connected with Harvard or MIT, now consider these public schools to be among the best elementary schools in the community. More to the point, many have even been willing to contemplate sending their children to such public schools rather than, as had been usual, to one or another of the private-market schools that, as a practical matter, had been the standard destination of most such children. That is the good news. The bad news, though, is that every year these schools get fewer applications from minority and especially poor families, despite the "controlled choice" system that guarantees all children an equal chance of getting in. Rightly or wrongly, these latter parents prefer a different style of education for their children.[49] Similarly, it should be obvious that an Afrocentric school sponsored by a public school system, even if formally open to any student in the district, is spectacularly unlikely to get more than a handful (if that) of non–African American students.

What these statistics and the civic and personal goals that diversity is supposed to help satisfy may suggest, then, is that receipt of public funds—in the form of direct funding of public schools or vouchers for private schools—should be contingent either on satisfying certain diversity criteria or on adopting strategies to increase diversity at the school. In the case of public schools, therefore, schools and districts might adopt the religious "magnet" programs discussed above as a way of increasing their religious diversity, while also continuing—or, more accurately, reviving—the pursuit of racial, ethnic, socioeconomic, and other forms of diversity. Private—both religious and nonsectarian—schools that wished to receive public vouchers would need to prove they were either already sufficiently diverse (and the meaning of this would obviously need to be debated and clarified in practice) or that they were taking practical, measurable steps to make themselves more so. Some schools would choose to comply; others would not, and therefore would not receive vouchers. And interestingly, as the data above suggest, some religious schools are more likely to be in compliance than some nonsectarian private schools are.

It is worth noting that these arguments strongly weigh against any support of home schooling. Almost by definition, home schooling works against the kinds of diversity that we, with many others, deem important. It is, obviously, not at all the case that specific home schooling parents might not be extremely sensitive to the kinds of concerns we are emphasizing and would, therefore, make special efforts to introduce their children to a wide array of people. But we are, to put it mildly, wary either of believing that there will be many such parents or, more importantly, of accepting as desirable a mode of education that limits the amount of contact that children will have with others during the "schooling" process itself. As several of our earlier anecdotes suggested, the presence of other children can be vital to appreciation of the dangers of facile stereotyping. It may be, for libertarian reasons, that parents should retain, legally, the right to home school their children. But any such decisions should receive no affirmative public support that might, indeed, serve as an incentive for yet other parents to choose that path.

Note well, though, that the major reason to reject public subsidies for home schooling must be the acceptance of some version of our argument about the desirability of diversity and its importance with regard both to civic education and development of an autonomous self. If education were merely instrumental—dealing, say, with the acquisition of certain knowledge capable of being tested for on standard examinations—then it is altogether possible that many home schooled children could do just fine. Indeed, supporters of home schooling point, with justifiable pride, to the academic success of many home-schooled children, though we have no good evidence about how representative these children are of the entire universe of home-schooled students. Interestingly enough, the voucher proposal that was submitted, and handily rejected by, the California electorate in 2000 included the possibility that home-schooling parents would be entitled to receive public funds to purchase school supplies and the like. That feature itself justified a vote against the proposal because of its encouragement of home schooling, even if someone accepting our overall argument could quite properly support at least some proposals for vouchers or other state aid to a wide variety of nonpublic, including religious, schools.

Conclusion

These arguments have not been balanced against other norms relevant to vouchers, such as equity or efficiency (and especially not legality). We would not argue, therefore, that our conclusions about the desirability of promoting religious diversity in public and private schools are definitive insofar as other public goals and goods may lead to other public policies that trump the ones we have put forward here. It is, nonetheless, worth emphasizing the significance—and possible counterintuitiveness—of our conclusions about the importance of religious diversity for both public and private school policy. Proceeding from explicitly liberal assumptions about the desirability of promoting children's development of civic toleration and individual autonomy, we demonstrated that many religious schools may actually be *more* deserving of vouchers than are many nonsectarian private schools, and that public schools can and should do much more to attract minority religious students. Our school communities should be religiously inclusive in addition to being racially, ethnically, and socioeconomically diverse. It is not easy (and may not be possible, even with the institution of creative voluntary measures) to promote all of these at once, and we certainly would not argue that we have provided any definitive guide to how to balance them. But it is a challenge worth taking on.

Six

Assessing Arguments for School Choice: Pluralism, Parental Rights, or Educational Results?

AMY GUTMANN

MANY AMERICANS who are products of our school system cannot understand simple jury instructions or summarize basic information about schools from a simple chart. Nor can they fill out a job application or understand a train schedule. Yet a central part of the historic mission of a democratically accredited school system is to educate citizens who are capable of sitting on juries, assessing public proposals (about schools, for example), exercising their rights, fulfilling their responsibilities, and seizing their opportunities to live a good life as they see fit. A publicly accredited school system that prepares all children for a life of equal liberty and opportunity is a defensible democratic ideal.[1]

A life of equal liberty and opportunity is made possible by an educational system that enables children to make informed choices both as individuals who have their own lives to lead and as citizens who are free to participate as civic equals in a representative democracy (which does not require them to participate in politics but depends no less— perhaps therefore more—on an educated and publicly concerned citizenry). An ideal of free and equal citizenship constitutes democracy as a moral conception, and it gives democratic citizens reason to support primary and secondary schooling that educates all children to be able to exercise their rights and responsibilities as adults by informed choice, not by force or indoctrination. Yet we know that each year in publicly accredited schools, tens of thousands of students fail to learn even the barest minimum that is necessary—never mind sufficient— for exercising the rights and responsibilities of democratic citizenship or for enjoying a life of equal liberty and opportunity.[2] Democracies are political projects that by their very nature will never achieve their full potential, since their potential is to be ever improved by their citizens. How can primary and secondary schooling in the United States be improved today?

Schooling tops the public's list of salient issues in American politics.[3] As usual, there is no shortage of suggestions for quick fixes. The reform proposal that has gained the most press and political ground in recent years is variously called vouchers or school choice. In the early stages of his presidential campaign, George W. Bush proposed a voucher plan that would transfer $1,500 per child, per year of federal Title I money from failing schools to parents, for use at any school of their choice, public or private, religious or secular.[4] Once the presidential campaign was in full swing, however, Bush refused to use the word *vouchers* or even speak about this plan. *School choice* has a better public resonance than vouchers, but even school choice has taken on negative connotations as a means to undermine public schools. But school choice is actually much broader than the idea of vouchers. Whereas the idea behind vouchers is to let parents decide among any school, public or private, school choice sometimes refers to parental choice within a public school system. Other times, however, school choice is simply a synonym for vouchers that would grant parents the right to choose any school at public expense. In this essay, I will focus on the voucher movement to reform schooling in the United States as a distinct part of a broader idea of school choice, and I will argue—among other things—that it is very important not to confuse the narrower (voucher) and broader (school choice) ideas.

Because vouchers are both the most celebrated and the most criticized of the new reform ideas for publicly funded schooling in the United States, anyone concerned about the issue would do well to carefully examine their promise. Let's begin with what has happened in practice with regard to school vouchers in this country. Most recently, a statewide voucher proposal—presented to California voters in a referendum accompanying the 2000 presidential election—was defeated by a wide margin.[5] But prior to the California referendum, several voucher plans in other states had already been put in place, although only one is publicly funded at a statewide level. With regard to statewide vouchers, California is not in the lead; Florida is. In Florida, George W.'s brother Jeb has initiated what the *New York Times* calls the "nation's boldest voucher experiment."[6] Citywide experiments in Cleveland and Milwaukee have been in place longer, and therefore enroll more students. This year, Florida's experiment enrolls only fifty-three students; Cleveland and Milwaukee together enroll over ten thousand. But the potential enrollment of the Florida voucher experiment is much greater: all parents of students whose public schools fail standardized tests twice in four years will be eligible for vouchers usable at the school of their choice, public or private, secular or parochial.

The vouchers are worth the lesser of the per-pupil cost of the failing public school or the private school's tuition ($3,400 on average in 2000).

Voucher plans like the one in Florida give a designated group of parents a certain amount of money that is tied to use at a school of the parents' choice, either publicly or privately run, religious or secular. The designated groups of parents can be all parents, or they can be means-tested (and thereby limited to a lower-income level), or they can be selected (as George W.'s plan would have done) according to whether their children attend a school that has failed for a number of consecutive years. Voucher schools are to be minimally regulated so that they do not become public schools in disguise. Most voucher advocates therefore put their trust in market forces and distrust public standards and values, such as the integrationist idea of bringing children from different backgrounds and with different perspectives together in learning as preparation for democratic citizenship. Voucher proponents would not require voucher schools to renounce racial, religious, or gender discrimination. Many also oppose the idea of even a permeable wall of separation between church and state. Some voucher proponents acknowledge that schools, as publicly funded and accredited institutions, should serve public purposes, but they minimize the public purposes of schooling. They argue that the public purposes of schooling are "minimal," and whenever they are controversial—as are many curricular standards, along with the principle of nondiscrimination—voucher advocates oppose public enforcement and defer to parental choice in the marketplace.[7]

What are the strongest arguments in favor of vouchers? Three very different kinds of arguments are commonly offered. I call them the arguments from pluralism, parental rights, and educational results. I begin with the argument from pluralism because it is the most general: let many more schools bloom by publicly subsidizing any school to which parents want to send their children. Michael McConnell defends vouchers primarily on pluralist grounds. The "core idea" behind vouchers, McConnell argues, is that "families [i.e., parents] be permitted to choose among a range of educational options . . . using their fair share of educational funding to pay for the schooling they choose."[8] Public funds for schooling, on the pluralist view, are fairly distributed when parents control the use of public funds and the funds are not tied to anything more than minimal public standards of what constitutes a good school. The idea is that individual parents, not citizens more generally (or even parents acting collectively), would then set the standards. They would do so indirectly through decentralized market forces. The pluralist argument for vouchers makes little or nothing of the fact that democratic citizens are expected to fully fund schools for all children while being prohibited from requiring anything more from the schools than minimal public standards. Why make the least of the practical or moral implications of public funding? Because, as McConnell puts it, "educational pluralism would be a mirage if the result were to yoke all schools to a single set of prescriptive standards." The idea that a democratic public has the right to expect more than minimal public standards from publicly funded schooling is defended on grounds that to expect more is "to yoke all schools to a single set of prescriptive standards."[9]

The argument from pluralism for vouchers raises two big questions that are rarely asked by voucher advocates. First, does a commitment to supporting many different kinds of schools uniquely support a voucher system? Second, is pluralism per se a primary goal of a system of primary and secondary schooling? Let's begin with the connection between pluralism and vouchers. Does the argument from pluralism uniquely support a voucher system? It is impossible to answer this question without saying more about what pluralism in schooling means. A pluralistic school system may be contrasted to a centrally controlled one, like the school system in France. Pluralism would mean many noncentrally coordinated schools, which would offer different curricula, although all would be publicly accredited. If this is what pluralism means, then the nonvoucher school system in the United States is certainly pluralistic. American public school systems are remarkably decentralized by states and school districts, and to this decentralization is added also heterogeneous private schools and some home schooling.

Voucher advocates may mean more by pluralism. They may mean a school system that has minimal public regulation, even if that regulation is largely decentralized.[10] But what constitutes "minimal" public regulation? Voucher advocates do not offer a rich account of the public's stake in schooling, and therefore they leave "minimal" standards minimally described and defended.[11] This means that pluralism is also sorely underdescribed and defended. I say "sorely" because if pluralism is the linchpin argument in defense of vouchers, it becomes essential to know what pluralism in schooling entails, beyond letting many schools thrive that meet defensible public standards. What are defensible public standards? What range of schools can and should thrive in a pluralistic democracy that is committed to educating all children for free and equal citizenship? To be a critic of introducing voucher plans is decidedly not to be a supporter of making all schools the same, or "yoking" them all to the same set of comprehensive standards. Defenders of vouchers no less than critics support some set of standards, and therefore we should be asking not whether publicly accredited schools should be required to meet some common standards, but what those common standards may justifiably be and who has the legitimate authority to set them.

As it turns out, most voucher advocates and critics alike tend to support a mixed system of public and private schooling. Voucher advocates tend to want publicly funded schools to be subject to market forces, and voucher critics want publicly funded schools to be democratically governed (within constitutional constraints), largely at the local level. The controversy does not pit pluralist advocates of vouchers against nonpluralist critics, but rather concerns what kind of mixed system is most defensible. And the answer to this question does not turn on whether we value educational pluralism. It turns on *what kind of educational pluralism* we value. The rhetoric of educational pluralism enlisted in the cause of vouchers against an already decentralized publicly funded public school system, supplemented by privately funded private schools, turns out to be just that: rhetoric. The rhetoric is misleading because a voucher system would not necessarily even incline toward—let alone ensure—pluralism of the sort that some pluralists seem to be seeking: a significant expansion of new schools that teach the widest range of comprehensive philosophies or thick theories of the good (secular and religious) to many students, and that thereby provide an antidote to consumerist or secular humanist perspectives on life (depending on the advocate's outlook). What parents will choose for their children when given market choices in schooling is no more foreordained to be schools that teach them thick theories of the good life than what they choose for themselves when they purchase other goods on the open market. At its best, tying vouchers to pluralism of this sort—a pluralism constrained by the idea that parents should choose schools that teach their children a single thick conception of the good life either for its own sake or as an antidote to the thin conceptions that seem to prevail in society—is wishful thinking. At worst, tying vouchers to a thickly constrained pluralism is an unintended way of devaluing to the point of denigrating the wide range of publicly defensible ideals in schooling—such as civic, scientific, literary, and other publicly important kinds of knowledge and understanding, along with civic virtues of toleration, mutual respect, nonviolence, honesty, and open-mindedness—that crosscut many (but by no means all) thick theories of the good life.

The pluralist argument for vouchers often targets not only the existing school system—which is far from ideal from any publicly defensible perspective—but also a democratic ideal like the one I defend in *Democratic Education*. There I criticize the existing school system for its failure to live up to publicly defensible ideals, including nondiscrimination in the way it teaches students and brings students together to associate with one another (which is an important part of learning to live together as free and equal citizens). Another publicly defensible ideal is nonrepression: children should not be indoctrinated; they should be taught to think for themselves as free citizens who are capable of living their own lives and sharing as equals in shaping the future of their society by among others ways, holding their democratic representatives accountable. Democratic education is consistent with a decentralized public-private school system in which publicly accredited schooling is constrained by more than minimal standards of literacy and numeracy. Free and equal citizenship in democracy today certainly demands a high (not merely a minimal) level of literacy, numeracy, and the capacity to understand politically relevant issues and deliberate with others who are affected by them. Free and equal citizenship also depends on an education that provides certain collective goods—such as toleration and mutual respect—that benefit all and therefore are not in the familial interest of particular parents to ensure in the education of their children (although many parents may happen to have more than their narrow familial interests at heart in educating their children). It takes conscious educational understanding and organization, which market forces do nothing to ensure, to create schools that educate students to toleration and mutual respect across different backgrounds and perspectives, not by preaching but by teaching them together in an environment that is conducive to understanding as well as practicing these civic virtues.

Here is one justifiable limit as well as defense of pluralism in schooling: A publicly accredited school system should do its best to teach and express the educational values of a constitutional democracy. It should not discriminate against students on educationally irrelevant grounds, and it should develop rather than repress their capacity to deliberate about politically relevant matters. It should educate children in a way that encourages them to engage with one another across a range of comprehensive perspectives on the good life by finding common ground in an integrated education, which is part of the common ground that the ideal of a constitutional democracy itself provides in seeking to secure liberty and opportunity for all. An integrated education may bridge several of many kinds of perspectives that might otherwise divide citizens in potentially destructive ways: divides of religion, race, class, ethnicity, gender, and sexual orientation. Proportional representation in schools is not necessary for a nondiscriminatory education, but nondiscrimination in admission for students who are members of negatively stereotyped (and otherwise discriminated against) groups is necessary. These ideals of democratic education are robust—thereby making sense of the sizable public investment in schools—but they are not comprehensive, thereby supporting a truly pluralistic system in a sense of pluralism that is publicly defensible. Such robust standards of democratic education leave a lot of room for discretionary decision making at the local level—by citizens in local communities, principals, and teachers within classrooms—about how to organize schools, and what and how to teach in the formal curriculum and outside it.[12]

Educational pluralism in a mixed system of democratic education therefore would not be a mirage. The kind of pluralism that democratic education would support—were it put into practice—is not just a matter of superficially exposing students to a smattering of difference and diversity. While publicly funded schooling at its best would not aim to immerse every (or any) student in a single comprehensive conception of the good life, whether it be the one preferred by her parents or a like-minded local community, neither would it subscribe to a single *comprehensive* set of prescriptive standards that precludes parents from deciding to so immerse their children. Nondiscrimination and nonrepression in schooling do not constitute anything close to a *comprehensive* set of prescriptive educational standards. They are necessary to justify public schooling, but they do not preclude teaching comprehensive conceptions of the good life that are consistent—as many are—with constitutional democratic values of schooling. Enforcement of a comprehensive set of standards by a central authority would make all schools educationally the same. Democratic education explicitly leaves a lot of discretion in different educational realms to parents (in the family), to principals and teachers (in the school and classroom), and to the democratically accountable representatives of citizens at local, state, and federal levels (in structuring school systems, funding and overseeing them), while leaving room for a private school sector that can teach religious and secular points of view that are too sectarian (and comprehensive) to be taught within publicly funded schools.

In a constitutional democracy, there are constitutional limits to the legitimate discretion that anyone—parents or public officials—may authoritatively exercise in publicly accredited schools to educate children as future citizens. For example, public schools should not discriminate in whom they admit and how they teach, nor should any accredited school repress the knowledge and understanding necessary for educating free and equal citizens. Public schools are constitutionally constrained not to discriminate on grounds of race, gender, ethnicity, and religion, while private schools are permitted to admit children and teach on comprehensive religious or secular humanist grounds as long as they also teach the skills and virtues necessary for first-class citizenship in a constitutional democracy. Selected admission is justifiable only insofar as it is consistent with an overall system of nondiscrimination in schooling. Democratic education supports such a pluralistic system of schooling, although it is not the only pluralistic system that could be designed. Voucher plans would also be pluralistic, but not uniquely so. Is the kind of pluralism supported by voucher plans better in some democratically defensible way?

The claim that a decentralized and mixed system of public and private schools makes educational pluralism a mirage cannot be sustained, but what may still be true is that a school system that is nondiscriminatory and nonrepressive would be less various than our present school system, which includes both privately and publicly controlled schools that together do not add up to a nondiscriminatory or nonrepressive system. The variety that would be missing should not be missed by anyone committed to providing a publicly defensible education for all children. Any publicly defensible system of schooling would lack the schools that today fall far short of teaching toleration, mutual respect, or anything close to a high level of literacy and numeracy; that discriminate on grounds of gender, race, religion, or sexual orientation; that aim to indoctrinate rather than to educate children; and that fail in other basic ways to educate children to be capable of exercising their rights, fulfilling their responsibilities, and seizing their opportunities as free and equal citizens. Because democracy at its best is a human project continually in the making, we should not expect perfection from even the best achievable system of democratic education at any given time—but the school system in the United States today is far from the best achievable given this society's resources, both material and human.

Saying that a decentralized and mixed public-private school system that aims to educate (and not indoctrinate) democratic citizens would be pluralistic therefore leaves open the question of whether *maximizing* educational pluralism is a fundamental aim of public schooling, as voucher advocates often suggest when they defend vouchers on pluralistic grounds, in contrast to the lesser pluralism of alternative systems. To fully assess the pluralist argument for vouchers, we therefore need to ask the second question: What speaks in favor of maximizing diversity among schools? The short answer is "not much." Maximizing diversity would be a rather senseless goal for an educational system. And no educational reformers therefore really aim to maximize diversity, even though their rhetoric sometimes suggests otherwise. This is because diversity per se—without substantive caveats attached—embraces a lot of blatantly bad education, whether it be in public, private, voucher, nonvoucher, religious, or secular schools. Yet the rhetoric of voucher advocates often indiscriminately trades on the contemporary resonance of the word *diversity*. Many kinds of diversity, as I have suggested above, are educationally valuable. But the diversity that is made possible by minimally constrained choice in schooling has yet to be shown to be educationally valuable. Market choice of schools in itself is certainly not educationally valuable for children.[13]

Rhetoric aside, what is it about maximizing school diversity that attracts voucher advocates and leads them to champion the cause of imposing no more than minimal standards on publicly funded schools? I suspect that maximizing diversity is attractive to voucher advocates because they distrust public standards beyond the minimum that they take to be right (and therefore required of all voucher schools). McConnell distrusts people who defend public control of publicly funded schools because, he says, they pretend to "know what principles are best for democracy."[14] He apparently wants to avoid what he considers the moral arrogance of people who defend nonvoucher conceptions of schooling. He therefore suggests that "maybe we are ready for educational disestablishment." Educational disestablishment here means disestablishing public standards of (publicly funded and accredited) schooling just as the liberal-democratic state once disestablished public standards of religion. The allusion of course is to the disestablishment of religion. This is a very strained allusion, since democratic societies like the United States were created and existed for a good deal of their early history without any public standards of education.

The rhetoric of disestablishing public standards of schooling is even more misleading than that of pluralism. Like everyone else who supports public funding of schools for children, voucher advocates cannot escape defending some publicly enforced requirements. (Surely they would not argue that those requirements that are publicly enforced should not be publicly defended, or that academics should not stoop to defend what they think is publicly defensible.) Without public requirements for what counts as a school worthy of public support, public funding of schools would be meaningless. Absent such public requirements, there would be no operative public understanding of what counts as an educational institution entitled to public funds. This means that voucher advocates no less than defenders of democratic education also must claim to "know what principles are best for democracy." They defend *different* principles in schooling entitled to public support: market choice constrained by minimal standards. But their defense of these principles counts no less as claiming to "know what principles are best for democracy."

Voucher advocates legitimately defend the principles that they think are best for democracy, but they apparently think that their principles can escape being tarred by the same rhetorical brush they use against critics of vouchers with whom they disagree. How can they think that they are not also claiming to know what principles are best for democracy? If this is not rhetoric (cleverly but deceptively) designed to make everyone who defends different standards seem arrogant, then it is an argument that prevents everyone—including voucher advocates—from saying what they think are better and worse principles for funding and governing schools in a constitutional democracy. The logical implication of the claim that "we are ready for educational disestablishment" is considerably more radical than McConnell's conclusion in favor of a voucher system of funding schools admits: if the time comes when citizens of a constitutional democracy should not as citizens say what principles we think are best for the education that we are publicly funding, then we will probably be ready for the end of public funding of schooling. This would be a sad day for constitutional democracy. It would signal the end of any public concern for the democratic education of children, with the possible exception of one's own.

The pluralist argument for vouchers, taken on its merits, therefore deconstructs the voucher advocates' defense of publicly funded vouchers. Here is how the logic of McConnell's argument deconstructs. Democratic citizens, he claims, would be arrogant to think that they can know what principles should guide democracy and therefore should guide the schooling of children at public expense. We therefore also would be foolish to support schooling at great public expense, which spells the end of vouchers since they rely every bit as much as does democratic education on public funding of schools. Voucher advocates think that parents know what is good for their children's education. But in order to defend public funding of vouchers, it is by no means enough to think parents know what is good for their own children. The claim of a voucher plan on the public purse depends on our also thinking that what parents want for their own children is so good for democracy that it is worthy of public funding through considerable taxation. To think this, however, is to think that we know what is good for democracy. Voucher advocates therefore need to think that they know what is good for democracy to defend vouchers no less than their critics need to think that they know what is good for democracy to criticize vouchers and defend an alternative.

Because voucher advocates would rather avoid saying what they think is good for democracy (since anything they say is bound to be controversial, and they criticize others for being controversial), voucher advocates tend not to say much about their minimal standards for funding a voucher school. But this leaves voucher schools almost entirely without definition. (Any definition of the civic minimum will be controversial, which is not a critique except according to what voucher advocates argue against their opponents.) Voucher advocates need to get more specific about what should count as a set of minimal educational standards. Without a substantive defense of a specific civic minimum, the minimalist standard for schooling is simply meaningless. In its abstract form, it stands as a hollow conception into which all citizens, including advocates of democratic education, can put their understanding of what constitutes publicly defensible standards of civic education and call it the civic minimum.

What do voucher advocates defend as a specific substantive conception of the civic minimum? Some defend little more than basic literacy and numeracy.[15] They reject requirements like that of racial integration, whereby children frcm different backgrounds learn together as preparation for associating together as democratic citizens. McConnell explicitly opposes a public requirement that voucher schools practice racial, religious, or gender nondiscrimination. Yet voucher schools would be publicly funded and accredited institutions. Why should the public fund racially segregated or religiously discriminatory schools, for example, just because some parents would choose such schools for their children? There may well be an argument for funding schools that discriminate on some grounds as long as they operate with a school system that taken as a whole is nondiscriminatory on these grounds. But the permission to discriminate then depends on an assessment based on a standard of nondiscrimination. Why does a constitutional democracy have a right to insist on nondiscrimination in publicly funded schooling? The short answer can be by way of another question: If publicly funded schools cannot be held up to a public standard of ensuring that all children receive an education adequate for becoming free and equal citizens, what reason is there for the *public* to fund them? A longer answer depends on a conception of democracy that treats all persons as free and equal citizens with rights to equal liberty and opportunity, and such rights depend critically on a nondiscriminatory system of schooling, as I argue in depth in *Democratic Education*.

Voucher proponents who do not rely on the argument from pluralism often argue that voucher schools should be publicly funded because citizens should recognize *a parental right to choose* a school in a free marketplace. I therefore turn now from the pluralist argument to the argument from parental rights. The first thing worth noting about the argument from parental rights is that the right at stake is not a matter of basic freedom, as are constitutional rights of free speech, press, association, and religion. What is at issue in the argument is not the personal freedom of parents but their power to determine their children's schooling. The legal scholar Charles Fried elides the difference between parental freedom and power by claiming that "the right to form one's child's values, [and] one's child's life plan . . . are extensions of the basic right not to be interfered with in doing these things for oneself." But Fried never adequately defends his claim that "the facts of reproduction" make children the extensions of their parents' personalities.[16] And which parent's personality should a child be considered the extension of when parents are divorced or disagree? We need not travel far down this road, because the basic claim that children are extensions of their parents' personalities is indefensible in the realm of publicly funded schooling.

When voucher advocates defend parental rights to control the education of their children, they succumb to one of the most searing critiques ever made by John Stuart Mill. In introducing the subject of state regulation of education in *On Liberty*, Mill writes:

> It is in the case of children that misapplied notions of liberty are a real obstacle to the fulfillment by the State of its duties. One would almost think that a man's children were supposed to be literally . . . a part of himself, so jealous is opinion of the smallest interference of law with his absolute and exclusive control over them, more jealous than of almost any interference with his own freedom of action: so much less do the generality of mankind value liberty than power.[17]

A constitutional democracy cannot fulfill its obligation to ensure an adequate education for every child if it treats parental power to control the education of children as if it were a basic constitutional freedom, and therefore immune from a consideration of the educational consequences of giving parents more or less control over the publicly funded education of their children. Treating parental power as if it were synonymous with constitutional liberty eclipses the importance of a child's right to an education adequate for first-class (free and equal) citizenship.

The parental rights argument sometimes takes a different turn, piggybacking on a claim about unfairness in the way public and private schools are differentially funded. Many voucher advocates argue that the present school system in the United States—in which only public schools are fully funded (while private schools are subsidized by tax exemption and smaller subsidies)—is unfair to parents who choose to send their children to private schools. Those parents pay twice, once when paying mandatory school taxes and twice when paying private school tuition. But this claim about unfairness to parents is parasitic on the morally indefensible claim that parents have a right, grounded in their own basic constitutional freedom, to choose at public expense whatever school among any they prefer for their children. The right that supports publicly funding and accrediting schools, however, is not a parental right but a child's right to an adequate education for first-class democratic citizenship.

We should still ask why the absence of public funding of private schools is not unfair to religious parents who for conscientious reasons want their children to attend a religious school. An answer consistent with the religious disestablishment clause of the U.S. Constitution is that democratic citizens have a constitutional duty not to fund schools that teach Christianity, Judaism, Islam, atheism, or any other religion or antireligion as a matter of faith or gospel, and a correlative duty not to fund institutions that give preference to children who have the true religious faith or eschew all faith.[18] (Although this still leaves open the possibility of public funding of private schools that do not violate these establishment strictures, voucher proponents almost universally oppose the idea that public funding of vouchers may be made conditional on use only at a school that abides by public standards of nondiscrimination and nonrepression.) In a constitutional democracy that protects both religious freedom and the disestablishment of any and all religions, private schools that teach religion are permitted to discriminate on religious grounds precisely (and only) because they are not publicly funded. Publicly funded schools, by contrast, must not discriminate in admissions on the basis of religion or its lack thereof.

The school system in the United States is unfair, but its unfairness is the result of its failure to provide an adequate education for all children rather than the public's refusal to fund any school preferred by parents for their own children. This argument from unfairness rejects the voucher advocates' claim that parents have a *right* to be maximally free of public regulation of publicly funded schools. Yet it is also an argument that can go some way toward supporting means-tested vouchers insofar as they can be shown to produce better educational results, judged by public standards, than the available alternatives. The central claim in defense of means-tested vouchers is that in their absence, children of poor parents will not have access to adequate schooling. Many lower-income parents, especially those who reside in inner cities where good public schools are scarcest, cannot take advantage of the good schools that exist in the suburbs and in the private sector of the city for their children. This disparity between lower- and higher-income parents is unfair to children. And this unfairness goes a long way to explaining the public appeal of vouchers to many lower-income Americans.

Many Americans rightly think it unfair that rich parents but not poor ones can opt their children out of a failing urban school system and send them to better suburban or private schools. A Supreme Court decision protected suburban schools from being forced to integrate across city-suburban lines, thereby closing off an important and fair means by which public schools could have otherwise provided a better education for the children of poor as well as middle-class Americans, and at the same time mitigated the unfair effects on children of white flight to the suburbs. Another alternative for inner-city children is the private sector of city schools. Many Catholic schools in inner cities—which are often integrated by race, gender, and even religion—are eager to admit more students, but most inner-city parents cannot afford even their relatively low tuition. Vouchers for poor parents may make a difference. That inner-city parents cannot find good public schools for their children has become a major source of the appeal of vouchers—particularly to these same parents, who are disproportionately African American and Hispanic American. It is certainly unfair to relegate children of poor parents to failing schools while children of affluent parents move to the suburbs or are placed in private city schools.

The unfairness of our present system thus resides not in the absence of choice per se, but in the presence of poverty and an inadequate public school system, which disadvantage the children of poor parents, who deserve better and are entitled to more. It is not only unfair but also unjust that people who are willing and able to work cannot find decent-paying jobs that cover child care and cannot afford to live in safe neighborhoods that provide good public schools for their children. The truly bold reform—one that is also clearly constitutional and would express as well as support public concern for schooling—would be for the public to support good public schools, decent-paying work, and a real safety net for everyone, including good child care and health care.[19] But this support has not been forthcoming from our government, even though majorities seem to support many of its elements and do not seem to support vouchers. The defensible alternatives to vouchers, however, are not yet visible on the political horizon. Are vouchers therefore a second-best or third-best response to a much broader problem of unfairness that federal and state governments do not have the will to address, and city governments—dependent on an unfavorable tax base that gives vastly disproportionate political weight to the wealthy—are often unable to address on their own?

The problem with defending vouchers as a second- or third-best response on grounds of fairness to poor children is that the inner logic of voucher proposals—and the aim of many proponents—is equal public financing for all parents, regardless of their income and wealth, to pick a private or public school for their children at public expense, not good schooling for all children. The most vocal voucher advocates think it is unfair that any parents, even the richest who can afford it, should have to pay more to send their children to private schools than they would to send their child to a comparably costly public school. The argument is that parents whose preferences tend toward private schools are doubly taxed. On the argument from parental choice, what fairness requires is that in any given school district the same tax dollars should follow all children—not just otherwise disadvantaged children—to private or public schools. The private schools would not be democratically governed, while the public schools would be. A successful voucher movement in this country would therefore provide an enormous subsidy to affluent parents. Would it significantly increase educational opportunity for disadvantaged children?

This question orients our focus, as it should be, on educational opportunity for children, bringing us to the third and most important argument in favor of vouchers, the argument from educational results. Let's start with the educational results that are the most morally troubling in this country, those of disadvantaged children in inner-city schools. If the citizens of this country were committed to giving low-income parents what most parents want for their children, we would not follow the voucher route. We would do whatever it takes to improve public schools. The vast majority of parents who can afford private education send their children to public schools. Poll after poll shows that they are quite satisfied with these schools. Even among the highest-earning fifth of American families, only about 15 percent of children attend private schools, and despite the skyrocketing incomes of the top quintile over the past twenty years, the proportion has actually decreased slightly.[20] Voucher advocates might say that this is because economic incentives push parents toward public schools. True enough. Public schools are publicly funded, while private schools are not. Private schools are significantly subsidized as tax-exempt institutions, but a big financial incentive still remains to send one's children to public schools. We should remember that if this is the complaint—that subsidizing public schools is unfair to parents who want to send their child to private schools—then the controversy is not about achieving parity between rich and poor children, but rather about whether private schools, in fairness to the rich more than the poor, must also be publicly funded.

John Chubb and Terrence Moe put the case for vouchers on grounds of educational results most pointedly when they say "Choice *is* a panacea." A voucher plan, they argue, "has the capacity *all by itself* to bring about the kind of transformation that, for years, reformers have been seeking to engineer in myriad other ways."[21] Vouchers uniquely have this capacity, advocates say, because competition in a free market is the only way of really improving the quality of just about anything people want in the world, and parents certainly want better schools for their children. They do not want to depend on state bureaucracies, which are surely not the best agents for satisfying consumer demand. A case in point, which I had the pleasure of confirming, was the difference between the old state-run restaurants and the new private ones in Prague, shortly after the collapse of communism. (The latter all displayed signs that proclaimed the same name: Private Restaurant.) Little doubt about it: Market choice in restaurants is a panacea for improving the quality of cuisine—or close enough to a panacea not to quibble.

The question then is whether market choice in schooling is also a panacea for improving the quality of education for disadvantaged inner-city children, or close enough not to quibble. Or is there a significant difference between improving schools in Chicago and restaurants in postcommunist Prague? Not according to Milton Friedman, who can be credited with getting the voucher ball rolling in this country. In *Capitalism and Freedom*, Friedman compared schools and restaurants. Beyond funding school vouchers, the sole role of government in education, he argued, should be to inspect schools to assure that they meet minimal curricular standards "much as it now inspects restaurants to assure that they maintain minimum sanitary standards."[22]

This analogy, which drives the market model, is more revealing than politicians defending vouchers may want to admit. If the public's interest in schools and restaurants is so similar, then citizens have no obligation to pay for schools for other people's children. We do not have a public obligation to pick up other people's restaurant tabs. At least as troubling from the perspective of a constitutional democracy, the analogy suggests that the public has no obligation to ensure that schools are desegregated, that they teach to high standards, or that they are otherwise structured to prepare children for free and equal citizenship. We do not have a public obligation to dine at a communal table together or to eat good food, and it borders on the absurd even to think about structuring or regulating restaurants in the service of educating adults for free and equal democratic citizenship. It is not at all absurd to think about schools in this way vis-à-vis children.

Unlike restaurants, primary and secondary schools are supposed to serve public purposes. They should ensure that all children—regardless of their socioeconomic status, gender, race, ethnicity, or religion—receive an education that prepares them to exercise their rights and fulfill their responsibilities as free and equal citizens. Again, advocates of parental choice and market control downplay the public purposes of schooling, and this is not accidental. It coincides with the idea of consumer sovereignty (although in a way that ultimately undermines the very cause of voucher advocates): the market should deliver whatever the consumers of its goods want. The problems with applying the market model to school vouchers should now be apparent. First, the market model is based on consumer sovereignty, but parents are not the consumers of education. Children are. And even the most ardent advocates of the market model do not argue that children's preferences are the ones that should be counted. Second, the market model is based on the idea that "he who pays the piper picks the tune." But democratic citizens, not parents, pay the piper. If their tune is that schools should serve public purposes, then the market model collapses into a defense of democratic control of publicly funded schooling. Ironically, if the market model takes any side in this controversy, it supports the public side. And it opposes the claim that the public purposes served by publicly funded schools must be minimal.

We are still left with the question of how to overcome the unfairness and other problems that plague the status quo of our society's vast and complex school system. We would do well to begin by locating where the system is actually failing. In many states and most suburban areas, students score higher on standardized tests than in any other country in the world, and the vast majority of these students attend public schools. Standardized tests are a sorely inadequate measure of the success of a school, but many voucher advocates—including George W. Bush—point primarily to low test scores as primary evidence of the failure of inner-city public schools. By this measure, many public schools are succeeding where inner-city public schools are failing. The public schools outside of inner cities have also improved over time in their teaching of civic values such as toleration and nondiscrimination. Although there is room for much more improvement even in the most successful schools, the morally and politically salient problem is the ongoing failure of public schools in our large inner cities.

In the absence of more promising ways of improving our school system—some of which were discussed above, and include public policies that go far beyond schooling—means-tested voucher programs in inner cities could represent a commitment to find some way to deliver a decent education to the most disadvantaged students. The problem is that the results of the few voucher programs in existence lend no support to the claim that school choice by itself is anything close to a surefire way of improving the education of a sizable proportion of students at risk. The results after three years of the private-public school voucher experiment in Milwaukee, which targets the least-advantaged students in the city, show modest improvements in the mathematics test scores but no improvement in English test scores over nonvoucher school students. According to C. E. Rouse, the improvements are more likely attributable to smaller class size than to competition or private control.[23] Her hypothesis is supported by the Project STAR experiment in Tennessee, where 11,600 students were randomly assigned to either small or regular-size classes within public schools. Alan B. Krueger and Diane M. Whitmore found that small class size significantly increased educational achievement, especially among disadvantaged minority students, and narrowed the black-white gap in college test taking by 54 percent. These are preliminary findings, but they offer another reason to doubt the claim that parental choice is the key to improving education.[24]

Is increasing parental choice important at all? Yes, but the most publicly defensible way of creating educationally productive competition in schooling is to give parents *educationally good choices* for their children among *public* schools. To do that, however, new schools need to be created and old schools radically reformed, often by breaking them up into smaller, more responsive units with smaller class sizes. More classrooms need to be built and more high-quality teachers have to be hired. The incentives should be increased to attract more of the ablest college students into the teaching profession, and additional incentives offered for teaching in inner-city schools. These reforms are democratically and educationally desirable, and they are also consistent with a politics that steers a moderate course on school choice, avoiding the extremes of creating a parental right to choose a minimally regulated school at public expense and of perpetuating a highly bureaucratized system of public schooling in our inner cities. These reforms are also doable; they are far from utopian.

The remaining question is not whether there is a way to improve public schools while giving parents choice among them, but whether there is a will to do what is needed for the least-advantaged children to make their educational improvement a reality rather than a pretext for defending market choice in schooling at public expense. Advocates of the California voucher proposal, roundly defeated in the 2000 referendum, could honestly promise to subsidize primarily affluent parents who already could afford private schooling for their children. Based on the available evidence to date, advocates could not promise improvements in educational results for disadvantaged children.

Over the past century, highly bureaucratized public schools that developed in inner cities have been largely (and often increasingly) unresponsive to the educational needs of the students they are supposed to serve. The movement to create small charter schools—sometimes as a school within a school—seems to be one positive step in a better direction. I say "seems to be" because the educational results of charter schools are as uncertain as those of voucher schools. The advantage of charter schools is that they still remain under public control, as voucher schools do not. They will therefore be measured by educational results, and not lauded simply because they are chosen by parents or represent the free market in action (they do not, but neither do voucher schools, as I argued earlier). And charter schools are far less likely to be permitted to discriminate on grounds of race, religion, gender, ethnicity, or sexual orientation, because they remain public schools. Charter schools have been multiplying far faster than voucher schools, and they now serve many more inner-city students.[25] Some charter high schools offer a special educational focus—for example, on computers, performing arts, science and technology, literature, or social studies—without neglecting the publicly required range of studies. Unlike voucher schools, they are typically required to choose by lottery from all the students who apply. Their educational accomplishments (or lack thereof) warrant far more attention than they have yet received.

Charter schools highlight a worry about parental choice that remains to be addressed. The worry is that parental choice—even among public schools—may drain away the best students from faltering or failing schools, creating two problems. First, the least-advantaged students may be made even worse off than they otherwise would be, since these students do better (by conventional measures of educational achievement) when they attend schools with more advantaged students. Second, the schooling of all students suffers when students are segregated by ability or by socioeconomic, ethnic, racial, or religious background. Integrated schools are a place where children from different backgrounds can learn from one another to respect one another. This kind of learning is every bit as important in a democracy as book learning; equal liberty and opportunity depend on it, since no government of a free people can afford to regulate adults so closely as to ensure that they treat others as civic equals. Yet democracies depend on fellow citizens so treating one another.

Are the worries about "creaming off" the best students and undermining integration sufficient reasons to oppose parental choice among public schools? Not if charter schools are no more segregated than existing schools (and many may be less segregated) and if some disadvantaged students will be better served than they would be by staying in their neighborhood schools. Neighborhoods in inner cities today are extremely segregated, so the ideal of the neighborhood school is not in practice an integrationist ideal even if it is presented as such in theory. The theory that assumes neighborhood schools to be integrated is at best sorely outdated, and at worst a piece of misleading nostalgia for a golden era that never (or briefly) was, at least not in the inner city. If the public's obligation is to make all schools good schools (for all students), voucher plans do not do this, and neither do public schools as they now exist. Until this obligation is honored, a good case can be made that as many students should be as well served as possible. This means that there is a lot to be said for small charter schools that provide a better education than do existing overbureaucratized public schools, and there is even something to be said on behalf of voucher plans that serve some disadvantaged students.

Nobody can tell an African American inner-city parent who wants to send her child to a better public (or private) school that her reasons are selfish, sectarian, or in any sense illegitimate. Her reasons are at least as good as the ones that lead her middle-class counterpart to move into a better school district, often in the suburbs. Moreover, there is no evidence that without public-school choice, failing schools will improve faster (or at all), or that with public-school choice, failing schools cannot be improved. There are ways to make public schools better and to give parents choice among them—as is demonstrated, for example, by the school system of Cambridge, Massachusetts, which years ago instituted a relatively effective program of public school choice. But the most defensible system of public school choice would not limit the choices of inner-city parents to schools in the inner city. The boundaries between city and contiguous suburbs are otherwise porous, and suburbanites, after all, draw heavily and asymmetrically upon the city's resources.

Still, public school choice is not an adequate remedy either. There is no simple or single way of improving inner-city schools. Rather there are many ways, no one of which is sufficient (and there are even more means of creating and maintaining bad schools). Pursuing "systemic reform" is far more promising than relying on a single remedy. Some of the most promising, mutually reinforcing improvements include decreasing class size, expanding preschool programs, setting high standards for all students, engaging students in cooperative learning exercises, empowering principals and teachers to innovate, increasing social services offered to students and their families, and providing incentives to the ablest college students to enter the teaching profession and, in particular, to teach in inner-city schools. The list could be longer, but it cannot be formulaic. There is no mantra—whether of parental choice or decentralized democratic control—for improving the schooling of all our children.

To summarize the argument so far: Both parental choice and decentralized democratic control are pluralistic, but maximizing pluralism (understood as limitless choice) makes no educational sense. Pluralism in itself cannot possibly promise good educational results. As far as the argument from a parental right to choose is concerned, parents do not have a basic right to choose whatever school they wish for their children at public expense. Publicly funded schooling at the elementary and secondary school level is fundamentally about the rights of children, not parents, to be educated as free and equal citizens. In considering schools that the public is expected to accredit and support, we should therefore keep in mind that neither pluralism nor parental choice is the primary aim of education.

At its best, pluralism is a valuable means for three reasons, which apply only to a pluralism that is constrained by defensible public standards of schooling. Pluralism within educational limits is valuable, first, because children learn in vastly different ways, and no single kind of school is therefore likely to be best for all children. Second, education is too complex for one kind of school to suffice to demonstrate how to educate even a single child as best as can be. Instead, many kinds of good schools contribute to the state of the art of schooling. Third, even if we suppose that there can in principle be a single best kind of school, there are in fact no philosopher kings and queens to create those schools for all children in our society, or any other. Fallible beings that educators all are, we are both educated and motivated to improve our teaching by some degree of competition among many kinds of good yet imperfect schools. Voucher advocates and their critics therefore can agree that some substantial degree of diversity and competition among schools (although not on a pure market model, since parents are not the "consumers" of schooling—children are) is valuable to satisfy the diverse educational needs of students and to support educational innovation, discovery, and effective implementation.

To avoid pluralism at its worst, we also need to keep in mind its limits as an educational value. Schools educate children not by how they are chosen, but by what and how they teach, and also by whom they teach together in classrooms, and how well children learn what is necessary for free and equal citizenship from both their teachers and their fellow students. Learning from the association of children in schools is an important and neglected democratic value of education. It is therefore important that we ask not only about the results of standardized tests, but a broader question as well: Do schools educate children from many backgrounds together in classrooms to a high level of literacy, numeracy, economic opportunity, and mutual respect for one another as free and equal citizens? These standards of excellence in education themselves admit of plural interpretations and ways of implementation, and they are also of course subject to challenge. All standards of schooling—those of voucher advocates, defenders of democratic education, and their critics—are open to challenge in a democratic society. The question, however, is not whether a constitutional democracy should act on standards of schooling—since standards are implicit in any school system—but what standards it should act on.

Taken as a whole, my analysis suggests that the persistent failure of our inner-city schools is attributable not to too little pluralism or parental choice or too much public control, but to political neglect. The privatizing impulse behind vouchers in their full-fledged ("free market") form threatens to increase this neglect by diminishing common concern about the children who are most at risk and by restricting the vision of a good education for all children to a good education for "my children." The vision of democratic citizens and governments will almost inevitably narrow if the market of parental choice—subsidized with minimal public standards—primarily determines the association of children within schools. Bringing together children from different backgrounds, and caring about their education as free and equal citizens, is a crucial feature of democratic education that will fade from public view if the market metaphor comes to dominate the theory and practice of publicly subsidized schooling in American democracy.

Reasonable hope for improving inner-city schools rests on using the link between public funding and public oversight as a means of fulfilling a civic obligation to offer high-quality, socially integrated education to all children. In recent years, Americans have ranked improving education as their first or second highest priority in politics, and a majority of all citizens also say they are willing to spend more money to improve public schools. The political will of these citizens, at state and national levels, is especially critical for improving inner-city schools, but the political will of public officials is also critical. Democratic citizens are right to be wary of proposals like the California referendum that threaten to erode public support for public schools, or that present themselves as substitutes for publicly judging the educational and democratic merits of schools.

Voucher programs that would give parents the right to choose any school for their own children at public expense have both these problems: These programs too threaten to erode public support for improving public schools, and they present themselves as substitutes for publicly judging the merits of publicly funded education. This said by way of criticism, it also must be said that some voucher programs—those which target the children most at risk in inner-city schools—offer long-awaited hope for at least some parents. If inner-city public schools do not improve and suburban schools continue to be off-bounds to inner-city parents, it will become politically harder and democratically less defensible to oppose subsidizing private schools that are willing and able to provide a better education on a nondiscriminatory basis to at least some otherwise at-risk students. Some private schools in our inner cities—Catholic schools especially—have demonstrated that they are able to do this for a small but significant number of inner-city students.

But politicians cannot honestly offer inner-city parents hope for their children without also offering them better public schools with smaller classes, stronger principals, more dedicated teachers, more challenging curricula, and whatever else it takes to create a good school. Good schools must be created before parents can choose them. There is no evidence that vouchers or any other scheme of parental choice alone will produce good schools for the vast majority of children who need them most. American constitutional democracy—if it is to be worthy of the name—needs public action to create the diverse *and* educationally sound schools that all children, not just some, deserve.

Response

DAVID HOLLENBACH, S.J.

THE AUTHORS of the essays in this book were asked to address the following questions: "Is there a 'common good' that, in the absence of a common school, is less likely to be realized? Are Americans better off when they can choose schools that best fit their own conception of morality, or should they be exposed to moralities other than their own?" Amy Gutmann, Meira and Sanford Levinson, and Nancy Rosenblum are all committed to some concept of the common good to which schools should prepare children to contribute. They do not believe that individual or parental choice is the premier or only value in the current debate. None of their chapters proposes a developed notion of the common good. But each presumes an implicit understanding of the shared good and how school choice would affect its achievement. Let me first suggest how an understanding of an achievable common good affects the authors' position on school choice and then, second, suggest my own view on this issue.

Amy Gutmann is explicit in arguing for a "robust" understanding of the social good that all schools should serve in a democratic society. This good goes beyond basic literacy and numeracy to include the "capacity to deliberate about politically relevant matters." This capacity for deliberation is required if children are to be prepared for active participation in the political life of a democratic society. Thus Gutmann presumes that active political participation by citizens is a part of the common good of democratic society. But schools should not seek to promote a "comprehensive" vision of the good life like the visions held by religious communities. Democratic respect for pluralism means that citizens must be tolerant of the comprehensive visions of other citizens even as they seek to deliberate with them about how to live together. To prepare such citizens, schools should teach tolerance, should not discriminate among students on educationally irrelevant grounds, and should not repress students' capacity to deliberate with others. Thus Gutmann's chapter is suspicious of any school that seeks to promote a vision of the good life that is more comprehensive or "thicker" than one based on tolerance, nondiscrimination, and nonrepression of the individual's capacity to deliberate about public affairs. Ideally, all public schools would contribute to the common good by promoting these values and thus preparing their students to play an active part in democratic life. Unfortunately, not all public schools achieve this ideal. Therefore, Gutmann is prepared to consider vouchers as a remedial step for students who are presently being deprived of the kind of education that they need to be active, democratic citizens. But this is at best a concession she makes very reluctantly; Gutmann is suspicious that private and especially religious schools may teach intolerance and promote understandings of the good life that are repressive of the capacity for deliberation. She is further concerned that the remedial step of vouchers for the inner-city poor, for example, is more like a treatment of a symptom than a cure for the disease itself—that is, inadequate education in inner-city public schools.

The Levinsons' vision of the common good of a democratic society is both similar to and different from Gutmann's. Like Gutmann, the Levinsons value toleration and autonomy as conditions of a good common life in a pluralist society. But they place a higher value on the interaction of people with diverse backgrounds as a precondition of the civic good than does Gutmann. Gutmann places strong emphasis on *toleration* for those who are different as key to an appropriate response to pluralism. Her worries about repression and exclusion reveal this. On the other hand, the Levinsons stress *engagement* with those who are different as key to the development of both the civic virtue and the capacity for autonomy needed in a successful democracy. This is evident by the way they invoke friendship among those with differing backgrounds as an analogy for what real diversity can accomplish. Engagement with others, not a live-and-let-live sort of tolerance, is central to their vision of a good democratic society. Further, they note that such engagement is important across a number of kinds of diversity—including the religious as well as those based on class, race, or ethnicity. Thus they reach the provocative conclusion that public schools should more actively seek to support religious diversity than they do, and that education in some schools sponsored by religious communities may be worthy of public financial support because their class and racial diversity may outstrip that of many public and nonsectarian private schools. This, I take it, is the result of the Levinsons' positive readiness to call for engagement across the many kinds of differences that in fact mark American life. It is in contrast with Gutmann's suspicion that differences in understanding of the good life are potential threats to toleration, especially differences based on religion. In other words, the Levinsons see diversity, including religious diversity, as a resource for a rich civic life, while Gutmann is predisposed to see religious visions of the good life as potential threats to the common good. Her call for education that is "nonrepressive" in the context of her discussion of religion reveals this suspicion. The difference between a vision of the common good based on engagement from one based on tolerance thus has very important consequences for the school-choice debate.

Rosenblum's chapter also implicitly affirms the importance of support for the common good in this debate. She suggests that arguments for school choice as a support for strong pluralism (i.e., that it will support communities built around particularistic values such as a religion or a distinctive culture) can be reduced to support for choice as such. Under the highly fluid conditions of social life in the United States today, arguments for vouchers would thus end up as support for choice, not for a pluralism of strong but distinctive communities. Rosenblum maintains that policies employing vouchers will in effect implement individualistic and libertarian values, along the lines that Milton Friedman proposed over forty years ago. They are therefore a threat to the common good of American society, not least because they will undercut perhaps the single strongest symbol of common life—the public school. We are a "people" whose lives are deeply intertwined, and our interconnections need to be sustained by such symbols. But our interactions have become so complex and impersonal that many citizens feel powerless to influence the institutions that shape the public good and are consequently drawn to see their own private good as the most they can realistically aspire to. Rosenblum's argument, therefore, implies that school choice would amount to an abandonment of one of the few remaining symbols of the hope that citizens can live good lives *together*. To invoke Robert Putnam's analysis, it would lead to the further diminishment of the social capital needed to make democracy work. In Rosenblum's view, support for vouchers is the educational equivalent of encouraging "bowling alone."

What is one to conclude on the basis of these three essays? It is significant that all three of them explicitly or implicitly reject Friedman's view that vouchers will make for better lives in America by giving everyone the resources required to make a market in schools function competitively. All three essays hold some implicit notion of the common good, for they all reject libertarian and market-based solutions to the problems facing education in the United States today. The policy stances taken by the authors, however, depend largely on whether their positions are driven by what they fear or by what they hope for. Gutmann's policy conclusions are shaped by her fear of discrimination, intolerance, repression, and "indoctrination"; Rosenblum's by her fear of a further weakening of public life and of confidence in public institutions. The Levinsons' recommendations, on the other hand, are founded on a hope that the common good of public life can be strengthened through deepened engagement across diversity, and that an appropriately designed voucher program could encourage such engagement.

I agree with Rosenblum that we have a serious problem of lowered commitment to the public good and loss of confidence in public institutions. For this reason I also share Gutmann's insistence that the public school system needs more financial and cultural support, not less. Nevertheless, I side with the Levinsons' hope that public schools could serve the common good by taking religion more seriously. I also agree with them that private schools, including religious schools, can in fact encourage the engagement across diversity that sustaining or even rebuilding the social capital of our democracy requires. This leads me to a both/and conclusion: both strengthened support for the public school system and vouchers seem compatible with the promotion of the common good as I understand it. Is that a cop-out? Not if one thinks that the sharp division between the private and public spheres is one of the major pathologies that threatens our culture and our political life today. If one does not hold to such a sharp division of spheres, one cannot hold similarly sharp distinctions between the private good and the common good or between private and public schools. Abandoning such sharp distinctions might be the new wisdom on the school question today.[1]

SCHOOL CHOICE AND SOCIAL ECOLOGY

Seven

Educational Choice and Pillarization: Some Lessons for Americans from the Dutch Experiment in "Affirmative Impartiality"

RICHARD J. MOUW

OUR PRESENT DEBATES about educational choice in the United States are characterized by a variety of arguments for and against the encouragement of educational pluralism. Some of the considerations presented on both sides are superficial ones, as when a voucher plan is defended by broadsides against a public educational system that is bent on brainwashing children into secular or "occult" thoughts and practices, or when vouchers are opposed on the grounds that they will encourage "outdated" religious teachings. At their best, however, the discussions are healthy ones that assess the challenges of contemporary pluralism, with one side insisting that we ought to promote a plurality of educational philosophies and programs, and the other worrying about the fragmenting impact of such a plan.

My purpose here is to explore some of the underlying issues relating to educational choice. Let me make it clear at the outset that my own sympathies are on the side of those who call for equitable funding for a variety of educational programs. But I must also confess that while I think a good case can be made for such an approach on the level of principle, I have some serious qualms about the feasibility of implementing a program of equitable funding in our present North American context.

In what follows I will explain my misgivings. I will begin by briefly discussing the "school settlement" that was established by law in the Netherlands in 1917, and the way in which it has influenced some patterns of thinking—including my own—about educational choice. Some defenders of a voucher system for North America have rightly pointed to the Dutch program as one where government-sanctioned educational choice has met with much success. I am convinced, though, that it is important to pay attention to the cultural circumstances that gave rise to the Dutch settlement; I will do this, comparing those conditions to the context of our own present-day North American debates. Finally, I will assess the recommendation, made by several commentators on educational choice policies, that the Dutch system can provide an instructive reference point for a voucher program in the United States—and in doing so, I will spell out some of my qualms about the applicability of the Dutch experiment to our own North American context.

The Dutch "Peace Treaty"

The 1917 Dutch agreement—which provided equitable funding for a variety of religious and nonreligious school systems—was engineered by several Calvinist thinkers in the Netherlands, with Abraham Kuyper leading the way. Kuyper (1837–1920) was an important figure in Dutch life during the last half of the nineteenth century and the opening decades of the twentieth—he founded two newspapers as well as the Vrije Universiteit (Free University) of Amsterdam. Also a prominent church leader, he headed a group that broke away from the state church in the 1880s to form the country's second-largest Dutch Reformed denomination. And he founded the Anti-Revolutionary Party, which he led as a member of the Dutch parliament, and eventually—for a few years just after the turn of the century—as prime minister of the Netherlands.

Kuyper has long had an influence among Dutch Calvinists in North America, especially in the Christian school system and higher educational institutions (the best known being Calvin College in Grand Rapids, Michigan) associated with the Christian Reformed denomination. In recent years, however, interest in his thought has spread in North America, especially with regard to Kuyper's social-political thought. John Bolt's recently published study of Kuyper's thought makes a special point of exploring the relevance of his ideas to the North American context—Bolt even chose as his subtitle *Abraham Kuyper's American Public Theology*.[1] Nor has this interest been restricted to people who share Kuyper's Dutch Calvinist convictions. In his 1979 presidential address to the Canadian Political Science Association, Kenneth McCrae proposed that his colleagues think about reshaping the typical curriculum in political studies so that attention can now be given thinkers who have been pretty much ignored thus far in the mainstream of North American discussions. Have we arrived at an appropriate time, he asked, when we might consider giving preference to "Althusius over Bodin, Montesquieu over Rousseau, von Gierke over Hegel, Acton over Herbert Spencer, Abraham Kuyper over T. H. Green, Karl Renner and Otto Bauer over Marx and Engels?"[2]

The 1917 educational policy that Kuyper was instrumental in forging is commonly referred to as a "peace treaty," and rightly so, since it was accepted only after a century of much controversy in Dutch society over the government's responsibility toward schools that had been established by religious groups. The controversies can be traced back to 1807, when the Dutch government effected a significant shift in the country's educational arrangement by assuming control over the system of elementary education.[3] Prior to that, the school system had been officially administered by the national Reformed Church. While there was little immediate change in the substance of religious education as a result of the new regulations of 1807—the practices of daily worship and regular catechetical instruction were continued in the schools—gradually the religious content moved in a more "generic" direction. These developments were especially troublesome to the dissident Reformed groups that emerged in the 1830s. Unhappy with the influence of Enlightenment thinking in both the state churches and the schools, they distanced themselves from both entities. The combined opposition on the part of both the state and the national church made their efforts difficult, however. Stringent conditions were imposed for the establishment of alternative schools, and even when permission was granted, the high costs had to be borne by the parents.

When a new Dutch constitution came into effect in 1848, the rights of alternative school systems were guaranteed—although the procedures for doing so were still difficult and no financial support was offered to these schools. The public debate heated up considerably in 1857, when a new educational law stipulated that the public schools were to teach "Christian and civic virtues." As Bolt observes, however, it soon became clear that "the former was understood in terms of the latter," so that "'Christian' came to mean nothing more that what is socially and civically important, [and] the schools became effectively de-Christianized."[4] As Kuyper emerged as a public leader, he took up the cause of the alternative schools, arguing for equitable financial support for all schools, religious and nonreligious. The 1917 agreement granted this full government funding for all schools, with the exact subsidies based on student numbers.

The social arrangement that provided the context for the school agreement is known as *pillarization (verzuiling)*. The Dutch sociologist J. P. Kruijt provides this fairly concise explanation of the use of the pillarization metaphor:

> A pillar or column is a thing apart, resting on its own base (in our case a particular religious or non-religious faith) separated from other pillars, which are units similar to the first: they are standing upright, perpendicular

sets of persons and groups separated from other sets. Perpendicular means that each pillar is cutting vertically the horizontal socio-economic strata that we call social classes. For a pillar is not a social class; it contains persons out of every social class or stratification. . . . Further, a pillar is solid; the ideological pillars of the Dutch nation are indeed strong super-organizations . . . [and] all the pillars together generally serve as a support to something resting on top; in our case that something is the whole Dutch nation.[5]

Each Dutch pillar, then, is encouraged to support its own pattern of primary and secondary education. It is important to emphasize the fact, however, that education is viewed in the Dutch scheme as only one among many pillarized activities. It is a part of a larger set of pillarized activity—held together by a fairly comprehensive understanding of what life is all about—that also includes such things as labor unions, farming organizations, radio stations, and political parties.

The Kuyperian Rationale

Kuyper had his own unique version of Calvinist thought that provided a rationale for this overall pillarization scheme. To be sure, other pillar groups also provided their unique philosophical underpinnings for pillarization. But Kuyper's perspective not only served to convince the Calvinist rank and file of the merits of pillarization; it also provided a benchmark for other groups to articulate detailed alternative rationales.

One of Kuyper's most original themes was his idea of "sphere sovereignty." God, he insisted, built into the creation a variety of cultural spheres, such as the family, economics, politics, art, and intellectual inquiry. Each of these spheres has its own proper "business" and needs its own unique pattern of authority. When we confuse spheres by violating the proper boundaries of church and state or when we reduce the academic life to a business enterprise, we trangress the patterns that God has set for created existence.

Kuyper's perspective on social issues has much in common with the views put forth today by thinkers who are concerned with the proper shape of "the good society." A number of North American social critics (Peter Berger, Robert Bellah, Mary Ann Glendon) have emphasized in recent years the important role that "mediating structures" play in providing a buffer zone between the individual and the state. Families, churches, and service organizations protect us from the all-encompassing tendencies of the state, on the one hand, and an isolated individualism, on the other.

Like these contemporary thinkers, Kuyper was eager to curb the power of the state. The various cultural spheres, he insisted, do not exist by governmental permission. They are established by God, and no human authority has the right to violate the Creator's intentions. Nor are the created "spheres," as he saw things, completely disconnected. They are a part of a larger created reality whose unity we can fully grasp only by developing a comprehensive "biblical world-and-life view" (one of his favorite phrases). And Christians are obligated, he argued, not only to ask the state to allow them to work out the implications of their own comprehensive vision of life; they must also demand that the state grant the same rights to other worldview groups, even if Christians have serious disagreements with the content of those alternative perspectives on life.

A key virtue of the Dutch educational settlement from the Kuyperian perspective, then, is its recognition that any educational program is inevitably guided by a "world-and-life view." The so-called public school system is not really "neutral" with regard to the basic issues addressed by religious and philosophical creeds. Such neutrality was viewed by Kuyper and his followers as impossible. In the Dutch case the public schools were shaped by the ideals of the Enlightenment. In a pluralistic society, Kuyper argued, people who genuinely embrace these ideals should be permitted, even encouraged, to educate their children in conformity to this philosophy of life. But parents with other worldviews should also be granted the right to give educational shape to their convictions. And the government should maintain a position of impartiality toward these various worldview pillars.

American Kuyperianism

Again, this perspective on educational pluralism has had some currency in the United States and Canada. One of the most carefully formulated statements of this view was set forth by Nicholas Wolterstorff in a pamphlet he published in the mid-1960s, *Religion and the Schools*. Wolterstorff argues that the government's primary educational aim is to see to it that all citizens are educated. There is no reason, he claims, why this aim cannot be met by the encouragement of a plurality of school systems based on a variety of pedagogical and philosophical perspectives. Wolterstorff calls for a governmental posture that supports schools in a way that respects their religious or nonreligious perspectives. The fact that this means that the government will provide aid to specifically religious programs of education ought not to bother us, argues Wolterstorff; the main concern must be that the government

not have *as its purpose* the favoring of a particular religious or philosophical perspective. Governments cannot be neutral in these matters.
Neither can they avoid doing things that will in fact promote the cause
of one or another religious or nonreligious perspective. Wolterstorff
advocates a governmental posture of "affirmative impartiality," where
nothing that a state "says or does manifests a lack of impartiality on
its part" with respect to the "religion or irreligion" of various groups.
"For the state to be affirmatively impartial," explains Wolterstorff, "it
is not necessary that it not say or do anything contrary to the tenets of
any irreligion or irreligion." He observes that municipalities that require peddlers to be licensed in fact violate the convictions of Jehovah's
Witnesses who stand on street corners selling copies of the *Watchtower*.
This need not be construed as a violation of governmental impartiality:
"In our society there can be no such thing as a state all of whose policies and practices are in accord with the conscientious convictions of
all its citizens." But what *is* required, he insists, is that the government
"not have *as it purpose* to lend support to any religion or irreligion; and,
in addition, what is demanded is that whenever one of its legitimate
purposes can be achieved without violating the tenets of some religion
or irreligion, it be so achieved."[6]

While Wolterstorff made his case long before the voucher question
became a matter of broad public interest, the applicability of his Kuyperian perspective on educational freedom to this contemporary discussion is obvious. And more recently the application has been made explicit by a number of writers. Stanley Carlson-Thies, for example, states
the case for the applicability of the Dutch arrangement to our context
in very direct terms. In North America these days, he argues, we are
facing "the same issues" that led to the Dutch plan. And for our own
situation, "vouchers represent the American way to make public education plural by funding every variety of school, secular or religious."[7]

What is intriguing about the case that Carlson-Thies makes for his
recommendation, however, is that he actually also makes much of the
differences between our present North American context and that of
nineteenth-century Holland. For one thing, he observers that while the
nineteenth-century Dutch dissidents generally agreed that the government should subsidize their alternative educational projects, it is not
the case that

> all those who reject the public schools as unsuitable on religious grounds
> favor pluralizing public education through vouchers. Many are proponents
> instead of home schooling, sometimes for financial reasons but often be-
> cause they interpret the biblical injunction that raising children is the respon-
> sibility of parents to mean that parents should not send their children out to

school. Home schoolers do not agitate for pluralized public schools but rather to be left alone by the government. Similarly, a growing number of supporters of non-public schools reject vouchers on the grounds that "government shekels" always bring "government shackles." Their goal is the "separation of school and state." Yet others are home-school [*sic*] or use private schools only until they can win the public schools back for God.[8]

Carlson-Thies admits that this kind of plurality of motives within the forces that are critical of public education means that it is not

clear what the broader social consequences might be if vouchers were widely adopted. In the Netherlands, the *schoolstrijd* [school struggle] catalyzed the formation of subcultures, and the adoption of equal funding for all schools established the precedent for pluralizing other state services. In America, concern about the public rights of believers is only one of the causes of the school wars, and defenders of the right of religious people to carry out their belief into the public square are divided between pluralists and theocrats.[9]

These are important observations—ones that, as I see things, raise some significant questions about the case for vouchers that Carlson-Thies means to be making. In order to weigh these considerations in more detail, however, it will be helpful to look a little more closely at some of the conditions that have given rise to the present debate over school choice in North America.

Suspicion of Public Education

When Wolterstorff made his case for affirmative impartiality in the mid-1960s he was doing so as a supporter of a Christian school movement that was very much on the margins of North American life. The folks who were then advocating a uniquely "Christian" pattern of elementary and secondary education were in a rather small minority. The most visible were the Roman Catholics; other school systems were maintained by the Missouri-Synod Lutherans, the Christian Reformed, some Mennonites, and Episcopalians; some Jewish groups also sponsored their own religiously based schools. And in that setting "home schooling" was pretty much the sort of thing that the Amish and some countercultural commune types tried to get away with.

Most fundamentalist and evangelical Christians at that stage were strong supporters of the public school system. Indeed, in many ways their commitment to the public schools was stronger than their commitment to the culture at large. Fundamentalist and evangelical Christians had long lived with a deep ambivalence toward the dominant patterns of American culture. As heirs of the Puritans, they nurtured the hope that the United States would someday return to its "Christian nation" status. But at the same time they were quite aware of trends that made this return an unlikely prospect. This ambivalence also characterized their relationship to public education. But both of the pulls—optimism and pessimism—seemed to dictate a "hang in there" posture regarding public education. If there was hope for a "Christian America," the public school system would be an important instrument of moral reform. But if the negative trends continued, it was still important to offer support to the public school system: even if they were critical of some of the practices and teachings in those schools, many Christian parents were still convinced that their children could be a good "Christian testimony" within that system for values that the believing community held dear.

In the early 1970s, however, things began to change significantly, and disillusionment with public education began to take hold. New Christian schools began to sprout up, many of them under the sponsorship of local Pentecostal and "Bible church"–type congregations. Many observers simply attribute this growth to racial issues, as busing and other programs for integrating the public schools became controversial topics. And racism was undoubtedly a factor. But it was not the whole story, and to attempt to make it so is to ignore some important topics that have a bearing on the present-day debates over school choice.[10]

Many Christian parents in the 1970s experienced a new sense of cultural alienation as secularism—the "secular humanism" that had long been a worrisome presence to many people of faith—began to display a new stridency in the form of the the the "sexual revolution." As pornography, homosexual rights, abortion on demand, the Pill, rising divorce rates, sex education in the schools, and the like, became increasingly prominent on the cultural agenda, many concerned parents feared that their defenses against secularism had been seriously damaged. Previously they had taken it for granted that a strong family life could inoculate their children against whatever secularism might be at work in public education. Now they began to suspect that public education had itself become a chief propagator of values that were antithetical to many of their most cherished convictions.

"Worldviews" and the American Context

While conservative Protestants are not the only ones who have established alternative schools during the past decades, they are among the most vocal advocates of educational choice these days. It is not clear, however, that their pleas for government support for their school programs are typically based on a nuanced philosophy of pluralism. Nor is it clear that the Kuyperian perspective set forth by Wolterstorff and Carlson-Thies—which calls for a government posture of impartiality to all schools, whether they are Christian, Muslim, Scientologist, atheist—applies well to the kind of plurality of educational experiments that prevail in contemporary North America.

One obvious difference between our own situation and that of nineteenth-century Holland is the nature of the entities with reference to which the government is asked to be impartial. As already noted, the key term in the Dutch arrangement has been *pillarization*. The "pillars" in the Netherlands have been relatively stable, long-standing patterns of life and thought. Kuyper's favorite term to describe this sort of pattern was *worldview*.[11] He saw his brand of Calvinism as the most coherent of competing worldviews, but he also attributed a coherence to the other pillar worldviews, the most prominent ones in the Dutch scheme being Roman Catholicism, Lutheranism, socialism, and secularism.

Governmental impartiality in North America, on the other hand, would have to make decisions regarding a very different range of perspectives. And the truth is that very few of them deserve to be thought of as pillars—or even as very coherent worldviews. Indeed, if anything, we seem to be experiencing considerable worldview fragmentation in American culture. This phenomenon was nicely illustrated for me by a leader of an evangelical ministry on university campuses, who reported that his organization is struggling with difficult questions about how to present the claims of the Christian faith to present-day students. In the not-so-distant past, he observed, evangelicals would employ an apologetic approach that placed a strong emphasis on the coherence of a Christian view of reality. The biblical perspective was shown to tie things together, to answer more questions adequately than other worldviews. Such an approach challenged students to make a clear choice between Christianity and, say, a naturalistic or an Eastern religious perspective. But today's students, he observed, do not seem to put much stock in coherence and consistency. They think nothing of participating in an evangelical Bible study on Wednesday night and then engaging in a New Age meditation group on Thursday night, while spending their daily jogging time listening to a taped reading of *The Celestine Prophecy*, with a stop for an infusion of nutrition at the local Holistic Herbal Healing Center—without any sense that there is anything inappropriate about moving in and out of these very different perspectives on reality.

The fragmentation phenomenon was raised for me in a poignant manner a few years ago by a brief comment from a person who called into a radio talk show. I was a guest on this particular program, and I was paired with another theologian in a discussion about the continuing fascination in our culture with the person of Jesus of Nazareth, as evidenced in frequent cover stories in weekly newsmagazines, television specials, and the like. My fellow guest was a very liberal Protestant who expressed some strong skepticism about the reliability of the New Testament accounts of the resurrection of Jesus. I strongly disagreed with his assessment, and made it clear that I believe that what occurred on Easter morning was a literal bodily resurrection. When we opened the discussion to questions from our listening audience, one of our callers was a teenager who identified herself as Heather from Glendale. Heather expressed herself in typical "Valley Girl" tones: "I'm not what you would call, like, a Christian," she began. "Actually, right now I am sort of into—you know—like, witchcraft and stuff? But I want to say that I agree with the guy from Fuller Seminary. I'm just shocked that someone would, like, say that Jesus wasn't really raised from the dead!"

I was taken aback by Heather's way of offering support for my position. Her comment still strikes me as rather bizarre—combining a fascination with "witchcraft and stuff" with a belief in the literal resurrection of Jesus. And the more I have thought about what Heather said, the more I worry about her and what she represents in our contemporary culture. I am concerned about the way she seems to be piecing together a set of convictions to guide her life. While I did not have the opportunity to quiz her about the way in which she makes room in her psyche for an endorsement of both witchcraft and the Gospel's resurrection narratives, I doubt that Heather suscribes to both views of reality, Wicca and Christianity, in their robust versions. She is placing fragments of worldviews side by side without thinking about their relationships. And it is precisely the fact that these disconnected cognitive bits coexist in her consciousness that causes my concern.

And my worries are reinforced by the realization that there are intellectual leaders who actually celebrate this kind of disconnected selfhood. Take the case of Kenneth Gergen, a psychologist who has written a much-discussed study of contemporary selfhood in his 1991 book, *The Saturated Self: Dilemmas of Identity in Contemporary Life.* There Gergen argues that traditional conceptions of how to understand personhood—that we do or do not have souls or unconscious minds, that people have "intrinsic worth" or "inherent rationality"—have been exposed by "the postmodern turn" as inappropriate: "These are, after all, ways of talking, not reflections of the actual nature of persons. In contrast to the narrow range of options and the oppressive restraints favored by totalizing systems of understanding, postmodernism opens the way to the full expression of all discourses, to a free play of discourses." From this way of viewing things, we help people best, says Gergen, by inviting them into an "endless wandering in the maze of meaning," in which they regularly experience "the breaking down of oppositions." To be sure, Gergen wants individuals to find some way of blending, through both internal and external dialogues, various "richly elaborated discourses into new forms of serious games that can take us beyond text and into life."[12] But it is not clear exactly what standards are to guide this process in a world in which all comparative judgments are arbitrary, indeed "imperialistic." Why should my Dodger-fan self have any less status in my life than the self that senses a need to serve the poor? Why should I prefer any instinct or preference over any other one? In such a world, what is the difference between a healthy and an unhealthy self? What would keep each of us from proclaiming, like the young demoniac whom Jesus encountered, "My name is Legion; for we are many" (Mark 5:9)?

Something like this same pattern—although in a more subdued form—prevails in the larger religious culture. Several commentators have pointed to a widespread cafeteria approach to religious belief these days. Of course, this metaphor takes on added significance in the light of the ways in which literal cafeterias have changed in recent years. For example, providers of campus food services have transformed college cafeterias, which were once places where people sat and "dined" together, into spaces containing a variety of "grazing stations." A student will first go to a salad bar, then to a sandwich preparation area, then to a dessert stand, and finally grab a cone from the frozen yogurt machine on the way out. Quite likely she will not actually sit and "dine" with a specific group of people during this time; instead she will touch down at a variety of points to eat various portions of her meal. Nor is this a substantial shift from the habits that she learned at home, where the family meal—as a regularly scheduled communal experience—was at best a rare occurrence.

Religious grazing, then, where people sample bits and pieces of a plurality of religious offerings, putting together their own personal combinations, is a part of a larger grazing culture. In the realm of educational choice, for example, it is not at all uncommon to find parents who are members of an evangelically oriented Presbyterian church and who also attend Catholic charismatic prayer meetings on Wednesday evenings, while sending the occasional contribution to a Southern Baptist television evangelist—and who, having sent their children for three years to a Lutheran school, now have enrolled them in a Christian school sponsored by a local Pentecostal congregration. What "pillar" does this family's religious perspective represent?

And even where we *can* identify long-standing pillars in American life—for example, Judaism, Roman Catholicism, Lutheranism, Islam—we still must take into account the greatly increased mobility *between* these pillars, in contrast to the stability of the Netherlands of Kuyper's day. People change religions frequently in our culture, so that even the relatively stable worldview pillars that do exist on the American scene are not populated by correspondingly stable constituencies. Furthermore, the very fact of this mobility suggests that in our context, a plurality of schools encourages a competitive educational market environment. And this is likely only to increase when the competition focuses on vouchers available to parents whose own sense of religious identity is not well defined.

Anyone, then, who wants to apply the lessons of the Dutch educational settlement to the North American context, must seriously wrestle with this important question: Where are the pillars to be found in our culture?

New Social Conditions

But there is another key item in the Dutch equation that must also be looked at carefully from the perspective of North American culture. It was *families* in the Dutch context who were expected to make their educational choices in the light of their worldview commitments. More specifically, it was assumed that the decisions would be made by *parents*.

This motif is also featured prominently in many American formulations, where a strong emphasis is placed on "parental choice." But how are we to think about parental decisions amid the shifting patterns of parenting in contemporary life?

Kuyper and his contemporaries spoke much of the fundamental right and obligation of parents to determine the basic patterns of the education of their children. This same formulation characterizes the cases made by Wolterstorff and Carlson-Thies. Wolterstorff, for example, praises the Supreme Court ruling in the case of *Pierce v. the Society of Sisters*, where the court struck down a 1920s law requiring all children to attend public schools. "The child is not the mere creature of the State," the justices wrote; "those who nurture him and direct his destiny have the right, coupled with the high duty, to recognize and prepare him for additional obligations."[13]

The problem with this way of putting things, of course, is that the patterns of American family life have changed significantly in recent decades: many children now live in single-parent or blended families, and increasing numbers are even moving back and forth between two or more family units. The question of what "parental choice" means in situations where *competing* parental choices are a fact of life for many children is one that cannot be ignored.

Societal Health

In the case that he set forth in the 1960s, Wolterstorff made a point of insisting that affirmative impartiality must always be carried on within a framework where "the good order and health of society must be preserved."[14] This concern must certainly figure prominently in our present debates. Will a voucher plan or some other strategy for encouraging school choice promote a healthy pluralism, or will such arrangements further fragment our culture in unhealthy ways?

The question of the relationship between educational choice and societal health is also being raised in the Netherlands these days.[15] The Dutch pillars have been visibly crumbling in recent decades, and while the educational patterns that were established on the basis of pillarization thinking do still remain intact, many people, including many Christian supporters of Dutch religious schools, wonder these days whether the effects of educational impartiality continue to be primarily beneficial for either religious groups or the larger culture. And as Dutch life continues to become more religiously and ethnically diverse, the Dutch educational arrangement must now distribute benefits over an increasing number of worldview units. At what point, many critics are asking, does the expansion of pillarization (*verzuiling*) actually become a force for depillarization (*ontzuiling*)?

Obviously, many of the issues being raised in these Dutch discussions parallel those which dominate our own North American discussions of pluralism. But it is significant that in the Dutch case the arguments are informed by many decades of actual experience with a system that is only in the advocacy stage in North America.

One issue that is never far from the surface, whenever and wherever these issues are discussed, is the question of religion's role with regard to the promotion of civic virtues. Here is one report about the way in which the concern is presently being articulated in the Netherlands:

> Nowadays, it is broadly accepted that all young people need to learn to cope with and fully accept ideological diversity in today's open and multicultural

society. In the light of the pervasive secularization and plurality of modern Dutch culture questions are being raised as to the advisability of so many still being sent to schools professing only one particular conception of "the good," even if all the teachers in any given school are required by law to introduce all their students to different ideas and cultures. All citizens should respect and value—or learn to respect and value—multiformity, and no student ought to be confined to the self-imposed ghetto of a denominational school, say the advocates of a uniform public multicultural school system.[16]

This is an important concern, and no defender of educational freedom can ignore the fact that religion has indeed often promoted a "ghetto" mentality in which the civic virtues of tolerance and respect for diversity have been ignored, and even on occasion aggressively undermined. This is not the place to explore the complexities of the relationship of religious conviction to what Woltertorff describes as "the good order and health of society." But I do want at least to offer a brief personal testimony on the subject.

Part of my own elementary education took place in a small Dutch Calvinist school in Paterson, New Jersey. Most of the students in that school came by bus, and we all brought our lunches. During our noon hour, the boys would play baseball in a nearby field at a time when groups of students would be returning from their lunchtimes at home to the local public school. These encounters were often not very peaceable. On one particular day, some taunting words between my friends and a group of African American public schoolers turned into a rock-throwing fight. A stone thrown by one of the blacks grazed my head, and I was enraged. I yelled out the N word in his direction, and ran back to the school.

Unbeknownst to me, the young stone-thrower followed me and marched into the principal's office to report my verbal insult. Soon the principal and I were facing each other, alone in his office. Mr. Dykstra told me how disappointed he was with me. Through my tears, I protested: "But he threw a *stone* at me! He *hit* me with it!"

Mr. Dykstra's response was kind but firm. "Yes, he should not have done that. I'm sorry it happened to you. But, Richard, you have done something much worse. He tried to harm your body. You responded by trying to harm his soul. God is much more saddened by what you did to that young man than by what he did to you."

A common punishment in that school was to "write lines"—the punishee was made to write a sentence, such as "I will not chew gum in class," a prescribed number of times. My punishment for saying the N word set a school record. I had to copy the Ten Commandments over one hundred times, and then return the result to the principal after the sheets were signed by my parents.

Mr. Dykstra's way of handling this case had a lasting impression on me. I came to see the theological wisdom of what he made me do. What I had done was not only an insult to the young stone-thrower, it was an offense against the God who had created both of us. My angry retort was an act of bearing false witness against my neighbor. I had violated God's Law.

This experience, in an all-white, predominantly Dutch-ethnic Christian school shaped my convictions about race relations in the way that was unmatched by any other lesson on the subject I was later to learn in the broader environs of multiculturalism. There is no question in my mind that religion can be a positive force in promoting civic virtues. Indeed, I believe that it has a crucial role to play in that endeavor.

"Thick" and "Thin"

Again, this is a complex topic that I have only touched upon with this example. But the larger picture has been nicely sketched out by Professor Bryan Hehir, of Harvard Divinity School. Father Hehir, who has been a key adviser to the U. S. Roman Catholic bishops on matters of public policy, acknowledges that he has been deeply influenced by the natural law tradition, which has led him to work as an ethicist with the assumption "that when speaking to the state, the church must use a language the state can comprehend." While he still basically adheres to this position, he tells us, he has come to see the limits of such an approach: "In surveying the principally social policy debates of the 1990s," he writes, "I am also struck by the limits of the ethical, that is to say the failure of the purely moral argument to address the underlying dimensions of our public policy disputes and decisions." It is important for us to attend especially to "the premoral convictions that must be addressed to confront the societal questions we face today." And on these matters, he says, "the comparative advantage is with communities that are convinced of the kind of theological truths the Christian community takes for granted. These are embedded convictions—capable of being articulated, so not unintelligible for public discourse." What this means in practice, Hehir suggests, is that we are severely limited in our use of theological language "when we finally address the state on law and policy. . . . But prior to stating the policy issue we can and should expansively engage the wider civil community in the deeper questions that undergird policy choices, and that may take theological argument to the surface, because they are about our basic relationships as a society and a human community."[17]

Hehir's suggestion here that it can be helpful to introduce theological language into our public discussions is an important one. He is right, of course, also to insist that this sort of "thick" language becomes less appropriate at that point where we begin directly to "address the state on law and policy"—here a "thinner" language becomes necessary.[18] But proposing formulas for the official policies that will guide our collective lives is not the only proper mode of public discourse. There are also many opportunities in public life for us to testify to each other about how our policy proposals connect to our deepest convictions about the human condition. Nor ought we even to pretend that those connections do not matter much, since for many of us—perhaps for all of us—it is precisely *in* the awareness of the particularities of our deepest convictions that we know the proper limits of our public discourse. We should never promote a ban, then, on all thick expressions in our public conversations, for the public square ought to provide us with a forum where—at least on important occasions—we talk to each other about the sources of the hope that lies within us. There are, to be sure, also moments when thin discourse becomes the important mode of conversation—especially when we come to those points when we must hammer out those consensus formulations that will allow all of us, people of faiths as well as those with no faiths at all, to live out our deepest commitments together with integrity.

I am convinced that faith-based schools can serve as important workshops for training in this kind of citizenship in a pluralistic society. Ronald Thiemann put it well when he observed that various sorts of particularistic Christian communities can function as "schools of public virtue," where people of faith work at forming "the kind of character [that is] necessary for public life."[19] All we need to add, so as to link his claim to our present discussion, is the insistence that actual faith-based schools be numbered among these "schools of public virtue." My own lesson about racism serves as a case in point. It is in the very thickness of the kind of theological language that can be freely employed in religious school settings that we are encouraged to reflect on the deeply human questions that are so crucial to the thinner discussions that take place in the public square. To be sure, religion at its worst, and even when it is functioning in a mediocre fashion, does not contribute in a healthy manner to this larger discussion. But in assessing the overall merits of religiously oriented school systems, we ought not simply ignore what might happen when religion is in fact functioning at its best.

I hasten to add the acknowledgment that there are Christian thinkers who get nervous when someone even hints that religion might be good for the larger pluralistic culture. Debates within the theological community can get pretty heated these days about the dangers of sacrificing the thick texture of Christian discourse for the alleged benefits of a thin ethical contribution to the larger public arena. And these worries are legitimate when they stem from a concern that we not assess the merits of religion exclusively with reference to the utilitarian benefits it can bring to the larger society. People of faith will serve the larger culture best by nurturing convictions that sometimes go against the cultural grain. But that does not rule out the real possibility that religious training can also lay the groundwork for healthy citizenship.

The Virtues of Sacrifice

My own musings on the issues of educational choice, then, are shaped by the strong belief that religiously oriented schools can make an important positive contribution to the health of society. But while I do believe, given my Kuyperian convictions, that affirmative impartiality is a healthy posture for government to take toward educational pluralism, I am also convinced that the actual policies for implementing the concerns associated with that posture—including the financial support systems that might be appropriate—must be decided on the basis of prudential considerations. One such consideration is the need for educating people for the common good—a task that, as I have just been arguing, *can* be accomplished by faith-based schools, but is not likely to happen without stronger worldview pillars than presently populate the scene in our American context. Another crucial consideration is the need to attend in special ways to what will promote the well-being of the disadvantaged. This need is not adequately provided for in most of the schemes being proposed these days—a fact that leaves me with nagging doubts about the prudence of moving ahead with a program of government support that relies too heavily on the Dutch model.

Not that I am pessimistic about finding productive new strategies for implementing some sort of affirmative impariality program. I see much wisdom in the idea, for example, that instead of a voucher plan, we should legislate in favor of tax credits for parents who send their children to nonpublic schools. But we must work harder than we have thus far to see to it that such a move would in fact be good for, say, the urban poor. In a helpful discussion in the *New Republic*, Sarah Wildman has argued that tax credits are the one measure most likely to gain bipartisan support. But she also makes a point of emphasizing the fact that such a strategy would not guarantee the "one clear benefit" of a voucher plan: that of "enabling low-income kids to get out of failing public schools." As she rightly notes, "since the vast majority of people who get a tax credit are the ones rich enough to pay income taxes, it does virtually nothing for the very poor."[20]

But my own fear is that even a voucher system will not do much to make quality education more available to the poor. To achieve that goal, a stronger sense of justice must be at work in our culture. That is best achieved, at least for people with the kinds of religious convictions that I hold dear, when we take seriously our obligations to live sacrificially on behalf of, and for the sake of, those who are victims of injustice. And this in turn could be helped by encouraging a spirit of sacrifice in the hearts and lives of those who want to support alternatives to the dominant patterns of education in our contemporary context—including the sacrifice of promoting the cause of the poor and the marginalized while also learning to live with the fact that we ourselves are receiving less than we believe is appropriate from a government that is obliged to act with affirmative impartiality to all of its citizens.

There is good biblical support for such an approach. The ancient prophet spoke wisely to the faith community when suddenly they found themselves to be strangers in Babylon: "Seek the welfare of the city where I have sent you into exile, and pray the Lord on its behalf," he preached, "for in its welfare you will find your welfare" (Jer. 29:7).

Eight

Protecting and Limiting School Distinctiveness: How Much of Each?

CHARLES L. GLENN

ONE OF THE CHARGES commonly brought against policies that would provide public funding to support parental choice of schools is that they could lead to a proliferation of schools of poor quality or harmful influence upon children. The appropriate response, of course, is that government would have a continuing responsibility to ensure that no school failed its pupils in either respect. But this leads to a second charge: that government oversight would have a blighting effect upon the distinctiveness and integrity of nongovernment schools.

Can policy makers find the right balance between protecting the distinctiveness of schools and at the same time keeping that distinctiveness within appropriate limits? Fortunately, we do not have to deal in hypothetical scenarios; we have plenty of examples available of government regulation of schools that government does not directly operate.

A European colleague and I have studied how twenty-six national systems of schooling balance freedom of parents and distinctiveness of schools against common standards and protection for human rights. In twenty-three of these countries, government provides funding for all or most of the cost of nongovernment schools to ensure that the ability of parents to make decisions about the education of their children is not limited by lack of resources, but the countries differ considerably in the constraints placed upon schools.[1]

Virtually every nation in the world allows parents to send their children to a school other than those operated by public authorities; reportedly, there are more private schools in China, under its communist regime, than in the United States. In some cases, as in China and the United States, this option is largely limited to those who can afford to pay tuition to a private school, in addition to their taxes for the support of the public system. Private-school choice, under those conditions, is arguably both a form and a source of injustice.

Almost all Western democracies, by contrast, seek to eliminate or at least to moderate this form of injustice by providing public funding to enable parents to exercise school choice without limitations imposed by their own lack of resources. That is the case in our neighbor Canada, as well as in Australia and New Zealand; it is the case in every member of the European Union with the exceptions of Greece and Italy; and it is the case in Russia and most of the postcommunist societies of Eastern and Central Europe.

While the debate in the United States is over "vouchers," most countries don't consider them necessary and provide funding directly to private schools, paying teacher salaries or giving a general subsidy based upon the number of pupils enrolled, adjusted for the characteristics of the pupils. In Italy, where the national government operates all public schools and does not assist private schools, several regional governments have begun to provide vouchers directly to parents for part of their tuition costs.

Not only is publicly supported school choice the norm in almost all countries with well-established systems of public education, but it is also strongly supported by the various international covenants that define what respect for human rights requires. For example, the Universal Declaration of Human Rights (1948) states that "parents have a prior right to choose the kind of education that shall be given to their children" (art. 26, sec. 3). According to the *International Covenant on Economic, Social, and Cultural Rights* (1966),

> the States Parties to the present Covenant undertake to have respect for the liberty of parents . . . to choose for their children schools, other than those established by public authorities, which conform to such minimum educational standards as may be laid down or approved by the State and to ensure the religious and moral education of their children in conformity with their own convictions (art. 13, sec. 3).

Similar language appears in the 1966 International Covenant on Civil and Political Rights, in article 13, which is concerned with freedom of thought, conscience, and religion.

Concern for justice, then, and for freedom have led many to call for public support of the choices that parents make for the education of their children. The idea that a government official should decide which school is appropriate for each child has lost its credibility.

As more and more voices are raised in support of leaving that responsibility in the hands of parents, however, we are also hearing more warnings about possible negative consequences. Supporters of the government monopoly who have previously evinced little concern for the religious or pedagogical distinctiveness of independent schools suddenly begin to speak of that distinctiveness as a precious but fragile part of the educational scene. After all, they argue, there is no reason to encourage parental choices if, in order to protect the interests of children, there is little difference among the schools available. In short, it is claimed that if nonpublic schools are not regulated by government, they are likely to do much harm to children and to the society; if they *are* regulated, on the other hand, they will quickly lose their reason to exist.

Is there no way out of this double bind? Well, we might start by asking whether the predictions of disaster are well founded. As it happens, we do not need to speculate, but can turn to extensive and well-documented experience in this and other countries.

The experience of the twenty-six countries we have studied to date can be read to confirm or to refute the warnings or, to put it more exactly, to refute the first set of warnings, about the harmful effects of schools that are not operated by government, but to lend support to the warning that, in some cases, subsidized schools may sacrifice some of their distinctiveness.

It all depends, we might say, on how you do it. What can we learn from experience about the dangers and how to avert them? We will consider the question under the three headings:

1. dangers to tolerance and social harmony
2. dangers to the quality of education
3. dangers to the integrity of distinctive schools

Dangers to Tolerance and Social Harmony

What about the charge that vouchers or other forms of public support could lead to a flourishing of all sorts of unhealthy and socially undesirable attitudes, that some schools might teach religious or racial intolerance? The argument, stated succinctly, is that all of the children of the society need to be taught the same set of values and loyalties, or the result will be *deux jeunesses*, two hostile groups of youth becoming adults who will, in mutual suspicion, embed conflict at the heart of the society.

The warning has been endlessly repeated, in Europe and in the United States, over the last two centuries and more, and yet it has never yet been validated by historical experience. Although millions of youth have received their education in Catholic and other nonpublic schools, in this and other countries, the level of mutual suspicion and conflict has dropped steadily. Northern Ireland is the exception that proves the rule, since the Catholic and Protestant parties in that province have received very little support from their co-religionists in other countries, almost all of whom deplore both sides in the sectarian conflict.

It is true that some parents would choose schools that teach beliefs regarded with distaste or hostility by the general public. This does not, in a free society, imply that we should deny them the right to have these beliefs taught to their children. In its 1943 *Barnette* decision, the U.S. Supreme Court pointed out that government is not entitled to impose any sort of orthodoxy of belief upon schoolchildren, even if they adhere to what was at that time the highly unpopular beliefs of Jehovah's Witnesses.

Despite this fundamental principle, there are those who would—ironically, often in the name of freedom itself—deny the right of parents to choose to send their children to a school with a religious character. For example, a legal scholar has recently argued that religious schools are inherently harmful to children and that society has a duty to prevent that harm, even if that involves violating the free exercise clause of the First Amendment.[2]

Most of us would agree that there are messages from which we might reasonably want children to be shielded in school, or messages from outside the school to which we would want teachers to present an alternative. Does that require a government monopoly on schooling or (what is the same thing for many families) on schooling made affordable through public subsidy? No, the need to protect children has been addressed by other countries within the framework of publicly supported school choice.

In Sweden, for example, independent schools (whether publicly subsidized or not) may receive approval only if the instruction they provide is based upon such democratic values as openness, tolerance, and objectivity. This does not preclude the school from having a confessional character. To receive permission to operate, schools must agree to accept the goals of the 1994 national curriculum for compulsory-level schooling, which states:

> Democracy forms the basis of the national school system. The School Act stipulates that all school activity should be carried out in accordance with fundamental democratic values. . . . In accordance with the ethics borne by Christian tradition and Western humanism, this is achieved by fostering in the individual a sense of justice, generosity of spirit, tolerance and responsibility. . . . All who work in the school should uphold the fundamental values that are stated in the School Act and in this curriculum, and should very clearly disassociate themselves from anything that conflicts with these values.[3]

The Norwegian national curriculum document specifies that "the school shall be based on the fundamental values of democracy," and many pages are devoted to providing specifics, including an entire chapter on equality between the sexes. "An attempt shall be made," the Ministry insists, "through the content of the teaching, to arouse and strengthen the pupils' sense of ethical and religious values. The teaching shall help the pupils to acquire all-round insight into moral and religious issues, and challenge them to deepen their own opinions."[4]

The organization and work of schools in Iceland are to be "guided by tolerance, Christian values, and democratic co-operation." The Compulsory School Act includes, among the curriculum requirements, "Christian instruction, ethics and religion" (art. 30).

The Spanish Constitution of 1978 (art. 27) requires that nonpublic schools provide instruction on the basis of respect for the principles of human and civil rights. Consistent with this requirement, the education law requires that schools (whether subsidized or not) include among their goals

1. the full development of the personality of the students and
2. their shaping (*formación*) in respect for the fundamental rights and freedoms and in the exercise of tolerance and freedom within the democratic principles of common life.[5]

A more recent law requires that schools develop "moral values in all areas of personal, family, social and professional life." Elementary schools must seek to ensure that each pupil "appreciate the basic values which govern human life and co-existence and *prove that he/she is in agreement with them*."[6] Secondary schools are required, in addition to teaching about human rights, to ensure that students "are familiar with the basic beliefs, attitudes and values of our tradition and cultural heritage, assessing them critically and choosing those options which are most favorable to their overall development as people."[7]

France requires that subsidized independent schools—almost all of which are Catholic—provide instruction "with total respect for freedom of conscience." The government inspection of independent schools that are *not* subsidized extends to the education provided only "to ensure that it is not contrary to morality, to the Constitution, and to the laws." Inspectors may, for example, examine the textbooks used to check whether they are inculcating unlawful messages.[8]

In the Netherlands, where nonpublic schools (mostly Catholic and Protestant but also Muslim, Jewish, and Hindu, as well as Humanistic) serve 70 percent of the pupils, they are reputed to be more open than are the country's public schools to the growing cultural diversity of the population and are, in consequence, commonly chosen by Muslim parents. The government oversight of independent schools that began with the Constitution of 1848, guaranteeing freedom to establish schools, was intended to ensure that they would not promote "theories dangerous to the State." While independent schools are free to determine their teaching methods and to choose the textbooks that best support their distinctive character, it would be considered an offense against public order if they chose books that called for overthrowing the government or encouraged unlawful behavior.[9]

The teaching of values is in fact an important aspect of Dutch education. Religious instruction is supplemented by a required course, in elementary schools, on the "spiritual currents" in the world and in Dutch society.

In Ireland almost all schools are denominational—mostly Catholic, as one would expect—and organizationally private though funded in full by the government. The boards of subsidized schools are required by the Education Act of 1998 (sec. 15e), in their oversight of instruction and school life, to "have regard to the principles and requirements of a democratic society and have respect and promote respect for the diversity of values, beliefs, traditions and ways of life in society."

Subsidized schools are required to follow a national curriculum; sex education is the area where this is most likely to cause conflict. Irish law recognizes that all schools need not provide such instruction in the same manner or from the same perspective. Among the "functions of a school," as defined by the Education Act (sec. 9d), is to "promote the moral, spiritual, social and personal development of students and provide health education to them, in consultation with their parents, having regard to the characteristic spirit of the school."

Finally, the Canadian provinces approach the funding and regulation of independent and faith-based schools in a bewildering variety of ways. To take a single example, independent schools in Alberta, in order to be eligible for public funding, may not "offer programs that in theory or in practice will promote or foster doctrines of racial or ethnic superiority or persecution, religious intolerance or persecution, social change through violent action, or disobedience of laws."

As these examples show, it is quite possible to attach conditions to the receipt of public funding in order to ensure that schools do not teach hate-filled messages. Those who warn that all sorts of bizarre schools could spring up in the United States to teach anti-Semitism or racism or witchcraft should be asked why, if such schools are in demand, we do not find them represented among the 27,223 private schools now operating in the United States, mostly with minimal government oversight? Why assume that the availability of public funding would suddenly stimulate a demand where none—or very little—exists at present?

Or we might ask the critics of school choice another question: If you are so concerned about the messages that nongovernment schools might teach to children, why has this concern been expressed only in the context of proposals for public subsidies? Surely the children are more important than the money, and yet it is only the prospect that private schools might be able to compete on equal terms financially with public schools that has elicited these warnings about dangerous teaching.

In fact, of course, there is no evidence that parents want or that non-public schools provide teaching that is out of line with the core American value of respect for others, whatever their beliefs or their ancestors. It is true that some evangelical and fundamentalist schools tell children that only those who put their faith in Jesus Christ will be saved from eternal punishment for their sin and rebellion against God; this is central to the beliefs that they profess. But where is the evidence that this leads to intolerance or social discord? Sociologist Alan Peshkin (himself a Jew) studied such a school, and found no evidence that the students had been turned into bigots by what they had been taught. When surveyed, "93 percent of the Bethany students compared with 80 percent of the public high school students responded that they would approve of a black family moving next door; . . . 93 percent of the Bethany and 95 percent of the public school students agreed that 'people who don't believe in God should have the same right to freedom of speech as anyone else' . . . 83 and 84 percent respectively disagreed with the statement that 'only people who believe in God can be good Americans.' Peshkin found also that the students at the fundamentalist school were "significantly less alienated" than those at the local public high school, and that "Bethany neither desires nor has automatons for students."[10]

Dangers to the Quality of Education

Does the encouragement of alternatives to the public system of schooling mean that the quality of education will decline, as it becomes more difficult to impose common standards and to require accountability for results? To this question, as to the other, we can bring considerable international evidence to bear.

In most countries, subsidized nonpublic schools are held to the same academic standards as are public schools, and these standards are enforced in most cases by school inspections and high-stakes national examinations.[11] A typical provision is that of the South African Constitution, which states nonpublic schools must "maintain standards that are not inferior to standards at comparable public educational institutions." In order to receive a public subsidy, they must agree to inspections without advance notice. Under the 1996 South African Schools Act (sec. 48), a secondary school may be considered for subsidy if

- its grade twelve pass rate is 50 percent or more of full-time candidates writing the examination in the prior year;
- the repetition rate in grades eleven or twelve is not more than 20 percent; and
- it does not engage in practices that are calculated to artificially increase the grade twelve pass rate (such as, presumably, encouraging weaker pupils to drop out).

In Australia, subsidized schools (almost 30 percent of total enrollment) receive a six-year approval whose renewal is contingent upon satisfactory inspection to determine whether staff are qualified and results satisfactory. With the nongovernment school-funding changes that are taking place in the next funding quadrennium, however (2001–4), there will be greater Commonwealth accountability arrangements established. These have yet to be specified, but the intent will be a greater focus on learning outcomes as a condition of Commonwealth funding.[12]

Nonpublic schools in Belgium—two-thirds of the total—must submit to government inspection that focuses upon the subjects taught, the level of instruction, and compliance with the country's strict language laws. This inspection does not, however, include the pedagogical methods used, which are entirely within the discretion of the school.

The Russian education law adopted in 1992 promises public funding for accredited nonpublic schools, but establishes such an elaborate process to gain accreditation that it has been compared to a combat course in military training. First a school must be registered with an acceptable charter, then licensed after review by a commission, then "attested" on the basis of evidence that at least half of its students have passed their final examinations for three years in a row, and only then, after a further evaluation of the level of instruction and conformity with programmatic requirements, is the school accredited and eligible for subsidy.[13]

Subsidized nonpublic schools in Sweden are held accountable to the national curriculum frameworks by the fact that their pupils take national examinations at the end of elementary and lower-secondary school in Swedish, mathematics, English, and civics. Beyond the external standard provided by national examinations, considerable discretion is left to local municipal authorities to build flexibility into the contracts that (since 1997) they establish with the nonpublic schools which they subsidize. There is no national school-inspection system. Grading is generally noncompetitive, and scores on standardized tests are not used to rank schools.

> Grades are awarded from the eighth year of compulsory basic school onwards and relate the pupil's achievements to the national objectives stated in the syllabus for the subject. throughout compulsory school. Pupils and their parents are to be given regular progress reports, including meetings to discuss development. At the end of year 9 national tests are held in the three subjects, Swedish, English and Mathematics, in order to assess pupils' level of achievement. The tests provide support for teachers in awarding grades. There are tests in the same subjects at the end of year 5, but it is not compulsory for the municipality to use them.[14]

Subsidized nonpublic schools must develop work plans showing how they will ensure that the national requirements are met. This makes it possible for the school to design its own education strategy to meet the common goals, while adding other goals that reflect its distinctive mission.

Danish nonpublic schools, while enjoying extensive freedom to shape their curriculum and teaching methods, are similarly accountable to their pupils and parents for good results on the national tests in Danish, mathematics, English, and elective subjects that pupils take at the end of lower-secondary school. The Education Act of 1995 (sec. 13.7) gives pupils themselves control over whether and how they will be assessed.:

> The school shall issue a leaving certificate for pupils leaving school at the end of the 7th form, or later. The leaving certificate shall contain information on the educational activities in which the pupil has participated as well as the most recent proficiency marks given. The leaving certificate shall furthermore include information on the assessment at examinations, if any. . . . A written statement and/or a mark for the obligatory project assignment may be indicated in the leaving certificate, if the pupil so wishes. An assessment of the free assignment, if any, may also be indicated in the leaving certificate, if the pupil so wishes. Any written assessment in other subjects than the examination subjects may be indicated in or enclosed with the leaving certificate as part hereof, if the pupil so wishes.

Section 14 of the Danish law specifies that

> (1) In each of the subjects of Danish, mathematics, English, German and physics/chemistry, the pupils can present themselves for the leaving examination of the Folkeskole on completion of the 9th form. On completion of

the 10th form, the pupils can in each of the subjects mentioned present themselves for either the advanced leaving examination of the Folkeskole or the leaving examination of the Folkeskole.

(6) It shall be up to the pupils themselves to decide whether they want to present themselves for examinations—upon consultation of the parents . . . and the school.

Finland has simplified the process of reviewing the adequacy of nonpublic schools by allowing them to deviate from the national curriculum frameworks if they are implementing an "internationally recognized" pedagogical system and if their efforts are judged to be useful to Finnish society.

The German Constitution (art. 7.4) provides that private schools must be approved if they "are not inferior to the public schools in their educational aims, their facilities and the professional training of their teaching staff."

In France, the system of public inspection extends to independent schools, but is concerned primarily to ensure that the national curriculum is followed, not that instruction produces satisfactory results. A comparative study of public and independent schools, however, found that the latter had a significantly lower rate of retention in grade and that, in consequence, their pupils were somewhat younger at a given grade. Comparing pupils who had received their entire education to date in public or in independent schools, the study found that it was in particular those at risk of failure and those from families of lower status who benefited most from independent schooling, a result consistent with the findings of Coleman and Hoffer and other researchers in the United States. There was almost no gap between the baccalaureate results of the children of workers (86.6 percent passed) and of senior executives (87.9 percent) who had attended exclusively independent schools, in contrast with a significant gap (78.7 percent versus 91.1) for those who had attended exclusively public schools. "It is incontestable that within independent education the difference in success based upon social origin has generally been reduced."[15]

The Dutch Constitution gives legislators the competence to impose quality standards in education. In 1993, Parliament established a series of national outcome standards, so-called core goals (*kerndoelen*), for which schools are to be held accountable. There is a considerable tension between these requirements and the freedom to organize teaching as the school's sponsors wish. For example, it would not be appropriate for government to include attitudinal or desired opinions among the required goals of schooling, even for public schools, which are required to respect each pupil's religious or other convictions about life. Prescribing particular books or materials could lead in the same direction.[16]

The Elementary Education Law (art. 8), lays out the basic principles and objectives upon which elementary education must be based. While there are no national examinations at the conclusion of elementary school, each school must specify, in its "school work plan," how it will address the core goals in fifteen curriculum areas and how the progress of pupils will be assessed and reported.[17] The school's plan—parallel in content to a "charter" in the United States—also spells out what instructional materials will be used, the teaching methods used, the means of integrating pupils with special needs, the use of additional resources provided for target groups like immigrant children, and the method of parent involvement. Every two years each school must make a report on how it has been meeting its goals—both those imposed by the government and those which are distinctive.

The school inspectors give particular attention to whether these provisions meet the requirements of the law. They can give advice about possible improvements, but have no authority to order changes.[18] Inspectors also visit schools periodically, observe instruction, and make recommendations, but they no longer have the authority to require changes.

Publicly funded independent schools in Spain must comply with government requirements as to materials and programs, minimum and maximum class sizes, the teaching methods employed, the levels to reach for graduates, and the means of evaluation of graduates. There has been considerable controversy over whether these requirements trespass upon the right of those operating such schools "to define their distinctive character and to ensure effectively that this is carried out as necessary in the educational process."[19]

The issue of the autonomy of independent schools was brought before the Constitutional Court, which ruled that the government could set standards but should do so with careful respect to the constitutional guarantee of educational freedom. While the schools were required to "conform to the minimums set by the public authorities with respect to the content of the various subjects, the number of hours of instruction, etc.," they were free to do so in a way that gave expression to the educational concepts on the basis of which the school had been established.[20]

Inspection of both public and independent schools in Spain is a responsibility of public-education authorities, and includes ensuring compliance with the laws, assessing the quality of the education provided, and working toward the improvement of teaching practice.[21]

In short, other countries have found a variety of ways to ensure that subsidized nonpublic schools meet quality standards equivalent to those of the public system. There is also reason to believe that in countries where full subsidization of nonpublic schools ensures that there are no income barriers to choosing them, the academic results of the nonpublic sector of schooling is higher than that in the public sector.

Dangers to the Integrity of Distinctive Schools

Are many supporters of faith-based and other independent schools in the United States justified in fearing that public subsidies in other countries have been gained at too high a price? Do these schools lose the freedom to have a distinctive pedagogical approach, or to express unapologetic religious convictions, or to admit pupils and employ teachers on the basis of their own criteria?

It is impossible to give a simple yes or no answer. In some countries the burden of government requirements and regulations can be heavy, and there are schools that refuse to seek public funding for that reason. On the other hand, lack of subsidy does not guarantee lack of government interference. In Greece, for example, despite the absence of public subsidies, nonpublic schools are required to conform closely to the curriculum of the public system. The situation in Italy is evolving rapidly, but it has generally been true that nonpublic schools are unsubsidized but closely regulated.

We need to distinguish among the ways in which independent nonpublic schools may find their autonomy limited, whether or not they receive public subsidies. These can be ranked from most to least acceptable to most supporters of the independent sector in education.

Accountability for Results

In most countries, independent schools are required to produce results generally equivalent to those of the public system. In some cases, as we have seen, this requirement of comparability is not exercised directly but created by the fact that they are preparing secondary students to take the same national examinations that students in public schools take. This form of accountability is of course present in the United States, as well, for that portion of the student population hoping to go on to college.

Generally, the requirement to produce comparable outcomes by some objective measure is accepted by independent schools, though there may be objections to the form or scope of the assessment.

Curriculum Requirements

More intrusive is the requirement to follow a national curriculum specifying what subjects will be covered and even how much time over the course of a year or of several years should be devoted to each. This often does not cause a problem for Catholic and other schools whose distinctiveness is religious, but may be difficult for schools that follow a distinctive pedagogical approach: Steiner, Montessori, or "alternative" schools. Countries that have such a requirement may also accept alternative curricula proposed by schools if they are judged to be of sufficient quality.

The Hungarian education law that came into effect in 1998 takes a particularly interesting approach to reconciling standards with school-level autonomy and diversity. The national curriculum sets a general framework for ten educational domains, but leaves it up to individual schools to fill this in with specific courses and teaching methods. Schools submit their curricula, once approved by education authorities, to a National Core Curriculum Bank, from which other schools, if unable or unwilling to develop their own approaches to the national framework, may draw and adopt them. Curricula in the "national bank" are considered preapproved and do not require review when adopted.

In Poland, similarly, all schools may choose between adopting a curriculum already approved by the Ministry of Education, and developing their own for government approval. Schools must also work closely with parents to develop a program for moral education.

Portugal is another country that recognizes, in its education law making, that the impulse to innovation and originality is not distributed evenly among schools. Some schools are allowed significant pedagogical independence, while others must follow the national curriculum more closely.

In an unusual provision for school autonomy, independent schools in Denmark can participate in selecting the person who will supervise their compliance with requirements for public subsidy

All that is demanded of private education is that it measures up to that of the municipal schools. The Ministry of Education confers on private schools the right to use the municipal schools' final examination and thereby exercises a form of indirect quality control. However, in principle it is not up to any government authority but to the parents of each private school to check that its performance measures up to the demands of the municipal schools. It is the parents themselves who must choose a supervisor to check the pupils' level of achievement in Danish, arithmetic, mathematics and English.

If a pupil's knowledge is found inadequate, the supervisor must report it
to the municipal council who may then assign the child to another school.
Individual parents who are dissatisfied with a private school may move
their child to another private school or to a municipal school. In extraordi-
nary circumstances, the Ministry of Education may establish special supervision, for example if there is reason to believe that the school teaches Danish
so poorly that the children's ability to cope with life in Denmark may be
impaired.[22]

The German requirement that the education provided in subsidized
nonpublic schools be equivalent in quality to that in public schools
does not require that their educational aims be identical with those of
the public system. Once equivalence has been established, nonpublic
schools enjoy considerable freedom to organize instruction as they
wish, though the need to prepare secondary students for the Abitur
examination before university creates inevitable constraints. The constitutionally protected right to "the free development of personality"
requires, Jach argues, that the State abstain from defining a single
model of maturity which all schools should strive to develop in their
pupils. In particular, it should recognize that the goal of individualiza-
tion does not necessarily point toward the liberal model of the free-
standing individual, but may rather require meaningful participation
in a community. Simply to proclaim "toleration" as the fundamental
principle of public schools does not satisfy the developmental need of
children to form secure identities in relationship to such communities.
The state is thus obligated to make it possible for young citizens to
have a variety of types of schooling, based upon different concepts of
the meaning of "development of personality," and to support independent schools to the extent that public schooling does not include the
necessary diversity.[23]

Since there is no system of national testing at the elementary level,
Dutch schools are free to promote pupils each year without pressure
about their grades. They are not required to teach particular material
at particular grade levels, but simply to ensure that pupils have mas-
tered the goals by the end of elementary schooling.

If a school's board believes that one or more of the attainment targets, as formulated by the government, conflicts with its distinctive
character, it may propose alternative goals for the same aspect of the
curriculum. If these are approved by the responsible school inspector
as of the same standard as the official attainment targets, they may be
implemented; if not, a decision is made by the nationwide Education
Council, whose role is to advise about conflicts between government
actions and constitutional protections.[24]

In most countries, the requirement of a national curriculum, like that of satisfactory academic outcomes, is not generally experienced as a problem by leaders in nonpublic education. While these requirements may create some additional burdens, they are rendered acceptable by the fact that parents would be satisfied with no less than comparable academic outcomes, and that provisions usually exist for alternative ways of organizing the curriculum.

The issues which seem most often to cause difficulties are those having to do with the admission of students and the employment of teachers, with the latter considered crucial.

Student Admissions

Most countries allow nonpublic schools, even those receiving public subsidies, to exercise some discretion in admitting pupils, though generally forbidding racial discrimination. In some cases, faith-based schools are allowed to use religious criteria in admissions, though usually with some limitations.

A problem caused by the near monopoly of subsidized Catholic schooling in Ireland is to protect the right of non-Catholic parents to send their children to the school of their choice. School leaders may legitimately be concerned about maintaining the distinctive character of their school if too many pupils are admitted who do not share the beliefs upon which it is based. The Education Act of 1998 gives explicit recognition to the need to protect the ethos of subsidized schools. The term used is "characteristic spirit," which is "determined by the cultural, educational, moral, religious, social, linguistic and spiritual values and traditions which inform and are characteristic of the objectives and conduct of the school." As a result, while they may not refuse to admit any applicants whose families are not practicing Catholics, they are allowed to draw the line if a heavy influx of non-Catholic pupils threatens to change the character of the school.[25]

Subsidized independent schools in Spain must admit pupils on the same basis as public schools, without applying religious criteria: "in no case may there be discrimination in admission on the basis of ideology, religion, moral, social, or racial reasons, or birth." In cases of oversubscription of a school, criteria are spelled out to determine which applicants should be given priority, based upon such considerations as place of residence, siblings already in the school, and financial need.[26] Efforts to establish residential attendance zones for subsidized independent schools have been struck down by the courts as inconsistent with the constitutionally guaranteed freedom of school choice for parents.[27]

When French parents enroll their child in a subsidized independent school, they sign a contract that requires them to respect the way the school operates and "implies a voluntary adherence to that which distinguishes the school from comparable public schools."[28]

Some subsidized nonpublic schools in Australia give enrollment preference to a student whose family is a member of the relevant church or religious body, particularly if the school has limited vacancies.[29]

In New Zealand, during the first two years of the universal choice model (1990 and 1991), oversubscribed schools were required to employ random selection to admit students, but this was changed the following year to allow them to adopt "enrollment schemes" specifying how applicants would be selected. These could not discriminate in violation of human rights standards but otherwise were at the discretion of the school's trustees. No approval was required from the government until 1998, when difficulties arising from this unregulated exercise of discretion on the part of schools led Parliament to modify the requirements for enrollment schemes. The method and criteria for admission to an oversubscribed school must now be worked out in consultation with the other schools affected, and must be approved by the secretary of education; parents have a right to enroll a child in a nearby school.[30] Publicly subsidized schools with a religious character must admit some applicants who are not of the same denomination, but not so many as to threaten their distinctive character.

The board responsible for each subsidized independent school or group of schools in the Netherlands has the authority to admit or deny admittance. This right was upheld in the case of a Jewish school that, on religious grounds, refused admission to a pupil.[31] It seems likely, however, that such decisions must rest upon clearly stated criteria adopted by the board, and cannot be exercised in an arbitrary way. Racial discrimination is forbidden.

As this brief sampling demonstrates, different countries have adopted different policies about whether subsidized schools may select among applicants on any other than a random basis. Spain, whose Constitution, adopted after the death of Franco, is especially explicit on human rights protections, seems to leave little room for selection, though the legal protection of the school's *ideario*, or set of ideas and beliefs, may ensure that parents do not seek a school at a strong variance with their own convictions. Other countries, though no less committed to equity, have built into their laws and policies protections for schools that seek to reinforce their distinctive character by selecting among applicants.

A distinction exists, in law or in policy or in practice, in most of the countries considered, between admissions decisions made on the basis of the family's acceptance of the religious or pedagogical character of the school, and decisions made on the basis of race—universally forbidden—or academic ability. Generally speaking, subsidized schools are allowed to be selective to preserve their educational character, but not to become educationally elite—unless that is an explicit and approved dimension of their mission.

Employment Decisions

Control over the hiring—and firing—of teachers is the issue that cannot be compromised for nonpublic school leaders in most countries.

The Dutch Constitution makes explicit provision to "respect in particular the freedom of private schools to . . . appoint teachers as they see fit" (art. 23.6). The goal of a particular school, if it is clearly stated in the school's mission statement, creates requirements for the teacher that are specific to a particular position. Postma points out that a teacher in a Montessori school does not have the right to teach by another method, nor can a teacher in a school with a religious character fail to take that into account. The model contract recommended by the coordinating organization for Protestant schools states that the teacher is expected to carry out his or her functions in a way consistent with the goals of Protestant schools; the applicant is given a copy of these to consider before signing the contract. Similarly, the model contract for Catholic schools states that the teacher will, in carrying out his or her responsibilities, work loyally for the fulfillment of the goals of the school, including those reflecting a distinctive worldview.[32]

There are definite limits, however, upon the freedom of a school board to require that a teacher uphold the mission of the school. For example, a teacher at a conservative Protestant school who had a baby out of wedlock could not be fired for that reason.[33]

The Irish Supreme Court concluded, in a 1997 case, that, despite the general prohibition against treating citizens differently on the basis of their religious beliefs, occasions may arise when it is necessary to do so "in order to give life and reality to the constitutional guarantee of the free profession and practice of religion."[34]

The Employment Equality Act of 1998 accords a special status to Irish schools (and religious and medical institutions) that are "under the direction or control of a body established for religious purposes or whose objectives include the provision of services in an environment which promotes certain religious values." Such a school is not discriminating illegally when "(a) it gives more favourable treatment, on the religion ground, to an employee or a prospective employee . . . where it is reasonable to do so in order to maintain the religious ethos of the institution, or (*b*) it takes action which is reasonably necessary to prevent an employee or a prospective employee from undermining the religious ethos of the institution" (sec. 37). Similarly, the school-management guidelines state that "a teacher shall not advertently and consistently seek to undermine the religious belief or practice of any pupil in the school."[35]

Teacher behavior outside of school can be grounds for dismissal if "might damage the school's efforts to promote certain norms of behaviour and religious principles which it was established to foster."[36]

French law provides two sorts of arrangements under which independent schools are subsidized. In the more common (the only one permitted for secondary schools), teachers in subsidized schools are employed directly by the government and not by the school. Until 1985, a prospective teacher was nominated by the school's director and approved by the state, but since 1985 the nomination is by the state and the director can accept or refuse it. Often, of course, there is prior consultation before a nomination is made. Since the director has responsibility for protecting the distinctive character of the school, he or she can take religion into account in deciding whom to accept for a teaching position in the school.[37]

Obviously, this arrangement creates a strong potential for difficulty in maintaining the mission of the school, though the courts have generally been willing to support the authority of the sponsoring organization (the diocese, in the case of Catholic schools) to enforce compliance with the school's character. In an important decision in 1977, the Constitutional Court concluded that educational freedom (and thus the right to protect the distinctiveness of a school) was rooted in the freedom of association, which it had asserted in a 1971 decision. Educational freedom (which was also an individual right) could be realized only under conditions of structural pluralism rather than pluralism internal to the school. Real pluralism rested upon differences, and differences could not be maintained without the right to take them into account in appointing staff. Teachers in an independent school could be required to respect its distinctive character.[38]

Teachers who work in subsidized independent schools are thus obligated to take the distinctive character of the school into account when teaching and otherwise comporting themselves. In its 1977 decision, the Constitutional Court made a distinction between an inappropriate requirement that a teacher pretend to beliefs which he or she did not hold, and an appropriate requirement that a teacher refrain from statements that might compromise the distinctive character of the school.[39]

Failure to comply with this requirement may make a teacher subject to disciplinary action such as suspension or dismissal, but in fact there have been almost no cases involving conflict over classroom behavior.[40] The controversial cases have arisen from discipline following actions of the teacher outside the school that are inconsistent with the character of the school. There have been several cases involving divorced teachers in Catholic schools who were dismissed for remarrying without permission of church authorities. While decisions have gone both ways, it appears that school authorities are legally justified when they take such actions.[41] The close connection, for confessional schools, between instruction and education in the broader sense makes it appropriate for these schools to be concerned about the message that children receive from the way of life and the moral choices of their teachers.

The laws providing public subsidies to independent nonpublic schools, supporters claim, have promoted the freedom of teachers as well as of families and schools. Teachers can now choose whether to work in a public or independent school without consequences for their salaries, benefits, or professional advancement.

The Belgian Constitutional Court, in a 1992 decision, pointed out that "the freedom of education encompasses the freedom of the organizing power to choose the staff employed, with a view to achieving their own educational objectives."

Teachers in public schools in Spain have a recognized "teaching freedom" (*libertad de cátedra*), though this does not extend to the right to promote any particular ideology through their instruction; they are obligated to maintain a neutral posture. Those in independent schools have an additional obligation, to show respect for the distinctive character or worldview (*ideario*) of the school which employs them. The distinctive character defined by the sponsors of the school is legally significant, since it may form the basis for selecting particular teachers and for insisting that teachers not undermine the mission of the school; for example, a teacher mocking Catholic doctrine would be dismissible from a Catholic school, though he or she could not be dismissed for refusing to endorse such doctrine contrary to conscience. (But note that a school's distinctive character must be consistent with Spain's constitutional principles of "liberty, equality, justice, pluralism.")

There are those who argue that the growing pluralism of beliefs and values in Spanish society should find its counterpart within each school, and that only a morally neutral school can teach the lessons essential to democracy—indeed, that only in such a school is there real educational freedom. This, others counter, is to use the idea of educational freedom to undermine its reality, as expressed in a diversity of educational offerings. It is absurd, they point out, to contend that in contemporary society the control of a religious organization over youth can be anything as extensive as that of the state, or that a church could be as much of a threat to freedom as a government with monopoly of the power to tax and to punish.[42]

The right of the sponsors of independent schools to require such respect, and to fire teachers who fail to comply with this obligation, has been upheld by the Spanish Constitutional Court several times. In 1981, the court pointed out, in upholding an education law against an attack by the Socialists, that conflict was possible between the distinctive character of a school and the teaching freedom of a teacher, but concluded that

> the existence of a worldview [*ideario*], accepted by the teacher upon freely joining the school . . . does not oblige him, obviously, to become an apologist for that [worldview] or to transform his teaching into indoctrination or propaganda . . . [but] the teacher's freedom does not entitle him to direct open or surreptitious attacks against that worldview. . . . The concrete effect [*virtualidad*] of the worldview will no doubt be greater when it comes to the explicitly educative or formative aspects of the instruction, and less when it has to do with the simple transmission of knowledge.

In another decision, in 1985, the court reiterated that "the existence of the school's distinctive character obligates the teacher to an attitude of respect which forbids attacking that character."[43] This second decision grew out of a case brought by a teacher who had been fired by a private schools because, according to the school authorities, he had not conformed his professional activities to the worldview of the school. The teacher complained that he had been discriminated against on ideological grounds, but he lost in the lower courts. The Constitutional Court ordered the teacher reinstated on the grounds that his failure to conform to fundamental aspects of the worldview had not been demonstrated clearly in his external behavior (*exteriorizado*), but upheld the principle that, with appropriate documentation, this would be an appropriate cause for disciplinary action.[44]

Martínez López-Muñiz points out that "an educational program which is definite and stable will permit a larger degree of identification [on the part of the teacher] than will a program in which there can be no single established and permanent orientation, as is the case in public schools, which 'must be open to all tendencies of thought and all standards of conduct which are allowed by law.'"[45]

The freedom of nonpublic schools to express a distinctive ethos and character is thus the guarantor of the freedom of those teachers who wish to teach in a way consistent with that ethos and character; public school teachers are not free to do so. As a result, "the internal pluralism of public schools is not a model which guarantees in itself the right to education in its full sense, nor the freedom of those who teach; in this way they are denied the possibility of adhering voluntarily to a specific educational project." It is therefore possible to speak of "the *collective* freedom of teaching or, what is the same thing, the right to direct the school which belongs to the sponsor of the school" and which supports the freedom of teachers *to the extent that they work in a school which corresponds to their own convictions about education.*[46]

In each of the countries considered, the right of subsidized schools to require that the teachers they employ respect the religious or pedagogical character of the school is well established. In France and Spain, this right does not extend to requiring that teachers be enthusiastic supporters of that character; it might well be questioned whether a passive acquiescence on the part of staff is enough to sustain the mission of a school.

In other countries, subsidized schools can expect considerably more. It appears that in many cases, whether from "loss of nerve" or from a lack of clarity about the distinctive education that they claim to offer, school leaders do not make full use of the authority that they in fact possess to ensure that their staff fully support that distinctiveness.[47]

What Does School Integrity Consist Of?

It turns out, in practice, to be difficult for many educators to explain how their schools and the education provided are distinctive. Much "slippage" occurs because the mission of a school has not been thought through clearly or translated into the specific details of school life. Government requirements—whether or not attached to funding—can create problems and the temptation of "preemptive capitulation," but these are probably not as great a problem as the daily press of business and the temptation to please every parent a little rather than some parents very much.

Despite the temptation to "mission creep," there are more distinctive schools than ever in the countries surveyed, and greater interest in how the distinctiveness works its way out in the way education is provided. New developments in policy and in society are making educational offerings more diverse. Charter schools in the United States, grant-maintained or foundation schools in England, and alternative curricula in a dozen countries respond to demand on the part of parents and interest on the part of educators. To an increasing extent, these differences are not religious but pedagogical, though religious schools continue to be the largest group of nonstate schools (more than half in most countries), and many are also pedagogically distinctive.

We have seen that Alan Peshkin's study of a fundamentalist Christian school did not reveal a hotbed of bigotry. But was this because in fact the school was a pale imitation of public education, not really offering a distinctive education? Not at all. Peshkin reports that at the first chapel session of the school year, the principal told the gathered students that "we try to be different in everything we do. We make no apology for that." And indeed it was for that reason that the parents had chosen the school, at considerable expense. "Bethany parents . . . knowingly send their children to a school that provides an intentionally deviant experience, one that is at odds with public schools and not 'a better expression of a common form.' " It is the shared religious convictions that all participants can take for granted, Peshkin concluded, that accounted for the strong group cohesion that he found among students, among faculty, and between the two groups.

> All participants . . . draw their prescriptions and proscriptions from the same ultimate authority. . . . Thus, the prevailing social distance between students and teachers coexists with an attachment to doctrine that joins both groups in a corporate life with shared ends and means. . . . No caste-like split characterizes the student-teacher relationship.[48]

Rather than spin out gloomy scenarios about what *might* happen with expanded parental choice of schools, supported by equitable public funding, we would do well to look at actual experience in this and other countries. Have societies been torn apart, and have new inequities been created? Or has conflict over schools been reduced, and the effect of residential segregation by income and sometimes by race been reduced as well? Evidence supports the second set of hypotheses.

And before we warn that the result of equitable public funding for parental choice would be new dangers from increased educational diversity or, conversely, new dangers *to* existing and valuable diversity among schools, we should consider carefully the characteristics of schools that are educationally distinctive. Would it be a good thing for children and for society to have more such distinctive schools? Evidence, experience, and our commitment to families and to a free and pluralistic society argue strongly that it would.

Nine

Catholic Schools and Vouchers: How the Empirical Reality Should Ground the Debate

JOSEPH M. O'KEEFE, S.J.

THIS CHAPTER EXPLORES the moral and normative aspects of vouchers through a study of the role of inner-city Catholic elementary schools. It begins with an exploration of the voucher debate, outlining the partisan positions, the state of research about the topic, and the role of Catholic schools in the political arena. Next, it discusses the contributions and needs of Catholic schools, especially those which serve children in poverty. Lastly, it recommends a way forward, in which partisan acrimony is replaced by a realistic reform agenda that is based on the needs of children in poverty.

The Voucher Debate: Political Certainty and Empirical Ambiguity

The voucher approach to school finance has been growing in popularity throughout developed nations.[1] Unlike most of its peers, the United States has, with a few notable exceptions, resisted the movement, due to lack of popular support at the ballot box and reigning interpretations of the separation of church and state. While the school voucher debate may lack conclusive research, it certainly has self-assured voices on both sides. At one end of the spectrum are the antivoucher people: the American Federation of Teachers, the National Education Association, the Democratic Party, and various other advocacy groups for public education. The other end consists of pro-market think tanks and political action organizations associated with the Republican Party, inner-city parents, and the Roman Catholic Church. The alliance is curious because the latter two groups have historically associated themselves with the Democratic Party. It is indeed ironic that the Church in the United States, with its pro-labor legacy, finds itself in a highly public and vociferous struggle with two of the largest unions in the nation.

Typifying the antivoucher side of the debate are arguments put forward by the American Federation of Teachers. The antivoucher position first tries to discredit the effectiveness of private schools, especially in regard to educationally at-risk populations—the selectivity argument. They rightly claim that private schools do not have the array of programs for special-needs students. However, they make serious unsubstantiated assertions about high admissions criteria and low retention rates in private schools. Second, they claim that private schools are not accountable and therefore educational quality is dubious. This argument may gain strength as state and federal government puts a high-stakes testing mandate on public schools. These tests, which provide data to compare the quality of schools, could become the sole criterion of effectiveness. Will schools outside of the system be able to use other criteria of excellence in a way that is convincing to an often skeptical and increasingly consumeristic public? Finally, they use the extreme case, a "setting up the straw man" approach:

> In a market system, some parents might choose top-notch schools, but others might choose cult schools or football factories. When a referendum on private school choice was called in California, a group of avowed witches announced plans to open a "pagan" school combining reading, writing and arithmetic, with magic. Indeed, vouchers would create a lot of chances for hocus-pocus.[2]

People for the American Way also engage in sound-bite rhetoric. In their position paper on the Milwaukee voucher experiment, tellingly entitled "Rolling the Dice for Our Children's Future," they slander those involved in this experiment in urban school reform, calling it "a story of unprotected constitutional and civil rights for children in private schools, lack of accountability to parents and public officials and corruption, theft and fiscal irresponsibility."[3]

Voucher advocates are no less strident, from the titles of some of Myron Lieberman's books (*Public Education: An Autopsy*: *The Teacher Unions: How the NEA and AFT Sabotage Reform and Hold Students, Parents, Teachers, and Taxpayers Hostage to Bureaucracy*) to newspaper articles and reports. Typical of the rhetoric of many advocacy groups is the following excerpt from the Web site of the Clare Boothe Luce Foundation:

> The last weapons in the public education monopoly's arsenal are fear and prejudice disguised as concern for the welfare of the disadvantaged. Thus its leaders insinuate (in politically correct terms, of course) that poor and minority parents won't make good decisions when it comes to their children's education. This argument not only underestimates America's struggling families but it also undermines the central value that makes this coun-

try great. In America, we must place out faith in freedom and in the ability of ordinary, often humble people to make the best decisions, by their own lights, for themselves and for their families.[4]

The pro-voucher side extols freedom, liberty, individual rights, parental prerogatives and the appeal of the market. It describes low-income children in public schools as trapped in underperforming schools, victimized by self-interested government bureaucrats, exposed to immorality or amorality. The voucher proposal is presented as a justice issue:

> Parental vouchers will allow all parents to again exercise their God-given right to extend their own educational mission. It will empower them to choose where to send their children to school, regardless of their income. No mother should have to send her child to a dangerous school and no child should be forced to endure a substandard education., The dynamic parental voucher movement is the next great human rights issue. It is a social justice movement reaching across racial, sectarian and socioeconomic lines.[5]

Racial politics plays a part here also. For example, the niece of Martin Luther King wrote in the *Wall Street Journal:*

> U.S. citizenship guarantees all parents an education for their children. This is a true civil right. Yet some children receive a better education than others due to their parents' ability to pay for benefits that are often missing in public schools. This inequity is a violation of the civil rights of the parents and children who are so afflicted by lack of income and by the mismanagement endemic to so many of the country's public school systems.[6]

In regard to African American involvement in the pro-voucher camp, one of the grass-roots leaders of the campaign in Milwaukee told a reporter from the *Boston Globe*: "I knew from the beginning that white Republicans and rich, right-wing foundations that paid me and used me to validate their agenda would do it only as long as it suited their needs. . . . I knew that once they figured they didn't need me as a black cover, they would try to take control of vouchers and use them for their own selfish interest.[7]

Ted Forstmann, who contributed millions of dollars to a private voucher program for inner-city children, used a racial allusion when he spoke at the National Press Club:

> By refusing to open this system up, we continue to perpetuate a kind of educational apartheid. While more affluent families can buy themselves better options—whether by sending their children to private schools or moving out to more expensive suburbs with better public schools—poor parents are stuck with no option other than government schools that can't teach or even protect their children.[8]

While the racial justice argument is important in pro-voucher rhetoric, the more essential element is the deep commitment to the free market as a solution to failing public schools. The basic argument is as follows: "If our market economy can help us be the leaders in computer technology, automobiles and telecommunications, there is no reason we can't lead the world in educational excellence."[9]

On either side of the debate, the high-minded rhetoric is not matched by empirical grounding. In places where voucher programs have been established, gains in academic achievement for voucher recipients are not consistent enough or conclusive enough to warrant wholesale adoption or rejection of the practice.[10] Most plans are not consistent enough and studies are not comprehensive enough to provide comparative evidence about key questions: Will vouchers be made available only to low-income families? Will vouchers be made available to children already in private schools? Will the voucher offer enough money to cover necessary expenses? What criteria will be used to select voucher recipients? What criteria will be used if the demand outstrips the supply? How will information be disseminated? How will hard-to-reach parents be contacted? How will the engagement of nonchoosers be enhanced? Will parents of all children be actively offered or required to choose? What will be the racial and ethnic balance? What provision will be made for students with special needs? Will private schools be required to admit students without consideration of past achievement and discipline problems? Will transportation be provided so that any child can attend the school of the parents' choice?[11]

Perhaps the most difficult problem in current studies is the application of findings from one sector or sample to a full-scale voucher plan or from a targeted plan to a universal plan.[12] Especially problematic is the application of past success in Catholic or other private schools to new schools that would be spurred by free enterprise or to the public schools that would be forced to improve because of competition. Sugarman and Kemerer explain:

> There are unresolved disagreements about whether the value added by private schools is sufficiently large and assured to warrant radical policy changes, whether observed gains are attributable to market forces or somehow uniquely tied to the religious orientation that characterizes most private schools, and whether the mechanisms that produce the gains are replicable in public schools.[13]

In conclusion, the voucher debate is vociferous but often vapid. It may have seen its heyday. Certainly, the resounding defeat of voucher referenda in Michigan and California in the November 2000 election had serious political consequences. Even if the courts gave more leeway to government support of religiously affiliated institutions, it seems unlikely that there is the political will to enact legislation. More devastating than defeat at the ballot box was President George W. Bush's decision to barter away the voucher provision in his education bill for other features such as states' rights and high-stakes testing. And it seems that the alternative proposals put forward by the Bush administration, such as tax credits, are either too small to make a difference or too politically risky to warrant serious lobbying efforts.[14]

Catholic Schools in the Political Arena

Catholic schools have figured prominently in the voucher debate; they have become, according to Youniss and McLellan, "a lightning rod in public discourse on education." The authors continue:

> Thus a repeating pattern has emerged. A study is published showing a Catholic school effect on achievement scores. It is immediately promoted by advocates of government vouchers as demonstrating the failure of public schools. Next, the anti-voucher movement publishes a critique showing that the methodology of the study was faulty and that the effect was due to the background characteristics of the students in the Catholic schools studied. With each new study, the pattern is played out again and neither side reaches satisfactory closure.[15]

The role of Catholic schools in the voucher debate is widely acknowledged.[16] In most cases, Catholic educators offer wholehearted support.[17] A recent statement by the president of the National Catholic Educational Association is typical of the official position:

> The truth about and validity of school choice is finally seeing the light of day. Two failed ballot initiatives cannot reverse this clear tide toward greater parental control in education. It is no longer a matter of *if* but rather *how* the barriers that prevent parents from choosing schools will come tumbling down—like the Berlin Wall. Instead of "Mr. Gorbachev, tear down this wall," it is, "Mr. Legislator, tear down this wall."[18]

Others in the Catholic community take a different position, though such opposing points of view are rare. These people are wary of the alliance between the Catholic Church and the Republican Party, evidenced by such vocal voucher advocates as the Catholic Alliance, a wing of the Christian coalition. Second, and related to the first, is opposition to the idea that market-based reforms will enhance justice and human dignity. A strident version of this position is found in the *Na-*

tional Catholic Reporter, a weekly newspaper generally considered to be on the left end of the Catholic spectrum:

> The single-minded pursuit of vouchers threatens to turn the Catholic Church, still by far the largest single private-school voice, into a vehicle for the profoundly anti-social, antidemocratic, anti-poor agenda of the right. Much as the Republican Party has become a bridge to respectability for far-right proposals from Star Wars to privatized prisons, the voucher movement has been a bridge of respectability for an ideological crusade against public schools. Ultimately our children will be educated not because there are markets to exploit and profits to be made, but because collectively, we as a society decide that it is right and just to do so. It is social justice that insists on the community's collective responsibility for educating all our children, just as we should insist that they have health care, food and a safe place to live.[19]

Of course, the Church should be supportive of schools that serve all children—but also of schools that serve its children. It is estimated that only 16 percent of Catholic school-aged children attend Catholic schools, down from 33 percent in 1950.[20] More significantly, the Church must be careful not to surrender its long-term goals for short-term financial relief for its schools.

Though a lengthy discussion of moral theology is beyond the scope of this essay, one can posit that Catholic social teaching clashes with the philosophy of the free market that undergirds the pro-voucher position, which is marked by competition and survival of the fittest—the best schools will survive and the worst will perish. Because of the reality of caveat emptor, vouchers could diminish the ability of the poor and powerless to work the system in favor of their children, thus perpetuating social stratification and limiting the ability of some to participate fully in public life. A moral theologian explains: "Keeping in mind the fundamental question about the conditions under which a Catholic might give a conditional moral endorsement to markets, it is clear that communal provision is a necessary addition to the moral logic of self-interested logic in the market."[21] A recent statement of the bishops of the United States echoes this sentiment: "The standards of the marketplace, instead of being guided by sound morality, threaten to displace it. We are now witnessing the gradual restructuring of American culture according to ideals of utility, productivity and cost-effectiveness."[22]

Catholic educators in England and Wales have written on the corroding effects of market-based reforms that were undertaken in the 1980s. Though the era and the setting differ, the underlying principles remain the same. The words of a British philosopher of education are telling:

Market forces cannot explain the broadly shared institutional purpose of advancing social equality or account for the efforts of Catholic educators to maintain inner-city schools (with large non-Catholic enrollments) whilst facing mounting fiscal woes. Likewise, market forces cannot easily explain why resources are allocated with schools in a contemporary fashion in order to provide an academic education for every student. Nor can they explain the norms of community that infuse daily life in these schools. . . . Individualism replaces community, consumer demand determines what is of value, competition replaces cooperation, utility replaces the best that has been thought and said. Diversity and choice are justified in terms of client satisfaction.[23]

Given the inconsistencies between Catholicism and the free-market philosophy that undergirds the pro–school choice position, vouchers cannot be the solution. Moreover, the political climate has evolved to the point where vouchers do not have a long life expectancy in any event. The philosophical and political realities shift the debate to focus on this question: How can U.S. society help all schools, Catholic included, better provide for the educational needs of children in poverty? Before answering that question, it is necessary to understand the empirical reality of the contemporary Catholic school.

The Contemporary Catholic School

In the mid-1960s, Catholic schools reached their peak enrollment. Along with the emergence of a more benevolent view of the secular world that emerged from the Second Vatican Council worldwide were the particular circumstances of the Church in the United States. European immigrants, marginalized from the mainstream because of their non-English ethnicity, their poverty, and their religion, built Catholic schools as protective fortresses for their children. By the mid-1960s many of these immigrants had moved in through ethnic assimilation and had moved out of urban ethnic ghettos as they moved up the socioeconomic ladder. Thus, the rationale for schools, appropriate for previous generations, was lost. Indeed, enrollment declined precipitously and many schools closed, in large part due to the demise of religious life, which had provided a cadre of lifelong volunteers—mostly nuns, with brothers and priests—to resource the educational needs of the community. Catholic schools were considered anachronistic but many of them survived, even in the inner cities that had been abandoned by the children of Catholic European immigrants.

In the 1980s researchers analyzed large federal data on academic achievement. To their surprise, they found a positive school effect for children in Catholic schools.[24] The major research studies indicated that Catholic schools were particularly effective for members of ethnic minority groups.[25] More recently, Gamoran discovered a positive Catholic school effect in his analysis of tests of academic achievement in the National Educational Longitudinal Study (NELS) data set.[26] In their analysis of NELS, Teachman, Paasch, and Carver discovered a low dropout rate in Catholic high schools.[27] In an analysis of the study High School and Beyond, Sander and Krautman found, after adjusting for self-selection that sophomores in Catholic schools were more likely to graduate with their class.[28] Jones, in an analysis of the National Assessment of Educational Progress data on math achievement of fourth graders, found that students from less-supportive family environments achieved higher scores when they attended Catholic schools.[29] Neal used census data and the annual survey from the National Catholic Educational Association to show higher graduation rates for Catholic school students.[30] In her psychological studies, Bempechat found a high degree of achievement and self-esteem among students of color who attend Catholic schools.[31]

In 2000 there were 8,146 schools serving 2.6 million students; in 1965, 13,500 schools served 5.6 million students. Catholic schools educated 49.5 percent of all private-school children and 5.5 percent of all school-aged children. But the percentage of students taught in major metropolitan centers, where Catholic schools constitute the vast majority of private schools, is much higher. In Philadelphia, private schools educate 31 percent of all children; in New York, 23 percent; in Chicago, 22 percent.[32] The savings to these public school districts are enormous.

In a host of areas, private schools are remarkably successful. They deserve their reputation as safe schools. According to a study conducted by the U.S. Departments of Education and Justice, a lower percentage of students ages twelve to nineteen reported criminal victimization at school, and far fewer gangs were present than in public schools.[33] A national survey of principals and administrators corroborates these findings; private schools experience fewer physical conflicts, fewer gang activities, and less student misbehavior.[34] It is not surprising that other studies have found that the most satisfied teachers tend to teach in private schools.[35] Certainly safety and good student behavior figure prominently here, but shared governance is an important factor. A recent study found that "public school teachers were consistently less likely than peers in private schools to agree that the principal in their schools communicated expectations to staff, was supportive and encouraging, recognized staff for a job well done, and talked with them about instructional practices."[36]

Though the findings cannot be generalized to a hypothetical free market for reasons described earlier, private school students do indeed outpace their public school counterparts in some significant areas. According to the Council on American Private Education, which presents statistics about private schools that are collected by the U.S. Department of Education, private school students have high expectations.[37] Nearly 88 percent of private high school students apply to college, compared to 57.4 percent of public high school students. Though private high school students comprise only 7.5 percent of that population nationally, they account for 20 percent of the nation's twelfth graders who took Advanced Placement examinations in 1998. Private school students scored higher on the SAT than did their public school counterparts. Private school students scored significantly above the national average on the International Math and Science Study (TIMSS), which measured math and science performance in thirty-eight countries around the world. Private school students also performed better on the National Assessment of Educational Progress in a range of subject areas, including reading), science, geography, and U.S. history.[38]

It is especially important to note that civics achievement is considerably higher in private schools, thus indicating that these schools contribute not only to the academic achievement of its members, but also to the formation of good citizens. In a national sample of tests given at grades four, eight, and twelve, students in nonpublic schools had higher average scores than did their peers in public schools. Students in Catholic schools had higher average scale scores than did students in public schools at all three grades. They discussed current events more regularly and were comparable to public schools in studying the Constitution, Congress, the executive branch, how laws are made, the court system, political parties, state and local government, other countries, and international relations. The report concludes:

> After controlling for a host of other factors described above, private school students tend to have higher political knowledge scores, are more likely to have confidence in their ability to speak at public meetings, are more likely to accept the presence of controversial books in public libraries than are public school students.[39]

In private schools, interest in politics is matched by community service. For both 1996 and 1999, students in public schools (47 percent in 1996 and 50 percent in 1999) were less likely to report participation in community service than were students in church-related private schools (69 percent in 1996 and 72 percent in 1999). In 1999, students attending public schools were less likely to participate in community service than were students in private non-church-related schools (50 percent compared to 68 percent). In addition, students from private church-related schools were more likely than those from public schools to report service-learning experiences for both 1996 and 1999.[40]

Despite their success, private schools in general and Catholic schools in particular face some daunting challenges, most of them driven by financial constraints. In the budget of most schools, four-fifths of the operating budget is devoted to salaries for the teaching staff. As a result, private schools are being hit especially hard by the teacher shortage. In a report on patterns of teacher compensation, the National Center for Educational Statistics reported that public school teachers earn between about 25 to 119 percent more than private school teachers earn, depending upon the private subsector.[41] On average, private school teachers earn two-thirds of the salary of their colleagues in public education and far fewer receive benefits. More alarming are data from the School and Staffing Survey 1993–94 and the Teacher Follow-Up Survey 1994–95 reported in NCES's *Condition of Education 1998*. Private schools are losing younger teachers in much higher percentages than are their public counterparts.

An article by Jeffrey Archer in the March 29, 2000, edition of *Education Week* illustrates the data presented above.

> When a 26-year-old teacher left, she was one of three St. Agnes teachers who made the switch from private to public education that year. In fact, one public school in the same neighborhood employs 10 former St. Agnes teachers, said Patricia Jones, the Catholic school's principal. "I've been seeing that here for 18 years," Ms. Jones said. "The average person can afford to work for us for about four years, until they start getting serious about life and have all the expenses that you then incur. I've pretty much accepted the fact that we're a training ground for the public schools."[42]

Later in the same article, Archer reports a claim by Richard M. Ingersoll that annual teacher turnover is 18 percent at Catholic schools, compared with 12 percent at public schools.

Catholic diocesan superintendents also feel the effects of the teacher shortage. According to a survey done in 1999, 94 percent of the respondents reported a shortage, which was acute in several cases.[43] Dioceses experience the greatest shortage in urban and rural areas and in the disciplines of math, natural science, computer science and Spanish. Moreover, many of the new hires were unfamiliar with Catholic education—few attended Catholic schools themselves and even fewer had experienced Catholic higher education. In addition, the problem of attracting teachers of color continues; whereas 26.5 percent of all students in Catholic schools are of color, only 3 percent of the teachers share that heritage.[44] It appears that the staffing problem will get worse in the future because of changing certification requirements in other school sectors.

The advantages that private schools enjoy may be diminishing. Charter schools present new opportunities for teachers to work in a "personalized teaching setting," but with salaries comparable to those in public schools. Also, many states are relaxing once-rigid certification requirements, which gave private schools the advantage of being the only possible employer of promising candidates with no formal teacher training or licensure. Given the supply and demand of the job market, most states have become much more flexible about licensure.[45]

Along with staffing, capital improvements are another area in which private schools are threatened, especially in the area of technology. Compared to public schools, private schools have more students per instructional computer, are considerably less likely to be connected to the Internet, have significantly fewer rooms connected to the Internet, and are less likely to report high-speed connections—21 percent of private schools versus 65 percent of public schools.[46] Finally, as tuition-charging institutions, private schools share with colleges the problem of accessibility; how can students from lower-income families attend these schools? Given its mission, accessibility is a serious problem in Catholic schools. According to Riordan, an eliting phenomenon is taking place in Catholic high schools.[47] In 1972, 12.3 percent of Catholic high-school students were from the lowest socioeconomic (SES) quartile; by 1992 only 5.5 percent of the students attending Catholic schools represented the lowest SES quartile. In contrast, while 29.7 percent of Catholic school students were from the highest SES quartile in 1972, close to 46 percent of Catholic school students were from this quartile by 1992. Given their history of providing educational opportunities to those from nonmainstream and low-income communities, and given the preferential option for the poor that is an essential characteristic of Catholic institutional life, the eliting phenomenon is a serious problem indeed. The incoming president of the National Catholic Educational Association put it well: "Catholic schools will not be able to serve all families who would choose them unless schools establish development and endowment programs that either reduce the percentage of their operating budgets supported by tuition or increase their capacity to provide financial aid to middle- as well as low-income families."[48]

It is reasonable to conclude that Catholic schools are effective and are challenged. They are effective insofar as they provide a good workplace for adults and, as a result, a positive formative environment for young people. They are threatened by financial constraints that manifest themselves in the socioeconomic status of students, staffing challenges, and capital expenditures. While all Catholic schools share these characteristics, they also differ greatly from each other by level, location, and type of governance structure.

It is the contention of this author that it is the inner-city Catholic elementary schools that make the greatest contribution. They are also the schools that have the greatest needs. During the 1980s and 1990s many of these schools closed.[49] In the 2000–2001 academic year inner-city schools were scheduled to close in Atlanta and New York, among other places. Newspapers report closings in a repeated pattern, showing how the school is an oasis for low-income children, complete with pictures of them in uniform weeping over their loss.[50]

In an attempt to understand better the contributions and the needs of inner-city schools, data were collected from a nationwide sample in the 1995–96 school year.[51] Major findings revolved around the following issues: a decoupling of the school from the parish and an increased dependence on the diocese for subsidies; a high level of students of color in schools; mismatch between the ethnicity of students and staff; low socioeconomic status of students; questionable fiscal viability; and issues of religious vitality.

From 1991 to 2001 new data have been collected from a larger number of inner-city schools. For the first round of data collection, schools chosen for analysis had the following characteristics: they were from large or medium cities; central city or urban fringe; elementary; Catholic; and 20 percent or more of their students were eligible for free or reduced lunch lived below the poverty line, or both ($n = 280$).

This study demonstrated anew that these schools are not elite. First, their schools have nearly open admissions and a small 7 percent attrition rate. In half of the schools, over 40 percent of the students are eligible for free or reduced lunch, are living below the poverty line, or both. One hundred eighty-six schools qualified for a telecommunications reduction (based on student SES); in sixty-two of the schools, they qualified for an 80 percent reduction. Sixty-two percent of the students are Hispanic or African American. Tuition is low (just under $2,200 per year), and 82.5 percent of the schools offer partial scholarships. Unfortunately, however, there are minimal special education services, and only 16 percent of the schools have students who receive IDEA (Individuals with Disabities Education Act) benefits.

In regard to staffing, these schools reflect the larger Catholic-school population, with a revolving door of young teachers and a cadre of older women who earn low salaries. Twenty-one percent of the teachers left their position in the last academic year; 42 percent of those went to public schools that offered higher salaries. Compared to constituting only 5 percent of the staff in all Catholic schools, women religious constitute nearly half of the principals in these schools. They are nearing retirement age and generally earn salaries much lower than their education and experience warrant. Given the precipitous decline in vocations to religious life, they will not be replaced by their own.

On average, the schools have filled 80 percent of their seats. They have limited capacity for growth. If vouchers were to be instituted, relatively few seats would be available. Despite good enrollments, most schools do not meet their operating costs through tuition; they tend to be subsidized by the diocese. Nearly 70 percent receive grants from other sources. Close to one-fifth of the schools have a full-time development director, a trend that will surely grow. The pivotal question for these schools is this: Will philanthropic efforts be significant enough or sustained long enough to ensure viability? Centralized diocesan philanthropic efforts have become widespread. In Boston, for example, the archdiocese is launching a $300 million capital campaign, $85 million of which will be devoted to Catholic education. Of that, $25 million will go to an endowment fund to supplement tuition income as a source of teacher salaries.[52] In other places, so-called private voucher programs have benefited Catholic schools. One wonders if these efforts will be sustained in the long term in light of the political demise of public voucher plans. Donors' intentions are crucial; are they more committed to capitalism than to Catholicism. If so, private voucher programs are politically motivated demonstration projects that provide convincing data for the privatization of all schools. Once the latter goal is unattainable, whither the future financial commitment?

The schools serve a religiously diverse population. Whereas 13.6 percent of students in all Catholic schools are non-Catholic, 30 percent of these students in this sample are non-Catholic.[53] Most of the non-Catholics are Baptist and African American. The schools do not serve narrow denominational interests, but provide educational opportunities for the greater community, as indeed they should, based on Catholic teachings on ecumenism, racial justice, and solidarity.[54]

The Way Forward:
Collaboration for the Common Good

As Catholic inner-city elementary schools face the future, they must realize that "society is generally grateful for the civic contributions of parochial education, but Americans are reluctant to provide public monies—even in the form of vouchers—to support parish schools. The hard truth is that Catholics will have to pay for parish schools them-selves.[55] Private philanthropy will undoubtedly be the key to the fu-ture. Nonetheless, government can enhance the services it provides to children in poverty, even those who attend sectarian schools. Can these services provide a via media between the two extremes of the voucher debate? Can children in poverty benefit from a recognition that, in re-gard to government aid to faith-based organizations, "perfect neutral-ity is an unachievable dream."[56]

To the surprise of the general public, a wide variety of government programs assist children in poverty no matter which school they attend. Provision of these services is easier because of the *Aguilar v. Felton* case in the mid-1990s. Already, 4,405 (54.5 percent) of Catholic schools have students who receive some services under Title I of the Elementary and Secondary Education Act. In addition, 3,124 (46.7 percent) of the schools have students who participate in the U.S. Agriculture Depart-ment's federal nutrition programs. Over 3,100 schools (38.3 percent) participate in the E-rate reductions of the 1996 Telecommunications Act. With enhanced funding, as well as assistance with onerous paperwork that inhibits strapped Catholic-school administrators from participat-ing in government programs, low-income students could benefit from a wide array of services that would arguably give their families added income to pay for tuition.

The Elementary and Secondary Education Act can provide the great-est assistance. Among its various entitlement programs, the following are available for students in Catholic schools: Title I, Part A, Helping Disadvantaged Children Meet High Standards; Title II, Eisenhauer Professional Development Program; Title III, Technology for Educa-tion; Title IV, Safe and Drug-Free Schools and Communities; Title VI, which supports a broad range of local activities in eight primary areas: technology related to implementing reform; acquisition and use of in-structional and educational materials, including library materials and computer software; promising education-reform projects such as mag-net schools; programs for disadvantaged and at-risk children; literacy programs for students and their parents; programs for gifted and tal-ented children; school reform efforts linked to Goals 2000; and Title VII, Bilingual Education Services.

Other federal government programs that can assist students in Cath-olic schools are the Goals 2000 Educate America Act. At the request of private school teachers and administrators, information related to goals, standards, materials, and assessments developed with Goals 2000 funds must be made available. In addition, professional develop-ment opportunities supported by Goals 2000 funds must be made available to teachers and administrators in private schools in proportion to the number of students attending private schools in the state. Students can receive special education services under the Individuals with Disabilities Education Act. Catholic school administrators can apply for other programs such as the Partnership for Family Involvement in Education, which is a coalition of hundreds of family, school, business, community, and religious organizations committed to working together to encourage and enable families to be more meaningfully involved in their children's education. The mission of the Partnership is to promote children's learning through the development of family-school-community partnerships. Another initiative is the Teacher Forum, which seeks to shift the focus of the education reform movement from teachers as objects of reform to teachers as partners in reform by building teacher leadership capacity. Still another, the Blue Ribbon Schools Program, established by the secretary of education in 1982, serves three purposes. First, it identifies and recognizes outstanding public and private schools across the nation. Second, the program makes research-based effectiveness criteria available to all schools so that they can assess themselves and plan improvements. Third, the program encourages schools, both within and among themselves, to share information about best practices based on a common understanding of criteria related to educational success. Blue Ribbon designation can be very helpful in attracting donors as well as foundation and corporate support. Catholic schools can participate in programs to transfer excess and surplus federal computer equipment and, as stated above, participate in the E-rate reduction program. They can apply for some assistance in energy conservation efforts from the Department of Energy. For staff development, Catholic school teachers can receive grants from National Endowment for the Humanities and National Endowment for the Arts. They can receive money from Americorps for teacher-corps programs and cancellation of their Perkins Loans for teaching in designated low-income schools. They can participate in the Teacher Next Door Program sponsored by the Department of Housing and Urban Development.

States can and do offer assistance to children in Catholic schools.[57] Textbook loans are available in seventeen states, nursing services in fifteen states, technology assistance in thirteen states, special education provision in thirteen states, and teacher benefits in six states.

These programs offer interesting possibilities for supporting children in poverty who are in sectarian schools. Because government funds are funneled through the local education authority, much would need to be done to enhance these processes, which are often stalled and stymied by hostile public school officials. Moreover, many of these programs are unknown and the paperwork for many of these pro-

Response

JOHN T. McGREEVY

THE THREE ESSAYS in this section all contain examinations of school vouchers or private choice. Professor Mouw offers a case study of the Dutch experiment in funding of religious schools; Professor O'Keefe provides a close examination of what Catholic schools in the inner city actually do and how they might better be understood; and Professor Glenn demonstrates the unusual character of American educational arrangements in comparative perspective.

All of this is useful. But the three essays also suggest the difficulty, although not the impossibility, of separating descriptions of our current situation from the normative and moral dimensions of our educational ecologies. The jump from social and institutional history to ethics and policy making is a short one.

Charles Glenn's important project, for example, begins with the assumption that comparing of American educational strategies with European counterparts will be illuminating. And his detailed comparison of the situation in most European countries with that of the United States emphasizes the singularity of the American situation, where public schools alone receive government funding. Professor Mouw offers an even more pointed comparison of the Dutch and American situations and the ironic effects of subsidizing religious schools in a culture of declining religiosity.

Mouw and Glen conclude their comparative and descriptive projects with normative claims in support of vouchers, and use comparative data to justify such proposals. Mouw offers a "chastened defense" to be sure, but also a basic sympathy with the view that the state's primary responsibility is to guarantee a certain acquisition of knowledge in its schools, not a particular patriotic or civic disposition. O'Keefe, similarly, urges government aid for all poor children, whether enrolled in public schools or not.

I find these analyses persuasive, but I suspect that many philosophers interested in these issues, including contributors to this volume, are less sanguine. Or to put in the form of a question: Does the sheer existence of multiple forms of aiding schools offer concrete wisdom for the particular American situation? Professor Macedo, for example, argues that public schools produce the best citizens, better able to tolerate social diversity in an increasingly diverse world. And implicit in Macedo's argument is the assumption that American society—because of its diversity on racial, religious, and ideological grounds—requires common shaping institutions. Neither he nor Professor Gutmann seem especially interested in comparative questions, simply because they want to narrow the focus of the debate to the American case, and the need to produce tolerant and informed American citizens. Both scholars believe in, even have faith in, the public school as an instrument of socialization in the United States and inculcator of values.

Do, in fact, religious schools produce good citizens and foster tolerance among their students? The Professors Levinson argue that private schools in fact display considerable racial diversity, a precondition to the civic tolerance urged by Professors Macedo and Gutmann. Similarly, the work of James Coleman and others on Catholic schools leads one to suspect that it would be difficult to prove that Catholic schools, for example, have produced less-informed, less-capable citizens than their public-school counterparts. Here the burden shifts to the philosophers, requiring them to explain why the state should not assist institutions capable of forming good citizens.[1]

The essays also reflect our particular historical moment. During the past two centuries the intensity of the voucher debate has neatly tracked the perceived societal need for strong public institutions. The first intense discussion of the question occurred in the 1850s, when fierce anti-Catholicism merged with a belief that public schools were the only means to propagate democratic and Protestant values in a diverse society. The second wave of anti-Catholicism and emphasis on public schools occurred in the 1870s, when Republican activists saw public schools as a key to assimilation of newly freed African Americans in the South and immigrant Catholics in the North. Without common schools, national cohesion, not just individual character, seemed at risk.[2]

The third discussion occurred immediately after World War II. Here Americans witnessed on explicitly secular defense of the public schools—not coincidentally the intellectual community now included numerous Jews and nonbelievers—often on the grounds that the cultural values students imbibed in public schools would prevent the kind of authoritarianism associated with fascism and Catholicism. The then-current vogue for cultural anthropology played an important role in this discussion, with its presumption that certain cultures produce certain kinds of politics. The culmination of this third intense discussion occurred in the late-1940s with the two Supreme Court decisions that established the putative "wall of separation" between church and state. And as the private papers of the justices indicate, fear of an aggressive Catholicism played an important, perhaps decisive, role in shaping the opinions of the court on this matter. [3]

None of this demonstrates that the present merely repeats the past. Instead, this historical synopsis suggests the difference between our own discussion and its predecessors. We write in an era where we have less confidence in public institutions generally, and this declining confidence has opened up the debate on school vouchers. Consider the groups now unwilling to entrust their own children to American public schools: home schoolers worried about secular liberalism; home schoolers worried about too rigid a curriculum and too violent a school subculture; affluent parents in large metropolitan areas (such as Bill Clinton and Al Gore) worried about the educational quality of public schools; religious parents (Catholic, Protestant, Jewish, and Muslim) eager for religious education or disenchanted with local public schools; impoverished parents of all races and religious backgrounds desperate for any public or private alternative to the neighborhood school.

Proponents of school vouchers, then, need to focus even more closely on why such programs make sense in the particular historical moment. The Jesuit John Courtney Murray's withering attack on what he called the "establishment" theology of Felix Frankfurter and American liberals of the 1940s had important uses (although it persuaded few Supreme Court Justices at the time), but that era's rigid interpretation of the establishment clause to the First Amendment already seems dated.[4] Advocates of vouchers now face a different bar. Put bluntly: in an era of declining confidence in public institutions—and this should worry all citizens—can religious schools serve at once private and public purposes?

SCHOOL CHOICE AND THE LAW

Ten

Parents, Partners, and Choice: Constitutional Dimensions of School Options

MARTHA MINOW

THE CONSTITUTION'S RELIGION clauses are not the only constitutional norms relevant to contemporary school-choice debates. Due process liberties protect the rights of parents to guide their children's education. Equal protection guarantees against discrimination must also guide the adoption of lawful policies and the resolution of litigation over policies. In this heady moment of school reform,[1] with experiments in public vouchers for private schooling, public charters to prompt the creation of new "charter" schools, public partnerships with nonprofit and for-profit companies, and choice options within public school systems, the rights of parents and the equality claims of students deserve as much attention as do the establishment and free exercise clauses of the Constitution.[2] Because the power of Congress and the states to adopt laws beyond what the Constitution requires is more up for grabs than in the past, I largely restrict the analysis to what the Constitution itself requires, although existing legislation comes in for discussion at some points as well.

Let me acknowledge several starting points. First, I am mainly engaging here in prediction of the Supreme Court's interpretation of the Constitution rather than development of ideal constitutional theory. Second, constitutional interpretation is relevant to determine both what kinds of actions are required and what kinds are permitted to legislatures, school boards, and other actors. Further, some features of the Constitution cannot be ordered by courts but can be undertaken only by other actors, so some of the analysis here involves conceptions of constitutional meaning that require actors outside of courts to realize.

Religion

In the crowded legal discussions of school choice, establishment clause issues predominate. The Supreme Court rejected the argument that voucher plans that allow election of parochial schools amount to impermissible public support for or public endorsement of religion.[3] Parents are merely conduits for the impermissible payment of public funds to religious institutions.[4]

Defenders of such programs argue that so long as such programs are neutral in relations between believers and nonbelievers, and as long as such programs do not directly aid religion, they can be constitutional.[5] Michael McConnell has creatively argued that First Amendment disestablishment—specifically the commitment to pluralism in educational provision—actually supports voucher plans that include religious schools.[6] McConnell has also led the efforts to challenge voucher schemes that exclude religious schools as unconstitutional incursions on the free exercise of religion by forcing individuals to choose public schools when they would rather pursue religious education.[7]

I am impressed by those who remind us that the religion clauses do not—and should not—provide bright lines for analysis. Instead, these elements of the First Amendment reflect deep and broad purposes, to be reinterpreted in specific contexts and specific eras.[8] I also think there is much to commend in demands for facts—facts about the state of relationships among religious groups, about the actual scope of choice available to parents, and even about the actual quality of public and private schooling—before conclusions are reached about the the legality or wisdom of particular voucher schemes under the religion clauses.[9] Whether a given scheme actually benefits one religion over others or benefits religious over secular options thus remain vital factual issues for states and localities considering or operating voucher plans.

Although the Supreme Court has spoken on the topic of religion and school choice, other constitutional issues related to school choice remain.

Due Process and Liberty

The fundamental constitutional commitment in the United States to parental choice in educating children is well established but also intricately linked to public values and frameworks. The Supreme Court in *Pierce v. Society of Sisters* faced a challenge to Oregon's law requiring parents to ensure their children attended public school; compulsory schooling could be satisfied only through public schooling.[10] The advocates framed the case as a contest over relations between groups—immigrants and long-term residents, secularists and the religiously affiliated, or as perhaps best reflected the historical context, Protestants and Catholics.[11] Using the due process clause of the Fourteenth

Amendment, the Court found the state's compulsion of children's attendance at public schools unconstitutional. The Court elevated the liberties of parents to choose not to accept the instruction provided by public schools because "the child is not the mere creature of the State; those who nurture him and direct his destiny have the right, coupled with the high duty, to recognize and prepare him for additional obligations."[12] Parental liberties must be recognized; the state does not have the authority to "standardize its children."[13]

Note, though, the possessive pronoun that the Court attached to children. They are "its children." I do not mean to make too much of it, but the irony is sharp, and therefore the liberty recognized is at best complex. The Court's full sentence reads: "The fundamental theory of liberty upon which all governments in this Union repose excludes any general power of the State to standardize its children by forcing them to accept instruction from public teachers only."[14] Do the children belong to the state, and not to their parents, or not even to themselves? The answer is a little of each, and hence the complexity.

The child is not the "mere" creature of the state and parents have the right and duty to prepare the child for "additional" obligations."[15] These terms signal the presumption—a presumption pervading the opinion—that state-defined elements will ånd must frame children's education, even as parents may elect additional educational features. The child thereby will be prepared for citizenship, and may, at the parents' election, also be prepared to fulfill additional obligations related to religion, military service, or other commitments.

Thus, even the profound commitment to pluralism, and rejection of Oregon's effort to rule out any but public schools, remains yoked to state supervision. In *Pierce*, the Supreme Court treated as a given, and thus as a central condition to its conclusion, that the state would retain the power to supervise private schools, their selection of teachers, and their curricular choices.[16] The state could prescribe some subjects for study and proscribe others.[17] Responding to contemporary fears of Bolshevism and political subversion by immigrants, attorneys for the private schools supported this approach by arguing to the court that "the private and parochial schools teach the same subjects as the public schools—whatever one does to inculcate and foster patriotism, the other can and does do quite well."[18]

What does this joint commitment to pluralism, guided by parental choice, and to state supervision of education mean for contemporary school choice reforms? By ruling that the state cannot make public schools the only avenue for satisfying compulsory schooling requirements, the Court ensured that the state must allow private school options; by presuming state supervision of private school options, the

Court located parental choice within a governing framework of state policy. The government, representing the society, is a partner with parents in preparing children for their obligations in society. Private school choice in a constitutional democracy is bound to involve governmental regulation of private schools.[19]

Pierce itself does not require funding to support any private school option because *Pierce* announces no right to governmental neutrality in schooling. Instead, it protects parents' rights to be free from criminal coercion in the education of their children.[20] Yet within this scheme, a polity—whether federal, state, or local—certainly can enhance private parental choice with a public subsidy through vouchers or tax credits or deductions. Indeed, the political branches can bolster their policy arguments with claims that they are assisting constitutionally protected choices. This kind of public assistance for private choice is not required, and indeed, the state need not even pretend to be neutral in arranging the options of public and private schooling.[21] And even where it is provided, the public subsidy for private-school choices can involve at least as much public regulation as would otherwise be permitted of private schooling receiving no public support.

Advocates of subsidized school choice should attend to the real risks that even greater public regulation might follow. The point is not only that he who pays the piper picks the tune. Because some degree of public supervision is already a given in private education, the political pressures to secure even more public benefit from governmental subsidy may be powerful, whether the benefit takes the form of reporting and accountability requirements, further curricular mandates, or conditions on admission and hiring practices.

Public schools, of course, are entirely saturated by public supervision, a mandated curriculum, and public rules governing student admissions and teacher hiring. It is intriguing to consider whether the due process protection for parental liberty requires not only the option of privately electing and paying for nonpublic schools, but also room for parental choice among public school options. Many public school systems already experiment with choice through magnet schools, additional types of choice options, and examination schools. More than thirty states have authorized entrepreneurial groups of teachers, parents, and businesspeople to compete for charters to start their own new public schools. The *Pierce* tradition suggests that these avenues for parental choice may have a constitutional dimension, especially if they enable parents to express deep values and prepare their children for "additional obligations." This is not to suggest that the Constitution guarantees parents the power to enroll their children in a particular school of their choice. Even choice of residence does not guarantee enrollment in the closest public school. Both the facts of scarcity and the lawful public control of the entire enrollment process by public officials counter that suggestion. But it does imply that parents must not face irrational or unfair obstacles in selecting from among public school choices—and even, perhaps, that once launched, public school choice options cannot be arbitrarily diminished.

What about a public school system that affords no latitude for parents to choose from among public schools, or a state without charter school authorization? I would not bet on any successful outcome, but a parent could challenge such systems for unduly curbing parental choice and influence in education. The space for parental input seems especially vital; a choice system or array of charter schools that did not accord to parents the selection option or did not attend to parental desires in their design would seem outside of at least the spirit of *Pierce*.

In addition to protecting the liberties of parents, choice options in education can promote responsible parenthood and democratic citizenship. By engaging parents in their children's education and encouraging their participation in the very selection of the school program, choice options can promote the kind of active participation that democratic government both encourages and requires.[22] Even if the Constitution cannot generate a judicial remedy,[23] school boards and state legislatures seeking to fulfill their constitutional obligations would be wise to enhance parental choice. This would respect parental liberties and engage parents with potentially important consequences for the quality of schooling and the vitality of democracy.

An additional feature of contemporary school reforms is the growing presence of partnerships between public and private actors—including for-profit actors—in the management of schools. Some charter schools are launched or managed by for-profit entities and some ordinary public schools have hired for-profit entities to perform a variety of management tasks within their schools.[24] The legacy of *Pierce* suggests that parents should have a role in the governance of these emerging public/private partnerships. It also reminds us of the presumption of continuing public supervision to achieve public educational goals.

Equal Protection

One vital public purpose for education is equality. Over the twentieth century, public policy elevated fights against discrimination and improvement of schools as gateways to equal opportunity. Since World War II, perhaps no domain of society has been so persistently subject to scrutiny by a particular constitutional provision besides public schools and the equal protection guarantee of the Fourteenth Amendment. Probably the most famous Supreme Court decision is *Brown v. Board of Education*[25] which rejected state-mandated racial segregation in public schools—although the Court subsequently permitted local districts to monitor slow implementation under the phrase "with all deliberate speed."[26] The courts have further ruled that the state cannot operate two systems, one integrated and one segregated, while allowing parental choice between them.[27] Nor may a school system offer any students the chance to transfer from a desegregated school back to a school in which their racial group holds a majority.[28] And a public system that has been formally segregated cannot use a freedom-of-choice plan to desegregate.[29] Moreover, a state or district that has created racially segregated public schools cannot close its public schools to avoid racial desegregation.[30]

What do these rulings mean where there is either no history of intentional segregation or where such a history has been deemed no longer relevant because of intervening steps taken by the public system? The Supreme Court recently ruled that any use of racial categories to produce racial balance triggers strict scrutiny and requires demonstration of both a compelling state interest and a means narrowly tailored to serve that interest.[31] In that light, district courts and courts of appeals have been rejecting uses of racial categories to promote racial balance in school programs.[32] It remains to be seen whether the Supreme Court will affirm this trend.

Ambiguities also arise in interpreting equal protection in terms of gender, religion, disability, and economic class. Nonetheless, I will sketch the potential issues affecting vouchers and tax benefits for parents electing private schools, public magnet schools, charter schools, and public-private education partnerships. Federal and state statutes and state constitutional provisions are likely to offer more determinate guidance—and more enforceable restrictions on school choice plans that affect equality.[33] But given the aggressive efforts by the Supreme Court to question the constitutional authority of Congress and the states to act in civil rights domains,[34] construing the federal Constitution has never been more central.

Even given doubts about the exact borders of federal constitutional interpretation in many areas of equality, choice schemes will be subject to overarching public obligations against intentional racial segregation, inequality in opportunities available to boys or girls, and unequal treatment for students of different religions. Less-stringent constitutional requirements would attach to protections for students with disabilities and students who are poor, but here state and federal legislation and state constitutions can provide more vigorous obligations.

Thus, the equality concerns set limits on the shape of various school choice reforms.

The federal government may also specify conditions necessary to satisfy tax-exempt status for a private school.[35] State regulations to guarantee a minimum quality of private education and commitment to educate children in democratic principles combine with federal statutes and with the Constitution to frame the terms that private schools must meet if they are to serve as settings to fulfill compulsory education. Parental choice can operate only within this framework.

Racial and Ethnic Equality

Intentional segregation by race is impermissible by public school officials, and the adoption of school choice plans that intentionally segregate by race and ethnicity would clearly be unconstitutional. In the absence of explicitly racially segregating school assignments, though, some choice systems may generate notable patterns of racial and ethnic segregation. If a public system creates an Afrocentric magnet school, an Asian-heritage magnet school, and a Hispanic culture-bilingual school,[36] it may seem to be inviting parental choices to self-segregate.[37] Will these kinds of programmatic choices, with foreseeable racial and ethnic sorting effects, give rise to a constitutional violation? Parents may make choices not based on their races, and even if they do, the fact that parents make the enrollment choice may shield the public system from charges of impermissible segregation, although other factors in the political and social context may bolster those charges.

A voucher plan or provision for tax relief for parents selecting private schools would violate equal protection on racial grounds only if it betrays intentional racial preference or animus. Disparate impact, benefiting more whites than others, would not produce a constitutional defect. At the same time, one line of judicial decisions indicates that public dollars cannot be used by private schools for an unconstitutional or unlawful purpose, such as racial discrimination.[38]

Nonetheless, citizens in a state may worry that a voucher scheme or tax-relief program could impair efforts to produce racially integrated schools. May a state (or district) go beyond the usual requirement that schools participating in such programs commit to nondiscrimination in admissions, and actually seek racial balance in their enrollments? Such elements would be part of a governmental policy, and thus potentially subject to as rigorous a review as if racial-balance goals were used in student assignments within public schools, charter schools, or magnet schools within the public system. (Racial balance goals

adopted unilaterally by private schools should not trigger any constitutional concerns, as they involve no state action; racial exclusionary
policies by a private school may sometimes jeopardize the school's tax-
exempt status.)[39] In the absence of findings of intentional governmental
discrimination, the Supreme Court in recent years has been highly
skeptical of deliberate use of racial categories, even when designed to
benefit members of minority groups.[40]

The context of elementary and secondary education may be treated
differently by the Supreme Court because of the relevance of a diverse
community to the missions of learning and preparation for citizenship
and adult roles.[41] The centrality of schools to combating historical practices of intentional and de facto racial segregation—and the willingness
of the society to pursue civil rights and public purposes in the context
of schooling—may convince the Court to treat the use of race-based
decision making differently in school settings. Courts could find that
even a stringent requirement of a compelling state interest is satisfied
by the importance of helping each next generation to learn alongside
people of different backgrounds, to cultivate mutual understanding,
and to prepare for working, voting, and living in a multiracial and
multicultural society.

Yet were I to advise a legislature today, the safer approach, even if
the goals include racial integration, is to use admission procedures that
stay clear of explicit consideration of race. Alternatives to race can be
tried to promote this kind of diversity; indicators of economic class and
a range of academic achievements and difficulties could be used as
elements of diversity when charter and magnet schools select from
applying students. Indeed, if lower-court opinions give a clue to where
the Supreme Court may be heading, states and districts seeking the
safest course should avoid using racial and ethnic categories in admissions even if racial diversity is the goal. One court recently ruled that
race cannot be used to prevent the transfer of a student to a magnet
school even if it would leave the student's existing school with a continuing racial imbalance; another recent decision concluded that diversity alone does not provide a compelling governmental interest justifying the use of racial categories in student school assignments.[42]

Yet earlier courts ruled that even parents' liberties to select a private
school and to choose with whom to associate cannot outweigh the
power of the federal government to require even a private school to
avoid racial discrimination in admissions.[43] And the Supreme Court
has not yet overturned *Regents of University of California v. Bakke*,[44]
where Justice Powell's crucial fifth vote for the majority approved of
the use of race among a range of factors used to achieve a diverse
college class. Accordingly, states still are permitted to require private

schools participating in voucher plans to avoid racial discrimination, and states can even require participating private schools to recruit for diversity along many dimensions of the student body. Such requirements cannot, however, force schools to use quotas or numbers of slots set by race, nor to set differential admission standards for students of different racial or ethnic groups. A court of appeals rejected the use of differential admission scores for public-exam schools to achieve racial and ethnic diversity.[45]

In sum, race as a factor in school assignment to promote racial balance has been permitted up until this point in elementary and secondary schools,[46] yet the Supreme Court will likely soon be addressing such issues in the context of higher education, and the ground rules could well change. Choice plans have real ability to promote racial and ethnic integration even without explicit use of these categories, largely because they break out of residential assignment to schools, and residential segregation is the key cause of school-based segregation.[47] School choice options may allow students of color who attend majority-minority schools to transfer to more integrated public and private schools.[48] Especially if they bridge districts and city/suburban borders, school choice programs could open more quality opportunities for more students while promoting integration across racial and class lines.[49]

The crucial point to acknowledge is that as long as good options remain relatively scarce, "school choice" will entail that schools pick students at least as much as parents pick schools.[50] If public support is involved, school choice programs must be vigilantly nondiscriminatory on racial grounds, and can seek racial diversity as part of a larger plan of diversity, at least until the governing courts rule otherwise.

Gender Equality

As a constitutional matter, gender differentiation does not trigger as rigorous constitutional protection as does racial classification, although Justice Ginsburg has written an opinion for the Supreme Court seeking to close the gap.[51] The legal basis for guarding against gender discrimination is more obvious under statutory than constitutional grounds. Yet even on constitutional grounds, public schools cannot offer demonstrably less of a given educational offering either to boys or girls compared with what is offered to children of the other sex. Where the sex difference is germane—as it is in setting the curriculum for a sex-education class—the instruction may be provided on a sex-segregated basis.

A school system can maintain single-sex schools where enrollment is voluntary and educational opportunities are essentially equal.[52] Sex-based classifications must be substantially tied to achieving important and legitimate public purposes, but enhancing diverse educational offerings is likely to provide just this sort of justification.[53] Therefore, a state or district can devise special single-sex programs, but only if essentially equal opportunities are available for members of the other gender. Even vouchers and tax benefits for election of private schools should be governed by this norm; the system can provide vouchers or tax benefits for single-sex schools, but only if it extends identical benefits to comparable schools for the other sex.

Religion and Equality

There may be a constitutional basis for permitting a religiously affiliated private school to discriminate on the basis of religion in its employment practices.[54] Discrimination in the selection of students is another matter, however. Since a religious school can create the character of its program through its curriculum and selection of teachers, it would be hard-pressed to justify exclusion of students on the basis of their or their parents' religions.

Historically, parochial schools have simply made participation in religious classes and ritual a condition of school enrollment rather than imposing a religious identity test for admission. If the parochial school's only public dimensions are its tax-exempt status and its eligibility to satisfy the compulsory schooling requirement, students not affiliated with the relevant religion would not be likely to be able to find sufficient state action to trigger the equal protection clause protections against discrimination on the basis of religion.

The situation could well change if public dollars are involved through a voucher scheme. Then, state action is involved at least at the level of the scheme itself. State approval of public payments to schools intentionally discriminating on the basis of students' religion would be illegal discrimination, and it would be difficult to justify, given the school's ability to set the curriculum, select the teachers, and set other requirements. With public support, the parochial school may face free exercise rights of students who do not wish to engage in the school's religious practices. Ensuring such students alternatives to required chapel attendance would be wise if the supervising public body wished to avoid constitutional challenge,[55] although the private schools should be able to preserve their character and distinctive curricular and programmatic features.

Disability and Equality

The constitutional status of persons with disabilities is ambiguous. The leading Supreme Court decision refused to accord persons with disabilities heightened constitutional scrutiny of official action designed to treat them disadvantageously, and yet simultaneously found a defect with a city's refusal to grant a permit for a residential group home for persons with mental retardation.[56] Protected in that one instance, persons with disabilities remain without an established doctrine of constitutional protection against unequal treatment.

Before that time, in the 1970s, lawsuits challenging public failures to provide educational opportunities for children with disabilities achieved consent decrees and encouraged state and federal legislative action to extend rights to them of statutory educational equality.[57] By now, it is simply unclear what the Supreme Court, in the absence of such statutes, would find today if a public school system denied children with disabilities educational programs. Even less clear would be the effects of a similar challenge to a voucher scheme that made no provision for educating children with disabilities in the eligible private schools.

If the level of constitutional scrutiny applied to students with disabilities simply requires a rational relationship between the legislation and a permissible end, it is conceivable that courts would uphold voucher plans, magnet schools, and charter programs that excluded students with disabilities. The defense would have to be that the new, individual schools cannot efficiently meet the needs of all students with disabilities and need not do so if other schools in the system can do so. If such plans resulted in no educational opportunities for students with disabilities, however, they would appear to be constitutionally defective.

The current federal statutory scheme makes public benefits for students with disabilities available to students in private schools, but only after students enrolled in public schools obtain relevant benefits.[58] One respected interpretation of federal law indicates that charter schools are subject to heightened, not lower, duties to serve students with disabilities,[59] although similar interpretations have not extended to specialized magnet schools.

Economic Class and Equality

The Supreme Court has rejected equal protection challenges to school finance systems that produce disparities in local school spending within a state.[60] Unequal expenditures are not invidiously discriminatory.[61] Yet the Court's refusal to treat poverty as a suspect classification calling for heightened equal protection scrutiny actually permits states and districts to take poverty into account in designing school choice programs. A voucher plan can have an income cap for eligible families without triggering an equal-protection problem. A school choice system can promote diversity within each school by coordinating parental choices with goals of economic diversity.[62]

This would involve a departure from the effects of school choice in the past. Studies show that parents with more education are more likely to know about choice options and more likely to enroll their children in them.[63] Some studies indicate that parents with higher incomes as well as higher education are more likely to exercise options for magnet schools and other choice features.[64] Studies of charter schools in particular indicate that there may be a bimodal pattern emerging, with some charter schools serving high percentages of at-risk and poor students, and others serving large percentages of relatively affluent students.[65]

Efforts to promote integration of students from different socioeconomic classes through school-choice mechanisms would be lawful and could also assist racial integration.[66] Yet, there is no obligation to promote socioeconomic integration, and without care, school choice programs could exacerbate segregation along these lines.

Closing Comments

The federal civil rights statutes and regulations, including the Individuals with Disabilities Act and Titles VI and IX of the Civil Rights Act, provide a thicker and more predictable normative context for assessing school choice plans. State statutes and regulations do as well, although many school choice plans are designed precisely to bypass complex webs of state regulation. State constitutional provisions are increasingly giving rise to ambitious judicial orders governing school expenditures and visions of equality.[67] All of these sources of law are vital to a full assessment of the constitutionality and legality of school choice reforms.

Nonetheless, the foundational federal framework clearly preserves a vital role for parents—as partners with the state—in children's education, and roots school choice in this constitutional base. The scarcity of good options makes schools choosers, and this pushes questions of equity and equality to the fore. Even with shrinking latitude for explicit use of racial and ethnic categories in school assignments, school choice plans must avoid worsening patterns of racial and ethnic segregation. Some plans hold promise for promoting integration along these and social-class lines.

Gender equality requires that any state or system engaging in school choice create comparable options for boys and girls. Preventing discrimination the basis of religion may support some arguments for school choice plans that include parochial schools. If public support is involved, however, antidiscrimination norms also should require accommodation by those schools for students of other religions, to the degree consistent with preservation of the character of the participating schools.[68] Children with disabilities should not be left out of the school choice possibilities, although the federal constitutional foundation for this idea is ambiguous at best.

These antidiscrimination and equality norms are simply some of the public obligations that accompany schooling in the constitutionally protected partnership between parents and the government. Other countries work out different relationships among government, parents, and religious groups in the vital project of educating children, and there no doubt are lessons—encouraging and discouraging—for us.[69] But the answers for the United States must be framed by our commitments to individual liberty, equality, and the public good.

The equation that ensures parents choice in their children's education also ensures public values in guiding any school able to satisfy the public requirement of compulsory schooling. Those values include combating discrimination along racial, ethnic, gender, religious, and disability lines, and enhancing equal opportunity for all students. Those values, in sum, include a continuing commitment to schooling as a common enterprise, one that may be enhanced but not waylaid by parental choice.

Many people at the vanguard of school choice reforms embrace this vision. Sara Kass, founder of Boston's City on a Hill Charter School, explained, "There are people in this so-called charter movement who really see this as a chance to break free of public education, [but] we are not among them. We don't take public money to escape from public education. There are 60,000 children in this city, and we have to determine what we are able to do as an institution to leverage wider school changes."[70] Some fear that vouchers and tax benefits for private schools threaten equal opportunity, and I myself have noted the eerie coincidence in timing: choice forms grow just as equality movements crest.[71] But others argue that well-designed privatization approaches can improve student achievement and open options for students the system seems to ignore.[72] If we understand schooling as not only governed by the Constitution but also the precondition for fulfilling constitutional commitments to liberty and equality, then the challenge comes sharply into focus. Parents must be partners with government to ensure that school reforms, including school choice reforms, help forge shared civic culture "in the face of normative diversity."[73]

lishment of religion, or prohibiting the free exercise thereof; or abridging the freedom of speech, or of the press; or the right of the people peaceably to assemble, and to petition the Government for a redress of grievances." Yet according to the authoritative case law—law that is constitutional bedrock in the United States[3]—it is not just "Congress" but all three branches of the national government that may not prohibit the free exercise of religion, abridge the freedom of speech, and so forth. Moreover, it is not just the (whole) national government but the government of every state that may not do what the First Amendment forbids. I have suggested elsewhere that there is a path from the text of the First Amendment, which speaks just of Congress, to the authoritative case law.[4] But even if there were no such path, it would nonetheless be constitutional bedrock in the United States that neither the national government nor state government may either prohibit the free exercise of religion or establish religion (or abridge "the freedom of speech, or of the press; or the right of the people peaceably to assemble, and to petition the Government for a redress of grievances").[5] For Americans at the beginning of the twenty-first century, the serious practical question is no longer whether the "free exercise" and "nonestablishment" norms (as I prefer to call them) apply to the whole of American government, including state government. They *do* so apply. And there is no going back. The sovereignty of the free exercise and nonestablishment norms over every branch and level of American government—in particular, their sovereignty over state government as well as the national government—is now, as I said, constitutional bedrock in the United States. For Americans today, the serious practical inquiry is what it means to say that government (state as well as national) may neither prohibit the free exercise of religion nor establish religion. I have addressed elsewhere, at length, what it means to say that government may not prohibit the free exercise of religion.[6] However, it is not the free exercise norm that bears on the principal question I address in this essay—the constitutionality of school vouchers—but the other constituent of the American constitutional law of religious freedom: the nonestablishment norm. In the United States, what does it mean to say that government may not establish religion? What does the nonestablishment norm forbid government to do?

The idea of an "established" church is a familiar one. For Americans, the best known example is the Church of England, which, from before the time of the American founding to the present, has been the established church in England.[7] (Though, of course, the Church of England was much more established in the past than it is today.)[8] In the United States, however, unlike in England, there may be no established church: The nonestablishment norm forbids government to enact any law or pursue any policy that treats one or more churches as the official church or churches of the political community; government may not bestow legal favor or privilege on one or more churches—that is, one or more churches as such—in relation to one or more other churches or to no church at all. More precisely: Government may not take any action that favors one or more churches in relation to one or more other churches, or to no church at all, on the basis of the view that the favored church is, as a church—as a community of faith—better along one or another dimension of value (truer, for example, or more efficacious spiritually, or more authentically American). The nonestablishment norm deprives government of jurisdiction to make judgments about which church(es), if any, is, as such, better than another church. The norm requires government to be agnostic about which church—which community of faith—is better; government must act without regard to whether any church is in fact better than another.[9] In particular, government may not privilege, in law or policy, membership in one or more churches—in the Fifth Avenue Baptist Church, for example, or in the Roman Catholic Church, or in the Christian church generally;[10] nor may it privilege a worship practice—a prayer, liturgical rite, or religious observance—of one or more churches.[11]

From 1947, when the U.S. Supreme Court first applied the nonestablishment norm to the states,[12] to the present, the justices of the Court have been divided about what it means to say that government may not establish religion.[13] They have been divided both about what the nonestablishment norm means as a general matter and, especially, about what the norm means, about what its implications are, for government aid to religiously affiliated schools. The division among the present justices is as great as it has ever been; the three most-relevant recent cases decided by the Court (in 1995, 1997, and 2000) were decided by a vote of five-to-four or six-to-three.[14] This state of affairs partly explains why I am not interested in ferreting out the Supreme Court's answer to the question of what the nonestablishment norm forbids government to do: There is no such animal. But even if there were such an animal, my principal concern here would not be the Court's answer. The preceding paragraph is meant to state not the Court's answer to the question of what, as a general matter, the nonestablishment norm forbids, but the best answer. Similarly, the paragraphs that follow are meant to present the best answer to the question what the nonestablishment norm means, what its implications are, for government aid to religiously affiliated schools—in particular, government aid in the form of school vouchers. Of course, the best answer may not be the answer a majority of the Court will give if and when the Court finally addresses the question of the constitutionality of school vouchers.

II

Assume that a state legislature, with the support of the governor, has responded to a growing, insistent demand for greater "school choice" in two main ways. First, the legislature has made state funds available to local school districts for the purpose of establishing charter schools.[15] Second, the legislature has funded a statewide voucher program designed to enable poor families to send their children to private (nonpublic) primary and secondary schools. Assume further that the state's new voucher program includes the following five features:

1. Only poor families—families that meet a strict standard of financial need—may participate in the voucher program.[16]
2. The amount of a voucher may not exceed, in any school year, the local school district's average per-pupil expenditure in the preceding school year.[17]
3. Only schools that meet strict requirements concerning curriculum, teacher certification, student performance, and the like may participate in the voucher program.
4. No school that engages in discrimination or other conduct that violates the public policy of the state, or that promotes such behavior, may participate in the voucher program.[18]
5. All private schools, including religiously affiliated schools, may participate in the voucher program if they meet the various requirements of the program.[19]

It is the fifth feature of the state's voucher program that concerns me here: Does the nonestablishment norm forbid the state to permit religiously affiliated schools to participate in the voucher program; that is, does the nonestablishment norm require the state to exclude from the program schools that are religiously affiliated? Or, instead, does the nonestablishment norm permit the state to include schools in the program without regard to whether or not they are religiously affiliated?

The state does not violate the nonestablishment norm by permitting religiously affiliated schools to participate in its voucher program; that is, the state does not necessarily violate the nonestablishment norm by doing do. The reason is simple. By including schools in its voucher program without regard to whether or not they are religiously affiliated, the state is not necessarily taking any action that favors one or more churches in relation to one or more other churches, or to no church at all, on the basis of the view that the favored church(es) is, as a church, truer, or more efficacious spiritually, or more authentically American, or otherwise better; nor, in particular, has the state privileged either membership in or a worship practice of one or more churches. The state may include religiously affiliated schools in its voucher program (or other aid program) if, and only if, two criteria are satisfied. The first criterion speaks to the design of the voucher program; the second criterion speaks to the basis of the political choice to adopt the program.

First: The eligibility requirements for school participation in the program are religiously neutral; school participation in the program does not depend on whether or not the school is religiously affiliated. If this criterion is not satisfied, it is fair for the courts to presume that the political choice to adopt the program is based on the belief that the favored church(es) is, as a church, truer, or more efficacious spiritually, or more authentically American, or otherwise better than one or more other churches or than no church at all. But even if this criterion is satisfied (as in the real world it surely will be), it still may be the case that the political choice to adopt the program is based on—that the program would not have been adopted but for—that belief.[20] In that sense, the program may be a subterfuge: a covert establishment of religion.[21] Hence, the need for this second criterion, which comes into play only if the voucher program satisfies the first criterion.

Second: The state's adoption of the voucher program, though it may operate in some jurisdictions to favor one or more churches (namely, those which in those jurisdictions sponsor many eligible primary or secondary schools) in relation to one or more other churches (those that do not sponsor many or even any such schools), is not based on the belief that the favored church(es) is, as a church, better (truer, etc.) than one or more other churches or than no church at all.[22]

The story of the evolution of the Supreme Court's nonestablishment jurisprudence—that is, its evolution in the context of constitutional controversies over government aid to religiously affiliated entities, especially schools—is an important one. But because the story has been well told elsewhere, there is no need to rehearse it here.[23] For present purposes, I want only to note that four justices of the present Supreme Court have recently espoused a position substantially like the one articulated in the preceding paragraph: Chief Justice Rehnquist and Justices Scalia, Kennedy, and Thomas.[24] The other five justices require that additional criteria be satisfied if a government-aid program is to survive review under the nonestablishment norm.[25]

According to one of the principal additional criteria, if government money is to end up in the pocket of a religiously affiliated school, it must do so not because government gave the money directly to the school, upon certification that an eligible child has enrolled there, but only because the person(s) to whom government gave the money chose to use it to pay expenses incurred in sending her child to that particular school.[26] This direct/indirect distinction seems to me entirely formalistic: I cannot fathom why it should make a constitutional difference that voucher money goes directly to a parent, who then gives it to the school, rather than directly to the school, upon certification that an eligible child has enrolled there.[27] If a voucher program would be constitutional in the former case, then it should be constitutional in the latter case too—and if unconstitutional in the latter case, then in the former case too.[28] But because five justices see the matter differently, no state should adopt a voucher program that does not include the requirement that the voucher money go directly to the parents.[29]

As I said, there is no need to rehearse here the story of the evolution of the Court's nonestablishment jurisprudence. One feature of the story bears brief mention, however: Anti-Catholicism animated not only Protestant opposition to Catholic schools but also judicial opposition (in the name of the nonestablishment norm) to government aid to such schools even when the aid program could not plausibly be said to establish religion.[30] The anti-Catholicism is now largely spent, but not the position, still defended by some Supreme Court justices,[31] some scholars,[32] and others,[33] that government aid to religiously affiliated primary and secondary schools can and often does violate the nonestablishment norm even though (*a*) participation by such schools in the aid program would be pursuant to eligibility requirements that are religiously neutral and (*b*) government's decision to include such schools in the aid program is not based on the belief that one or more churches are, as churches, truer, or more efficacious spiritually, or more authentically American, or otherwise better than one or more other churches or than no church at all.[34] That position took root in the soil of anti-Catholicism, as hisorian John McGreevy and legal scholar Douglas Laycock have each explained.[35] Laycock notes, near the end of his discussion, that

> [r]espectable anti-Catholicism faded in the 1950s and all but collapsed in the 1960s in the wake of the Kennedy presidency and Vatican II. But even at the time of Lemon v. Kurtzman, [403 U.S. 602 (1971)], some justices were influenced by residual anti-Catholicism and by a deep suspicion of Catholic schools. This appears most clearly in Justice Douglas's citation of an anti-Catholic hate tract in his concurring opinion in Lemon [403 U.S. 602, 635 n. 20 (1971)] and in Justice Black's dissenting opinion in Board of Education v. Allen [392 U.S. 236, 251-52 (1968)]. The Court's opinion in Lemon is more subtle and arguably open to more charitable interpretations, but it relied on what it considered to be inherent risks in religious schools despite the absence of a record in Lemon itself and despite contrary fact-finding by the district court in the companion case.[36]

III

The position identified in the preceding paragraph is tantamount to the position that the nonestablishment norm sometimes (often) requires the state to discriminate against religiously affiliated schools vis-à-vis private schools that are not religiously affiliated.[37] As Akhil Amar has recently observed, it is the position of the three justices who dissented in *Mitchell v. Helms*[38]—Justice Souter, who wrote the dissenting opinion, and Justices Stevens and Ginsburg, who joined it—that

> the government may not, pursuant to a genuinely secular law, give computers on a completely evenhanded basis to all public schools and private schools. To put it yet another way: The Constitution requires that if the government decides to give computers to private schools, it may give them to the Secular School and the Indifferent Institute but must withhold them from various religious schools. If a given private school eligible for certain computers later decides to add prayer to its curriculum, while otherwise continuing to teach all the basics, that school must forfeit the computers. The Constitution requires this discrimination, depriving religious schools, and only religious schools, of a benefit that all other schools receive.[39]

Amar's response to this position is correct: "The Constitution, however, requires no such thing, at least if the test is the best reading of its words, history, and structure, as opposed to the many outlandish (and contradictory) things that have been said about it in the United States Reports."[40]

The Mitchell dissenters' construal of the nonestablishment norm is indeed troubling—not only as a matter of the Constitution's "words, history, and structure," but also as a matter of what we may call, for want of a better term, political morality. We can all agree that the state should not discriminate in favor of religiously affiliated schools (because there is no good reason for it to do so). That is, we can all agree that the state should not privilege, in law or policy, either (*a*) some religiously affiliated schools in relation to some other religiously affiliated schools or (*b*) some or all religiously affiliated schools in relation to private schools that are not religiously affiliated. But that the state should not discriminate in favor of religiously affiliated schools does not entail that the state must discriminate against such schools. That it is wrong for government to discriminate in favor of an activity does not mean that it is right for government to discriminate against the activity—any more than that it is wrong for government to discriminate against an activity means that it is right for government to discriminate in favor of the activity. There is no good reason for concluding that the state should discriminate against religiously affiliated schools.

Nor is there any good reason for concluding that the nonestablishment norm should be construed to require the state to discriminate against religiously affiliated schools.[41] In particular, the fact that some persons object to their taxes being spent in a way that has the effect of supporting religiously affiliated schools (even though their taxes are not being spent in a way that discriminates in favor of such schools) no more justifies according constitutional status to their objection, however conscientious it may be, than the fact that some persons object to their taxes being spent in a way that has the effect of supporting—indeed, that is designed to support—military activities, for example, or capital punishment, or abortion (etc.), justifies according constitutional status to *their* objection. "As citizens we are taxed to support all manner of policies and programs with which we disagree. Tax dollars pay for weapons of mass destruction that some believe are evil. Taxes pay for abortions and the execution of capital offenders, that some believe are acts of murder. Taxes pay the salaries of public officials whose policies we despise and oppose at every opportunity. Why is religion different?"[42] Religion does not seem to be different in any relevant way. (Michael McConnell has observed that "religious differences in this country have never generated the civil discord experienced in political conflicts over such issues as the Vietnam War, racial segregation, the Red Scare, unionization, or slavery."[43]) To assert, at this point, that the nonestablishment norm accords constitutional status to the objection of some to their taxes being spent in a way that has the effect of supporting religiously affiliated schools, is to beg the question here, which is whether the nonestablishment norm should be so construed. My argument here is that the nonestablishment norm should not be so construed.[44] Moreover, the claim that permitting religiously affiliated schools to participate in a school voucher program "would compel some taxpayers to support religious schooling with which they disagree"[45] is problematic:

> As long as the voucher amounts do not exceed the value of the secular components of religious schooling, taxpayers in reality will be subsidizing K–12 education, not religion. Given the combination of low tuition and relatively high academic achievement that characterizes the average religious school, it seems clear that the public would almost always get its secular money's worth.[46]

Now, none of this is to deny that one's objection to taxes being spent, whether one's own taxes or someone else's, to fund a state program that "establishes" religion—an aid program whose eligibility criteria are religiously partial rather than religiously neutral or that is based on a belief that one or more churches are, as such, better than one or more other churches or than no church at all—does have constitutional status, in this sense: The nonestablishment norm forbids the state to have such a program. But the nonestablishment norm does not forbid a state to have an aid program whose eligibility requirements are religiously neutral and that is not based on any such belief. And, therefore, one is not constitutionally entitled, under the nonestablishment norm, to have taxes not spent in a way that has the effect of supporting religiously affiliated schools. Thus, the claim pressed by Kathleen Sullivan, the Baptist Joint Committee on Public Affairs, the American Civil Liberties Union, and others, that one's objection to taxes being spent in aid of religious activities has constitutional status is simply mistaken.[47]

Moreover, and unsurprisingly, this mistaken claim has no warrant in American constitutional history. As Justice Thomas explained in his concurring opinion in *Rosenberger v. Rectors and Visitors of University of Virginia*:

> The history cited by the dissent cannot support the conclusion that the Establishment Clause "categorically condemn[s] state programs directly aiding religious activity" when that aid is part of a neutral program available to a wide array of beneficiaries. Even if Madison believed that the principle of nonestablishment of religion precluded governmental financial support for religion per se (in the sense of government benefits specifically targeting religion), there is no indication that at the time of the framing he took the dissent's extreme view that the government must discriminate against religious adherents by excluding them from more generally available financial subsidies.... The dissent identifies no evidence that the Framers intended to disable religious entities from participating on neutral terms in evenhanded government programs. The evidence that does exist points in the opposite direction.[48]

IV

Again, one is not constitutionally entitled, under the nonestablishment norm, to have taxes not spent in a way that has the effect of supporting religiously affiliated schools, because the nonestablishment norm does not require a state to exclude such schools from an aid program whose eligibility requirements are religiously neutral and that is not based on a belief that one or more churches are, as such, better than one or more other churches or than no church at all. That is, the nonestabishment norm does not require a state to discriminate against religiously affiliated schools. Indeed, it is not only inaccurate that, under the nonestablishment norm, the state, in its voucher program, must discriminate against religiously affiliated schools. It is open to serious question whether the state may discriminate against such schools.

Some states do choose to discriminate against religiously affiliated schools. Indeed, in some states this choice has been enshrined in the state constitution, so that as a matter of state constitutional law, the state must discriminate against religiously affiliated schools.[49] But, of course, the U.S. Constitution trumps a state constitution: If the U.S. Constitution forbids a state to discriminate against religiously affiliated schools, no state may do so even if its own constitution requires it to do so; if the U.S. constitution forbids a state to discriminate against religiously affiliated schools, a state constititional provision, insofar as it requires the state to discriminate against such schools, is itself, under the U.S. Constitution, unconstitutional. Assume for the sake of discussion that the Supreme Court has ruled that a state is not required by the nonestablishment norm to discriminate against religiously affiliated schools. Does it then follow that a state is not constitutionally free to discriminate against religiously affiliated schools? More precisely: Does it then follow that the U.S. Constitution forbids a state to exclude religiously affiliated schools from a program of aid for private schools—a program that, were it to include religiously affiliated schools, would not violate the nonestablishment norm? The answer, in my judgment, is that if a state is not constitutionally required to discriminate against religiously affiliated schools, neither is it constitutionally free to discriminate against religiously affiliated schools by excluding them from such an aid program. The strongest argument in support of that answer is a simple one, and it is based on the American constitutional doctrine of freedom of expression.

Here is a bare sketch of the argument: In adopting a program of aid to nonpublic schools, a state is not constitutionally free to discriminate against (by excluding) a nonpublic school because it espouses a particular view, whether partisan or agnostic, on a certain issue. That is, a state is not constitutionally free to do so *unless the school's espousing the view is a state of affairs from which a state must dissociate itself and therefore may not support.* An example of such a state of affairs: a school's espousing white supremacy. Why must a state dissociate itself from a school's espousing white supremacy? Why is a state required to do so, both consitutionally and morally? A state is *constitutionally* required to do so because for a school to espouse white supremacy is for it to reject a fundamental aspect of the constitutional morality of the society, according to which no person is to be deemed inferior to another by virtue of skin color; a state may not cooperate with, it must dissociate itself from, such a view.[50] A state is *morally* required—that is, as a matter of human rights it is required—to dissociate itself from a school's espousing white supremacy because for a school to espouse white supremacy is for it to reject the very idea of human rights, according to which each and every person is sacred and no person is less sacred than another by virtue of skin color.[51] Now, that a state must dissociate itself from a state of affairs—here, a group's espousing a particular ideology—does not entail that the state may outlaw the state of affairs. Perhaps a constitutional provision—for example, the First Amendment's protection of freedom of expression—forbids the state to do so. (With some exceptions not relevant here, the right to freedom of expression surely does forbid the state to outlaw a group's espousing a particular ideology.) But that a state must dissociate itself from a state of affairs *does* entail that a state must not subsidize or otherwise support the state of affairs.[52]

However, there is no reason to think that a state must dissociate itself from a school's espousing the view that God exists, or that Jesus is Lord, or that the Roman Catholic Church is the one true church—any more than it must dissociate itself from a school's espousing the view that God does not exist, or that Jesus is not Lord, or that Roman Catholicism is a false religion, or the view that we do not and perhaps cannot know if God exists, or if Jesus is Lord, or if the Roman Catholic Church is the one true church. In espousing any of these views, a school is not rejecting a fundamental aspect of the constitutional morality of the society. Because a state is not constitutionally required to dissociate itself from a school's espousing any of these views, no state, in adopting a program of aid for private schools, may discriminate against (by excluding) a private school because it espouses any of these views.[53]

Are there other arguments that support the claim that a state may not discriminate against religiously affiliated schools?[54] One possibility: an argument based on the constitutional rule that government not prohibit the free exercise of religion. The free-exercise norm is, whatever else it may be, an antidiscrimination norm. According to my understanding of the norm (or perhaps I should say, according to my understanding of the Supreme Court's understanding),[55] which I have elaborated elsewhere, if a state's exclusion of religiously affiliated schools from its voucher program is based on hostility to one or more churches, then the exclusion—the discrimination—violates the free-exercise norm.[56] It is undeniable—history is clear—that many state policies against extending aid to religiously affiliated schools were originally and conspicuously adopted on the basis of hostility to Roman Catholicism.[57] But today it seems likely that the maintenance of such

policies is based less, if at all, on anti-Catholicism than on one or more
other factors, the principal one of which is an inaccurate understanding of what the nonestablishment norm forbids—an inaccurate understanding abetted by many decisions of the U.S. Supreme Court.[58]

Assume, however, that the Supreme Court changes course and rules
that no state is required by the nonestablishment norm to exclude religiously affiliated schools from its voucher program (or other program
of aid for private schools)—and that a state nonetheless persists in excluding such schools from its voucher (or other aid) program. Does
that make the free-exercise argument more promising? Not necessarily.
The fact remains that a state legislature might well have reasons other
than hostility to one or more churches for continuing to exclude religiously affiliated schools from its voucher program. First, the legislature might disagree with the Court's change of course; it might believe
that, contrary to the Court's new ruling, the nonestablishment norm,
correctly understood, requires the exclusion of religiously affiliated
schools. Second, there might be a provision in the state's own constitution that requires the exclusion of religiously affiliated schools; at least,
the legislature might believe that the provision requires their exclusion.
Third, the legislature might believe that, whether or not the federal
nonestablishment norm or any state constitutional provision requires
their exclusion, it is wiser, all things considered, to exclude religiously
affiliated schools from the state's voucher program than to include
them. One could claim that each and every one of those legislative beliefs—about what the nonestablishment norm requires, about what the
state constitutional provision requires, and about what good public
policy requires—is embedded in hostility to one or more churches,[59]
and that, therefore, excluding religiously affiliated schools on the basis
of one or more of the beliefs violates the free-exercise norm. But surely
it would be difficult, at best, to sustain such a claim. The free-exercise
argument is, at best, problematic.

But even if the free-exercise argument were not problematic, the argument based on freedom of expression would be preferable, for this
reason: Unlike the free-exercise argument, the freedom of expression
argument does not invite judges to inquire into the subterranean attitudes of legislators or other policy makers toward one or more religions or religion generally; it does not require litigants or, if they are
to accept the argument, judges to impute religious hostility (prejudice,
bigotry) to those who defend exclusion of religiously affiliated schools
from state voucher programs.[60] Rather, the freedom of expression argument requires only that litigants claim and judges conclude that in excluding religiously affiliated schools, the state has drawn a line it may
not draw, it has employed a criterion of selection—here, a criterion of

exclusion—it may not employ.[61] In that sense, the freedom of expression argument is focused on legislative "outputs"; the free-exercise argument, by contrast, is focused on legislative "inputs." Unlike the free-exercise argument, therefore, the freedom-of-expression argument avoids what Steve Smith has aptly called "the discourse of disrespect." As Smith has explained, minimizing, in constitutional argument and decision making, the discourse of disrespect is an important virtue.[62]

It is not true that a state must exclude religiously affiliated schools from its voucher program: The nonestablishment norm, correctly understood, does not forbid a state to include such schools. In this respect, a state is constitutionally free to take the path that other liberal democracies have taken. "The United States is one of the few modern democracies that does not provide publicly supported options for parents who prefer to have their children educated in schools that reflect their religious values.[63]

But may a state nonetheless choose to exclude religiously affiliated schools from its voucher program or other program of aid to nonpublic schools? In my judgment, in providing aid to nonpublic schools, no state may discriminate—no state is constitutionally free to discriminate—against religiously affiliated schools. It is not only false that a state *must* discriminate against such schools; it is also false that a state *may* discriminate against them. Again, this is not to deny that there are some ideologies—a racist ideology is the clearest example—from which government should and indeed must dissociate itself, even if the ideologies are religious in character.

Twelve

Charting a Constitutional Course between Private Values and Public Commitments: The Case of School Vouchers

ROSEMARY C. SALOMONE

THE MODERN-DAY STORY of school choice begins three-quarters of a century ago with *Pierce v. Society of Sisters*.[1] The Supreme Court's decision in *Pierce* was a crucial event in the history of American schooling. In striking down the Oregon Compulsory Education Law, the Supreme Court made clear that the state cannot standardize children by forcing them to accept instruction from "public school teachers only." To do so would violate the "liberty" of parents protected under the Fourteenth Amendment due process clause.[2] At the same time, the Court recognized the state's authority to impose reasonable regulations on private schools.

Here the justices struck an uneasy compromise between private values and public commitments. On the one hand, they implicitly affirmed that compulsory schooling should respect the private values that flow from individual conscience and belief. On the other, they acknowledged that since private schools perform a critical public function in promoting the purposes of compulsory education, they must meet minimal standards. The state may require studies that are "essential" and prohibit teaching of anything that is "manifestly inimical" to the public welfare—a very basic concept of education for citizenship.

Pierce essentially granted parents an abstract constitutional right, a freedom to choose private schooling at their own expense for their children. For private schools nationwide, many of them operated by religious and ethnic minorities, this was a monumental victory. More importantly, it was a victory for parents who saw the cost of private school tuition as negligible when compared to the personal benefits gained. In a day when faith in the common school held sway and hostility toward cultural outliers ran high, the *Pierce* compromise seemed reasonable. At the time of the decision, the *New Republic* commented, "Thus came to an end the effort to regiment the mental life of Americans through coerced public instruction."[3] But as the historian David

Tyack much later observed, the *Pierce* decision ended only this chapter of coercion. "The schools would remain a ready target for those who saw perils in pluralism."[4] *Pierce* addressed the immediate crisis, but it also left unresolved deeper and enduring tensions that would intermittently surface through the coming decades.

The rabid nativism and overt anti-Catholicism that gave rise to the statute struck down in *Pierce* have dissipated over the years. Nevertheless, widespread discomfort with and even distrust of religion and faith-based institutions continue to permeate public policy and judicial decision making. The pervasiveness and depth of those feelings have crystallized in recent years in public discussion on state aid to religiously affiliated elementary and secondary schools. That discussion has reached a feverish pitch in the school voucher debate, where legal, political, and policy dimensions are intricately intertwined.

The voucher concept is part of a larger national movement to afford families more choice and voice in the education of their children. Once considered a heresy against the creed of the common school, public funding for attendance at private schools gradually gained cautious support through the 1990s, reaching a high of 44 percent in 1997 and 1998. Since then it seems to be on a slow decline, down to 34 percent in 2001.[5] Vouchers remain by far the least understood and the most controversial among choice options.[6] The shift from a market to an equity model has forged a fragile alliance among business leaders, advocates for the poor, and African American political leaders and clergy who see vouchers as a ticket out of failing inner-city public schools. Yet skepticism toward vouchers still runs high, especially among white suburban voters.

Of all the arguments raised against voucher proposals, support for public schooling has proven the most politically compelling. As a nation of immigrants, we share a sentimental faith in the unifying power of a common school open to all. The charge that substantial state aid to private education might result in cultural isolation and balkanization understandably stirs fear in the hearts of many Americans. Tied to that argument, particularly in urban areas, is the inclusion of religiously affiliated schools. That aspect has proven the most contentious and legally salient focal point for opposition. Religious schools comprise 79 percent of the private school market nationwide and are the most likely to benefit from vouchers, at least for the short run. Existing programs are concentrated in poor communities, where low tuition costs closely match the value of the "scholarship" or voucher. Voucher opponents have used the First Amendment establishment clause and various state constitutional provisions to ward off the forces of pluralism initially unleashed in *Pierce*.[7] In recent years, publicly funded voucher programs have generated litigation in Florida, Illinois, Maine, Ohio, Vermont, and Wisconsin.

The Supreme Court is poised to bring some legal clarification to the voucher issue in a case challenging the constitutionality of the state-funded program operating in Cleveland, Ohio.[8] The likelihood of a favorable Supreme Court ruling is now more probable than it has been since the school-aid wars over a century ago.[9] Throughout the past decade and a half, membership on the Court gradually has become more accommodating toward government aid to religious schools, to the point of overturning prior decisions.[10] With that shift, the broad holding of *Pierce*, that parents have the constitutional right to direct the education of their children, has gained renewed life.

This is not to suggest that the Court would compel the states to fund private education as a matter of constitutional right. Such a ruling would run contrary to the deference the Court historically has shown toward state autonomy over educational policy. While the Court has repeatedly cited *Pierce* to support a private realm of family life protected from state interference, and most recently affirmed that the Fourteenth Amendment due process clause "protects the fundamental right of parents to make decisions concerning the care, custody, and control of their children," it has consistently declined requests to extend these rights into the educational arena.[11] That being said, the promise implicit in *Pierce*, loosened from its moorings in substantive due process liberty, is now searching for qualified reality in alternative constitutional arguments grounded in freedom of religion, equality, and freedom of speech. Assuming even a narrowly favorable Court ruling lifting establishment clause impediments, the way would open for collateral claims whereby any government aid program that defrays the expenses in whole or in part for a student to attend nonreligious private schools must include religious schools as an available option for all unless there exists a compelling governmental reason, apart from church-state separation, for excluding them.

Whether funding for religious schools is merely permissible or mandatory within a larger voucher program, either possibility for some spells near doom for the republic. Whichever way you look at it, vouchers cross the traditional divide between public and private education, lay bare our deepest feelings about religion, and over time could dramatically change schooling as we have come to know it. But we have not yet reached that point. Even setting aside the constitutional question, the underlying political and policy concerns may prove at least equally contentious and difficult to resolve.

In this essay I use the Supreme Court's establishment clause decisions as a framework for examining the tension between private values and public commitments that pervades the voucher debate on all levels. My intent is to push the discussion beyond "religion per se," which has become a flashpoint in a far more complex political conflict, and open the way for a constructive dialogue on vouchers and family choice. In pursuit of that end, I draw upon the nature and function of schooling, evolving views on religion in public life, and the changing realities and increasing diversity within religious education.

The discussion focuses on two constructs that have divided the Court and will likely continue to fragment public policy and discourse even beyond a Court decision. The first is the notion of *private choice* and its relation to the distinction between direct and indirect aid. The second is the concept of *pervasively sectarian* schools and the arguable dangers of religious indoctrination when state aid flows to these schools. I maintain that the first construct is not merely a legal fiction, as some voucher supporters argue, but an important consideration with clear political consequences. At the same time, contrary to what voucher opponents contend, the second is misguided, while the fears that flow from it are misplaced. On this last point I argue that beneath the concerns with religious indoctrination lies a deep skepticism toward religion, which masks and diverts attention from the more probable dangers of political indoctrination irrespective of religious affiliation.

I begin with the premise that among contemporary understandings of the establishment clause is the view that it protects evenhandedly freedom of religious conscience and belief among all members of the political community by minimizing government's influence over personal choices. In that sense, the clause promotes religious equality in terms of equal respect, dignity and inclusion, which at the same time preserving liberty and autonomy. Although not universally accepted, this presents a plausible reading as applied to present-day realities.[12] Those realities include the administrative state with its vast network of benefits and regulations as well as mass compulsory schooling, neither of which existed at the time of the nation's founding. From there I examine the Supreme Court's school-aid cases and especially *Mitchell v. Helms* as a starting point for charting a course on school vouchers that is both constitutionally sound and politically coherent.

Schooling as Values Inculcation

The Supreme Court has affirmed repeatedly that the primary end of state-supported education is to prepare the young for democratic citizenship. In case after case, the justices have noted that schools are the mechanism through which society "inculcate[s] the habits and man-

ners of civility as . . . indispensable to the practice of self-government,"
that they are "vitally important 'in the preparation of individuals for
participation as citizens' and . . . for inculcating fundamental values
necessary to the maintenance of a democratic political system," and
that they are "the most pervasive means for promoting our common
destiny."[13] Among our shared fundamental values, the Court has recognized tolerance for diverse political and religious views, even unpopular ones.[14]

The Court has suggested, however, that while the state has unfettered discretion to enforce the legitimacy of its own views, the interests
of society sometimes outweigh tolerance for the views of individuals
and minority groups. In fact, the Court has made many of these broad
pronouncements on values inculcation in the course of limiting individual rights in favor of government authority. Whether we agree or
disagree with this evolving Court perspective—from a rights-based to
a governance-based ideology of schooling—the truth remains that education is inherently a process of cultural and political normalization
that conveys explicit and implicit messages.

This idea has deep historical roots. The indissoluble link between
education and a good society dates back to ancient Greece. The Greek
paideia, or concept of education, joined citizenship and learning around
a shared set of norms and values under the legal and moral authority
of the *politeia*, or prevailing culture. But for the Greeks, religious life
was bound up with public life, and so religious and civic values were
one and the same. In modern times, Thomas Jefferson fervently believed that republican government demanded citizens of virtue and
intelligence. He promoted government-supported schooling as an instrument for creating citizens who could realize republican and democratic ideals.[15] Jefferson, a nominal Episcopalian but at the same time
an exemplar of Enlightenment rationality, was ahead of his time in de-
parting from the religious and moralistic paradigm of schooling that
prevailed in the colonies.

The connection Jefferson drew between an educated citizenry and a
republican form of government gradually attracted broader acceptance
over the course of the next century. The Northwest Ordinance of 1787,
granting land for the maintenance of schools to new state governments
formed out of the territories west of the Appalachians, directed that
"Religion, Morality, and Knowledge being necessary to good government and the happiness of mankind, Schools and the means of education shall forever be encouraged." Several newly admitted states, including Kentucky and New Mexico, also incorporated into their
constitutions a clause supporting the purposes of public education.[16]

The notion of education for democratic citizenship was the guiding force behind the common school movement of the mid-nineteenth century. For Horace Mann and the early school reformers, universal education was largely a mechanism for social control. Mass compulsory education would instill in children of all classes, religions, and ethnic backgrounds, particularly the foreign-born, the virtues, understandings, and political commitments to function as citizens in a democratic society. The schools would be common in that they would be open to all free of charge, and they would inculcate a common core of values that would serve as the bedrock of an American public philosophy.

This concept was particularly appealing to the emerging Protestant middle class, who saw public education as a way to sustain their values and patterns of life against the onslaughts of immigration. For them, the common school became a means to assimilate the waves of poor, uneducated immigrants, particularly Catholics but also Lutherans and later Jews, washing up on American shores. It was a mechanism for churning out newly minted citizens and maintaining peace and social unity.[17] They fervently believed that public control was essential to the success of their project. In this way they could avoid the dangers of partisanship.[18]

As the common school gradually took hold, it gained a monopoly over public funds for education and effectively abolished the practice of direct government support for private and predominantly religious schooling. At the same time, reformers struck what they believed was a nonsectarian compromise. In an attempt to teach some form of moral and civic values, they infused the school curriculum with what they considered to be widely accepted religious truths. In reality, these truths represented a pan-Protestant-Republican ideology. From the *McGuffey Readers* to history, science, and geography textbooks, references to God and his goodness permeated the curriculum. These "guardians of tradition" taught by rote and as moral absolutes such values as love of country, love of God, and duty to parents. They also inculcated the values of laissez-faire capitalism, urging children to develop habits of thrift, honesty, and hard work as a way to accumulate property.[19]

As the number of immigrants swelled in the second half of the century, the myth behind the neutrality ideal became increasingly more evident. The mainstream Protestant ideology pervading the public school curriculum proved especially offensive to Catholics and Lutherans, who saw it as merely sectarianism in disguise. The Catholic clergy challenged the very premise underlying the common school—that moral education could be separated from religious beliefs. They unsuccessfully pressed for a share of public funds to operate their own schools.

The Catholic question gained national attention in the 1870s in congressional debates surrounding the proposed Blaine Amendment. The amendment would have carved into constitutional stone a prohibition against direct or indirect aid to any religious group and would have prohibited the teaching in public schools of any "religious, atheistic, or pagan tenets." The amendment failed by just several votes in 1876. Yet that did not put to rest overt hostility toward state aid to religious schools. That same year, President Ulysses S. Grant urged that "every child in the land [be given] a common school education unmixed with atheistic, pagan, or sectarian teaching."[20] Congress enacted legislation that required all states admitted into the Union after 1876 to adopt in their constitutions a requirement to maintain a school system "free of sectarian control." By that point in time, fourteen states had adopted laws restricting the use of public funds for "sectarian" schools. By 1890, twenty-nine states had incorporated similar provisions into their state constitutions.[21]

By the turn of the century, as the public school population became more culturally and religiously diverse, there was increased pressure to minimize sources of disagreement. The religious content of the common school curriculum gradually declined under pressure not only from religionists but also from avowed secularists, who publicly urged that moral instruction be grounded in secular rather than religious values. It became less important to Protestantize than to Americanize. The bottom line for school reformers, then as now, was the continued stability and survival of the common school. Overt forms of religious teaching disappeared from the curriculum (although Bible reading and prayer were still commonplace), while moral and particularly political training remained at the core of the public school project.

From here John Dewey and the Progressives more clearly defined the role of the common school to nurture good citizens. They too believed that education should develop in students a common identity, but one secular in nature and based in rational thought. In effect, the religion of the public schools became the religion of democracy. As one commentator has noted, in the wake of religious warfare between Catholics and Protestants, "what seemed to be needed was a 'common faith' which would emerge from the democratic community itself and which would have little or nothing to do with church religion or even with the supernaturalism of Enlightenment deism."[22] In the common school the Progressives also found common ground with a broader populist reform agenda where education would level differences in race, class, and alienage.

Three-quarters of a century later, we still view public education in this light. As new and different waves of immigration render us increasingly diverse, schools continue to serve as a bulwark for preserving our public ideology, an engine of assimilation and social leveling, and a vehicle for interpreting the popular culture and managing the tensions among competing values. Next to the family, public education is the most powerful socializing agent in society, normalizing a dominant ideological perspective that affects both consciousness and behavior.[23] Looked at more critically, public schools have been called "a communications theorist's dream: the audience is captive and immature . . . the messages are labeled as educational (and not as advertising) . . . and a system of rewards and punishments is available to reinforce the messages."[24] The extent of that influence reaches far beyond mere education for citizenship and the transmission of political understandings and culture. From sexual abstinence, to environmental conservation, to the harms of smoking and the merits of capitalism, government schools "prescribe what shall be orthodox."[25]

Both the overt and the "hidden" curriculum undeniably affect the formation of children's self-image, beliefs, and worldviews. The governance structure of the school (hierarchical or democratic); the grading system (numbers, letters, or anecdotal reports); the range and perspective of extracurricular activities (community service, entrepreneurship, sports, or the arts); the role models that teachers provide, including their mode of dress and affect; the importance and substance of exams; the student dress code, if any; the layout of classrooms (lecture or seminar style)—all of these factors are value-laden and send subtle but potent messages to students.[26] It is not surprising, therefore, that some parents decide to educate their children in private schools. There they can exercise greater control over the values their children adopt beyond those essential for democratic participation. Sometimes these private values are tied to religious beliefs, making the matter of choice all the more compelling.

The Constitutional Backdrop

A half-century ago, in *Everson v. Board of Education*, the Supreme Court cast the modern-day template on state aid to religious schools. Here the Court forged a particular historical understanding grounded in church-state separation tempered with neutrality. It also sent a definitive signal to the states that they too would be held to these principles. In *Everson* the justices made clear that the "'establishment of religion' clause" means at the least that "neither a state nor the Federal Government can pass laws which aid one religion, aid all religions, or prefer one religion over another."[27]

In subsequent years the Court has struggled to apply the "no aid" prohibition to a series of state educational initiatives that have progressively challenged traditional notions of public and private. In the process, the Court has selectively and at times inconsistently applied various tests and factors that, in the Court's own words, "sacrifice clarity and predictability for flexibility."[28] The result has been a trail of ad hoc decisions that prove difficult to reconcile on any principled basis. The Court is now laboring to rescue doctrine from an apparent 1950s time warp, squaring case precedent with changing political sensibilities and demographic realities.

The voucher question has put to the acid test the Court's mettle on this score. In reaching a consensus on vouchers, the Court must resolve the public-private tension underlying the principles of neutrality and no aid. Under one, government may provide aid in ways that indicentally benefit religious organizations, while under the other, government may not support an organization's religious purposes. The concept of *private choice* with its tie to the direct-indirect aid distinction as well as the notion of *pervasively sectarian* schools with their alleged dangers of religious indoctrination have loomed large in the Court's deliberations and have proven especially divisive among its members. Both constructs employ conflicting and powerful imagery that draws on the public-private distinction with significant legal and political implications for school vouchers. Both are legacies of the past, the second a remnant of the Court's 1970s fixation on the infusion of religious values throughout the curriculum of parochial schools and the first developed in the 1980s to reconcile a more accommodationist position with prior rulings. And both address the "effect" prong of the three-part test articulated back in 1971 in *Lemon v. Kurtzman*—that is, whether the program has the effect of advancing religion—or a subsequent variant of that test, whether from the perspective of a reasonable observer the program send a message that government is endorsing religion.[29]

Advancement looks toward the institutional relationship between church and state and the substantive effect of government action on religion. Endorsement looks toward the symbolic message conveyed by government action and its effect on how adherents and nonadherents of the controlling denomination perceive their place in the political community. While the *Lemon* test has received wavering support on the Court over the years and four sitting justices have indicated that they would like to set it aside, it still surfaces in some form in state-aid cases. In a similar way, commentators have maligned the endorsement test and particularly its reliance on the "reasonable observer."[30] Nevertheless, it maintains the support of five members of the Court while the remaining four justices have indicated that they too can live with some version of endorsement inquiry, at least for the sake of reaching majority consensus.[31]

Assuming that the soothsayers are right and the voucher question moves in some measure beyond the religion clauses, it will meet strong political resistance in moving beyond religion. Three decades of intense Court wrangling have established a certain tone, language, and set of opposing arguments that have profoundly influenced public discourse on state aid to religious institutions. That being said, the same presumptions, misconceptions, and myths that now cloud the Court's thinking will, if left to fester, turn the post–establishment clause political debate into a war of ideologies and preclude any reasoned discussion on the public and private dimensions of family choice in education.

The Value of Private Choice

The concept of private choice plays a key role in the discussion. But before getting there, the distinction between direct and indirect aid first needs to be unraveled. The Court's continued use of these opposing terms proves thoroughly confusing unless one recognizes that they apply in two contexts. The first examines the end result or effect of government aid. Here the Court often uses the word *direct* along with *substantial* and the word *indirect* along with *incidental* to indicate the degree to which the aid advances the religious mission of the school. The second context considers the path by which the aid reaches the school, whether directly from the government or indirectly through the independent decisions of parents and students. Often the justices elide the two meanings in the same discussion.

Throughout the 1970s the Court followed the rule that all government aid that directly supports the educational function of religious schools is invalid. Many of the cases that the Court addressed in that period concerned elementary and secondary religious schools, most of them Catholic. The justices assumed that the secular and religious functions of these schools were inseparable. Their primary concern was the end result or effect. They believed that, with few exceptions, any aid that went to the school inevitably would become diverted to support the school's religious mission and therefore should be considered direct aid.

Beginning in the 1980s the Court developed a more nuanced position in an attempt to distinguish various programs from those struck down in earlier cases. The Court first set upon this road in *Mueller v. Allen*, upholding a state tax deduction awarded to parents for public and private school expenses even though over 95 percent of the children attending tuition-charging schools were enrolled in religiously affiliated institutions. Here five of the justices gave express constitutional life to "family choice," a concept originally developed in the early 1970s when John Coons and Stephen Sugarman called for the redistribution of education decision making to families across the economic divide. In *Mueller* the justices noted that establishment clause concerns are reduced where "public funds become available only as a result of numerous, private choices of individual parents and school-age children."[32]

The Court drew upon this rationale in subsequent decisions often cited by voucher supporters. In *Witters v. Washington Department of Services for the Blind*, the Court unanimously upheld a state vocational rehabilitation tuition grant paid to a blind student. It was immaterial as far as the Court was concerned that the student used the funds to attend a Christian college that would prepare him for a career as a pastor, missionary, or youth director. In *Zobrest v. Catalina Foothills School District*, a five-member majority, including three new members on the Court (Justices Kennedy, Scalia, and Thomas), upheld the provision of a sign-language interpreter to a deaf student attending a Catholic school. Subsequently five justices affirmed the "private choice" factor in *Agostini v. Felton*, upholding a program that used federal funds to send public school teachers into religious and other private schools to provide remedial instruction to disadvantaged students.[33] Unlike decisions from the 1970s, these latter decisions reflected the Court's opinion that the fact that these institutions might be pervasively sectarian was of little constitutional consequence so long as the aid program was religiously neutral.

The language of "private choice" evokes images of parents and students as free agents in an educational market that includes religious and secular institutions. In that sense it appeals to political conservatives, harkening back to Milton Friedman's free-market voucher proposal almost four decades ago.[34] At the same time, it plays to the liberal imagination, creating a vision of the autonomous individual making unencumbered decisions, the implication being that religion is no more a burden on free choice than any other perspective or source of beliefs. But this linguistic spin has more than symbolic value. In the end, the term "private choice" releases the old "no direct aid" rule from its doctrinal moorings and effectively lays the foundation for a new "neutrality" rule that better supports the desired result. And it does so in a most compelling way.

In each of these post-*Mueller* cases, at least five members of the Court considered the path of the funding stream (through the student) as one among several relevant factors, including the indirect or incidental effect.[35] Meanwhile, in *Agostini* four justices made clear that "even formally individual aid must be seen as aid to a school system when so many individuals receive it that it becomes a significant feature of the system."[36] By the late 1990s, the Court's thinking on this issue had become so muddled and divided that any argument on the "directness" of government aid, either in form or effect, could not be resolved on its own terms.[37]

In *Mitchell v. Helms* in 2000, the Court seemed to break "new ground on crucial issues" but was still divided on several key questions, including private choice. In examining a materials and equipment loan program where no government money ever reached the coffers of religious schools, a plurality of justices essentially abandoned the direct-indirect distinction as both ends and means. In doing so, they gave a more inclusive meaning and more central position to "private choice." Speaking for the plurality, Justice Thomas viewed private choice as a measure of neutrality which, along with that broader principle, has replaced the "no direct aid" rule in preventing government aid to religion. As long as aid is neutally provided pursuant to private decisions, then it is not problematic that the program could fairly be described as providing direct (substantial) aid to the school's religious educational function. As for the path taken by the aid, he admitted that private choice is "easier to see when aid literally passes through the hands of individuals," but to make that an absolute requirement, he noted, "demonstrate[s] the irrelevance of such formalism."[38]

For the plurality, a significant feature of the federal grant program was the per-capita allocation scheme. The state awarded the funds based on school enrollment, which in turn was determined by the independent choices of families. According to this rationale, students and parents retained decision-making control through their initial choice of school and ultimately determined who would receive the funds. The fact that they did not have to apply for the aid for the school to receive it was constitutionally unimportant. The plurality's understanding was that the principles of neutrality and private choice might provide sufficient coverage to allow even cash grants distributed directly to religious institutions. That suggestion, although relegated to a footnote, has significant implications not only for school vouchers but also for other forms of "charitable choice" in the provision of social welfare and health care services.[39]

Justice O'Connor, in a concurring opinion joined by Justice Breyer, also recognized the principle of private choice but was far more concerned about the path by which the aid reaches the school. For her, the distinction between a per-capita aid program and the true private choice programs upheld in previous cases is significant for purposes of advancement and endorsement. When the government provides aid directly to the student, the student who chooses to use the aid at a religious school can "retain control over whether the secular government aid will be applied toward the religious education." In *Mitchell*, the effect of any aid to religious education was the result of private and not government decisions. The opinion weighed in upon the public's perception of the program, applying the principle of the "reasonable observer" who is not "likely to draw from the facts . . . an inference that the State itself is endorsing a religious practice or belief."[40]

If we step back from the *Mitchell* opinions, we see that the distinction between aid distributed directly to religious institutions and a true private choice program is more than the irrelevant formalism that the plurality would have us believe. It has interconnected constitutional and policy dimensions. First, using the family as the conduit for the aid is a factor in preserving First Amendment values and promoting religious freedom. This is so particularly in the case of monetary grants, where indirect funding may strengthen neutrality and evenhandedness. Even with clearly earmarked funds, direct aid lends itself to certain dangers and abuses less obviously present when aid is controlled by individual choice. As in any governmental grant program, the state's decisions are somewhat discretionary and subjective and perhaps could even be biased toward large denominations with existing school organizations while disadvantaging smaller and more decentralized groups. Schools also are more likely to divert direct aid toward capital projects and away from the instructional program, thereby creating even greater dependency on government largesse.[41]

Indirect aid, on the other hand, sends a clear and repeated message to the school that the aid is there for a specific secular public use. It serves as a check against government support to religion-based activities that do not substantially serve a public purpose. In that sense, it helps to assure that government gets "full secular value" for its money.[42] It empowers families and not institutions. When parents believe that they hold the decision-making power on where the aid is expended, they have a higher stake in the outcome. In that sense, they are more likely to hold schools accountable for fully and adequately providing the secular academic components of the program. If not pleased, they can take their voucher elsewhere. As a matter of policy, that level of accountability in turn creates a dynamic climate for innovation where new and existing schools, both religious and secular, compete in an ever-changing market.

Filtering funds through the private decisions of individual families avoids the symbolic union of church and state, which would suggest that government is endorsing particular denominations. In that regard, it protects minority or disfavored religions by minimizing the risk of both perceived and actual government favoritism toward the majority. While procedures, such as requiring parents to endorse voucher checks that the state sends directly to the school (as done in Cleveland), might seem to create a fiction of detachment, they serve a purpose. When it comes to state involvement in religion, not only do appearances matter, but they also help shape reality.

Much of this analysis hinges on endorsement inquiry that admittedly falls far short of providing a bright-line test. In fact, it depends largely on the proclivities and sensibilities of judges standing "in the shoes" of the hypothetical objective observer, who in turn assesses the likely perception of endorsement among members of the community. Over the years, various members of the Court have critically mused as to whether the "reasonable observer" might be "intelligent," "informed," "ideal," or "prescient."[43] More recently, in *Good News Club v. Milford Central School,* the Court attempted to offer some clarity but missed the mark. Upholding the right of an outside group to use public school classrooms immediately after school for activities that arguably included evangelical worship, a majority of the justices (the *Mitchell* plurality plus Justice O'Connor) reaffirmed that such an observer must be "aware of the history and context of the community and forum in which the religious [activity takes place]." As they saw it, the concern here was with the "political community writ large" and not with the *"perceptions of particular individuals"* nor with *"saving isolated nonadherents from discomfort."*[44]

This analysis, however, still leaves serious questions unanswered. Is the reasonable observer a disinterested but informed outsider or the archtypical member of the community? Does he or she have any particularly ideological or political perspective? What defines the political community in the first place? Is it necessarily the larger geographic community, or could it be the community of the school? If the latter, then should the reasonable observer ever take into account the perceptions of arguably "uninformed" children whose understanding of their position within the school community, as either insiders or outsiders, is nonetheless significant? On this last point, Justice Breyer in *Good News Club* parted ways with Justice O'Connor. For him as well as for the dissenting justices, the child's perception was the critical question.[45] But that was in the context of religious speech in a public school setting, where the Court has recognized the impressionability of young students. In the case of state aid to religious schools, the perceptions of the wider community are equally important.[46]

But before leaving the direct-indirect distinction, one final point needs to be made. In *Mitchell*, five of the justices suggested that it may be of some constitutional consequence if the aid actually reaches the coffers of the religious school. Yet if that factor were dispositive, it would undeniably preclude school vouchers or any system of cash grants and severely undercut the principle of private choice. In effect, it would permit only aid in the form of services, materials, and equipment. Even funds that pass through the hands of parent and students inevitably end up on the religious institution's balance sheet. The Court has overlooked this factor in the context of higher education, and there is no apparent justification for considering it in other contexts.[47]

For some members of the Court, however, the result here may turn on the special concerns surrounding government aid to religious elementary and secondary schools. Those concerns include the "pervasively sectarian" nature of at least some of these schools, the risks of diverting aid to the school's religious mission, and the arguable dangers of "religious indoctrination," particularly in the case of younger and more impressionable students.[48]

The Pervasively Sectarian Problem

Over the past three decades, the term *pervasively sectarian* has served as a kind of shorthand among members of the Court for expressing a certain fear that state aid might be used for purposes of "religious indoctrination." As in the case of private choice, here we see the justices using language laden with imagery that gives symbolic force to their doctrine. In doing so, they constitutionally legitimize a legal and political discourse on state aid that continues to hold remarkable currency despite its subjective and outdated assumptions about religion and religious schools.[49]

The term *sectarian* itself demands careful examination for its dark history and its negative connotations. In the nineteenth century, the ruling majority used it to exclude and marginalize groups whose religious beliefs did not match their own standards of cultural appropriateness and respectability. For Horace Mann, President Grant, and various Blaine Amendment supporters, *sectarian* meant the "wrong kind of religion." In the mid-1800s, it was the sectarianism of the evangelical Protestant denominations that gave rise to the allegedly nonsectarian (i.e., mainstream Protestant) curriculum of the common schools. Later in the century, as German and particularly Irish immigration swelled, *sectarian* became a mark of anti-Lutheran and especially anti-Catholic intolerance manifested most clearly in Blaine-type amendments expressly targeting "sectarian" schools in the states. Through the early-twentieth century, even the state courts considered sectarian instruction to be something other than the prayer and Bible reading that was common occurrence in the public schools.[50] The Supreme Court of Nebraska captured the prevailing sentiment when it noted back in 1911, "This is a Christian country, Nebraska is a Christian state, and its normal schools are Christian schools; not sectarian."[51]

In subsequent years, *sectarian* became neutralized or sanitized in ordinary parlance as the equivalent of *religious* in the sense of referring to affiliation with a particular denomination. For the past half-century, the Supreme Court has repeatedly used the term in this contemporary and ostensibly neutral sense. Nevertheless, among the word's common dictionary meanings are a list of pejorative synonyms including "bigoted," "narrow-minded," "heretical," "parochial," and "dogmatic." One wonders to what degree these remnants of past usage continue to subconsciously color the way some of the justices and others involved in the public debate over government aid view the relationship between religion and public life. If religion per se is narrow and bigoted, then it becomes easy to dismiss as harmful to the public good.[52]

When we join "pervasively" with "sectarian," additional issues arise. As an analytical construct, together they speak in absolutist terms. The implication is that these schools are permeated with "sectarianism" through and through, creating a uniform picture of "privateness" and "isolation" that negates their important public function. In the past this concept came into play when the government was allocating funds directly to faith-based institutions and particularly to religious schools. It first appeared in 1973 in the case of *Hunt v. McNair*, where the Court defined such an institution as one in which "religion is so pervasive that a substantial portion of its functions are subsumed in the religious mission."[53] Subsequently the Court has considered factors such as the institution's degree of autonomy from a religious organization, the presence or absence of religious indoctrination, the degree of compliance with normal academic standards, the proportion of faithful followers among students and faculty, and the relevance of religion in the selection of students and faculty.[54] How many of these factors might be determinative and which, if any, carry more weight remains open to question. In *Mitchell v. Helms* the dissent relied on a corollary to the *Hunt* definition, quoting from the Catholic Code of Canon Law and concluding that "religious teaching in such schools is at the core of the instructors' individual and personal obligations."[55]

It was fairly straightforward for the justices to apply the *Hunt* definition in a time when they could do so formulaically, assuming that all religious schools that could potentially benefit from aid programs could not separate their secular from their religious functions. That might have been the case in the 1970s, when Catholic schools were the primary potential beneficiaries of aid programs challenged in the courts and when these schools as a group more closely fit the definition. Fast forward three decades to the heterogeneous and almost idiosyncratic realities of religious schools today, and this factor becomes judicially unmanageable. It also becomes constitutionally inconsistent and even suspect in view of the protection that the Court now affords religious speech as viewpoint under the First Amendment free speech clause. And as a matter of policy, it is difficult to reconcile with a more recent national consensus on the role of religious expression, activities, and study in the public schools.

Given the increasingly wide diversity among religious schools, exactly how might a court determine what constitutes a *substantial* portion of the school's functions and whether it is *subsumed* into the school's religious mission without probing into the significance of the school's religious tenets and making subjective and potentially arbitrary determinations on its policies and curriculum? It is reasonable to assume that all accredited private schools at least partially serve a public function. Why must the public function be totally separable from the religious function? Given the fact that values pervade the entire educational enterprise, is separability a reasonable requirement? Outside of prayer and religious worship or clear instruction in religious doctrine, some and perhaps many of the values infused into the curriculum of religious schools are not solely religious and are equally justifiable on secular grounds. Although religious values may suffuse the secular concerns of many religious schools, secular welfare is the direct goal of much religious teaching.[56] The Court itself has noted that the mere fact that views espoused on particular subjects may coincide with the religious views of an organization is not sufficient to show that the aid is advancing religion.[57] Where the dividing lines are so unclear, it is understandably difficult if not impossible for religious schools to segregate the secular from the religious.

Public education, in fact, has violated that mandate in recent years with the approval of all three branches of the federal government. As public schools have opened their doors to religious subjects and practices, the line between the sacred and the secular has become increasingly blurred. In 1995 and again in 1998 and 2000, the secretary of education at the request of President Clinton distributed to the nation's fifteen thousand school districts a set of guidelines for accommodating religion. The president himself publicly stated that "nothing in the First Amendment converts our public schools into religion-free zones or requires all religious expression to be left at the schoolhouse door." For over a decade and a half, the federal Equal Access Act has permitted public school secondary students to meet on school grounds during noninstructional time even for purposes of religious worship. A decade ago, the Court upheld the act against an establishment clause challenge. In the meantime, groups from across the political and religious spectrums have endorsed several important and far-reaching documents affirming the role of religion in public education.[58] Religious pluralism has now replaced the public school norm of separationism.[59] Yet if state aid can facilitate a wide range of religious curricular and extracurricular activities in public schools without running afoul of the establishment clause, it defies reason to use that very legal argument as the basis for denying aid to private religious schools.

This is not to overlook several important differences between these two sectors. In an official sense, public schools *teach about* various religions from a historical and cultural viewpoint while religious schools *foster belief in* a particular religion from a doctrinal perspective. And under current case law, religious speech or worship on public school grounds during the schoolday is permissible only where it is organized by the students and not school officials.[60] In the context of public education, the school and the state are one entity and the perception of government endorsement is a relevant factor. Here we use the student as the "causative agent" to soften or mute the message of such endorsement.[61] Religious schools present a different picture. While some religious speech might be initiated by students, much of it is initiated by the school, which engages in a significant amount of religious speech. There is no question that the school is endorsing religion. However, that fact is irrelevant for establishment clause purposes because the school is a private entity and not the state.

At least at the elementary and secondary school levels, a significant establishment clause concern in the religious speech cases turns on the coercive effect that school-sponsored speech has on public school students who do not embrace the majority's religious views.[62] This goes back to the "captive audience" argument. Parents are compelled under state law to send their children to school. For those who lack either the economic resources to choose a private alternative or the ability or interest to home school their children, the public schools are the only available option. The endorsement and coercion tests have related aims—that is, to protect religious minorities from feeling like political outsiders in the given community or feeling pressured into a religious practice contrary to their own beliefs. These factors gain heightened importance in the case of schoolchildren and adolescents where peer pressure and the push toward conformity constitute a potent influence on their behavior and psychological well-being.

In the public school context, the Court's analysis has been contextual, whether it is prayer at football games and graduation ceremonies or the right of student groups to meet or distribute religious literature on school grounds. The resolution seems to hinge not only on government endorsement, but also on voluntarism versus coercion. Religious speech per se does not offend the establishment clause, but it may for example, where it has a coercive or negative impact on other students. Most recently, however, in *Good News Club v. Milford Central Schools*, five members of the Court including Justice O'Connor stretched the outer bounds of coercion and religious speech rights. To their mind, the relevant community was the parents who chose whether or not their children would participate, and not the children themselves, who could not join without their parents' permission.[63]

The argument can be made that the dangers of coercion do not arise in the context of religious schooling. Here the community is substantially homogeneous from a religious perspective, while those students who do not adhere to the institution's beliefs have agreed voluntarily (or at least their parents have agreed) to attend under these conditions. Therefore, the fact that school officials are organizing the activities in religious schools does not impose the same harmful coercive effect on students as it would in the public school setting.

So if religious ideas per se are not impermissible in *public* schools and the problem of coercion does not exist in *religious* schools, the only issue that remains is the danger of government endorsement. And the fact that religious speech may be intricately intertwined with the secular speech funded by the government does not necessarily implicate the state in the religious message or divert state aid to religious teaching per se. This is so particularly where the amount of the voucher is less than the per-capita allocation to the public schools. In this case, school officials do not clearly represent the state, while any danger that the public might interpret state aid as religious endorsement could be addressed by neutrally allocating funds to families and not directly to religious schools. If the program is indirectly available to religious and other schools, if parents determine where the funds end up, and if the government arguably funds only the value of secular instruction, then the public would not reasonably attribute to the government the religious content of the private school curriculum.[64]

Fears of Religious Indoctrination

Public funds now support religious expression and discussion in the public schools as long as the expression does not appear to coerce non-believers into participation or affirmation or convey a message of government endorsement. Then why not afford similar state support to religion in the private sector? The answer seems to lie in the dangers of religious indoctrination. As some members of the Court have viewed the matter, those dangers become heightened in pervasively sectarian schools. On this point *Mitchell v. Helms* sheds interesting light on the current distinct views among the current justices on religion and religious institutions. Some of these views are obsolete in their absoluteness.

For Justices Souter, Ginsburg, and Stevens, the dangers of religious indoctrination loom so large that any form of secular aid that might conceivably be diverted to religious use would be constitutionally suspect. Even aid that presents no appearance of endorsement would still "violate a taxpayer's liberty of conscience, threaten to corrupt religion, and generate disputes over aid."[65] And while Justice O'Connor's fears were more measured, she nevertheless expressed some discomfort with religion. She correctly appreciated that neutrality is not enough and that there are differences among religions and religious institutions. But rather than assume that pervasively religious schools would inevitably divert funds to their religious mission, she would require evidence that the aid actually has been diverted substantially for religious purposes. At the same time, she suggested that if the aid goes to the entirety of the program, any religious indoctrination that takes place could be "directly attributable to the government." This could pose a problem for school vouchers. Yet it seems that she also would consider other factors, including the neutrality of the selection criteria, the directness of the aid, and the degree to which the voucher supplements rather than supplants the basic educational program.[66]

Here again the loaded terminology creates a perception and mindset toward religious schools that admits of few exceptions. Why "indoctrination" and not "religious teaching"—a more neutral term? Why not distinguish between teaching from a religious viewpoint and religious proselytizing or worship? Indoctrination suggests that religion imposes some palpable harm that ultimately reaches into society. But the specific harm remains unclear. Does it lie in the potential erosion of religious autonomy when the government extracts concessions in exchange for funding? If that is the case, assuming the concessions are reasonable and do not infringe on constitutional rights, any negative impact on the religious mission is the result of private choices made by parents and participating schools. Is the establishment clause intended to save religion from weighing its own priorities and assessing its own needs?

Some commentators have argued that government funding of religious beliefs and activities may violate the conscience of taxpayers who find offense in the ideas and values taught.[67] That argument falls apart when you consider the numerous tax-supported programs, from environmental conservation to military spending and drug education, that offend the beliefs and sensibilities of countless taxpayers. Where the government funds a wide range of private schools that have a secular purpose (i.e., education) and religious schools are included on a neutral basis, the taxpayer argument has little merit.[68] Of course, it can also be argued that religion is far more central to an individual's "reason for being" than philosophical or political beliefs on policy issues, no matter how deeply felt, yet any of the above-mentioned objections reasonably could stem from religious motives.

Is there a potential danger of political divisiveness along religious lines? In recent years, it appeared that the Court had swept this factor into the dustbin of history. Yet the dissent in *Mitchell* warns us that "the more generous the support, the more divisive would be the resentments of those resisting religious support, and those religions without school systems ready to claim their fair share."[69] Such fears might have carried more credibility four decades ago when Catholic schools comprised 65 percent of all private schools and 75 percent of all religious schools nationwide and educated 90 percent of the students attending religious schools. With those figures now down to 30 percent of the private schools, 38 percent of religious schools, and 59 percent of religious school students, the religious fault lines have become less distinct. Meanwhile, the time-worn concern over Catholic versus Protestant religious conflict has outrun its course.[70]

The dramatic change in these figures represents a renewed interest in religious education among various groups. It also reflects shifting migration patterns transforming us into a more religiously diverse nation. Both factors have broadened the potential support base for aid to religious education. Today, evangelical and fundamental Christians, various African American denominations, Orthodox and Conservative Jews, and a growing population of Muslims operate almost half of the religious schools nationwide, with the largest enrollment among them in conservative Christian schools. Considering the growing population of non-Catholics in Catholic schools, it can safely be said that Catholics no longer dominate the student population of religious schools.[71]

The fear of "religious side effects," while questionable in itself, seems peripheral to the argument when you consider the language of indoctrination. If that is the case, then the use of the term seems gratuitous at best. But given its emotive power, this is no mere linguistic lapse. To the contrary, similar to the "pervasively sectarian" question, it reveals a deep-seated, unspecified, and probably unconscious lingering fear among some of the justices. And what they fear is not merely religious worship, but the teaching and learning from a religious viewpoint that arguably takes place in religious schools. They seem to imply that there is something inherently dangerous, or as Stephen Carter has stated, "scary" about religion, that religious ideas and values are inevitably contrary to the public values that we share as a nation.[72] This position negates the fact that religious schools perform an important public function in developing secular understandings that prepare future citizens. Unlike race discrimination or bigotry, religion is not "intrinsically evil."[73]

The dissent in *Mitchell* underscored this slowly fading undercurrent in the Court's thinking. Here three of the justices singled out one denomination, the Catholic Church, and drew selectively from the *Catholic Code of Canon Law*. I raise this here not to impute any anti-Catholic animus on the part of the justices, but merely to demonstrate their failure to appreciate the variations within and among religious schools, the nuances of religious teaching, and their abiding belief that the secular must be totally separated from the sacred to justify state aid. They use Catholic schools as an example of institutions that are "pervasively sectarian" and therefore pose the danger of "religious indoctrination." To support this conclusion, they specifically cite a requirement within the *Code* that bishops establish and regulate schools "imparting an education imbued with the Christian spirit." Yet one has to ask whether such an education is necessarily antithetical to democratic values. It can certainly be argued that many Christian beliefs, such as concerns for social justice and the poor, actually affirm those values.

Research evidence bears this out. More than three decades ago, Andrew Greeley and Peter Rossi challenged the assumption that religious subcultures are harmful to society. To the contrary, they found higher degrees of tolerance among Catholic school students than others.[74] Subsequent findings confirm that Catholic schools embrace the very social and political purposes, including belief in the dignity of all human beings and "a shared responsibility for advancing a just and caring society," that once lent public schools the title of "common schools."[75] More recent data compiled by the federal government indicate that nonpublic school students in general are more likely to participate in community service than are public school students. Among all high school seniors, 22.3 percent of students in Catholic schools, 31.2 percent in nonreligious private schools, and only 9.7 percent in public schools report that they engage in these activities on a weekly basis.[76] These findings confirm those drawn from the 1996 National Household Education Survey, a nationally representative survey of parents and children. Here Catholic school students were not only more active in voluntary community service, but they displayed more political knowledge and political tolerance than those attending public schools, although students attending religious/non-Catholic schools scored substantially lower than either group. Particularly in light of recent terrorist attacks stemming from religious extremism, it is tempting to conclude from these findings that some religious schools might breed intolerance. That might be so, but an alternative explanation is that students' attitudes are influenced at least as much by family background as by the schools they attend.[77]

For many religious schools, social morality and civic virtue are mutually supportive. As a concrete example of this synergy, I offer the five educational goals articulated by a highly regarded religious school in San Francisco: developing in its students "personal and active faith in God," a "deep respect for intellectual values," and a "social awareness which implies action," while at the same time "building community as a Christian value" and "fostering personal growth in an atmosphere of wise freedom."[78] I doubt if these goals, common among religious schools, would bring the term *indoctrination* to the minds of most reasonable people.

In *Mitchell*, the dissenting justices noted that the "youth" of the students in primary and secondary religious schools "makes them highly *susceptible* to religious indoctrination."[79] The imagery here is indeed powerful. It suggests that religious teaching is something akin to "brainwashing," conjuring up visions of innocent children forcefully accepting a body of closed beliefs at the hands of manipulating authority figures. Again, this may indeed be true for a minority of religious schools. From an objective perspective, such fears were also reasonable when parochial schools were largely staffed by women dressed in medieval garb and who had little contact with the outside world, when Catholics were thought to owe their first allegiance to the Pope and not to their country, and when they were bound by church law to educate their children in Catholic schools. It goes without saying that Catholic schools have departed significantly from that profile. Fears of totalistic papal control over secular views died with the 1960 presidential election and Vatican II's Declaration of Religious Freedom, while the *Code of Canon Law* now offers Catholics various options in providing their children with religious education. Laypersons far outnumber the clergy among the faculty of Catholic schools, nuns can barely be distinguished, if at all, by their mode of attire while many live and work in daily confrontation with the harshest realities of urban life, and the instructional programs and materials used in the schools are within the educational mainstream.[80]

Over the past three decades, Catholic schools in particular have become the "model" religious schools in terms of their acquiescence to state regulation, their utilization of conventional instructional practices, their willingness to educate students regardless of religious background, their relatively high achievement test scores, and the key educational and social role they now play in urban communities. Data show that the percentage of non-Catholics among the Catholic school population is now significant, particularly in poor urban communities: 19.5 percent in the Archdiocese of New York, 20 percent in Detroit, 20.5 percent in Newark, 22.4 percent in Baltimore, and 23.7 percent in Washington, D.C.[81] Most of these students are racial minorities whose families seek for their children a value-based, intellectually rigorous, and physically safe education, and not necessarily one grounded in Catholic doctrine.

As these schools have come increasingly to serve the inner-city "working poor," they have relied more heavily on government funding. At the same time, increased government aid, including state textbook-loan programs; student transportation reimbursement; and federally funded remedial, drug awareness, and special education programs have moved the Catholic school curriculum to resemble more closely that of the public schools. Whether these changes serve the religious mission of these schools in the end is debatable. Vouchers may indeed be the Trojan Horse coming into town, but that question is unrelated to the constitutional issue. The dissenting justices in *Mitchell* nonetheless noted that "parochial schools, in large measure, do not accept the assumption that secular subjects should be unrelated to religious teaching." That assumption itself is wide open to challenge, based as it is on the questionable belief that religion is harmful or dangerous. Must secular instruction be totally devoid of any religious references to be eligible for state aid? But on a more practical level, although Catholic schools might strive to relate secular subjects to religious teaching, that may say little about the realities of their everyday practices.[82]

This failure to distinguish between the aspirations and the widely recognized facts of Catholic education suggests that Catholic schools have become the "straw men" in the state-aid controversy. They present an acceptable public example, for argument's sake, in a more com-

plicated political debate. That debate touches on fears not only of religious and political conservatism, but especially of views expressed and
values espoused by less mainstream religious groups for whom the
cultural separatism of vouchers might hold particular appeal. Whatever perceived threat arose from state aid to Catholic schools over the
past century now resides in less-familiar minority and immigrant religions and, principally, forms of fundamentalism that have moved into
the private school market. The concerns raised in the public debate
now raging over proposals to award grants to faith-based organizations and community groups lend credence to that conclusion. One of
the repeated questions asked is whether government should fund so-
cial-welfare programs sponsored by controversial groups such as the
Nation of Islam or the Church of Scientology.[83] This and similar contentious issues aired in that context undoubtedly will influence public
opinion and perhaps dampen political enthusiasm for school vouchers.

I assume that what the justices mean by religious indoctrination is
values inculcation. But schooling by its nature is inherently value-
laden in the interests of what can be considered "political indoctrination." The core purpose of the common school since its beginnings has
been to socialize, indoctrinate, and assimilate. That history and continuing reality differentiate schools from other mediating institutions of
civil society. It also goes to the heart of the religion clauses—to prevent
government compulsion in matters of conscience. While values might
influence the type of services offered and the approaches taken by
other faith-based institutions, the inculcation of values is not necessarily integral to the purpose of the services that they render—that is, the
services have a secular public purpose not based in personal values.

Yet this comparison also contains a paradox. In the case of schooling
the political stakes (the preservation of democracy and social stability)
are much higher and the state's interest is more compelling as compared with other social services such as health, or drug rehabilitation,
or homeless shelters. Schooling, like no other social program, serves a
vital public function to the point where the state has made participation compulsory. In contrast with most forms of charitable choice, education raises more serious state concerns related not only to the quality
of the services provided but also to the messages conveyed. At the
same time, however, the compulsory nature of schooling and its profound influence on shaping the child's character and worldview demand greater sensitivity to the private values implicit in individual
family beliefs.

But if we agree that private schools serve an important public purpose and that religion is not inherently harmful to the social order, then
underlying fears of religious indoctrination lose their grounding, es-

sentially bankrupting the religion argument against government aid to education. With that argument removed from the discussion, we then can appreciate the real danger in state aid to nongovernmental schools, which is not religious but political indoctrination. The problem is not that taxpayers may disagree with the religious ideas that these schools convey, as some have argued, but that largely insulated from public view, they may undermine important public values at public expense.

This is not to deny that conventional voucher proposals support the core educational program, which at least some religious schools infuse with religious teachings. Some of those teachings might promote values that are outside the cultural and social mainstream, such as highly gendered roles for women and men. Others might undermine core political and legal commitments, such as racial equality and religious tolerance, commonly developed in the crucible of the common school. Although this problem might prove more easily identifiable in religious schools, it is not unique to them. The same potential holds for private independent schools. In fact, it even holds for some public schools, as history continues to demonstrate, depending on the values of the ruling majority in the community. Certainly resistance toward racial integration and persistent efforts to inject prayer into the public schools lend credence to that point. And while some commonly contested values, such as those concerning the role of women in society, or alternative lifestyles, or child discipline, might stem from deeply held religious beliefs, both these and others might have no grounding whatsoever in religion.

Nevertheless, a mass infusion of state aid to private schools, religious or otherwise, in the form of vouchers will inevitably give rise to constitutionally and politically significant equality, privacy, and justice issues. Should state aid go to groups, such as the Ku Klux Klan and the Aryan Nations, that teach racial hatred? What about schools that teach the subordination of women, or discriminate against homosexuals, or deny students basic due process protections? Should participating schools be prohibited from using religion as a criterion for faculty hiring or student admissions? Must schools provide an opt-out from religious activities that students find offensive? Will the state monitoring necessitated by vouchers excessively intrude into the affairs of religion?

These are indeed complicated questions, some of which admit of no easy answers. Private values, however, must at times yield to important public commitments, and state regulation of secular activiites inevitably will be the necessary price to be paid for public funding. The state might address these problems through constitutional norms under the Fourteenth Amendment equal protection clause and federal and state civil rights statutes that place constraints on the expenditure of government funds, or through state testing requirements and financial incentives such as textbook loan programs and consortiums organized for enrichment activities. Meanwhile, individual schools might challenge such restrictions as unconstitutional conditions on their ability to enjoy the benefits generally available to the public.[84]

The details of these strategies and potential responses are beyond the scope of this discussion. Yet when we scratch beneath the surface of the traditional arguments against state aid to religious schools, it becomes increasingly clear that whatever legal or policy problems such aid programs might bring, the source is not religion per se and the solution is no longer to be found in the establishment clause of the First Amendment.

Conclusion

Education serves a crucial public purpose in preparing young people for democratic citizenship. From the very beginnings of the republic, privately operated schools have played an important role in promoting that end. Government aid to such schools undeniably presents risks that may jeopardize that purpose. Contrary to popular perception, however, religious beliefs are only one source of those risks. It therefore is unreasonable to single out all religious schools or even the most "pervasively" religious and deny them government funds as a matter of constitutional law if, as a society, we are truly committed to equality of respect and freedom of conscience. In fact, to do so would set the establishment clause on a collision course with equality and free speech principles. As the Supreme Court inches toward a majority consensus and moves beyond religion, the politically constructive alternative is to explore policies that address specific conflicts between private values, religious or otherwise, and the public commitments that justify reasonable government regulation within a program of evenhanded support.

Response

PATRICK McKINLEY BRENNAN

THE CONSTITUTION OF THE UNITED STATES, architectonically among the components of our *legal* order, would constitute us a people and a people of a certain sort—persons who through state action must or may do some things, persons who must not do others. The three essays comprised in this section concern the implications of that Constitution for how we constitute ourselves specifically through schooling, that cardinal component of the overall architectonic through which we humans make ourselves the sort of people we shall be. The authors are exploring what *our Constitution* means for vouchers, regimes of government funding that would allow parents to choose their children's schooling, even schooling that advances religion. They ask, in effect, whether we are a people who can constitutionally constitute ourselves—or are rather a people who would render ourselves unconstitutional—issuing vouchers and redeeming some of them in schools that teach, say, that Jesus *is* Lord.

These are weighty considerations, most aptly undertaken in the face of a hot-button issue touching religion and neutrality, parents and children, poverty and equality, civic order and toleration. It is a strength of these essays that they all give voice to the sober judgment that our Constitution is meant to be a weight, a heavy weight, in favor of some ways of living and against others. It is also a strength of theirs that their authors know that the Constitution is, nonetheless, only a piece of paper—almost weightless and a suitable resting place for a paperweight—unless and until it be given weight. Constitutions that are nobody's repose under glass in museums. A constitution constitutes a people when it is given the weight of incarnation, when it shapes the minds and lives of the women and men who call it their own.

The passage from the black marks on the constitutional page to living arrangements that are *constitutional*, is—if a question of constitutionality arises and is pressed—through judicial judgment as to whether arrangement *x* "meets," as they say, "constitutional muster." Which just means that sonorous phrases must be made—or rather, judges and then justices looking to sonorous phrases must choose hon-

estly—to answer the question, Does this specific scheme satisfy the enacted aspiration of the American people to constitute themselves according to their Constitution? While the activity of interpreting the
Constitution cannot go forward in a vacuum of practical reasoning,
still Professor Perry is right to insist, as he does at the outset, that "we
disserve careful analysis of difficult issues by conflating, or confusing,
the question of the constitutionality of a government program with the
different question whether, apart from the question of its constitutionality, the program is sound public policy."

The process of discerning constitutionality is freighted in a peculiar
way when the sonorous phrases at issue include "establishment of religion" and "the free exercise thereof." Written into the Constitution's
First Amendment, ratified by the several states, they were to be limitations on "Congress," limitations on the legislative arm of the central
government. It was only in the 1940s that the Supreme Court of the
United States held them to be limitations, moreover, on the power of
state and local government—the governmental arms ordinarily closest
to the intimate creations that are schools and religious instantiations.
From that moment, and all of a sudden, the judges and justices of
courts created under Article III of the United States Constitution found
themselves, along with members of states' judiciaries, called upon to
decide the constitutionality of a whole range of local creations touching the most sensitive parts of life. Wise counselors today note that the
Supreme Court entered without doing the requisite homework.[1] The
result, as to which there is scholarly unanimity or close to it, is that the
Supreme Court has entangled the religion clauses of the First Amendment in a web of antinomies.[2]

But that's the way it is, and so we should be particularly grateful
that Professors Perry, Salomone, and Minow enter where angels are
prudently absent. They write as friends of the Court, keenly aware that
ineluctably from within a morass of its own creation, the Supreme
Court, after years of avoidance, is likely soon to say yes or no to school
vouchers that will have the effect of advancing religion. From a welter
of conflicted and sometimes confused precedents, as good lawyers
they write briefs for the Court, and as seekers of worthy constitutional
ways they plot for us all possible next steps in what John Noonan has
aptly described as the "pilgrim's process,"[3] by which the American
constitutional experiment goes whither it will go. Each of these essays
evinces a deep deployment of the insight that we are all, citizens and
amici curiae along with judges, "part of an experiment," what James
Madison called the American "experiment" in freedom of religion, and
that by now we "have two hundred years of experience" in a "process"
that "has [already] replaced religious war with litigation."[4]

Professor Perry zeros in on the religion question, seeking "the best answer to the question what the nonestablishment norm means, what its implications are, for government aid to religiously affiliated schools—in particular, government aid in the form of school vouchers." Professor Salomone, also pursuing the religion question, begins with the "contemporary understanding" of the "establishment clause"—which she characterizes as a "reasonable reading"—according to which "it protects individual freedom of conscience and belief by minimizing government's influence over personal choices." She then uses the 2000 Supreme Court decision in *Mitchell v. Helms*,[5] where a sharply divided Court upheld against an establishment clause challenge to a federal materials and equipment loan program that benefited religious as well as nonreligious private schools, "as a starting point for charting a constitutional course on school vouchers." And Professor Minow, finally, facially more concerned to "predict Supreme Court interpretation of the Constitution . . . than [to] develop ideal constitutional theory," wisely insists upon the unexceptionable point that the constitutionality of voucher schemes must be assessed not just in light of their religious dimensions, but also in light of their capacity to advance or retard equality and liberty, which of course the Constitution also protects.

Professor Minow notes, in this connection, "the fundamental constitutional commitment in the United States to parental choice in educating children." The reference is to the venerable 1925 case of *Pierce v. Society of Sisters*,[6] in which the Supreme Court held unconstitutional an Oregon statute requiring that all eligible students attend public schools. The Court reasoned, on the strength of the due process clause of the Fourteenth Amendment, that parents enjoy a constitutional liberty to choose not to send their children to public schools because "the fundamental theory of liberty upon which all governments in this Union repose excludes any general power of the State to standardize its children by forcing them to accept instruction from public teachers only." The Court continued, in its next sentence: "The child is not the mere creature of the State; those who nurture him and direct his destiny have the right, coupled with the high duty, to recognize and prepare him for additional obligations."[7]

Professor Minow nicely catches the "sharp" "irony" in the Court's use of the possessive pronoun "its" to describe "children" as at least in part the state's. She then notes the salutary result of this sharing of the child: "The child thereby will be prepared for citizenship, and may, at the parents' election, also be prepared to fulfill additional obligations to religion, military service, or other commitments." In this Minow finds a laudable American commitment to "pluralism." I find in addition, ironically in the same language, an affirmation of a *duty*, a "high duty," to assist the child to recognize and observe "obligations." Right and duty arise together, or at least they did in *Pierce*.

Talk about duty—not to mention "high duty"—will rankle in ears enamored of a certain sort of rights talk. But our very right to free exercise of religion, written into our Constitution, and the correlative exigence that government not establish religion, arose in the mind of its father, James Madison, from that highest duty of man to his creator. Madison fought for free exercise for everyone, as John Noonan has shown so elegantly, from a "mere duty": "The duty was mere; the prescribing authority was supreme. It was supreme because it was not just an inner tickle, a subjective unease: it was for [Madison] the actual voice of another, a communication, a command. . . . The radicalness of [Madison]—should we say the madness of Madison—was to suppose that each individual has a zone in which he or she responds to the voice of God, a zone beyond political authority."[8] That zone was what Madison called "conscience," of which in his *Memorial and Remonstrance* he wrote: "The Religion then of every man must be left to the conviction and conscience of every man; and it is the right of every man to exercise it as these may dictate. This right is in its nature an unalienable right. It is unalienable; because the opinions of men, depending only on the evidence contemplated by their own minds, cannot follow the dictates of other men: It is unalienable also, because what is here a right towards men, is a duty towards the Creator."[9] Madison was realistic enough to be certain that people would hear the voice of the Creator in conscience differently, and this too was for him a firm reason to free people to follow the God they heard.

To read Madison, to follow his line of reasoning to religious freedom and disestablishment, is to be elevated. To read what the Supreme Court has done to the religion clauses of the First Amendment is to be cast down. Many of its opinions reaching religion breathe prejudice and misunderstanding. Just the other day, in the 2000 *Mitchell* case, the fear that Catholic grammar schools are crucibles of "'pervasively sectarian'" indoctrination sent Justice Souter scurrying to the *Code of Canon Law* for evidence for the credulity-straining conclusion that aiding a Catholic school is "akin to aiding a church service."[10] Examples of cultured misunderstanding could be multiplied. They grow in a rhetorical chamber of the Court's creation—deftly and fairly deconstructed by Professor Salomone—that makes religion seem spooky and just the sort of thing best early and often exiled from education.

But the Justices misconceiving religion, like those who have grasped its essence, are, all of them, right if they conclude that religiously supported education is about conveying values, what in an older idiom would be respectfully described as imparting true doctrine. As Professor Salomone insists, however, all "schooling is by its nature . . . value laden in the interests of what can be considered 'political indoctrination.' The core purpose of the common school since its beginning has been to socialize, indoctrinate, and assimilate. That history and continuing reality differentiate schools from other mediating institutions of civil society. It also goes to the heart of the religion clauses—to prevent government compulsion in matters of conscience." The constitutional question cannot be, Who indoctrinates? The constitutional question—or at least the first one—is, Do some or all forms of government financial subsidy to schools teaching religious values, from religious motives, satisfy the constitutional proscription of establishment of religion?

To that question, sharply framed, Professor Perry replies with a resounding and carefully qualified "yes." Perry argues rigorously—a point that would have seemed too obvious to merit argument, except that it has often eluded the Supreme Court—that, quite simply, "in providing aid to private schools, no state may discriminate—no state is constitutionally free to discriminate—against religiously affiliated schools. It is not only false that a state *must* discriminate against such schools; it is also false that a state *may* discriminate against them." Perry protects against forbidden establishment of religion by insisting, first, that in doling out aid the state be neutral as between religious and nonreligious schools, and second, that the state's adoption of the voucher program not be based on a belief that the church or churches that may happen to be particularly favored by the program (because, say, they run most of the religious schools in that place) is or are "better (truer, etc.)" than other churches or no church at all. Professor Perry's position, as he notes, resembles that of four members of the current Court: Chief Justice Rehnquist and Justices Scalia, Kennedy, and Thomas. And in a case decided after the conference for which these papers were prepared, that same quadrumvirate, joined by Justice O'Connor and in part by Justice Breyer, considered a statute creating a program that permitted religious groups to use school facilities after hours. In his opinion for the Court, Justice Thomas had this to say about neutrality: "Because allowing the [Good News] Club to speak on school grounds would ensure neutrality, not threaten it, Milford [Central School] faces an uphill battle in arguing that the Establishment Clause compels it to exclude the Good News Club." It was a battle the school lost.

Neutrality may be the wise next jurisprudential step in the Court's pilgrim process of disestablishment, a prudent tool with which to bring the range of relevant constitutional guarantees—from free exercise and disestablishment to equal protection and free speech—to bear in the

modern administrative maze where state action reaches and seeps
deep into the interstices of civil society.[11] But as an image in which to
constitute ourselves, it misses, I think, some of the constitutional
point.[12] As John Witte has argued eloquently, it was the "eighteenth-
century founders' most elementary and most essential insight—that religion is special and is accorded special protection in the Constitution."[13] This priority of the good over the right may appear to flirt with
unsettling a settled first principle of liberalism, but still it was the judgment upon which the first of our liberties was written into our fundamental positive law.[14] And as John Witte continues, quoting Douglas
Laycock, "'We cannot repudiate that decision . . . without rejecting an
essential feature of constitutionalism, rendering all constitutional
rights vulnerable to repudiation if they go out of favor.' The founders'
vision was that religion was more than a peculiar form of speech and
assembly, privacy and autonomy. Religion is a unique source of individual and personal identity, involving 'duties we owe to our Creator,
and the manner of discharging them,' as Madison put it."[15] This is not
to repudiate at all the same founders'—and particularly Madison's—
insight that true freedom in discharging these duties requires that government not establish religion, but it is rather to insist that when the
state acts, it acts in ways that protect people's freedom to constitute
themselves as religious people.

Constituting ourselves people of a certain kind is, finally, quintessen-
tially the purpose and aim of education. "The annual crop of infants,"
as Bernard Lonergan observes, "is a potential invasion of barbarians,
and education may be conceived as the first line of defense."[16] Americans have tended to delegate responsibility for that line of defense to
the state. But as the Supreme Court acknowledged in *Pierce*, parents
have a duty to their child, and surely that duty includes their best efforts to communicate to the child, for his or her own maturing judgment, what is worthwhile, what is worth doing, worth living for, worth
being. A Supreme Court on the verge of deciding under what circumstances, if any, nonrich parents will have the freedom rich parents now
possess to choose their children's schooling might ponder what the international community said about parents and children in the 1959
United Nations Declaration of the Rights of the Child: "The best interests
of the child shall be the guiding principle of those responsible for his
education and guidance; that responsibility lies in the first place with
his parents."[17] Society, of course, for the reason Lonergan noted, "has
a legitimate interest in ensuring children are properly educated, but
whether families choose religious or secular education is their own af-
fair."[18] But the point is not, as John Coons reminds us, that "parents

are necessarily good deciders. They are merely the best."[19] And they are the best for reasons that run deep, as John Coons explains:

> The right to form families and to determine the scope of their children's practical liberty is for most men and women the primary occasion for choice and responsibility: One does not have to be rich or well placed to experience the family. The opportunity over a span of fifteen or twenty years to attempt the transmission of one's deepest values to a beloved child provides a unique arena for the creative impulse. Here is communication of ideas in its most elemental mode. Parental expression, for all its invisibility to the media, is an activity with profound First Amendment implications.[20]

These three chapters are timely reminders that when the Constitution is made to speak to the intersection of religion and education, parent and child, it shall speak to constitution in the most profound sense: "In a faint echo of the divine, children are the most important Word most of us will utter."[21]

Contributors _____

Patrick Brennan is Professor of Law and Associate Dean for Academic Affairs and Research, Arizona State University College of Law. He is the author of *By Nature Equal: The Anatomy of Western Insight*, with John Coons (Princeton: Princeton University Press, 1999), and articles in numerous law journals. Currently he is completing a book on the place of the "human subject" in the rule of law, and is a member of the Pew Charitable Trust's study on the "human person" in modern law.

Charles L. Glenn is Professor and Chairman of Administration, Training, and Policy Studies at Boston University. From 1970 to 1991 he was Director of Urban Education and Equity Efforts for the Massachusetts Department of Education. Glenn is author of a number of studies in educational history and comparative policy, including *The Myth of the Common School* (Amherst: University of Massachusetts Press, 1988): *Choice of Schools in Six Nations* (U.S. Department of Education, 1989); *Educational Freedom in Eastern Europe* (Washington, D.C.: Cato Institute, 1995); *Educating Immigrant Children: Schools and Language Minorities in Twelve Nations* (New York: Garland, 1996); and *The Ambiguous Embrace: Government and Faith-Based Schools and Social Agencies* (Princeton: Princeton University Press, 2000), as well as the article on school choice in the *International Encyclopedia of Education*, and several hundred articles, book chapters, and monographs. He is currently writing, with Professor Jan De Groof of Ghent, a study of the arrangements in thirty countries for balancing educational freedom with common standards and accountability.

Amy Gutmann is Laurance S. Rockefeller University Professor of Politics and Provost of Princeton University. Among her books are *Liberal Equality* (Cambridge: Cambridge University Press, 1980); *Democratic Education* (Princeton: Princeton University Press, 1987); *Democracy and Disagreement* (Cambridge: Harvard University Press, 1996), coauthored with Dennis Thompson; and *Color Conscious: The Political Morality of Race* (Princeton: Princeton University Press, 1996), coauthored with Anthony Appiah). Gutmann is also editor of *Freedom of Association; Multiculturalism: Examining the Politics of Recognition; Democracy and the Welfare State; Ethics and Politics* (in its third edition, coauthored with Dennis Thompson), and many other volumes. Gutmann's essays have appeared in such journals as *Ethics; Philosophy and Public Affairs; Politi-*

cal Theory; New York Times Book Review; Washington Post; Dissent; and *Times Literary Supplement.*

David Hollenbach, S.J. is the Margaret O'Brien Flatley Professor of Catholic Theology at Boston College, where he teaches theological ethics and Christian social ethics. His publications include *Catholicism and Liberalism: Contributions to American Public Philosophy,* edited with R. Bruce Douglass (Cambridge: Cambridge University Press, 1994); *Justice, Peace, and Human Rights: American Catholic Social Ethics in a Pluralistic World* (New York: Crossroad, 1988, 1990); *Nuclear Ethics: A Christian Moral Argument* (New York: Paulist, 1983); *Claims in Conflict: Retrieving and Renewing the Catholic Human Rights Tradition* (New York: Paulist, 1979). He has written numerous chapters in books and articles in journals such as *Theological Studies; Theology Today; Human Rights Quarterly; Annual of the Society of Christian Ethics;* and *America.* He is presently completing a book titled *The Common Good and Christian Ethics,* which will be published by Cambridge University Press.

Meira Levinson is an Eighth Grade Teacher and Social Studies Department Chair at John W. McCormack Middle School in Boston. She received her D.Phil. in Politics at Nuffield College, University of Oxford, and her first book is *The Demands of Liberal Education* (Oxford: Oxford University Press, 1999). She has also published articles in the *Oxford Review of Education* and the *British Journal of Political Science.*

Sanford Levinson is W. St. John Garwood and W. St. John Garwood, Jr. Centennial Chair in Law and Professor of Government at the University of Texas School of Law. He is author of *Constitutional Faith* (Princeton: Princeton University Press, 1988); and *Written in Stone* (Durham, N.C.: Duke University Press, 1998), and editor or coeditor of *Constitutional Stupidities, Constitutional Tragedies* (New York: New York University Press, 1998); *Responding to Imperfection: The Theory and Practice of Constitutional Amendment* (Princeton: Princeton University Press, 1995); and *Interpreting Law and Literature: A Hermeneutic Reader* (Evanston, Ill.: Northwestern University Press, 1988). His many articles have appeared in *Yale Law Journal; Constitutional Commentary; Ethics; Philosophy and Public Affairs,* and elsewhere. He is currently working on the fourth edition of *Processes of Constitutional Decisionmaking* (New York: Aspen).

Stephen Macedo is Laurance S. Rockefeller Professor of Politics and the University Center for Human Values, Princeton University Politics Department. He has authored *Diversity and Distrust: Civic Education in a Multicultural Democracy* (Cambridge: Harvard University Press,

1999); *Liberal Virtues: Citizenship, Virtue, and Community in Liberal Constitutionalism* (Oxford: Clarendon Press, 1990); and *The New Right versus the Constitution* (Washington, D.C.: Cato Institute, 1987). He has also edited *Deliberative Politics: Essays on Democracy and Disagreement* (New York: Oxford University Press, 1999); and *Reassessing the Sixties: Debating the Political and Cultural Legacy* (New York: W.W. Norton, 1997). Additionally, he has edited several NOMOS volumes and sits on the editorial boards of *Political Theory; American Political Science Review; Ethics;* and *Polity.* Macedo is currently working on manuscripts on liberal civil society, and on liberalism and sexuality.

John T. McGreevy is John A. O'Brien Associate Professor of History at the University of Notre Dame. He has authored *Parish Boundaries: The Catholic Encounter with Race in the Twentieth-Century Urban North* (Chicago: University of Chicago Press, 1996), and published articles in the *Journal of American History; Commonweal; Religion and American Culture;* and *Pacific Historical Review.* He is currently completing *Thinking On One's Own: Catholicism and American Liberalism from Slavery to Abortion* (New York: W. W. Norton).

Martha Minow has taught since 1981 at Harvard Law School, where she is a Professor of Law. The courses she has taught include Civil Procedure, Family Law, Law and Education, Children and Their Social Worlds, and Inclusionary Education. Her books include *Between Vengeance and Forgiveness: Facing History after Genocide and Mass Violence* (Beacon Press, 1998); *Not Only for Myself: Identity, Politics, and Law* (New York: New Press, 1997); *and Making All the Difference: Inclusion, Exclusion, and American Law* (Ithaca: Cornell University Press, 1990). She coedited *Law Stories* (Ann Arbor: University of Michigan Press, 1996) with Gary Bellow, and has also coedited casebooks on civil procedure, women and the law, and family law. Her research focuses on the legal treatment of children, women, immigrants, persons with disabilities, and members of ethnic, racial, and religious minorities.

Richard J. Mouw is President and Professor of Christian Philosophy at Fuller Theological Seminary. He is a Beliefnet.com columnist, has served on the editorial boards of numerous publications, including the *Journal of Religious Ethics* and *Books and Culture,* and is the author of many books including *The God Who Commands* (Notre Dame, Ind.: University of Notre Dame Press, 1990); *Uncommon Decency: Christian Civility in an Uncivil World* (Downers Grove, Ill.: InterVarsity Press, 1992); and *Consulting the Faithful: What Christian Intellectuals Can Learn from Popular Religion* (Grand Rapids, Mich.: Eerdmans, 1994), and most recently *The Smell of Sawdust: What Evangelicals Can Learn from Their Fundamentalist Heritage* (Grand Rapids, Mich.: Zondervan, 2000).

Joseph O'Keefe, S.J. is Associate Professor of Education at the Lynch School of Education, Boston College. With Peter Steinfels and James Youniss, he is currently writing *The Legacy and Future of Catholic Schools* (Chicago: University of Chicago Press), and has coedited the last five volumes for the National Catholic Educational Association's Conversations in Excellence series. Additionally, he has published over twenty-five articles and chapters in edited volumes. He has been the recipient of numerous grants, including most recently one from the McGivney Foundation for the Conversations in Excellence Conference on Teacher Recruitment and Formation in Catholic Schools.

Michael J. Perry holds the University Distinguished Chair in Law at the Wake Forest University School of Law. He has published seven books, including *We the People: The Fourteenth Amendment and the Supreme Court* (New York: Oxford University Press, 1999); *The Idea of Human Rights: Four Inquiries* (New York: Oxford University Press, 1998); *Religion in Politics: Constitutional and Moral Perspectives* (New York: Oxford University Press, 1997); *Constitution in the Courts: Law or Politics?* (New York: Oxford University Press, 1994); *Love and Power: The Role of Religion and Morality in American Politics* (New York: Oxford University Press, 1991); and over fifty articles and essays. Perry's scholarly interests include American constitutional studies—in particular, the Fourteenth Amendment, the relationship of morality and religion to law and politics, and the idea of human rights.

Nancy Rosenblum is a Professor of Government at Harvard University. She has authored *Membership and Morals: The Personal Uses of Pluralism in America* (Princeton: Princeton University Press, 1998); *Another Liberalism: Romanticism and the Reconstruction of Liberal Thought* (Cambridge: Harvard University Press, 1987); and *Bentham's Theory of the Modern State* (Cambridge: Harvard University Press, 1978). Additionally, she has edited *Civil Society and Government* (Princeton: Princeton University Press, 2001), with Robert Post; *Obligations of Citizenship and Demands of Faith: Religious Accommodation in Pluralist Democracies* (Princeton: Princeton University Press, 2000); *Thoreau: Political Writings* (Cambridge: Cambridge University Press, 1996); and *Liberalism and the Moral Life* (Cambridge: Harvard University Press, 1989). She is currently at work on a book on representations of political parties in America and a study of American individualism, communitarianism, and separatism in political theory, history, and literature.

Rosemary Salomone is Professor of Law at St. John's University School of Law. From 1985 to 1995 she served as a member of the Board of Trustees of the State University of New York. She is a fellow of the Open Society Institute and the author of *Same, Different, Equal: Rethinking Single-Sex Schooling* (New Haven: Yale University Press, forthcoming 2003); *Visions of Schooling: Conscience, Community, and Common Education* (New Haven: Yale University Press, 2000); and *Equal Education under Law* (New York: St. Martin's Press, 1986); as well as numerous articles, book chapters, and commentaries on education law and policy.

Joseph P. Viteritti is Research Professor of Public Policy at the Robert F. Wagner Graduate School of Public Service, New York University. He is the author of *Choosing Equality: School Choice, the Constitution, and Civil Society* (Washington, D.C.: Brookings Institution Press, 1999) and *Across the River: Politics and Education in the City* (New York: Holmes and Meier Publishers, 1983). He has co-edited *Making Good Citizens: Education and Civil Society* (New Haven: Yale University Press, 2001) and *New Schools for a New Century: The Redesign of Urban Education* (New Haven: Yale University Press, 1997). He gave expert testimony in the Cleveland school voucher case decided by the U.S. Supreme Court (*Zelman v. Simmons-Harris*, 2002), and has been a senior advisor to school superintendents in New York, San Francisco, and Boston.

Paul Weithman is Associate Professor of Philosophy at Notre Dame University. He has edited *Religion and Contemporary Liberalism* (Notre Dame, Ind.: University of Notre Dame Press, 1997); *The Philosophy of John Rawls* in 5 volumes (New York: Garland Press, 1999), coedited with H. Richardson; and is currently at work on *Religion and the Obligations of Citizenship* (New York: Cambridge University Press). He has also published articles in *Faith and Philosphy*; *Philosophy and Public Affairs*; and the *Journal of the History of Philosophy*. His areas of research are contemporary political philosophy, ethics, and medieval political philosophy, and he has published articles on Aquinas, Augustine, and John Rawls.

Alan Wolfe is Professor of Political Science and Director for the Boisi Center for Religion and American Public Life at Boston College. He is the author or editor or more than ten books, including *Marginalized in the Middle* (Chicago: University of Chicago Press, 1997); *One Nation, after All* (New York: Viking Penguin, 1998); and *Moral Freedom: The Search for Virtue in a World of Choice* (New York: W. W. Norton, 2001).

Notes

Chapter One
Defining Equity: Politics, Markets, and Public Policy

1. A recent elaboration on this approach is Andrew Coulson, *Market Education: The Unknown History* (New Brunswick, N.J. Transaction Publishers, 1999).

2. This approach is presented in Joseph P. Viteritti, *Choosing Equality: School Choice, the Constitution, and Civil Society* (Washington, D.C.: Brookings Institution Press, 1999).

3. "The Brown Center Annual Report on American Education" (Washington, D.C.: Brookings Institution, 2000).

4. See David Berliner and Benjamin J. Biddle, *The Manufactured Crisis: Myths, Fraud, and the Attack on America's Public Schools* (Reading, Mass.: Addison-Wesley, 1995); Richard Rothstein, *The Way We Were: The Realities of America's Student Achievement* (Washington, D.C.: Century Foundation, 1998).

5. Christopher Jencks and Meredith Phillips, eds., *The Black-White Test Score Gap* (Washington, D.C.: Brookings Institution Press, 1998).

6. Kate Zernike, "Gap Widens Again on Tests Given to Blacks and Whites," *New York Times*, August 25, 2000.

7. "Quality Counts, '98: The Urban Challenge," *Education Week*, January 8, 1998.

8. See Jencks and Phillips, *The Black-White Test Score Gap*; Susan E. Mayer and Paul E. Peterson, eds., *Earning and Learning: How Schools Matter* (Washington, D.C.: Brookings Institution Press, 1999); Norman H. Nie, Jane Junn, and Kenneth Stehlik-Berry, *Education and Democratic Citizenship in America* (Chicago: University of Chicago Press, 1996).

9. Gerald W. Bracey, *The War against America's Public Schools: Privatizing Schools, Commercializing Education* (Needham Heights, Mass.: Allyn and Bacon, 2001).

10. See Dinesh D'Souza, *The Virtue of Prosperity: Finding Values in an Age of Techno-Affluence* (New York: Free Press, 2000), pp. 111–34.

11. Jeffrey R. Henig and Stephen D. Sugarman, "The Nature and Extent of School Choice," in Stephen D. Sugarman and Frank R. Kemerer, eds., *School Choice and Social Controversy: Politics, Policy, and Law* (Washington, D.C.: Brookings Institution Press, 1999).

12. Milton Friedman, "The Role of Government in Education," in Robert A. Solo, ed., *Economics and the Public Interest* (New Brunswick, N.J.: Rutgers University Press, 1955). See also Milton Friedman, *Capitalism and Freedom* (Chicago: University of Chicago Press, 1962).

13. Milton Friedman and Rose Friedman, *Free to Choose: A Personal Statement*, rev. ed. (New York: Harcourt Brace, 1980).

14. Quoted in Friedman and Friedman, *Free to Choose*, p. 172. Kenneth B. Clark, "Alternative Public School Systems," *Harvard Educational Review* 38 (winter, 1968).

15. John E. Chubb and Terry M. Moe, *Politics, Markets, and America's Schools* (Washington, D.C.: Brookings Institution Press, 1990).

16. Chubb and Moe, *Politics, Markets and America's Schools*, p. 65.

17. See, for example, Anthony Bryk and Valerie E. Lee, "Is Politics the Problem and the Market the Answer?" *Economics of Education Review* 11 (1992); James Liebman, "Voice, Not Choice," *Yale Law Review* 101 (1991).

18. In my own study of the New York City school system seven years earlier, I described the problem as a dichotomy between "constituents and clients." See Joseph P. Viteritti, *Across the River: Politics and Education in the City* (New York: Holmes and Meier, 1983), pp. 317–22. See also Joseph P. Viteritti, "Public Organization Environments: Constitutents, Clients, and Urban Governance," *Administration and Society* 21 (1990).

19. See the interesting exchanges in Edith Rasell and Richard Rothstein, *School Choice: Examining the Evidence* (Washington, D.C.: Economic Policy Institute, 1993); William H. Clune and John F. Witte, *Choice and Control in American Education*, vols. 1 and 2 (Bristol, Penn.: Falmer Press, 1990).

20. Edward B. Fiske and Helen F. Ladd, *When Schools Compete: A Cautionary Tale* (Washington, D.C.: Brookings Institution Press, 2000); Bruce Fuller and Richard F. Elmore, *Who Chooses? Who Loses? Culture, Institutions, and the Unequal Effects of School Choice* (New York: Teachers College Press, 1996); Jeffrey R. Henig, *Rethinking School Choice: Limits of the Market Metaphor* (Princeton: Princeton University Press, 1993).

21. John E. Coons and Stephen D. Sugarman, *Education by Choice: The Case for Family Control* (Berkeley and Los Angeles: University of California Press, 1978). Other proposals were put forward by Theodore Sizer and Christopher Jencks. See Viteritti, *Choosing Equality*, pp. 54–56.

22. John E. Coons, William H. Clune and Stephen D. Sugarman, *Private Wealth and Public Education* (Cambridge: Harvard University Press, 1970).

23. See Rosemary C. Salomone, *Visions of Schooling: Conscience, Community, and Common Education* (New Haven: Yale University Press, 2000).

24. I have addressed the legal issues elsewhere: see Viteritti, *Choosing Equality*, pp. 117–79; Joseph P. Viteritti, "Choosing Equality: Religious Freedom and Educational Opportunity under Constitutional Federalism,"*Yale Law and Policy Review* 15 (1996); Joseph P. Viteritti, "Blaine's Wake: School Choice, the First Amendment, and State Constitutional Law," *Harvard Journal of Law and Public Policy* 21 (1998); Joseph P. Viteritti, "School Choice and American Constitutionalism," in Paul E. Peterson and David Campbell, eds., *Charter Schools, Vouchers, and Public Education* (Washington, D.C.: Brookings Institution Press, 2001).

25. For a recent iteration of their thinking, see John E. Coons and Stephen D. Sugarman, *Making School Choice Work for All Families* (Pacific Research Institute, 1999).

26. John E. Coons and Stephen D. Sugarman, "It's Not a Good Choice for Our Poor Families: A California Initiative on School Vouchers Would Benefit Students Who Least Need Help," *Los Angeles Times*, July 27, 2000.

27. See Viteritti, *Choosing Equality*, pp. 98–113.

28. See Paul T. Hill, "Contracting in Public Education," in Diane Ravitch and Joseph P. Viteritti, eds., *New Schools for a New Century: The Redesign of Urban Education* (New Haven: Yale University Press, 1997).

29. See Joseph P. Viteritti, "Risking Choice, Redressing Inequality," in Diane Ravitch and Joseph P. Viteritti, eds., *Making Good Citizens: Education and Civil Society* (New Haven: Yale University Press, 2001).

30. See, for example, Brian P. Gill, P. Michael Timpane, Karen E. Ross, and Dominic J. Brewer, *Rhetoric versus Reality: What We Know and What We Need to Know about Vouchers and Charter Schools* (Santa Monica, Calif.: RAND, 2001); Peterson and Campbell, *Charters, Vouchers, and Public Schools*; John F. Witte, *The Market Approach to Education: An Analysis of America's First Voucher Program* (Princeton: Princeton University Press, 2000); Kim K. Metcalf et al., "Evaluation of the Cleveland Scholarship Program: Second Year Report, 1997–1998" (Indiana Center for Evaluation, Indiana University, November 1998); Paul E. Peterson and Bryan Hassel, eds., *Learning from School Choice* (Washington, D.C.: Brookings Institution Press, 1998); Terry Moe, ed., *Private Vouchers* (Stanford, Calif.: Hoover Institution Press, 1995).

31. James S. Coleman, Thomas Hoffer, and Sally Kilgore, *High School Achievement* (New York: Basic Books, 1982); James S. Coleman and Thomas Hoffer, *Public, Private, and Catholic Schools: The Importance of Community* (New York: Basic Books, 1987).

32. Terry Moe, *Schools, Vouchers, and the American Public* (Washington, D.C.: Brookings Institution Press, 2001), pp. 43–72.

33. See especially Caroline M. Hoxby, "Does Competition among Public Schools Benefit Students and Taxpayers?" *American Economic Review* 90 (December 2000).

34. See especially Mark Schneider, Paul Teske, and Melissa Marschall, *Choosing Schools: Consumer Choice and the Quality of American Schools* (Princeton: Princeton University Press, 2000).

35. See Joseph P. Viteritti, "A Truly Living Constitution: Why Educational Opportunity Trumps Strict Separation on the Voucher Question," *New York University Annual Survey of American Law* 57 (2000).

Chapter Two
The Irony of School Choice: Liberals, Conservatives, and the New Politics of Race

Special thanks to Joseph Viteritti for offering comments on the paper and to Thornton Lockwood for research assistance as well as critical commentary.

1. Joseph P. Viteritti, *Choosing Equality: School Choice, the Constitution, and Civil Society* (Washington, D.C.: Brookings Institution Press, 1999), p. 209.

2. Milton Friedman, "The Role of Government in Education," in Robert A. Solo, ed., *Economics and the Public Interest* (New Brunswick, N.J.: Rutgers University Press), p. 130.

3. John E. Chubb and Terry M. Moe, *Politics, Markets, and America's Schools* (Washington, D.C.: Brookings Institution Press, 1990), p. 217, emphasis in the original.

4. Howard L. Fuller, "The Continuing Struggle of African Americans for the Power to Make Real Educational Choices" (paper prepared for the Second Annual Symposium on Educational Options for African Americans, March 2–5, 2000 [http://www.schoolchoiceinfo.org/research/research.jsp?c=12]).

5. Felicia Wong, "The Good Fight: Race, Politics, and Contemporary Urban School Reform" (Ph.D. dissertation, Department of Political Science, University of California, Berkeley, 2000), pp. 4–5.

6. Louis Hartz, *The Liberal Tradition in America: An Interpretation of American Political Thought since the Revolution* (New York: Harcourt, Brace, and World, 1955).

7. Robert Putnam, *Bowling Alone: The Collapse of Revival of Community in America* (New York: Simon and Schuster, 2000).

8. Putnam, *Bowling Alone*; Everett Carll Ladd, *The Ladd Report* (New York: Free Press, 1999).

9. Seymour Martin Lipset, *American Exceptionalism: A Double-Edged Sword* (New York: W. W. Norton, 1996), p. 22.

10. Lipset, *American Exceptionalism*, p. 145.

11. Stephen Thernstrom and Abigail Thernstrom, *America in Black and White: One Nation, Indivisible* (New York: Simon and Schuster, 1997); Andrew Hacker, *Two Nations, Black and White: Separate, Hostile, Unequal* (New York: Scribner's, 1992); Melvin L. Oliver and Thomas Shapiro, *Black Wealth/White Wealth: A New Perspective on Racial Inequality* (New York: Routledge, 1995).

12. Donald R. Kinder and Lynn M. Sanders, *Divided by Color: Racial Politics and Democratic Ideals* (Chicago: University of Chicago Press, 1996).

13. Jennifer Hochschild, *Facing Up to the American Dream: Race, Class, and the Soul of the Nation* (Princeton: Princeton University Press, 1995), pp. 98–102, 144; Jim Sidanius, Pam Singh, John J. Hetts, and Chris Federico, "It's Not Affirmative Action, It's the Blacks," in David O. Sears, Jim Sidanius, and Lawrence Bobo, eds., *Racialized Politics: The Debate about Racism in America* (Chicago: University of Chicago Press, 2000), pp. 191–235. For a contrary view, see Paul M. Sniderman and Thomas Piazza, *The Scar of Race* (Cambridge: Harvard University Press, 1993), pp. 15–58.

14. Philip A. Klinker with Rogers M. Smith, *The Unsteady March: The Rise and Decline of Racial Equality in America* (Chicago: University of Chicago Press, 1999), p. 313. See also Stephen Steinberg, *Turning Back: The Retreat from Racial Justice in American Thought and Policy* (Boston: Beacon Press, 1995).

15. For a review of the relevant data see Ruy Teixeira, "Critical Support: The Public View of Public Education," in Richard D. Kahlenberg, ed., *All Together Now: Creating Middle-Class Schools through Public School Choice* (Washington, D.C.: Brookings Institution Press, 2000), pp. 251–79.

16. Lawrence Hardy, "Public School Choice," *American School Board Journal* 187 (2000), pp. 22–26.

17. Public Agenda, "On Thin Ice: How Advocates and Opponents Could Misread the Public's Views on Vouchers and Charter Schools" (press release, November 17, 1999 [http://www.publicagenda.com/specials/vouchers/voucherhome.htm]).

18. Michael X. Delli Carpini and Scott Keeter, *What Americans Know about Politics and Why It Matters* (New Haven: Yale University Press, 1996), pp. 73–82.

19. Jeffery R. Henig and Stephen D. Sugarman, "The Nature and Extent of School Choice," in Stephen D. Sugarman and Frank R. Kemerer eds., *School Choice and Social Controversy: Politics, Policy, and Law* (Washington, D.C.: Brookings Institution Press, 1999), p. 29.

20. Lowell C. Rose and Alec M. Gallup, "The 32nd Annual Phi Delta Kappa/Gallup Poll of the Public's Attitudes toward the Public Schools," *Phi Delta Kappan* 82 (September 2000) (on-line at http://www.pdkintl.org/kappan/kpol0009.htm).

21. Public Agenda, "On Thin Ice," p. 2.

22. Rose and Gallup, "The 32nd Annual Phi Delta Kappa/Gallup Poll." See also Gallup Organization, "No Public Consensus Yet on School Voucher Programs" (poll releases, January 15, 2000, p. 2 [http://www.gallup.com/poll/releases/pr010115.asp]).

23. Terry Moe, *Schools, Vouchers, and the American Public*, (Washington, D.C.: Brookings Institution Press, 2001).

24. Rose and Gallup, "The 32nd Annual Phi Delta Kappa/Gallup Poll."

25. Pew Research Center for the People and the Press, "Faith-Based Funding Backed, but Church-State Doubts Abound" (April 10, 2001 [http://www.people-press.org/rel01rpt.html]).

26. Gallup Organization, "No Public Consensus Yet on School Voucher Programs."

27. Lowell C. Rose and Alec M. Gallup, "The 31st Annual Phi Delta Kappa/Gallup Poll on the Public's Attitudes toward the Public Schools," *Phi Delta Kappan* 81 (September 1999), p. 46 (http://www.pdkintl.org/kappan/kpol9909.htm).

28. Brian C. Hassel, *The Charter School Challenge* (Washington, D.C.: Brookings Institution Press, 1999).

29. Rose and Gallup, "The 32nd Annual Phi Delta Kappa/Gallup Poll."

30. Rose and Gallup, "The 31st Annual Phi Delta Kappa/Gallup Poll," p. 46; "The 32nd Annual Phi Delta Kappa/Gallup Poll."

31. Jennifer Hochschild and Bridget Scott, "Governance and Reform of Public Higher Education in the United States," *Public Opinion Quarterly* 62 (spring 1998), p. 88; Sammis White, "Black Public Opinion in Milwaukee," *Wisconsin Policy Research Report* 8 (February 1995); David A. Bositis, "National Opinion Poll—Education, 1999," (Washington, D.C.: Joint Center for Political and Economic Studies), (http://www.jointcenter.org/selrpts.htm); Moe, *Schools, Vouchers, and the American Public*; Public Agenda, "On Thin Ice," p. 3.

32. Barbara Schneider et al., "Public School Choice: Some Evidence from the National Education Longitudinal Study of 1988," *Educational Evaluation and Policy Analysis* 18 (spring 1996), pp. 19–29.

33. Amy Stuart Wells, "African-American Students' Views of School Choice," in Bruce Fuller and Richard F. Elmore, eds., *Who Chooses? Who Loses? Culture, Institutions, and the Unequal Effects of School Choice* (New York: Teachers College Press, 1996), pp. 25–49.

34. Bositis, "National Opinion Poll—Education, 1999," p. 9.

35. Rose and Gallup, "The 31st Annual Phi Delta Kappa/Gallup Poll," p. 55.

36. Albert J. Menendez, "Voters versus Vouchers: An Analysis of Referendum Data," *Phi Delta Kappan* 81 (September 1999), pp. 76–80.

37. *Los Angeles Times* Exit Poll, "How Californians Voted," November 9, 2000 (http://www.latimes.com/news/timespoll/state/446pa2an.htm).

38. Martha Groves, "*Times* Poll: Voters Ready to Give Vouchers a Drubbing," *Los Angeles Times*, October 26, 2000 (http://www.latimes.com/news/timespoll/state/lat_poll001026.htm).

39. Wong, "The Good Fight."

40. Viteritti, *Choosing Equality*, p. 211.

41. Robert C. Bulman and David L. Kirp, "The Shifting Politics of School Choice," in Sugarman and Kemerer, *School Choice and Social Controversy*, p. 60.

42. Thernstrom and Thernstrom, *America in Black and White*.

43. David A. Bositis, "2000 Opinion Poll—Politics" (Washington, D.C.: Joint Center for Political and Economic Studies) (http://www.jointcenter.org/selrpts.htm).

44. John David Skrentny, *The Ironies of Affirmative Action: Politics, Culture, and Justice in America* (Chicago: University of Chicago Press, 1996).

45. John F. Witte, *The Market Approach to Education: An Analysis of America's First Voucher Program* (Princeton: Princeton University Press, 2000), p. 159.

46. Gary Orfield, "Turning Back to Segregation," in Gary Orfield and Susan Eaton, eds., *Dismantling Desegregation: The Quiet Reversal of "Brown v. Board of Education"* (New York: New Press, 1996), p. 7.

47. Gary Orfield, "Segregated Housing and School Resegregation," in Orfield and Eaton, *Dismantling Desegregation*, citing *Foss v. Houston Independent School District*, 669 F.2nd, 218, 288.

48. Hochschild and Scott, "Governance and Reform," pp. 83–85; Ronald P. Formisano, *Boston against Busing: Race, Class, and Ethnicity in the 1960s and 1970s* (Chapel Hill: University of North Carolina Press, 1991).

49. Paul A. Minorini and Stephen D. Sugarman, "School Finance Litigation in the Name of Educational Equity: Its Evolution, Impact, and Future," in Helen F. Ladd, Rosemary Chalk, and Janet S. Hansen, eds., *Equity and Adequacy in Education Finance: Issues and Perspectives*, (Washington, D.C.: National Academy Press, 1999), pp. 50–51.

50. Melissa C. Carr and Susan H. Fuhrman, "The Politics of School Finance in the 1990s," in Ladd, Chalk, and Hansen, *Equity and Adequacy in Education Finance*, p. 151.

51. Margaret Weir, "The American Middle Class and the Politics of Education," in Olivier Zunz, Leonard Schoppa, and Nobuhiro Hiwatari, eds., *Postwar Social Contracts under Stress: The Middle Classes of America, Europe, and Japan at the Turn of the Century* (New York: Russell Sage Foundation, forthcoming).

52. Robert Berne and Leanna Stiefel, "Concepts of School Finance Equity, 1970 to the Present," in Ladd, Chalk, and Hansen, *Equity and Adequacy in Education Finance*, p. 26.

53. Orfield, "Turning Back to Segregation," p. 26.

54. Klinker and Smith, *The Unsteady March*, p. 321.

55. Klinker and Smith, *The Unsteady March*, p. 343.

56. PollingReport.com, "Education," p. 7 (www.pollingreport.com/educatio.htm).

57. Alan Wolfe, *One Nation, after All: What Middle-Class Americans Really Think about God, Country, Family, Racism, Welfare, Immigration, Homosexuality, Work, the Right, the Left, and Each Other* (New York: Viking, 1998), pp. 180–85.

58. Martin Gilens, *Why Americans Hate Welfare: Race, Media, and the Politics of Anti-Poverty Policy* (Chicago: University of Chicago Press, 1999), p. 7.

59. Paul M. Sniderman and Edward G. Carmines, *Reaching beyond Race* (Cambridge: Harvard University Press, 1997); Sniderman and Piazza, *The Scar of Race*.

60. Ira Katznelson and Margaret Weir, *Schooling for All: Class, Race, and the Decline of the Democratic Ideal* (New York: Basic Books, 1985), p. 24.

61. Jeffrey R. Henig, *Rethinking School Choice: Limits of the Market Metaphor* (Princeton: Princeton University Press, 1994), p. 193.

62. Peter W. Cookson, *School Choice: The Struggle for the Soul of American Education* (New Haven: Yale University Press, 1994), pp. 101–2, 199.

63. Wolfe, *One Nation, after All*, pp. 198–202.

64. Amy Gutmann, *Democratic Education* (Princeton: Princeton University Press, 1987).

65. Harold L. Wilensky, *The Welfare State and Equality: Structural and Ideological Roots of Public Expenditures* (Berkeley and Los Angeles: University of California Press, 1974), pp. 59–61.

66. Gary Sykes, David Plank, and David Arsen, *School Choice Policies in Michigan: The Rules Matter* (East Lansing: Michigan State University Press, 2000).

67. Klinker and Smith, *The Unsteady March*, pp. 324–25.

68. Edward B. Fiske and Helen F. Ladd, *When Schools Compete: A Cautionary Tale* (Washington, D.C.: Brookings Institution Press, 2000); Witte, *The Market Approach to Education*; Paul E. Peterson and Bryan C. Hassel, eds., *Learning from School Choice* (Washington, D.C.: Brookings Institution Press, 1998).

69. William G. Bowen and Derek Bok, *The Shape of the River: Long-Term Consequences of Considering Race in College and University Admissions*, (Princeton: Princeton University Press, 1998); Clifford Adelman, "The Rest of the River," *University Business* 2 (January–February 1999), pp. 43–46.

70. Introduction to Kahlenberg, *All Together Now*, p. 1.

71. Rose and Gallup, "The 32nd Annual Phi Delta Kappa/Gallup Poll."

72. Richard Rothstein, "Equalizing Education Resources on Behalf of Disadvantaged Children," in Richard D. Kahlenberg, ed., *A Notion at Risk: Preserving Public Education as an Engine for Social Mobility* (New York: Century Foundation Press, 2000), pp. 31–92; Peterson and Hassel, *Learning from School Choice*.

Chapter Three
Equity and School Choice: How Can We Bridge the Gap between Ideals and Realities?

1. An excellent discussion of the practical difficulties of enforcing public regulations against private religious schools can be found in Neal Devins,

"State Regulation of Christian Schools," *Journal of Legislation* 10 (1983), pp. 351–81.

2. I explore the complex motives at play in shaping common schools in *Diversity and Distrust: Civic Education in A Multicultural Democracy* (Cambridge: Harvard University Press, 2000), pt. 2.

3. Michael W. McConnell, "Education Disestablishment: Why Democratic Values Are Ill-Served by Democratic Control of Schooling," forthcoming in Stephen Macedo and Yael Tamir, eds., *Moral and Political Education*, NOMOS XLIII (New York: New York University Press, 2002). I should emphasize that while McConnell argues that public schools run afoul of some constitutional values, he does not argue that the courts should strike down school laws on constitutional grounds.

4. Joseph P. Viteritti, "Defining Equity: Politics, Markets, and Public Policy" chapter 1, this volume.

5. Note that McConnell and others play heavily on emphasizing that what purports to be a public or common school actually embodies values that are narrowly sectarian and indefensible as a public matter: the close equivalent of a religious view. This has sometimes been true to some substantial degree: public schoolchildren in the nineteenth century read the King James Bible, and more recently they have recited "nondenominational" prayers. It is at least worth noting that the reading of "nonsectarian" Bible passages inculcating ordinary moral virtues was typically defended not as a way of teaching them to be Protestant, but rather as a way of teaching them to be moral (I do not defend these practices, but the nineteenth-century common schools were not quite so objectionably sectarian as critics of public schooling such as McConnell like to argue). Likewise, McConnell may object to public-school exercises that teach children the value of "self-actualization" (whatever that means), but such exercises are unlikely to amount to the inculcation of a religious view: teaching children to actively develop their capacities would certainly be supported by a wide range of reasonable public arguments. I discuss these matters in *Diversity and Distrust*.

6. This point has been made by Amy Gutmann, *Democratic Education* (Princeton: Princeton University Press, 1987).

7. See for example the much-discussed case of *Mozert v. Hawkins County Board of Education*, 827 F. 2d., 1058 (6th Cir. 1987).

8. The emphasis here—that public institutions are for public purposes that must be justified in public terms—is a very old one, running through the social-contract tradition from John Locke to John Rawls.

9. For a discussion that places much greater weight than I think warranted on the imperative that public policies should have neutral effects on the variety of worldviews that support basic liberal-democratic values, see John Tomasi, *Liberalism beyond Justice: Citizens, Society, and the Boundaries of Political Theory* (Princeton: Princeton University Press, 2001).

10. Robert C. Bulman and David L. Kirp, "The Shifting Politics of School Choice," in Stephen D. Sugarman and Frank R. Kemerer, eds., *School Choice and Social Controversy* (Washington, D.C.: Brookings Institution Press, 1999).

11. I have benefited from the discussion in Howard Gardiner, "Paroxysms of Choice," *New York Review of Books*, October 19, 2000.

12. In the mid-1990s, the City of Cleveland School District faced an educational and fiscal crisis so severe that the state was ordered by a federal court to take over the administration of the district. The Ohio legislature responded with a scholarship program, which provided a tutorial program for children attending Cleveland public schools, and a school voucher program providing scholarships (or vouchers) to students from Cleveland to attend "alternative schools" that registered for the program. These alternative schools could be private schools in Cleveland or public schools adjacent to the City of Cleveland School District. Students whose family income was not more than 200 percent of the federal poverty level received 90 percent of their school tuition; all other students with higher incomes could receive up to 75 percent of their tuition, but there was a fixed ceiling for all students of $2,500. The state placed no restrictions on how the schools could use the money. The level of funds appropriated by the state of Ohio limited the number of students that could apply for the program. As of the beginning of the 1999–2000 academic year, 3,801 students were enrolled in the program. Sixty percent of those students were from families at or below the poverty level. See *Simmons-Harris v. Zelman*, 54 F. Supp.2d, 725, 728–29 (N.D. Ohio 1999); and *Simmons-Harris v. Goff*, 711 N.E., 203 (Ohio 1999). See the U.S. Supreme Court's reversal, *Zelman v. Simmons-Harris*, 122 S. Ct. 2460 (2002).

13. *Simmons-Harris v. Goff*, 210–11.

14. See *Jackson v. Benson*, 570 N.W.2d, 407, 413 (Wis. Ct. App. 1997); for a critical discussion of these provisions see Joe Laconte, "Paying the Piper: Will Vouchers Undermine the Mission of Religious Schools?" *Policy Review* (January–February, 1999), pp. 30–36, esp. p. 34.

15. Some of the schools appear to have had a pervasively sectarian character: one school's informational material states that "total religious instruction is the major focus of the educational program. . . . Lessons learned in formal religious classes are purposefully carried over into all subject areas." *Simmons-Harris v. Zelman*, 728–29.

16. See his observations on school choice in his book: John O. Norquist, *The Wealth of Cities: Revitalizing the Centers of American Life* (Reading, Mass.: Addison-Wesley, 1998).

17. See Harry Brighouse, *School Choice and Social Justice* (New York: Oxford University Press, 2000).

18. See Brighouse, *School Choice and Social Justice*, p. 184.

19. Of course, the fact that some families value educational achievement more than others is quite independent of their unequal ability to pay for more expensive schooling. Some have proposed ingenious schemes that allow parents to express the greater value they place on education by spending more, while equalizing the results. The idea is called "family-power equalization," and it would scale parental add-ons according to family income, so that there is a proportionality between families' desire to sacrifice more for the education of their children and the real burden they bear as a consequence of the sacrifice (the underlying principle is one of "equal pain for equal gain"). This lessens

children's dependence on family income but leaves children's educational funding sensitive to the values and choices of parents and to their willingness to sacrifice for their children's education. If top-ups are to be allowed, it is probably preferable to try to equalize them in this way, but it might be better to provide challenging opportunities for talented and engaged students that they can take advantage of without counting on their parents to pay for them. See Stephen D. Sugarman, "School Choice and Public Funding," in Sugarman and Kemerer, *School Choice and Social Controversy.*

20. Sugarman, "School Choice and Public Funding," esp. pp. 118–24.

21. Christopher Jencks and Meredith Phillips, "America's Next Achievement Test: Closing the Black-White Test Score Gap," *American Prospect* 9, no. 40 (September–October 1998).

22. The cited statistics, drawing on Justice DeGrasse's opinion, are from Anemona Hartocollis, "Legal Portrait of System that Cheats Pupils," *New York Times*, January 12, 2001; and "The Unforeseen Costs of Raising Standards," Richard Rothstein, *New York Times*, January 11, 2001.

23. Justice Leland Degrasse, in *Campaign for Fiscal Equity et al. v. The State of New York et al.*, 719 N.Y.S.2nd 475 (Sup. Ct. New York County, January 31, 2001); reversed in *Campaign for Fiscal Equity v. State of New York*, 2002 N.Y. App. Div. LEXIS 7252 (June 25, 2002).

24. *Lakeview School District, No. 25 v. Mike Huckabee* (VS. No. 1992–5318), sec. 84.

25. In the short run because the more experimental charter schools may discover better practices that redound to the benefit of public schools generally— and of course the very fact that better students get creamed off may encourage other public schools to work harder. Sorting out short- and long-term consequences is bound to be extremely difficult.

26. Douglas Reed, *On Equal Terms: The Constitutional Politics of Educational Opportunity* (Princeton: Princeton University Press, 2001).

Response
Paul Weithman

1. *New York Daily News*, January 21, 1999.

2. *Garrett v. Board of Education of the School District of the City of Detroit*, 775 F. Supp., 1004.

Chapter Four
Separating the Siamese Twins, "Pluralism" and "School Choice"

I want to thank David Hollenbach, S.J., for his comments, Lucas Swaine for his suggestions, and Ionnis Evrigenis for his research assistance.

1. The figures on public schools come from the U.S. Department of Education Web site, 1998–99 data (http://nces.ed.gov/pubs2000/quarterly/summer/2feat/q2–5.html); on private schools from the USDOE National Center for Education Statistics, Private School Survey 1997–99 (http://nces.ed.gov/pubs99/1999319.pdf). In Massachusetts there are thirty-four Common-

wealth charter schools with an enrollment of roughly 13,000 students and five Horace Mann charter schools. There is a cap of fifty. Thousands of students are on waiting lists.

2. Frances Fitzgerald, *America Revised: History Schoolbooks in the Twentieth Century* (Boston: Little, Brown, 1979).

3. *Pierce v. Society of Sisters*, 268 U.S., 510 (1925): "that certain studies plainly essential to good citizenship must be taught, and that nothing be taught that is manifestly inimical to the public welfare." Michael A. Rebell, "Values Inculcation and the Schools: The Need for a New *Pierce* Compromise" in Neal E. Devins, ed., *Public Values, Private Schools* (New York: Falmer Press, 1989), pp. 37–62. On the other side are those who think *Pierce* was wrongly decided and would enforce exclusively public schooling (like the early Klan-inspired referendum in Oregon after World War I), outlaw all public support for private schools (along the lines of the "little Blaine Amendments"), or mandate specific "thick" public content for all schools.

4. Public funding includes not only voucher plans but also tax incentives in the form of tax deductions for private-school expenses, tax credits, and educational savings plans. I leave aside privately funded scholarship programs like the one started in Washington, D.C. See Patrick Wolf, William Howell, and Paul Peterson, "School Choice in Washington, D.C.: An Evaluation after One Year" (Program on Educational Policy and Governance, Harvard University, 2000). On the role of businessmen as policy entrepreneurs and political activists supporting state initiatives see Hubert Morken and Jo Renee Formicola, *The Politics of School Choice* (New York: Rowman and Littlefield, 1999).

5. Justice O'Connor distinguished private-choice programs from "per-capita school-aid programs" in *Mitchell v. Helms* 120 S. Ct. 2530 (2000), 2559. The contrast with educational pluralism in Europe is summarized in Charles L. Glenn, *Choice of Schools in Six Nations* (Washington, D.C.: U.S. Department of Education, 1990). On the Reagan switch of focus from vouchers to choice within public systems, with his symbolic 1988 speech at a public magnet school, see Jeffrey R. Henig, *Rethinking School Choice* (Princeton: Princeton University Press, 1994), pp. 78ff.

6. As in the 1995 Ohio Pilot Project Scholarship Program struck down by the Sixth Circuit in *Simmons-Harris et al. v. Zelman et. al.* (December 2000).

7. On voucher systems aimed at the poor: John Coons and Stephen Sugarman, *Scholarships for Children* (Berkeley, Calif.: Institute of Government Studies Press, 1992). The latest statewide plan is Florida's, which to date has enrolled very few students.

8. Ryan in *Simmons-Harris*, 32.

9. The phrase is used almost as an incantation to refer to schools "that succeed in promoting academic achievement and other educational goals," by John E. Chubb and Terry M. Moe, "Effective Schools and Equal Opportunity" in Devins, *Public Values*, p. 163.

10. The dominant alternative, of course, is greater funding for public schools. For a case study of the limitations on reform imposed by financial resources see Marion Orr, *Black Social Capital: The Politics of School Reform in Baltimore, 1986–1998* (Lawrence: University Press of Kansas, 1999).

11. Here, *declinism* refers to traditional educational outcomes, with a particular focus on large urban school systems. The decline thesis has been challenged, most effectively by questioning the baseline. See Kevin B. Smith and Kenneth J. Meier, *The Case against School Choice: Politics, Markets, and Fools* (Armonk, N.Y.: M. E. Sharpe, 1995). Other refutations of declinism look at the balance between success and failure of decades of egalitarian reform on racial segregation in schools, gender equity, programs for the disabled, education for children with limited knowledge of English, and school financing.

12. Carl Kaestle, "Toward a Political Economy of Citizenship: Historical Perspectives on the Purposes of Common School" (typescript), p. 27.

13. *Committee for Public Education v. Nyquist*, 413 U.S. 756 (1973). Twenty percent of the state's elementary and secondary students attended private schools. The Catholic Church makes it a practice to publicly advertise how much parochial schools are saving taxpayers; the Philadelphia archdiocese posts signs outside school buildings. See Morken and Formicola, *The Politics of School Choice*, p. 106.

14. Kaestle argues against the thesis that there has been a wholesale historical shift to economic concerns in "Toward a Political Economy of Citizenship."

15. Key examples of the first three are the NEH project on history teaching in the mid-1980s, the *Nation at Risk* manifesto of 1983, and the National Defense Education Act of 1958.

16. Cited in Howard Gardner, "Paroxysms of Choice," *New York Review of Books*, October 19, 2000, p. 44.

17. Facilitating litigation over school funding in terms not of equal spending or disparities of spending per se, but of spending adequate to meet announced state standards.

18. The "standards movement" cannot be identified exclusively with advocacy of academic excellence; it is more closely tied to accountability. See Nicholas Lemann, "Dumbing Down," *New Yorker*, September 25, 2000, pp. 89–91.

19. John E. Chubb and Terry M. Moe, *Politics, Markets, and America's Schools* (Washington, D.C.: Brookings Institution Press, 1990), p. 162.

20. Chubb and Moe, *Politics, Markets, and America's Schools*, p. 2. Their argument hinges on the politics of social groups that have a hand in educational governance and resist affording schools the independence they need to create the conditions of quality education. They list the characteristics of effective schools: "clear school goals, rigorous academic standards, order and discipline, homework, strong leadership by the principal, teacher participation in decision-making, parental support and cooperation, and high expectations for student performance" (p. 16).

21. Chubb and Moe, *Politics, Markets, and America's Schools*, pp. 189, 217. Challenging this are Smith and Meier, *The Case against School Choice*, p. 123; confirming are Wolf, Howell, and Peterson, "School Choice in Washington, D.C.," p. 4 (68 percent of parents who took advantage of a private voucher plan listed academic quality first; 38 percent, religion and discipline.)

22. Chubb and Moe, *Politics, Markets, and America's Schools*, p. 189.

23. Deborah Meier, *The Power of Their Ideas: Lessons for American from a Small School in Harlem* (Boston: Beacon Press, 1995), pp. 95–96.

24. On Chubb and Moe's view, that would require public policy to put public education beyond the reach of public authority, creating an educational universe of public funding and limited oversight.

25. Studies cited in Orr, *Black Social Capital*, p. 7.

26. For a review of recent assessments of the educational superiority of private and charter schools over public schools see Gardner, "Paroxysms of Choice." Among the many issues is the salience of income to results, made more acute by the specific population that actually takes particular, relevant tests. Among recent contributors to the debate see Smith and Meier, *The Case against School Choice*; Henig, *Rethinking School Choice*; Wolf, Howell, and Peterson, "School Choice in Washington, D.C." It is fair to say that positive indications where some sort of control group was used to measure differentials are short run and modest at best and pertain chiefly to elementary-school students; Wolf, Howell, and Peterson emphasize the adjustment problems of older students moved to private schools.

27. Chubb and Moe, *Politics, Markets, and America's Schools*, pp. 170, 172.

28. A rough estimate is that 10–12 percent of children attend private schools, 85 percent sectarian schools. Of the roughly 52 million school-age in religious schools, half, or around 2.6 million, attend Catholic schools, and the second-largest enrollment is in conservative Christian schools. The fastest-growing private element nationwide is Christian schools, many "fundamentalist"; roughly 1.5 million, or 30 percent, of children in religious schools are in these schools. Among some groups, Orthodox Jews for example, about 80 percent attend yeshivas, cited in Warren A. Nord, *Religion and American Education* (Chapel Hill: University of North Carolina Press, 1995), pp. 355–56; and James Dwyer, *Religious Schools versus Children's Rights* (Ithaca: Cornell University Press, 1998), pp. 15–16.

29. Joseph Coleman, "Civic Pedagogies and Liberal-Democratic Curricula," *Ethics* 108 (July 1998), pp. 746–61.

30. Jay P. Greene, "Civic Values in Public and Private Schools," in Paul E. Peterson and Bryan Hassel, eds., *Lessons from School Choice* (Washington, D.C.: Brookings Institution Press, 1999).

31. Christopher Jencks and Meredith Phillips, "America's Next Achievement Test: Closing the Black-White Test Score Gap," *American Prospect* (September–October 1998), pp. 44–53.

32. Henig, *Rethinking School Choice*, pp. 67, 225. Henig comments on the redefinition of *public* to include "any school that serves the public interest and is ultimately accountable to public authorities" (p. 94). The political point here is that the real battle is not between government and parents, but between parents and educational interest groups.

33. Martha Minow, "Reforming School Reform," *Fordham Law Review* 68 (1999), p. 270.

34. The popular assumption is that states closely monitor and regulate private education. In practice, Dwyer argues, state regulation and supervision of private secular and sectarian schools and of home schooling varies greatly, as have state supreme court rulings in these contests; some states abdicate even a minimal role. Some Christian schools have self-paced instruction without

teachers at all. In some states, home-schooling parents need not have high school diplomas, and so on.

35. Religious educators produce internal critiques of the quality of their schools; see, for example, Thomas C. Hung and Norlene M. Kunkel, "Catholic Schools: The Nation's Largest Alternative School System," in James C. Carper and Thomas C. Hunt, eds., *Religious Schooling in America* (Birmingham, Ala.: Religious Education Press, 1984), pp. 11ff.

36. These are from Dwyer, *Religious Schools versus Children's Rights*, pp. 14–15, 147; the first is a citation at p. 16.

37. I do not consider parental authority as a separate category of argument for choice; it generally enlists one of the three discussed here.

38. Cited in Nancy L. Rosenblum, *Membership and Morals: The Personal Uses of Pluralism in America* (Princeton: Princeton University Press, 1998), p. 242.

39. At the same time the Court outlawed the compulsory flag salute as an unconstitutional measure coercing citizens into affirming faith in orthodoxy. Justice Jackson in *West Virginia State Board of Education v. Barnette*, 319 U.S. 624 (1943). Justice Jackson added, inconsistently, "Free public education, if faithful to the ideal of secular instruction and political neutrality, will not be partisan or enemy of any class, creed, party, or faction." See Michael McConnell, "Believers as Equal Citizens," in Nancy Rosenblum, ed., *Obligations of Citizenship and Demands of Faith* (Princeton: Princeton University Press, 2000), pp. 90–110.

40. Stephen Arons, *Short Route to Chaos: Conscience, Community, and the Reconstitution of American Schooling* (Amherst: University of Massachusetts Press, 1997), p. 52. Statistics from 1992 show that 55 percent of local government employees and 45 percent of state employees work in education; local school districts spent $241 billion; the manufacture and sale of K–12 textbooks is a $2 billion per year industry; testing and certification of teachers is a large outpost; the overall testing business claims a significant but undocumented share of the expense of public education—to say nothing of the amount families choose to expend; just two teachers' unions have over 3 million members; plus the professional journals and so on.

41. "Since Goals 2000 had its origin with Republican and Democratic members of the National Governors' Conference, and continues to rely on the power of states to create and implement reforms . . . the assurances of voluntary participation are all but meaningless to families and individuals." Arons, *Short Route to Chaos*, pp. 70, 77.

42. More specifically, theoretical arguments today adopt the language of "political liberalism." Theorists ask whether the contested elements of liberal democracy inculcated through education amount to a closet "comprehensive" ethical doctrine? If so, how threatening are they to religious faith and moral traditionalism? If not, how "thin" or modest are they? How accommodating of exit and opt-outs? See, for example, Eamonn Callan, "Political Liberalism and Political Education," *Review of Politics* 58 (winter 1996), pp. 5–33; and on the other side of the argument, Stephen Macedo, "Liberal Civic Education and Religious Fundamentalism: The Case of God versus John Rawls," *Ethics* 105 (April 1995), pp. 468–96.

43. If preference for charter over public schools rests on the relative ease of lifting onerous regulations, preference for charter over private schools rests on the relative ease of imposing appropriate restrictions.

44. What we do not find are proposals informed by many European systems, which absorb religious and other private schools into the public system with attendant strictures on curriculum or hiring qualifications and with national achievement testing. Glenn suggests that in these systems schools typically lose their "denominational flavor." *Choice of Schools in Six Nations*, p. 125. In Vermont, however, towns may satisfy the constitutional requirement to provide high-school education by designating secular private schools to function as a town's high school.

45. See Nancy L. Rosenblum, "Pluralism and Democratic Education: Stopping Short by Stopping with Schools," in Stephen Macedo and Yael Tamir, eds., *Moral and Political Education*, NOMOS XLIII (New York: New York University Press, 2002). Sharing this assessment, and exemplifying it, is William Galston in "Expressive Liberty, Moral Pluralism, Political Pluralism: Three Sources of Liberal Theory," *William and Mary Law Review* 40 (1999), p. 869.

46. Chubb and Moe, in their hypothetical choice plan, would prohibit supplementing scholarship amounts in order to limit disparities and inequalities within what they call "the public system." *Politics, Markets, and America's Schools*, p. 220.

47. Stephen Arons, "Educational Choice as a Civil Rights Strategy," in Devins, ed., *Public Values, Private Schools*, p. 74.

48. Again, we hear the argument that if private school students were to enroll in public schools, local and state school taxes would increase "by at least 10%." Arons, "Educational Choice as a Civil Rights Strategy," p. 186 n. 8.

49. For a discussion of the baseline question see Cass R. Sunstein, *The Partial Constitution* (Cambridge: Harvard University Press, 1993), pp. 298ff. A key comparison is access to abortion: whether withholding federal funding amounts to a penalty or unconstitutional obstacle to the exercise of a right. See Kimberly M. Deshano, "Educational Vouchers and the Religion Clauses under *Agostini*: Resurrection, Insurrection, and a New Direction," *Case Western Reserve Law Review* 49 (summer 1999), pp. 747–99; and Nord, *Religion and American Education*, pp. 366–67.

50. They are overwhelmingly segregated in practice and mainly white, with the exception of black Christian academies. See Paul F. Parsons, *Inside America's Christian Schools* (Macon, Ga.: Mercer University Press, 1987). "The evidence suggests that the primary motivation for the continued existence of Christian schools is religious and not racial" (p. 126). On the other side, public magnet schools originated as a way to temper racial segregation by inviting voluntary integration.

51. Jeremy Rabkin points out that these measures do not speak to the consequences of private-school enrollment on public-school desegregation—white flight. "Taxing Discrimination," in Devins, *Public Values, Private Schools*, p. 141.

52. See the discussion of Minnesota's open-enrollment plan in Henig, *Rethinking School Choice*, pp. 112–13.

53. McConnell, "Education Disestablishment," in Stephen Macedo and Yael Tamir, eds., *Moral and Political Education*, NOMOS XLIII (New York: New York University Press, 2002).

54. Clifford W. Cobb, *Responsive Schools, Renewed Communities* (San Francisco: ICS Press, 1992), p. 9.

55. On the other side, there is hardly a trace of individualism in any of these frameworks for choice. Self-development, say, makes no appearance among the avowed goals. "Progressive" models of education take a backseat to conservative pedagogies. The "special education" model of assessment of learning patterns, resource-rich services, and individualized education plans—its cost and controversy—may haunt these discussion as well. An exception is Meier, *The Power of Their Ideas*.

56. These are not always distinguishable: German Lutherans, for example, created schools focused on the preservation of language; Swedish Lutherans focused on faith alone. See Jon Diefenthaler, "Lutheran Schools in America" in Carper and Hunt, *Religious Schooling in America*, pp. 35–56.

57. Hence sometimes overt repudiation of choice; cited in Morken and Formicola, *The Politics of School Choice*, pp. 169ff. The priority assigned pluralist education over other moral and family issues, which is not as high as it is for other groups, sets evangelical organizations apart as well.

58. See the discussion of Nebraska cases in Parsons, *Inside America's Christian Schools*, pp. 140ff.

59. Rebell, "Values Inculcation and the Schools," p. 49. For a discussion of the how to discern religious-based conscience, see Greenawalt, "Five Questions Judges Are Afraid to Ask," in Nancy Rosenblum, ed., *Obligations of Citizenship and Demands of Faith: Religious Accommodation in Pluralist Democracies* (Princeton: Princeton University Press, 2000).

60. As urged by advocates of identity politics: "Groups cannot be socially equal unless their specific experience, culture, and social contributions are publicly affirmed and recognized." Iris Marion Young, *Justice and the Politics of Difference* (Princeton: Princeton University Press, 1990), p. 95.

61. Michael W. McConnell and Richard A. Posner, "An Economic Approach to Issues of Religious Freedom," *University of Chicago Law Review* 56 (1989), p. 57.

62. The policy implications of this logic of equal citizenship extend far beyond education. Entitlements would extend to a limitless range of church-state partnerships, beginning with current legislation enabling "charitable choice," which would allow religious ministries to administer government grants in areas of welfare, job training, drug rehabilitation, and so on. "Charitable choice" promises direct public support for religious missions and proselytizing. And *choice* is a misnomer since there is no guarantee that beneficiaries would have options among service providers.

63. In "Pluralism and Democratic Education: Stopping Short by Stopping with Schools" I argue that there is another direction open to those whose principal theoretical commitment in educational matters is to democracy, but who want to strike a different balance between democracy and pluralism. We can argue that pluralist education is consistent with democratic education, and

with a (bare) civic minimum, if we do not look on schools as the sole educational contexts but rather at the effects of a wide range of institutions in civil society. My criticism of this argument is contained in the same essay.

64. McConnell assumes irreducible pluralism but not deep balkanization of the sort that "threatens to tear the nation apart." If that were the case, he would accede to education that was not divided along religious lines. McConnell, "Education Disestablishment," p. 65.

65. Parsons, *Inside America's Christian Schools*, p. 134. In their first-year study of the Washington, D.C., voucher plan, Wolf, Howell, and Peterson could find no difference in religious attendance outside of school between students at private schools and their public-school control group, and a negative effect after the sixth grade (p. 35).

66. Graham Walker, "Illusory Pluralism, Inexorable Establishment" in Rosenblum, *Obligations of Citizenship and Demands of Faith*, pp. 111–26.

67. See the essays on denominational schools in in Carper and Hunt, *Religious Schooling in America*, dealing with Catholics, Protestant denominations, and internal divisions among Jews on the subject of religious education in general and public support for pluralist education in particular.

68. When it came to legislation creating an exclusive public-school district for the community, the Supreme Court overturned it as an impermissible establishment of religion. *Board of Education of Kiryas Joel v. Grume* 512 US687 (1994).

69. Of course "value pluralism" is preserved in the same way: local school boards "are permitted to establish and apply their curriculum in such a way as to transmit community values"; "there is a legitimate and substantial community interest in promoting respect for authority and traditional values be they social, moral, or political." *Board of Education v. Pico*, 457 U.S. 853 (1982), at 864.

70. So long as discretion is not exercised in a "narrowly partisan or political manner" and, contradictorily, does not foster "a homogeneous people"; see *Board of Education v. Pico*, 457 U.S. 853 (1982), pp. 5, 7, 12.

71. Stephen V. Monsma and J. Christopher Sopher, *The Challenge of Pluralism: Church and State in Five Democracies* (New York: Rowman and Littlefield 1977).

72. Political moves to establish secular control of schools has been one of the precipitants of stepped-up establishment of religious schools, of religious political activism, and, more, specifically of the formation of religious parties. See Nancy L. Rosenblum, "Religious Parties in Contemporary Democracies" (typescript); and Stathis N. Kalyvas, *The Rise of Christian Democracy in Europe* (Ithaca: Cornell University Press, 1966).

73. Glenn, *Choice of Schools in Six Nations*, pp. 100ff., 73ff., 77.

74. Arons, *Short Route to Chaos*, p. 6.

75. Cobb, *Responsive Schools, Renewed Communities*, p. 194.

76. Cited in Minow, "Reforming School Reform," p. 281.

77. Chubb and Moe, *Politics, Markets, and America's Schools*, p. 213. Note that this logic does not extend to public subsidy for home schooling, though networks of Christian home schoolers undercut the individualist ethos and gives the "movement" a communal character.

78. Gardner, "Paroxysms of Choice," p. 49.

79. *Simmons-Harris*, p. 24. If participating schools are predominantly parochial, it undercuts the argument that public funds channeled to religious schools are of no constitutional consequence if they are a result of genuinely private choice, that "parental choice is a determining factor which breaks a government-church nexus" (p. 25). The same would be true for tax deductions available for all practical purposes only to parents sending children to sectarian schools. The Vermont example indicates why *Agostini* does not apply to vouchers; private choice does not transform aid from "direct and substantial" to "indirect and incidental"; it is still part of unrestricted funds to religious schools.

80. Wolf, Howell, and Peterson point out the considerable percentage of winners of the D.C. voucher lottery who did not use the vouchers because the $1,700 did not cover full tuition, which averaged $3,113. "School Choice in Washington, D.C.," p. 22.

81. In addition to figures for the U.S., consider analysis of New Zealand's nationwide public-choice system in Edward B. Fiske and Helen F. Ladd, "The Invisible Hand as Schoolmaster," *American Prospect*, May 22, 2000, pp. 19–21.

82. The Cleveland experiment was limited to schools within the district boundaries that met the state's educational standards and did not discriminate on the basis of race, religion, or ethnic background, or advocate or foster unlawful behavior, or teach hatred of any person or group on the basis of race, ethnicity, national origin, or religion.

83. Chubb and Moe, *Politics, Markets, and America's Schools*, pp. 183, 201.

84. Meier, *The Power of Their Ideas*, p. 115. For a case study of resistance to school-based management, see Orr, *Black Social Capital*. "By 1993 more than 95% of the fifty largest urban school districts in the United States had similar SBM programs in at least some of their schools (p. 5). This is the general scheme favored by Chubb and Moe, who cite the East Harlem District along with Cambridge public-school districtwide "controlled choice" as exemplary. *Politics, Markets, and America's Schools*, pp. 210ff. Meier focuses on her own institution, Central Park East, but notes that District 4 in Harlem had at publication fifty-two schools in twenty buildings with a population of 13,000 students, mostly under fourteen—a group of alternative schools bigger than the vast majority of school districts in the country. *The Power of Their Ideas*, p. 27. The district has no geographically zoned junior high schools, i.e., attendance requires parent choice. Reformers point out that school autonomy cannot be captured by the phrase "school-based management," which puts the bureaucratic concept of "management" at the center of what teachers and administrators do.

85. Cited in Meier, *The Power of Their Ideas*, p. 123.

86. Meier, *The Power of Their Ideas*, p. 187.

87. *Helms v. Picard*, 5th Circuit, overturned in *Mitchell v. Helms*, 530 U.S. 793 (2000).

88. See the description in Arons, *Short Route to Chaos*, pp. 16ff. The conflict was exacerbated by the fact that historically, key reforms have been promoted by one or another party in state legislatures: antebellum reforms by Whigs,

Progressive reforms in the early-twentieth century, civil-rights-related reforms by a Democratic Congress, and so on.

89. Gardner, "Paroxysms of Choice," p. 49.

90. It is a historical irony that the development of common schools was inseparable from anti-Catholic and nativist movements, and that separationist constitutional amendments in the states prohibiting public funding of sectarian schools were promoted by "Know-Nothings," among others. See Joseph P. Viteritti, "Blaine's Wake: Schools Choice, The First Amendment, and State Constitutional Law," *Harvard Journal for Law and Public Policy* 21 (1998), p. 657.

91. Which is not to say that recent voter rejection of voucher initiatives in California, Michigan, and Washington reflects confidence in public schools.

92. The Hippocrates alternative was suggested to me by Lucas Swaine.

Chapter Five
"Getting Religion": Religion, Diversity, and Community in Public and Private Schools

1. William G. Bowen and Derek Bok, *The Shape of the River: Long-Term Consequences of Considering Race in College and University Admissions* (Princeton: Princeton University Press, 1998), p. 228.

2. Neil L. Rudenstine, "The Uses of Diversity," *Harvard Magazine* (March–April 1996), p. 50. Rudenstine goes on to offer as a key example the fact that Henry Adams's class of 1858 at Harvard included three Virginians, including the son of Robert E. Lee. As Adams put it, writing in the third person, "for the first time Adams's education brought him in contact with new types and taught him their values. He saw the New England type measure itself with another" (p. 51). Rudenstine goes on to note that his experience "altered Adams' consciousness, and forced him to confront and assess a type of person had had never before known. It drove him to reach new conclusions about himself and his own limitations" (p. 51).

3. See, e.g., Jeff Spinner-Halev, "Extending Diversity: Religion in Public and Private Education," in Will Kymlicka and Wayne Norman, eds., *Citizenship in Diverse Societies* (New York: Oxford University Press, 2000), pp. 68–95. He suggests that "one of the basic worries" about parochial schools and their increase (especially if they receive additional public support) is that "the more parochial schools there are, the less students of different backgrounds will mix with one [an]other; the less they will learn how to cooperate with one another or realize that others with different views exist. This leaves the children in private schools isolated" (p. 81). Spinner-Halev's interesting essay in part tracks our own concerns, especially insofar as he rightly insists that "[a] diversity that excludes religion and religious students is not very diverse" (70). Unfortunately, we became aware of his essay only after preparing our own and therefore do not give it the extended attention that it deserves. The same is true, alas, of another essay in that book, Eamonn Callan, "Discrimination and Religious Schooling," pp. 45–67, which offers an especially interesting discussion of educational policy in Canada, which takes a considerably different approach to state funding of religious schools than is found in the United States.

4. See Sanford Levinson, "Diversity," *University of Pennsylvania Journal of Constitutional Law* 2 (2000), p. 573.

5. See Gary Orfield, Susan E. Eaton, and the Harvard Project on School Desegregation, *Dismantling Desegregation: The Quiet Reversal of "Brown v. Board of Education"* (New York: New Press, 1996), esp. chaps. 11–12; Jeffrey Rosen, "The Lost Promise of School Integration," *New York Times*, April 2, 2000.

6. 406 U.S. 205 (1972).

7. The key opinions are those presented in *Mozert v. Hawkins County Board of Education*, 827 F.2d 1058 (6th Cir. 1987), cert. denied, 484 U.S. 1066 (1988).

8. See Levinson, "Diversity," pp. 573, 594.

9. *Hopwood v. Texas*, 78 F.3d 932, 965–66 (6th Cir. 1996)(Weiner, J., concurring).

10. This point is made at length in the recent decision involving the admissions program at the University of Michigan Law School. *Grutter v. Bollinger*, 137 F. Supp. 2d 821 (E.D. Mich., Southern Div., 2001), where Judge Friedman expressed strong reservations about the coherence of the law school's claimed commitment to "diversity." He wrote, for example, that

> there is no logical basis for the law school to have chosen the particular racial groups which receive special attention under the current admissions policy.... During some of the years at issue in this lawsuit, the law school bulletin indicated that special attention has been given to "students who are African American, Mexican American, Native American, or Puerto Rican and raised on the U.S. mainland." The law school has failed to offer a principled explanation as to why it has singled out these particular groups for special attention. Certainly, other groups have also been subjected to discrimination, such as Arabs and southern and eastern Europeans to name but a few, yet the court heard nothing to suggest that the law school has concerned itself as to whether members of these groups are represented "in meaningful numbers." No satisfactory explanation was offered for distinguishing between Puerto Ricans who were raised on the U.S. mainland from Puerto Ricans who were raised in Puerto Rico or elsewhere. No satisfactory explanation was offered for singling out Mexican Americans but, by implication, excluding from special consideration Hispanics who originate from countries other than Mexico. A special "commitment" is made to African Americans, but apparently none is made to blacks from other parts of the world. This haphazard selection of certain races is a far cry from the "close fit" between the means and the ends that the Constitution demands in order for a racial classification to pass muster under strict scrutiny analysis. (851–52).

11. See generally Orfield, *Dismantling Desegregation*.

12. We call these schools "special emphasis" following the National Center for Education Statistics' *Private School Universe Survey, 1997–1998*. See p. 28 of that survey, where the various categories of schools are defined.

13. This is not to say that diversity is concomitant with, or even necessary to, educational quality; although our focus in this essay is on the implications of the diversity argument for religious education, it may well be that other goals, such as achievement or equity, are more important. Be that as it may, it is not our purpose here to balance diversity claims against other educational or social norms.

14. Bushnell in Rush Welter, ed., *American Writing on Popular Education: The Nineteenth Century* (New York: Bobbs-Merrill Co., 1971), p. 182.

15. Quoted in Stephen Macedo, *Diversity and Distrust: Civic Education in a Multicultural Democracy* (Cambridge: Harvard University Press, 2000), p. 93.

16. Macedo, *Diversity and Distrust*, p. 194.

17. We put it this way because it might be too heroic an aspiration that everyone accept the substantive "reasonableness" of the views—and, even more so, the behavior—of others. One need not believe, for example, that it is truly "reasonable" not to mix milk and meat in order to respect the reasons that lead observant (and even some non-Orthodox) Jews to maintain adherence to this tradition of kashruth.

18. See Sanford Levinson, "Some Reflections on Multiculturalism, 'Equal Concern and Respect,' and the Establishment Clause of the First Amendment," *University of Richmond Law Review* 27 (1993), p. 989 (noting also the costs of growing up in a segregated society that meant that all of these friends were white).

19. Levinson, "Some Reflections on Multiculturalism," pp. 995–96.

20. This means, among other things, that (liberal) society as a whole almost certainly benefits from the "intermarriages" that are often bewailed by leaders of particular groups. To take what some would consider an extreme example, every marriage of an Israeli Jew with an Israeli Arab, whether Christian or Muslim, would be a cause for rejoicing on the part of any liberal.

21. Which is, in fact, true of at least some Chinese; see, e.g., Peter Hessler, "A Rat in My Soup," *New Yorker*, July 24, 2000, pp. 38–41. However, the student's assertion was not made by way of pointing to the remarkable culinary differences among cultures but, rather, as a sign of the true Otherness of all Chinese.

22. *Gratz v. Bollinger*, 122 F. Supp. 2d 811, 822 (2000), citing the "Gurin Report," p. 3. It should be obvious that this decision patently conflicts with Judge Friedman's decision several months later in *Grutter v. Bollinger*, 137 F. Supp. 2d 821 (2001). Presumably, the Sixth Circuit Court of Appeals will choose between them (and then, inevitably, the Supreme Court will be given an opportunity to weigh in).

23. *Gratz v. Bollinger*, at 822, quoting the Gurin Report at p. 5.

24. Meira Levinson, *The Demands of Liberal Education* (Oxford: Oxford University Press, 1999), pp. 101–6; Amy Gutmann, "Civic Education and Social Diversity," *Ethics* 105 (April 1995), pp. 516–34; Harry Brighouse, "Is There Any Such Thing as Political Liberalism?" *Pacific Philosophical Quarterly* 75 (1994), pp. 318–32; Eamonn Callan, *Creating Citizens* (Oxford: Oxford University Press, 1997), chap. 1, esp. pp. 39–42.

25. *Gratz v. Bollinger*, at 822, citing the Gurin Report, p. 5.

26. *Gratz v. Bollinger*, at 822, citing the Gurin Report, p. 5.

27. *Gratz v. Bollinger*, at 822, citing Brief for the United States, p. 20–21.

28. Whose suspicions of each other is, one suspects, are easily as great as any suspicion directed at Jews from outside these communities.

29. Compare, for example, James Davidson Hunter, *Culture Wars* (New York: Basic Books, 1991); and James Davidson Hunter, *Before the Shooting Begins : Searching for Democracy in America's Culture War* (New York: Free Press,

1994), with Alan Wolfe's considerably more optimistic assessment in *One Nation after All: What Middle-Class Americans Really Think about God, Country, Family, Racism, Welfare, Immigration, Homosexuality, Work, the Right, the Left, and Each Other* (New York: Viking, 1998).

30. Bowen and Bok, *The Shape of the River*, p. 228.

31. Emily Buss, "The Adolescent's Stake in the Allocation of Educational Control between Parent and State," *University of Chicago Law Review* 67 (2000), p. 1233.

32. These arguments are spelled out in Levinson, *The Demands of Liberal Education*, chaps. 1 and 2.

33. Levinson, *The Demands of Liberal Education*, pp. 144–45; Levinson, "Some Reflections on Multiculturalism," p. 1011.

34. 268 U.S. 510 (1925).

35. One might also be tempted to describe it as not only heavy-handed, but unconstitutional. If, though, racial preferences, which are presumptively unconstitutional, can nonetheless be justified because of the "compelling interest" of diversity, as many of their proponents allege, then it would seem that an identical argument would legitimize the otherwise prohibited taking into account of religion when designing catchment areas. See Levinson, "Diversity," pp. 602–5; Eugene Volokh, "Diversity, Race as Proxy, and Religion as Proxy," *UCLA Law Review* 43 (1996), pp. 2059, 2070–76.

36. See Jodi Wilgoren, "On Campus and on Knees, Facing Mecca," *New York Times*, February 13, 2001, which describes efforts that MIT has made with regard to the increasing number of Muslims on its campus. Indeed, it turns out that the University of Texas Law School, unlike MIT a decidedly state institution, has reserved a room within its library that serves as a chapel for students who wish to make use of it.

37. They also need not be seen as coercing other students into religion. In Meira Levinson's experience in teaching in Atlanta, at least, where Georgia law mandates forty seconds (!) of daily silent reflection, middle schoolers often stopped for silent reflection in the most absurd physical posture possible (in midstep, for example, balanced on one foot, or perched precariously on a desk) as teachers snapped repeatedly, "Quiet! Close your mouths! Silent reflection!" In what at other times felt like an emphatically religious (Christian) setting, especially for a public school, "silent reflection" never seemed to acquire any religious overtones.

38. National Center for Education Statistics, *Private Schools Universe Study,* 1997–1998, pp. 1–2.

39. According to the National Center for Education Statistics, there were 5.97 million students in private schools and 47 million in public schools in 1999 (http://nces.ed.gov/fastfacts). The numbers of schools—89,508 public and 27,402 private—as of 1997–98, are available in *Digest of Education Statistics, 1999*, chap. 2 (http://nces.edu.gov). The American School Directory (ASD.com) states that there are 108,000 public schools, which is, of course, a considerably higher number than that provided by the NCES.

40. *Private Schools in the United States*, table 1, p. 3.

41. *Private Schools in the United States*, tables 2.3a, 2.3b, 4.1, 4.2.

42. *Private Schools in the United States*, table 16, p. 21.

43. *Digest of Education Statistics*, 1999, table 45 "Enrollment in Public Elementary and Secondary Schools, by Race or Ethnicity and State, Fall 1986 and Fall 1997" (http://nces.ed.gov/pubs2000/digest99/d99t045.html). This table offers interesting insights about American demography when it breaks down the percentages by states. Consider, for example, the beginning and end of the alphabet, Alabama and Wyoming. In fall 1997, Alabama's public schools were 61.7 percent white and 36 percent black, together with 0.8 percent Hispanic, 0.7 percent Asian or Pacific Islander, and 0.8 percent American Indian; Wyoming, on the other hand, was 88.6 percent white, and the largest minority groups were Hispanics (6.6 percent) and American Indians (2.95 percent). Blacks accounted for only 1.1 percent of the enrollment. Texas was 45 percent white, 37.9 percent Hispanic, 14.4 percent black, 2.4 percent Asian, and 0.3 percent American Indian; while Massachusetts was 77.5 percent white, 9.7 percent Hispanic, 8.5 percent Black, 4.1 percent Asian, and 0.2 percent American Indian. Perhaps most striking is California, where Hispanics in 1997 comprised 40.5 percent of all students and whites 38.8 percent; Asian/Pacific Islanders were 11.1 percent of the total, Blacks, 2.5 percent, and American Indians 0.9%.

44. See, e.g., James Patterson, *Brown v. Board of Education: A Civil Rights Milestone and Its Troubled Legacy* (New York: Oxford University Press, 2001), p. 212.

45. Jay Greene, "Why School Choice Can Promote Integration," *Education Week* 19, no. 31 (April 12, 2000), pp. 72, 52 (also available at www.edweek.org/ew/ewstory.cfm?slug=31greene.h19); Jay Greene, "Civic Values in Public and Private Schools," in Paul E. Peterson and Bryan C. Hassel, eds., *Learning from School Choice* (Washington, D.C.: Brookings Institution Press, 1998); Sue Ellen Henry and Abe Feuerstein, "'Now We Go to Their School: Desegregation and Its Contemporary Legacy," *Journal of Negro Education*, 68, no. 2 (spring 1999), pp. 164–81.

46. *Private Schools in the United States*, tables 8, p. 12; 17, p. 22; 2.6.

47. *Private Schools in the United States*, tables 2.5, 2.6.

48. It would be interesting to find out how many Dalton or Shady Hill children voted for George W. Bush in "mock elections" in 2000, given that such student votes are a fairly reliable proxy for the views they pick up at home. Meira Levinson can report that only one of her 24 students (and only 19 out of 730 students in the school overall) voted for Bush, with the remainder voting overwhelmingly for Al Gore. This presumably reflects the dominantly poor and working-class composition of the school at which she teaches, given that Bush managed to get approximately 20 percent of the Boston vote and, within the state as a whole, approximately 30 percent. See http://www.state.ma.us/sec/ele/eleidx.htm, which is the entry point for the Web page of the Massachusetts Secretary of State and the relevant election statistics for the year 2000. In any event, few of her students have ever confronted other children or adults who actually support the current occupant of the White House, as is evidenced by their frequent declarations that "nobody supports Bush." One assumes that there were schools elsewhere in the country (even if not in Massachusetts)

where student opinion was equally unbalanced in favor of Governor Bush, leading to the impression that "everybody supports Bush."

49. Partly as a result, the Cambridge City Council recently mandated that as of the 2002–03 school year, students' socioeconomic status (as measured by their eligibility for free or reduced-price meals) will be taken into account when assigning them to schools. By 2004, each grade in each elementary school is expected to have a student population that is no more than 5 percent above or below the district rate of students eligible for free and reduced-price meals. "Seats may be held in an individual school based on free and reduced meals in order to achieve socioeconomic diversity" (Cambridge Public Schools, *Controlled Choice Plan*, December 18, 2001, p. 8). This has become necessary in part because few poor parents were choosing progressive schools and few wealthy parents were choosing more traditionally oriented schools.

Chapter Six
Assessing Arguments for School Choice:
Pluralism, Parental Rights, or Educational Results?

1. I offer a defense of this ideal in *Democratic Education*. This essay draws on ideas developed in *Democratic Education* (Princeton: Princeton University Press, 1999), but also goes beyond those ideas to pursue additional arguments for and against school choice.

2. Recent evidence is available on the National Assessment of Educational Progress (NAEP) Web site (http://nces.ed.gov/nationsreportcard, June 13, 2001.) See also Michael A. Fletcher, "Test Shows Wider Gap in Reading Skills," *Washington Post*, April 4, 2001; and Martha Groves, "Student Scores Stalled in 90s in Two Key Areas," *Los Angeles Times*, August 25, 2000. For an analysis of the NAEP math and reading test results from 1990 to 1996, see David W. Grissmer, Ann Flanagan, Jennifer Kawata, and Stephanie Williamson, *Improving Student Achievement: What State NAEP Test Scores Tell Us* (Washington, D.C.: RAND Corporation, 2000).

3. See Gallup poll, January 10–14, 2001.

4. See, for example, "The Real Test," *New Republic*, February 5, 2001, p. 7.

5. See, for example, Carey Goldberg, "The 2000 Elections: The Ballot Initiatives," *New York Times*, November 9, 2000.

6. Jodi Wilgoren, "Florida's Vouchers a Spur to Two Schools Left Behind," *New York Times*, March 14, 2000.

7. See Stephen Gilles, "On Educating Children: A Parentalist Manifesto," *University of Chicago Law Review* 63 (Summer 1996), p. 937. See also Keith Syler, "Parental Choice versus State Monopoly: Mother Knows Best—A Comment on America's School and Vouchers," *University of Cincinnati Law Review* 68 (summer 2000), p. 1331; and Neal Devins, "Social Meaning and School Vouchers" (paper presented at the Institute of Bill of Rights Law Symposium, "Religion in the Public Sphere"), *William and Mary Law Review* 919 (March 2001), p. 919.

8. Michael W. McConnell, "Education Disestablishment: Why Democratic Values Are Ill-Served by Democratic Control of Schooling," in Stephen Macedo

and Yael Tamir, eds., *Political and Moral Education*, NOMOS XLIII (New York: New York University Press, 2002.)

9. McConnell, "Education Disestablishment."

10. See Nancy Rosenblum's essay in this volume for more on this kind of pluralism.

11. Gilles, "On Educating Children," pp. 937–1032.

12. See Gutmann, *Democratic Education*, pp. 71–94.

13. See, for example, Harry Brighouse, *School Choice and Social Justice* (New York: Oxford University Press, 2000); Meira Levinson, *The Demands of Liberal Education* (New York: Oxford University Press, 1999); Jeffrey Henig, *Rethinking School Choice: Limits of the Market Metaphor* (Princeton: Princeton University Press, 1994); Stephen Macedo, *Diversity and Distrust: Civic Education in a Multicultural Democracy* (Cambridge: Harvard University Press, 2000). See also Jeffrey Henig, *The Color of School Reform: Race, Politics, and the Challenge of Urban Education* (Princeton: Princeton University Press, 1999).

14. McConnell, "Education Disestablishment."

15. See, for example, Milton Friedman, "The Role of Government in Education," in Robert Solo, ed., *Economics and the Public Interest* (New Brunswick, N.J.: Rutgers University Press, 1955), pp. 123–45. See also Milton Friedman, *Capitalism and Freedom* (Chicago: University of Chicago Press, 1962), pp. 85–107; and Gilles, "On Educating Children," pp. 937–1032.

16. Charles Fried, *Right and Wrong* (Cambridge: Harvard University Press, 1998), p. 152.

17. John Stuart Mill, *On Liberty and Other Essays* (New York: Oxford University Press, 1998), chap. 5.

18. Amy Gutmann, "Religion and State in the United States: A Defense of Two-Way Protection," in Nancy L. Rosenblum, ed., *Obligations of Citizenship and Demands of Faith : Religious Accommodation in Pluralist Democracies* (Princeton: Princeton University Press, 2000).

19. See, for example, William Julius Wilson, *The Truly Disadvantaged: The Inner City, the Underclass, and Public Policy* (Chicago: University of Chicago Press, 1987).

20. See Richard Rothstein, "An Allegiance to Public Schools," *New York Times*, March 15, 2001.

21. John E. Chubb and Terry M. Moe, *Politics, Markets, and America's Schools* (Washington, D.C.: Brookings Institution Press, 1990), p. 217.

22. Friedman, "The Role of Government in Education," pp. 123–45. See also Friedman, *Capitalism and Freedom*, pp. 85–107.

23. Cecilia Elena Rouse, "School Reform in the 21st Century: A Look at the Effect of Class Size and School Vouchers on the Academic Achievement of Minority Students," (working paper no. 440, Industrial Relations Section, Princeton University, June 2000). (Paper can be downloaded at http://www.irs.princeton.edu/pubs/working_papers.html; June 13, 2001.)

24. Alan B. Krueger and Diane M. Whitmore, "Would Smaller Classes Help Close the Black-White Achievement Gap?" (working paper no. 451, Industrial Relations Section, Princeton University, March 2001). (Paper can be down-

loaded at http://www.irs.princeton.edu/pubs/working_papers.html, June 13, 2001.)

25. See, for example, Jodie Morse, "Do Public Schools Pass the Test?" *Time Magazine*, May 29, 2001 (on-line version; no page number); and Marc Fisher, "To Each Its Own: Are Charter Schools Providing Customized Education, a Breakdown in Curricular Coherence, or Both?" *Washington Post*, April 8, 2001.

Response
David Hollenbach, S.J.

1. For further treatment of my views see: "The Common Good, Pluralism, and Catholic Education" in Terence H. McLaughlin, Joseph O'Keefe, S.J., and Bernadette O'Keefe, eds., *The Contemporary Catholic School: Context, Identity, Diversity,* (Washington, D.C.: Falmer Press, 1996), 89–103; "The Catholic University and the Common Good," *Current Issues in Catholic Higher Education* 16, no. 1 (summer 1995), pp. 3–15; "Virtue, the Common Good, and Democracy," in Amitai Etzioni, ed., *New Communitarian Thinking: Persons, Virtues, Institutions, and Communities* (Charlottesville: University of Virginia Press, 1994), pp. 143–53.

Chapter Seven
Educational Choice and Pillarization: Some Lessons for Americans from the Dutch Experiment in "Affirmative Impartiality"

1. John Bolt, *A Free Church, a Holy Nation: Abraham Kuyper's American Public Theology* (Grand Rapids, Mich.: Wm. B. Eerdmans Publishing Co., 2001).

2. Kenneth D. McRae, "The Plural Society and the Western Political Tradition" *Canadian Journal of Political Science* 12 (December 1979), p. 682.

3. For my brief sketch here of nineteenth-century developments I am drawing on more detailed discussions in Bolt, *Free Church*, pp. 332–39; and on John Sturm and Siebren Miedema, "Kuyper's Educational Legacy: Schooling for a Pluralistic Society," in Cornelis van der Kooi and Jan de Bruijn, eds., *Kuyper Reconsidered: Aspects of His Life and Work*, VU Studies on Protestant History, vol. 3 (Amsterdam: VU Uitgeverij, 1999), pp. 239–43.

4. Bolt, *Free Church*, p. 336.

5. J. P. Kruijt, "The Netherlands: The Influence of Denominationalism on Social Life and Organizational Patterns," in Kenneth McRae, ed., *Consociational Democracy: Political Accommodation in Segmented Societies* (Toronto: McClelland and Stewart, 1974), p. 130.

6. Nicholas Wolterstorff, *Religion and the Schools: A Reformed Journal Monograph* (Grand Rapids, Mich.: Wm. B. Eerdmans Publishing Co., 1965, 1966), pp. 22–23.

7. Stanley W. Carlson-Thies, "The Meaning of Dutch Segmentation for Modern America," in Goerge Harinck and Hans Krabbendam, eds., *Sharing the Reformed Tradition: The Dutch-North American Exchange, 1846–1996*, VU Studies on Protestant History, vol. 2 (Amsterdam: VU Uitgeverij, 1996), pp. 164–65.

8. Carlson-Thies, "Meaning," p. 165.

9. Carlson-Thies, "Meaning," p. 167.

10. The complex motivations for increased support for religiously based schools are nicely charted by David Sikkink in his essay "The Social Sources of Alienation from Public Schools," *Social Forces* 78, no. 1 (1999), pp. 51–86.

11. For a good summary of Kuyper's use of this concept, see Peter S. Heslam, *Creating a Christian Worldview: Abraham Kuyper's Lectures on Calvinism* (Grand Rapids, Mich.: Wm. B. Eerdmans Publishing Co., 1998), pp. 88–96; for more extensive discussions of the Kuyperian notion of worldview, see the essays in Paul A. Marshall, Sander Griffioen, and Richard J. Mouw, eds., *Stained Glass: Worldviews and Social Science* (Lanham, Md.: University Press of America, 1989).

12. Kenneth J. Gergen, *The Saturated Self: Dilemmas of Identity in Contemporary Life* (New York: Basic Books, 1991), p. 247, 256, 259.

13. Quoted by Wolterstorff, *Religion*, p. 34.

14. Wolterstorff, *Religion*, p. 12.

15. See the summary of these present-day discussions in Sturm and Miedema, "Kuyper's Educational Legacy," pp. 243–46

16. Sturm and Medema, "Kuyper's Educational Legacy," p. 245.

17. J. Bryan Hehir, "Personal Faith, the Public Church, and the Role of Theology," *Harvard Divinity Bulletin* 26, no. 1 (1996), p. 5.

18. My use of "thick" and "thin" here follows the pattern employed by many commentators in recent years. The imagery was made popular by Clifford Geertz, who in turn borrowed the terms from Gilbert Ryle. Cf. Clifford Geertz, "Thick Description: Toward an Interpretive Theory of Culture," in his *Interpretation of Cultures* (New York: Basic Books, 1973), pp. 3–30.

19. Ronald Thiemann, *Constructing Public Theology: The Church in a Pluralistic Culture* (Louisville, Ky.: Westminster/John Knox Press, 1991), p. 43.

20. Sarah Wildman, "Who Says Conservatives Like Vouchers?" *New Republic*, February 26, 2001, p. 16.

Chapter Eight
Protecting and Limiting School Distinctiveness:
How Much of Each?

1. Charles Glenn and Jan De Groof, *Finding the Right Balance: Freedom, Autonomy, and Accountability in Education*, vols. 1 and 2 (Utrecht: Lemma, 2002).

2. James G. Dwyer, *Religious Schools v. Children's Rights* (Ithaca: Cornell University Press, 1998).

3. On-line at www.skolverket.se/pdf/lpoe.pdf.

4. Ministry of Education (1990), 19, 26–38, 50.

5. Francesc Riu i Rovira de Villar, *Todos tienen el derecho a la educación* (Madrid: Consejo General de la Educación Católica, 1988), pp. 109, 166. It is worth noting that an official translation of this provision tones down the implication that the schools should shape the worldview of students: "knowledge of basic rights and liberties." General Law, 21.

6. General Law, 22, italics added.

7. General Law, 32.

8. Sabine Monchambert, *La liberté de l'enseignement* (Paris: Presses universitaires de France, 1983), p. 82.

9. Andries Postma, *Handboek van het nederlandse onderwijsrecht* (Zwolle, The Netherlands: W.E.J. Tjeenk Willink, 1995), pp. 112, 148.

10. Alan Peshkin, *God's Choice: The Total World of a Fundamentalist Christian School* (Chicago: University of Chicago Press, 1986), pp. 332–34, 189, 221.

11. For a full discussion, see Charles L. Glenn, "Common Standards and Educational Diversity," in Jan De Groof, ed., *Subsidiarity and Education: Aspects of Comparative Educational Law* (Leuven, Belgium: Acco, 1994).

12. Briony Scott and Stephen Crump, "Funding and Regulating School [in Australia]" (typescript prepared for the author, 2000).

13. Charles L. Glenn, "Organizing the Russian Educational System for Freedom and Accountability," in Jan De Groof, ed., *Comments on the Law on Education of the Russian Federation* (Louvain, Belgium: Acco, 1993).

14. On line at www.skolverket.se/english/system.

15. Gabriel Langouet and Alain Leger, *Public ou privé?* (Nanterre: Publidix, 1991), pp. 65–66, 71, 82.

16. Postma, *Handboek*, p. 136.

17. Postma, *Handboek*, p. 373.

18. Frank-Rüdiger Jach, *Schulverfassung und Bürgergesellschaft in Europa* (Berlin: Duncker and Humblot, 1999), p. 163.

19. Riu i Rovira, *Todos*, p. 53.

20. Ruling of the Tribunal Constitucional on February 13, 1981, reprinted in Riu i Rovira, *Todos*, p. 107.

21. Ley Orgánica de Ordenación General del Sistema Educativo 61.2, General Law 62.

22. On line at www.uvm.dk/eng/publications/factsheets/fact9.htm.

23. Frank-Rüdiger Jach, *Schulvielfalt als Verfassungsgebot* (Berlin: Dunker and Humblot 1991), pp. 64–65, 81.

24. Jo van Ham, "The Position of Minorities in Education in the European Union: The Netherlands," in Jan De Groof and Jan Fiers, eds., *The Legal Status of Minorities in Education* (Leuven, Belgium: Acco, 1996), pp. 360–61.

25. Dympna Glendenning, *Education and the Law* (Dublin: Butterworths, 1999), p. 174.

26. J. Alfonso Aisa Sola, "Los conciertos educativos," *in Cuadernos de Derecho Judicial: Aspecto Juridicos del Sistema Educativo* (Madrid: Consejo General del Poder Judicial, 1993), p. 257; Isabel de los Mozos Touya, *Educación en libertad y concierto escolar* (Madrid: Editorial Montecorvo, 1995), pp. 557–66; text in Riu i Rovira, *Todos*, pp. 189, 229.

27. Riu i Rovira, *Todos*, p. 191.

28. H.-C. Amiel, quoted by Jacques Georgel and Anne-Marie Thorel, *L'enseignement privé en France* (Paris: Dalloz, 1995), p. 207.

29. Education Department of Western Australia (www.des.wa.gov.au/services/nongov).

30. Edward B. Fiske and Helen F. Ladd, *When Schools Compete* (Washington, D.C.: Brookings Institution Press, 1999), pp. 62, 58, 182. 284.

31. Postma, *Handboek*, p. 124.

32. Postma, *Handboek*, pp. 351–52

33. Postma, *Handboek*, p. 142.

34. Quoted by Glendenning, *Education and the Law*, pp. 412–13.

35. Quoted by Glendenning, *Education and the Law*, p. 418.

36. Glendenning, *Education and the Law*, p. 430.

37. Monchambert, *La liberté de l'enseignement*, p. 160; Georgel and Thorel, *L'enseignement privé en France*, pp. 223–25.

38. Monchambert, *La liberté de l'enseignement*, pp. 60–63.

39. Monchambert, *La liberté de l'enseignement*, p. 179.

40. Georgel and Thorel, *L'enseignement privé en France*, p. 211.

41. Monchambert, *La liberté de l'enseignement*, pp. 181–84.

42. de los Mozos Touya, *Educación en libertad y concierto escolar*, pp. 255–58.

43. Text and commentary in Riu i Rovira, *Todos*, p. 135

44. Riu i Rovira, *Todos*, pp. 168–69; de los Mozos Touya, *Educación en libertad y concierto escolar*, p. 305.

45. Quoted by de los Mozos Touya, *Educación en libertad y concierto escolar*, p. 248.

46. José Luis Martínez Lopez-Muñiz, "El art. 27 de la Constitución: Analisis de su contenido, doctrina jurisprudencial. Tratados internacionales suscritos pos España," in *Cuadernos de Derecho Judicial*, p. 29.

47. See Charles L. Glenn, *The Ambiguous Embrace: Government and Faith-Based Schools and Social Agencies* (Princeton: Princeton University Press, 2000).

48. Peshkin, *God's Choice*, pp. 259, 49, 273.

Chapter Nine
Catholic Schools and Vouchers: How the Empirical
Reality Should Ground the Debate

1. D. J. Hoff, "School Choice Programs Growing More Rapidly outside the U.S.," *Education Week*, June 18, 2001, p. 5.

2. American Federation of Teachers, "Myths and Facts about Private School Choice" (http://www.aft.org/research/vouchers/vouchers/myths/myths.html).

3. People for the American Way, "Milwaukee Voucher Experiment: Rolling the Dice for Our Children's Future" (http://www.pfaw.org/issues/education/milwaukee.shtml).

4. L. Tuttle, "School Choice and Vouchers: Education Reform Begins with Alternative Choices" (http://www.cblpolicyinstitute.org/choice_and_vouchers.htm).

5. K. Fournier, "What Is Right about Parental Vouchers," *Catholic Alliance* (http://www.catholicvote.org/faith&culture/parental_vouchers.html).

6. A. King, "Fighting for School Choice: It's a Civil Right," *Wall Street Journal*, September 11, 1997.

7. D. Jackson, "The Corruption of School Choice," *Boston Globe*, October 28, 1998.

8. Ted Forstmann, "Make Education Look More Like America: Put Parents in Charge" (speech delivered at the National Press Club, April 3, 2001; (http:// www.putparentsincharge.org/speech_apr3.html).

9. N. Weller, "Private Scholarships Expand School Choice," *Cascade Commentary* 13 (2001), p. 2.

10. John F. Witte, *The Market Approach to Education: An Analysis of America's First Voucher Program* (Princeton: Princeton University Press, 2000); P. J. McEwan, "The Potential Impact of Large-Scale Voucher Programs," (occasional Paper no. 2, National Center for the Study of Privatization in Education, Teachers College, Columbia University, 2000).

11. E. Adelsheimer, *What We Know about Vouchers: The Facts Behind the Rhetoric* (San Francisco: WestEd, 1999).

12. Witte, *The Market Approach to Education.*

13. Stephen D. Sugarman and Frank R. Kemerer *eds., School Choice and Social Controversy: Politics, Policy and Law* (Washington, D.C.: Brookings Institution Press, 1999), p. 91.

14. R. Rothstein, "Lessons: Vouchers Dead, Alternatives Weak," *New York Times,* June 20, 2001.

15. J. Youniss and J. McLellan, "Catholic Schools in Perspective: Religious Identity, Achievement and Citizenship," *Phi Delta Kappan* 81, no. 2 (1999), pp. 105–6.

16. McEwan, "The Potential Impact of Large-Scale Voucher Programs.

17. Witte, *The Market Approach to Education.*

18. L. DeFiore, "Message from the President: School Choice, the Turned Tide," *Momentum* 32 (2001), p. 4.

19. S. Karp, "Justice Issues Are Common Ground for Catholic, Public School Alliance," *National Catholic Reporter,* March 27, 1998 (http://www.natcath. com/NCR_Online/archives/032798/032798b/htm).

20. B. T. Froehl and M. Gautier, *A Portrait of the Catholic Church in the United States* (Maryknoll, N.Y.: Orbis Books, 2000).

21. D. R. Finn, "John Paul II and the Moral Ecology of Markets," *Theological Studies* 59 (1998), p. 675.

22. National Catholic Conference of Bishops, *Sharing Catholic Social Teaching: Challenges and Directions* (1998, http://www.nccbuscc.org/sdwp/projects/ socialteaching/socialteaching.htm).

23. R. Pring, "The Market and Catholic Schools," in T. McLaughlin, J. O'Keefe, and B. O'Keeffe, eds., *The Contemporary Catholic School: Context, Identity, and Diversity* (Washington, D.C.: Falmer, 1996).

24. J. Convey, *Catholic Schools Make a Difference: Twenty-Five years of research* (Washington, D.C.: National Catholic Educational Association, 1992), pp. 59–65; D.E.D. York, "The Academic Achievement of African Americans in Catholic Schools: A Review of Literature," in J. J. Irvine and M. Foster, eds., *Growing Up African American in Catholic Schools* (New York: Teachers College Press, 1996), pp. 21–26.

25. J. S. Coleman, T. Hoffer, and S. Kilgore, *High School achievement: Public, Catholic and Private compared* (New York: Basic Books, 1982); J. S. Coleman and T. Hoffer, *Public and Private High Schools: The Impact of Communities* (New York:

Basic Books, 1987); A. M. Greeley, *Catholic High schools and Minority Students* (New Brunswick, N.J.: Transaction Books, 1982); A. S. Bryk, V. E. Lee, and P. B. Holland, *Catholic Schools and the Common Good* (Cambridge: Harvard University Press, 1993).

26. A. Gamoran, "Student Achievement in Public Magnet, Public Comprehensive, and Private City High Schools," *Educational Evaluation and Policy Analysis* 18, no. 1 (1996), pp. 1–18.

27. J. D. Teachman, K. Paasch, and K. and K. Carver, "Social Capital and the Generation of Human Capital," *Social Forces* 75, no. 4 (1997), pp. 1343–59.

28. W. Sander, and A. C. Krautmann, "Catholic Schools, Dropout Rates, and Educational Attainment," *Economic Inquiry* 33, no. 2 (1995), pp. 217–33.

29. A. M. Jones, "Differential Effectiveness: Catholic and Public School Fourth Graders' Performance on the 1992 NAEP mathematics assessment" (Ph.D. diss., Boston College, 1997).

30. D. Neal, "The Effects of Catholic Secondary Schooling on Educational Achievement," *Journal of Labor Economics* 15, no. 1 (1997), pp. 98–123.

31. J. Bempechat, *Against the Odds: How "At-Risk" Students Exceed Expectations* (San Francisco: Jossey-Bass, 1998).

32. J. M. O'Keefe, "Teacher Recruitment and Retention," *NCEA Notes* 33 (2001), p. 15.

33. P. Kaufman, X. Chen, S. P. Choy, S. A. Ruddy, A. K. Miller, J. K. Fleury, K. A. Chandler, M. R. Rand, P. Klaus, and M. G. Planty, *Indicators of School Crime and Safety, 2000*, U.S. Departments of Education and Justice, NCES 2001–017/NCJ-184176 (Washington, D.C.: GPO, 2000).

34. U.S. Department of Education, National Center For Education Statistics, *Students' Report of School Crime, 1989 and 1995* (1998, http://nces.ed.gov/pubs98/crime/98241–2.html).

35. M. Perie, and D. P. Baker, *Job Satisfaction among America's Teachers: Effects of Workplace Conditions, Background Characteristics, and Teacher Compensation* (Washington, D.C.: U.S. Department of Education, National Center for Education Statistics, 1997).

36. R. R. Henke, S. P. Choy, X. Chen, S. Geis, and M. N. Alt, *America's Teachers: Profile of a Profession*, 1993–94 U.S. Department of Education, National Center For Educational Statistics, NCES 97–460 Washington, D.C.: GPO, 1997), p. 82.

37. Council on American Private Education, *Private School Facts* (2001) (*http://www.capenet.org/facts.html*).

38. T. D. Snyder and C. M. Hoffman, *Digest of Education Statistics, 2000*, U.S. Department of Education, National Center for Education Statistics, 2001 (Washington, DC: GPO) p. 138.

39. C. Chapman, K. Chandler, and R. G. Niemi, *The Civic Development of Ninth through Twelveth Grade Students in the United States*, U.S. Department of Education, National Center For Educational Statistics, 1998 (Washington, D.C.: GOP).

40. C. Chapman and B. Kleiner, *Statistics in Brief, November 1999: Youth Service Learning and Community Service among Sixth and Twelveth Grade Students in the United States, 1996 and 1999*, MCES publication no 2000–028, U.S. Depart-

ment of Education, National Center For Educational Statistics, 1999 (Washington, D.C.: GPO).

41. S. Bobbit, *The Patterns of Teacher Compensation* U.S. Department of Education, National Center for Education Statistics, 1996 (Washington, D.C.: GPO).

42. J. Archer, "Catholic School Teachers Tempted by Public School Wages," *Education Week*, March 29, 2000.

43. J. M. O'Keefe, "Teacher Recruitment and Retention," *NCEA Notes* 33 (2001).

44. D. McDonald, *United States Catholic Elementary and Secondary Schools, 2000–2001* (Washington, D.C.: National Catholic Educational Association, 2001).

45. C. Gewertz, "Teacher Need Hits Private Schools Hard," *Education Week*, May 23, 2001, pp. 1–18.

46. B. Parsad, R. Skinner, and E. Farris, "Advanced Telecommunications in U.S. Private Schools," *Educational Statistics Quarterly* 3, no. 1 (2001), pp. 45–50.

47. N. Riordan, "Trends in Student Demography in Catholic Secondary Schools, 1972–1992," in J. Youniss and J. J. Convey, eds., *Catholic Schools at the Crossroads: Survival and Transformation* (New York: Teachers College Press, 2001), pp. 33–54.

48. M. Guerra, "Key Issues for the Future of Catholic Schools," in T. Hunt, T. Oldeski, and T. J. Wallace, eds., *Catholic School Leadership: An Invitation to Lead* (New York: Teachers College Press, 2000), p. 86.

49. J. M. O'Keefe, "No Margin, No Mission," in T. H. McLaughlin, J. M. O'Keefe, and B. O'Keeffe, eds., *The Contemporary Catholic School: Context, Identity, and Diversity* (Washington, D.C.: Falmer, 1996), pp. 177–97.

50. D. Herszenhorn, "Preparing to Grieve for a Catholic School," *New York Times*, April 29, 2001, p. 41.

51. J. M. O'Keefe and J. Murphy, "Ethnically Diverse Catholic Schools: An Overview of Students, Staffing and Finances," in Youniss and Convey, *Catholic Schools at the Crossroads*, pp. 117–36.

52. S. Galang, "Campaign: Funds Will Make More Schools Competitive," *Pilot* June 15, 2001, p. 1.

53. McDonald, *United States Catholic Elementary and Secondary Schools, 2000–2001*.

54. J. M. O'Keefe, "The Challenge of Pluralism: Articulating a Rationale for Religiously Diverse Urban Roman Catholic Schools in the United States," *International Journal of Religion and Education* 1, no. 1 (2000), pp. 64–88.

55. T. Walch, "The Past before Us: Three Traditions of the Recent History of Catholic Education," in J. Youniss, J. Convey, and J. McLellan, eds., *The Catholic Character of Catholic Schools* (Notre Dame, Ind.: University of Notre Dame Press, 2000), p. 186.

56. W. Raspberry, "Separation or Discrimination?" *Washington Post*, July 10, 2000.

57. United States Office for Catholic School Parental Rights Advocacy, 2001, *Directory for Catholic School Advocacy* (United States Catholic Conference, November 1, 2001).

Response
John T. McGreevy

1. James S. Coleman, *High School Achievement: Public, Catholic, and Private Schools Compared* (New York: Basic Books, 1982); Anthony S. Bryk, Valerie E. Lee, and Peter B. Holland, *Catholic Schools and the Common Good* (Cambridge: Harvard University Press, 1993).

2. Ward M. McAfee, *Religion, Race, and Reconstruction: The Public School in the Politics of the 1870s* (Albany: State University of New York Press, 1998).

3. John T. McGreevy, "Thinking on One's Own: Catholicism in the American Intellectual Imagination, 1928–1960," *Journal of American History* 84 (1997), pp. 97–131.

4. John Courtney Murray, S. J., "Law or Prepossessions?" *Journal of Law and Contemporary Problems* 14 (winter 1949), pp. 31, 37.

Chapter Ten
Parents, Partners, and Choice: Constitutional Dimensions of School Options

Thanks to Nina Wong, Dan Losen and Laurie Corzett for research assistance.

1. Probably the most fundamental reforms in U.S. schooling involve not the introduction of choice alone but the spreading use of accountability measures for teachers and students.

2. I have addressed the religion clauses in the context of school choice elsewhere. See Minow, "Choice or Commonality: Welfare and Schooling after the End of Welfare as We Knew It," *Duke Law Journal* 49 (1999), p. 493.

3. *Zelman v. Simmons-Harris*, 2002 U.S. LEXIS 4885 (June 27, 2002). Scholarly works before the decision include Ira C. Lupu, "The Increasingly Anachronistic Case against School Vouchers," *Notre Dame Journal of Legal Ethics and Public Policy* 13 (1999), p. 375; Laura S. Underkuffler, "Vouchers and Beyond: The Individual as Causative Agent in Establishment Clause Jurisprudence," *Indiana Law Journal* 75 (2000), p. 167: Eugene Volokh, "Equal Treatment Is Not Establishment," *Notre Dame Journal of Legal Ethics and Public Policy* 13 (1999), p. 341. See *Bagley v. Raymond School Department*, 728 A.2d 127 (Me. 1999).

4. See *New York University Law Review* "Contemporary Challenges Facing the First Amendment's Religion Clauses," 43 (1999), p. 101, 107 the comments of Steven Green.

5. See Stephen Macedo, "Constituting Civil Society: School Vouchers, Religious Nonprofit Organizations, and Liberal Public Values," *Chicago-Kent Law Review* 75 (2000), pp. 417, 432–42. Vital elements of this argument are the distinction between direct and indirect aid; see *Witters v. Washington Dept. of Services for the Blind* (upholding program allowing aid to a student who then selected a Christian college); see Michael McConnell, "Vouchers: Legal and Constitutional Issues," in C. Eugene Steuerle, Van Doorn Ooms, George Peterson, and Robert D. Reischauer, eds., *Vouchers and Related Delivery Mechanisms: Consumer Choice in the Provision of Public Services* (Washington, D.C.: Brookings Institution Press, 1999).

6. Michael W. McConnell, "Education Disestablishment: Why Democratic Values Are Ill-Served by Democratic Control of Schooling," forthcoming in Stephen Macedo and Yael Tamir, eds., *Moral and Political Education*, NOMOS XLIII (New York: New York University Press, 2002).

7. Michael McConnell, "The Selective Funding Problem: Abortions and Religious Schools," *Harvard Law Review* 104 (1991), p. 989.

8. See Marci A. Hamilton, "Power, the Establishment Clause, and Vouchers," *Connecticut Law Review.* 31 (1999), pp. 822–28.

9. See, e.g., Rachel Pine, "Speculation and Reality: The Role of Facts in Judicial Protection of Fundamental Rights," *University of Pennsylvania Law Review*, 136 (1988), p. 655.

10. *Pierce v. Society of Sisters*, 268 U.S. 510 (1925). This decision built upon the reasoning in *Meyer v. Nebraska*, 262 U.S. 390 (1923).

11. *Pierce v. Society of Sisters* 268 U.S. at 529 (counsel for the governor defending the Oregon compulsory public education law as a measure against religiously based separation); id., at 517 (representatives of the Society of Sisters responded to fears that foreigners would send their children to private schools or fail to be assimilated in private schools). See Merle Curti, *The Social Ideas of American Educators* (Patterson, N.J.: Littlefield, Adams and Co., 1965), pp. 348, 350 (describing Protestant-led opposition to Catholic parochial schooling).

12. *Pierce v. Society of Sisters*, 535.

13. *Pierce v. Society of Sisters*, 535.

14. *Pierce v. Society of Sisters*, 535.

15. See *Pierce v. Society of Sisters*.

16. "No question is raised concerning the power of the State reasonably to regulate all schools, to inspect, supervise and examine them, their teachers and pupils; to require that all children of proper age attend some school, that teachers shall be of good moral character and patriotic disposition, that certain studies plainly essential to good citizenship must be taught, and that nothing be taught which is manifestly inimical to the public welfare." *Pierce v. Society of Sisters*, 534.

17. *Pierce v. Society of Sisters*, 534.

18. Argument of William D. Guthrie, in *Pierce v. Society of Sisters*, 517.

19. Cf. Rosemary Salamone, *Visions of Schooling: Conscience, Community, and Common Education* (New Haven: Yale University Press, 2000), p. 260 (public funding for private schools generally brings public regulation in countries outside the United States).

20. Sunstein, quoted in McConnell, "Selective Funding Problem," p. 1036 n. 183.

21. Michael McConnell drew the comparison between abortion funding—which the state need not provide—and private school funding. See "Selective Funding Problem."

22. See Suzanna Sherry, "Responsible Republicanism: Educating for Citizenship, *University of Chicago Law Review* 62 (1995), pp. 131, 201 (arguing that constitutional democracy implies an active role for parents in their children's education).

23. See Lawrence G. Sager, "Fair Measure: The Legal Status of Underenforced Constitutional Norms," *Harvard Law Review* 91 (1978), p. 1212; see also Lawrence G. Sager, "Justice in Plain Clothes: Reflections on the Thinness of Constitutional Law," *Northwestern University Law Review* 88 (1993), p. 410.

24. See Lewis D. Solomon, "The Role of For-Profit Corporations in Revitalizing Public Education: A Legal and Policy Analysis," *University of Toledo Law Review* 24 (1993), p. 883, 891; see also Jennifer L. Romer, "Attacking Educational Inequality: The Privatization Approach," *Boston College Third World Law Journal* 16 (1996), p. 245 (considering impact of privatized options in education on equality); Jean J. Chang, "Note: The Hazards of Making Public Schooling a Private Business," *Harvard Law Review.* 112 (1999), p. 695.

25. 347 U.S. 483 (1954).

26. *Brown v. Board of Education (II)*, 349 U.S. 294 (1955).

27. See *Lee v. Macon County Board of Education*, 267 F. Supp. 458, 475 (Ala. 1967).

28. *Gross v. Board of Educ.*, 373 U.S. 683 (1963).

29. *Green v. County School Board*, 391 U.S. 430 (1968).

30. *Faubus v. Aaron*, 361 U.S. 197 (1959).

31. *Adarand Constructors, Inc. v. Pena*, 515 U.S. 200 (1995).

32. See below.

33. See, e.g., Jay Heubert, ed., *Law and School Reform: Six Strategies for Promoting Educational Equity* (New Haven: Yale University Press, 1999) (discussing state constitutions and statutes involved in contemporary school reforms).

34. See *City of Boerne v. P. F. Flores*, 521 U.S. 507 (1997); *Board of Trustees of the University of Alabama v. Garrett*, 531 U.S. 356 (2001); *United States v. Morrison*, 529 U.S. 598 (2000); Tomiko Brown-Nagin, "Toward a Pragmatic Understanding of Status-Consciousness: The Case of Deregulated Education," *Duke Law Journal* 50 (2000), p. 753.

35. *Virginia Education Fund v. Commissioner*, 799 F.2d 903 (4th Cir. 1986). See also *Bob Jones University v. United States*, 461 U.S. 574 (1983) (upholding IRS decision to withhold tax-exempt status under section 50c[c][3] of the federal tax code for a university engaged in racial discrimination).

36. It is difficult even to imagine a "white-heritage" school, but its inclusion in a choice plan would render the scheme even more vulnerable to challenge by making the racial distinctions more transparent.

37. See "Note, Segregating Schools: The Foreseeable Consequences of Tuition Tax Credits," *Yale Law Journal* 89 (1979), p. 168; "Note: The Judicial Role in Attacking Racial Discrimination in Tax-Exempt Private Schools," *Harvard Law Review* 93 (1979), p. 378. See also Hamilton Lankford and James Wyckoff, "Why Are Schools Racially Segregated? Implications for School Choice Policies" (paper prepared for Teachers College, Columbia University Conference on School Choice and Racial Diversity, May 22, 2000, p. 17). (Research indicates that minorities and whites have distinctive preferences for various dimensions of education, and therefore if racial integration is a goal, "the design of school choice plans should account for the underlying preferences"; "Failure to do so ignores the behavior that has led to the current highly segregated system.")

38. See *Grove City College v. Bell*, 465 U.S. 555 (1984) (sex discrimination); *Norwood v. Harrison*, 413 U.S. 555 (1973) (state cannot loan textbooks to students in public and private schools without checking whether private schools pursue racial discrimination). See "Note: Segregation, Academics, and State Action," *Yale Law Journal* 83 (1973), p. 146.

39. See *Bob Jones University v. United States*, 461 U.S. 574 (1983).

40. See *City of Richmond v. J. A. Croson Co.*, 488 U.S. 469 (1989); *Adarand Constructors, Inc. v. Pena*, 515 U.S. 200 (1995); *Hopwood v. Texas*, 78 F.3rd 932 (5th Cir. 1996); *Shaw v. Hunt*, 517 U.S. 899 (1998); *Shaw v. Reno*, 509 U.S. 630 (1993).

41. See arguments in *Hopwood v. Texas*, 78 F.3d 932 (5th Cir., 1996); *Grutter v. Bollinger*, 188 F.3d 394 (6th Cir. 1999); Jodi S. Cohen, "U-M Decision Is Weeks Away," *Detroit News*, February 18, 2001; see also Wiliam Bowen and Derek Bok, *The Shape of the River* (Princeton: Princeton University Press, 1998); Alice Dembner, "Harvard President Leads Stand for Affirmative Action," *Boston Globe*, April 24, 1997.

42. *Eisenberg v. Montgomery County Public Schools* 197 F.3rd 123 (4th Cir. 1999), cert. denied, 120 S.Ct. 1420 (2000); *Tuttle v. Arlington County School Board*, 195 F.3d 698 (4th Cir. 1999), cert. dismissed 120 S.Ct. 1552 (2000).

43. *Runyon v. McCary*, 427 U.S. 160 (1976). The question has not been conclusively treated if the racial discrimination is conducted by a religious school as a result of religious belief; see *Brown v. Dade Christian Schools, Inc.*, 556 F.2d 319 (5th Cir. 1977) (en banc), cert. denied, 434 U.S. 1063 (1978), although even in such a case, the federal government could deny the school tax-exempt status. *Bob Jones University v. United States*, 461 U.S. 574 (1983).

44. 438 U.S. 265 (1978).

45. *Wessmann v. Gittens*, 160 F.3d 790 (1998); Beth Daley, "City to Appeal Latin Ruling to High Court," *Boston Globe*, December 3, 1998.

46. See, for example, the controlled-choice plan in Cambridge, Massachusetts, described in Robert S. Peterkin and Dorothy S. Jones, "Schools of Choice in Cambridge, Massachusetts," in Joe Nathan, ed., *Public Schools by Choice: Expanding Opportunities for Parents, Students, and Teachers* (St. Paul, Minn.: Institute for Learning and Teaching, Bloomington, Ind., 1989).

47. See Hamilton Lankford and James Wyckoff, "Why Are Schools Racially Segregated? Implications for School Choice Policies" (paper prepared for Teachers College, Columbia University Conference on School Choice and Racial Diversity, May 22, 2000); see also Robert W. Fairlie, "Racial Segregation and Private/Public School Choice" (paper prepared for Teachers College, Columbia University Conference on School Choice and Racial Diversity, May 22, 2000) (noting tendency of whites and Hispanics to choose private schools in reaction to high concentrations of blacks in public schools).

48. See Jay P. Greene, "Why School Choice Can Promote Integration," *Education Week*, April 12, 2000, p. 72 (commentary).

49. In contrast, choice plans with nonparticipation by neighboring school can be a defect, as one court found in Cleveland: "The upshot of this drama is that the Ohio Legislature, the courts, and the suburban school districts have put many Cleveland parents and children eager to take advantage of school choice in a cruel situation. The real problem with the Scholarship Program . . .

is that Ohio has failed to require suburban public schools to participate in the program and give parents a real choice among schools." Stephen Macedo, "Symposium II. The Constitution of Civil Society B. Religion and Civic Education Constituting Civil Society: School Vouchers, Religious Nonprofit Organizations, and Liberal Public Values," *Chicago-Kent Law Review* 75 (2000), pp. 417, 436. Ohio later changed the plan by legislation. Ohio Revised Code Annotated 3313.974-.979 (West 1999).

50. See Carol Ascher and Nathalie Wamba, "Charter Schools: An Emerging Market" (paper prepared for Teachers College, Columbia University, conference on School Choice and Racial Diversity, May 22, 2000).

51. Compare *United States v. Virginia*, 518 U.S. 515 (1996 opinion for the Court by Ginsburg, J.) (calling for an "exceedingly persuasive justification" for excluding women from a public military academy) with *Frontiero v. Richardson*, 411 U.S. 677 (1973) (reviewing sex-based classifications under an intermediate scrutiny analysis). Commentators indicate that the Court has not actually shifted to strict scrutiny of sex-based classifications. See, e.g., Denise Morgan, "Antisubordination Analysis after *United States v. Virginia,*" *University of Chicago Law Review* 1999, pp. 381, 383, 408–17.

52. See *Vorchheimer v. School District of Philadelphia* 532 F.2d 880 (3rd Cir. 1976), affirmed by an equally divided court, 430 U.S. 703 (1977).

53. See Morgan, "Antisubordination Analysis," p. 419.

54. The free exercise clause has been read to permit religious enterprises the power to conduct their activities autonomously, to select their own leaders, to run their own institutions. See *NLRB v. Catholic Bishop* 440 U.S. 490 (1979); *Serbian Eastern Orthodox Diocese v. Milovojevich*, 426 U.S. 696 (1976). See *Corporation of the Presiding Bishop of the Church of Jesus Christ of Latter-Day-Saints v. Amos*, 483 U.S. 327 (1987) (statutory grounds); *NRLB v. Catholic Bishop*, 440 U.S. 490 (1979) (statutory grounds).

55. Compare Michael McConnell, "The Selective Funding Problem," pp. 1042–43 (groups need to be able to self-segregate to develop themselves) with Macedo, "Symposium II," p. 440 (opt-out from religious practice alters the character of the religious school but assists the public voucher experiment in Milwaukee).

56. *City of Cleburne v. Cleburne Living Center*, 473 U.S. 432 (1985).

57. See Minow, *Making All the Difference: Inclusion, Exclusion, and American Law* (Ithaca: Cornell University Press, 1990) (describing cases and statutes).

58. See IDEA 1997 amendments, IDEA Amendments of 1997, Pub. L. No. 105–17, 1997 U.S. Code Annotated (111 Stat.) 37 (amending Individuals with Disabilities Education Act, 20 U.S.C. 1400–1491(o) (1994)).

59. Jay P. Heubert, "Schools without Rules? Charter Schools, Federal Disability Law, and the Paradoxes of Deregulation," *Harvard Civil Rights–Civil Liberties Law Review* 32 (1997), p. 301.

60. *San Antonio Independent School District v. Rodriguez*, 411 U.S. 1 (1973).

61. *San Antonio Independent School District*.

62. See John Charles Boger, "Willful Colorblindness: The New Racial Piety and the Resegregation of Public Schools," *North Carolina Law Review* 78 (2000), pp. 1719, 1792 (commending school board's decision in Wake County, North

Carolina, to assign students to public schools to prevent any school from having more than 40 percent eligible for free or reduced-price lunch and no more than 25 percent reading below grade level).

63. Claire Smrekar and Ellen Goldring, "Social Class Isolation and Racial Diversity in Magnet Schools" (paper presented at Teachers College, Columbia University (Conference on School Choice and Racial Diversity, May 22, 2000), p. 20) (citing studies of Minnesota Open Enrollment Option, Milwaukee Voucher Plan, and other voucher programs).

64. Srmrekar and Goldring, "Social Class Isolation," p. 21.

65. Ascher and Wamba, "Charter Schools: An Emerging Market," pp. 33, 45 (reporting studies of New York University Institute for Education and Social Policy database, including 801 charter schools operating in 1997–98).

66. There should be room for experiments but also learning from past experiments. See Joshua E. Kimerling, "Black Male Academies: Reexamining the Strategy of Integration," *Buffalo Law Review* 42 (1994), p. 829.

67. See, e.g., *Sheff v. O'Neill*, 678 A.2d 1267 (Conn. 1996)(state constitution requires remedial action in the case of extreme racial and ethnic isolation, bound up with poverty and right to equal educational opportunity); Tom Beimers, "Note, A Wrong Still in Search of a Remedy: Educational Adequacy after *Sheff v. O'Neill*," *Minnesota Law Review* 82 (1997), p. 565.

68. Should a religious school be allowed to govern its employment practices by its religious teachings—which may, for example, direct against hiring "out" homosexuals as teachers? Nothing in the current interpretations of the Constitution would forbid application of such teachings. Yet if a legislature adopts laws protecting homosexuals from employment discrimination, there would be a potential conflict with freedom of association and free-exercise claims asserted by the school. These kinds of issues are bound to emerge if there is public funding of private religious schools.

69. Compare encouraging views of Finn, others, with Edward B. Fiske and Helen F. Ladd, *When Schools Compete: A Cautionary Tale* (Washington, D.C.: Brookings Institution Press, 2000), pp. 278–309 (warning, based on New Zealand's experience, that school-choice strategies can produced oversubscribed schools with rationing problems, low-performing schools, self-governance failures when combined with competition, racial, and class polarization). See also William Green, "Schools, Signs, and Separation: Quebec Anglophones, Canadian Constitutional Politics, and International Language Rights," *Denver J. International Law & Policy* 27 (Summer 1999), pp. [449 ff?] (assigning students to linguistic/religious schools based on percentage).

70. Kathleen Koman, Preparing Students for the Real World, 18, 19 *Hope Magazine* (spring 1999).

71. Minow, "Reforming School Reform," *Fordham Law Review.* 68 (1999), p. 1.

72. *See Jennifer L. Romer, "Attacking Educational Inequality: The Privatization Approach," Boston College Third World Law Journal* 16 (1996), pp. 245, 265.

73. *Stephen Macedo, Diversity and Distrust: Civic Education in a Multicultural Democracy* (Cambridge: Harvard University Press, 2000), pp. 51–100.

Chapter Eleven
What Does the Establishment Clause Forbid?
Reflections on the Constitutionality of School Vouchers

This essay is my contribution to the conference on the moral and legal aspects of the "school choice" controversy that was sponsored by and held at the Boston College Boisi Center for Religion and American Public Life, March 9–10, 2001. I discussed a draft of this essay in two other venues: in a faculty workshop at Wake Forest University School of Law and at the Rockefeller Center of Dartmouth College, where the essay served as the basis of a lecture—the annual Roger Aaron Lecture—that I was privileged to deliver on April 30, 2001. I am grateful for the comments I received from friends and colleagues in all three venues. I am especially grateful, for their written comments, to Dan Conkle, Michael Curtis, Rick Garnett, Fred Gedicks, Scott Idleman, Doug Laycock, Bob Nagel, Steve Smith, Laura Underkuffler, and Ron Wright. I know that I have not yet responded adequately to all the questions and cautions my colleagues have raised. See, e.g., Daniel O. Conkle, "The Path of American Religious Liberty: From the Original Theology to Formal Neutrality and an Uncertain Future," *Indiana Law Journal* 75 (2000), pp. 1, 22–24.

1. To date, the most important court decisions addressing the question of the constitutionality of school vouchers are these: *Jackson v. Benson*, 578 N.W.2d 602 (Wisc. 1998) (Milwaukee voucher program does not violate federal nonestablishment norm), cert. denied sub nom. *Gilbert v. Moore*, 119 S.Ct. 467 (1998); *Simmons-Harris v. Zelman*, 2000 FED App. 0411P (6th Cir.) (Cleveland voucher program violates federal nonestablishment norm). See also *Kotterman v. Killian*, 193 Ariz. 273, 972 P.2d 606 (Ariz. 1999) (state law allowing state tax credit of up to $500 for donations to "school tuition organizations," including religiously affiliated school tuition organizations, does not violate federal nonestablishment norm), cert. denied, 120 S.Ct. 42 (1999).

In my contribution to a symposium "Religion in the Public Square," I addressed a different aspect of the question, What does the establishment clause forbid? See Michael J. Perry, "Why Political Reliance on Religiously Grounded Morality Does Not Violate the Establishment Clause," *William and Mary Law Review* 42 (2001), p. 663. See John Hart Ely, "Another Such Victory: Constitutional Theory and Practice in a World Where Courts Are No Different from Legislatures," *Virginia Law Review* 77 (1991), p. 833.

2. A voluminous and growing literature addresses the question whether, even if constitutional, school vouchers are, all things considered, a good idea. On school vouchers and other kinds of "school choice" programs, especially charter schools, see, e.g., Paul E. Peterson and Bryan C. Hassel, eds., *Learning from School Choice* (Washington, D.C.: Brookings Institution Press, 1998).

3. On the idea of constitutional "bedrock," see Michael J. Perry, *We the People: The Fourteenth Amendment and the Supreme Court* (New York: Oxford University Press, 1999), pp. 20–23.

4. See Michael J. Perry, *Religion in Politics: Constitutional and Moral Perspectives* (New York: Oxford University Press, 1997), pp. 10–12. On the controver-

sial question whether the Fourteenth Amendment was meant to make the First Amendment's "free exercise" and "nonestablishment" norms applicable to the states, see Kurt T. Lash, "The Second Adoption of the Free Exercise Clause: Religious Exemptions under the Fourteenth Amendment," *Northwestern University Law Review* 88 (1994), p. 1106; Kurt T. Lash, "The Second Adoption of the Establishment Clause: The Rise of the Nonestablishment Principle," *Arizona State Law Journal* 27 (1995), p. 1085. Lash argues that the Fourteenth Amendment was meant to make applicable to the states both a broad free-exercise norm and a nonestablishment norm. For a recent instance of the argument that the Fourteenth Amendment was not meant to make the First Amendment's nonestablishment norm applicable to the states, see Jonathan P. Brose, "In Birmingham They Love the Governor: Why the Fourteenth Amendment Does Not Incorporate the Establishment Clause," *Ohio Northern University Law Review* 24 (1998), p. 1. For the argument that the Fourteenth Amendment was not meant to make any First Amendment norm applicable to the states, see Jay S. Bybee, "Taking Liberties with the First Amendment: Congress, Section 5, and the Religious Freedom Restoration Act," *Vanderbilt Law Review* 48 (1995), p. 1539.

5. See Michael W. McConnell, "Accommodation of Religion: An Update and Response to the Critics," *George Washington Law Review* 60 (1992), pp. 685, 690: "The government may not 'establish' religion and it may not 'prohibit' religion." McConnell explains, in a footnote attached to the word "establish," that "the text [of the First Amendment] states the 'Congress' may make no law 'respecting an establishment' of religion, which meant that Congress could neither establish a national church nor interfere with the establishment of state churches as they then existed in the various states. After the last disestablishment in 1833 and the incorporation of the First Amendment against the states through the Fourteenth Amendment, this 'federalism' aspect of the Amendment has lost its significance, and the Clause can be read as forbidding the government to establish religion" (690 n. 19).

6. See Michael J. Perry, "Freedom of Religion in the United States: Fin de Siècle Sketches," *Indiana Law Journal* 75 (2000), pp. 295, 297–302.

7. Cf. Akhil Reed Amar, "Foreword: The Document and the Doctrine," *Harvard Law Review* 114 (2000), pp. 26, 119: "Let us recall the world the Founders aimed to repudiate, a world where a powerful church hierarchy was anointed as the official government religion, where clerics ex officio held offices in the government, and where members of other religions were often barred from holding government posts."

8. What is the present reality? See Cheryl Saunders, "Comment: Religion and the State," *Cardozo Law Review* 21 (2000), pp. 1295:

> The special status of the Church of England manifests through legal links with the British crown. Under legislation, the reigning queen or king is "supreme governor" of the church and swears a coronation oath to maintain it. As such, the monarch may not be a Catholic, or marry a Catholic, and must declare on accession to the throne that he or she is a Protestant.

This is surprising enough in a western liberal democracy at the end of the twenti-eth century. But there is more. The monarch also appoints the archbishops and other reigning church dignitaries. Twenty-six of these "Lords Spiritual" sit in the upper house of the legislature, the House of Lords. The British Parliament can legislate for the church and can prescribe modes of worship, doctrine and discipline. And the church has delegated legislative authority in relation to church affairs. Measures initiated by the church may be accepted or rejected, but not amended, by the Parlia-ment and override earlier inconsistent law.

Professor Saunders then states:

As usual with the British system of government, however, what you see is not ex-actly what you get. In advising the crown on appointments to church positions, the prime minister draws names from a list provided by church authorities. As a practi-cal matter, Parliament is unlikely to veto legislative measures initiated by the church, or to act unilaterally in relation to other church affairs. Vernon Bogdanor draws attention to a House of Commons debate on the ordination of women priests in 1993, in which several Members expressed the view that the House should not be discussing the view at all. (1295–96)

Clearly, and happily, that England has an established church does not mean everything it once meant. But that England still has an established church is problematic. See Clifford Longley, "An Act That Hold Us Back," *Tablet* (Lon-don), March 17, 2001, p. 362. Cf. Brian Barry, *Justice as Impartiality* (New York: Oxford Clarendon Press, 1995), p. 164 n. *c*:

We must, of course, keep a sense of proportion. The advantages of establishment enjoyed by the Church of England or by the Lutheran Church in Sweden are scarcely on a scale to lead anyone to feel seriously discriminated against. In contrast, denying the vote to Roman Catholics or requiring subscription to the Church of England as a condition of entry to Oxford or Cambridge did constitute a serious source of grievance. Strict adherence to justice as impartiality would, no doubt, be incompatible with the existence of an established church at all. But departures from it are venial so long as nobody is put at a significant disadvantage, either by having barriers put in the way of worshipping according to the tenets of his faith or by having his rights and opportunities in other matters (politics, education, occupation, for example) materially limited on the basis of his religious beliefs.

9. However, neither the nonestablishment norm nor the free exercise norm (which is an antidiscrimination norm; see n. 56) should be understood to call into question the following proposition: Government may make a policy choice on the basis of a position that one or more churches happen to reject, even though the policy choice has the effect of disfavoring those churches rela-tive to other churches that do not reject the position. (For a discussion of this in connection with the free exercise norm, see Perry, "Freedom of Religion in the United States," pp. 297–302). An example of such a position: Racist ideolo-gies are false and evil. Another: The theory of evolution should be presented to high school students. (This does not entail that competing perspectives on evolution shouldn't be presented too.) Thus, a state may exclude from its

voucher program any school, whether or not religiously affiliated, that teaches that some persons are "naturally" inferior to others by virtue of race. (The Ohio Pilot Project Scholarship Program, recently struck down by the U.S. Court of Appeals for the Sixth Circuit, excluded schools that "discriminate on the basis of race, religion, or ethnic background; advocate or foster unlawful behavior; or teach hatred of an person or group on account of race, ethnicity, national origin, or religion." *Simmons-Harris v. Zelman*, 2000 FED App. 0411P [6th Cir.]) To say that government may not take any action that favors one or more churches in relation to one or more other churches, or to no church at all, on the basis of the view that the favored church is, as a church—as a community of faith—better along one or another dimension of value (truer, for example, or more efficacious spiritually, or more authentically American) is not to say that government may not take a stand on an issue that is opposed to a stand that one or more churches happen to take. Obviously, such a rule would be not merely extreme, but extremely silly.

10. For an example of a position that privileges the Christian church generally, see "Other Faiths Are Deficient, Pope Says," *Tablet* (London), February 5, 2000, p. 157: "The revelation of Christ is 'definitive and complete', Pope John Paul affirmed to the Congregation for the Doctrine of the Faith, on 28 January. He repeated the phrase twice in an address which went on to say that non-Christians live in 'a deficient situation, compared to those who have the fullness of salvific means in the Church'." The harsh doctrine that there is no salvation outside the church has been revised, however. "[Pope John Paul II] recognised, following the Second Vatican Council, that non-Christians can reach eternal life if they seek God with a sincere heart. But in that 'sincere search' they are in fact 'ordered' towards Christ and his Church" p. (157).

11. Cf. Douglas Laycock, "Freedom of Speech That Is Both Religious and Political," *University of California, Davis, Law Review* 29 (1996), pp. 793, 812–13 (arguing that "at the core of the Establishment Clause should be the principle that government cannot engage in a religious observance or compel or persuade citizens to do so").

What the nonestablishment norm forbids is one question. Another, and different, inquiry arises when we have answered the question what the nonestablishment norm forbids: Is it a good thing that the nonestablishment norm is part of our constitutional law, or is it a bad thing? I have argued elsewhere that it is a good thing. See Perry, "Freedom of Religion in the United States," pp. 326–32. Most Americans believe that it is a good thing. But there is, among Americans, not just one answer to the question why it is a good thing, and not every answer will appeal to every person. For example, although some secular answers may appeal to some religious believers, religiously grounded answers will not appeal to nonbelievers.

12. See *Everson v. Board of Education*, 330 U.S. 1 (1947).

13. Justice Thomas has noted that "our Establishment Clause jurisprudence is in hopeless disarray." *Rosenberger v. Rector and Visitors of University of Virginia*, 515 U.S. 819, 861 (1995) (Thomas, J., concurring). Many scholars concur in this judgment. See, e.g., Jesse H. Choper, *Securing Religious Liberty: Principles for Judicial Interpretation of the Religion Clauses* (Chicago: University of Chicago

Press, 1995), pp. 174–76. Akhil Amar has recently referred to "the many outlandish (and contradictory) things that have been said about [the nonestablishment norm] in the United States Reports." Amar, "Foreword," p. 119.

14. See *Rosenberger v. Rector and Visitors of University of Virginia*, 515 U.S. 819 (1995) (five-to-four decision); *Agostini v. Felton*, 521 U.S. 203 (1997) (five-to-four decision); *Mitchell v. Helms*, 120 S.Ct. 2530 (2000) (six-to-three decision; no majority opinion).

15. On charter schools programs and differences among them, see Paul E. Peterson, "School Choice: A Report Card," in Peterson and Hassel, *Learning from School Choice*, pp. 3, 7. For an argument in support of charter schools, see Bryan C. Hassel, "The Case for Charter Schools," in Peterson and Hassel, *Learning from School Choice*, p. 33.

16. The Ohio Pilot Project Scholarship Program ruled unconstitutional in *Simmons-Harris v. Zelman* gave "'preference to students from low-income families,' defining them as families whose income is less than 200% of the poverty line." *Simmons-Harris v. Zelman*, 2000 FED App. 0411P (6th Cir.).

17. Cf. n. 24.

18. The Ohio Pilot Project Scholarship Program excluded schools that "discriminate on the basis of race, religion, or ethnic background; advocate or foster unlawful behavior; or teach hatred of an person or group on account of race, ethnicity, national origin, or religion." *Simmons-Harris v. Zelman*, 2000 FED App. 0411P (6th Cir.).

19. For "A Model Voucher Plan," see Ronald J. Sider, *Just Generosity: A New Vision for Overcoming Poverty in America* (Grand Rapids, Mich.: Baker Books, 1999), pp. 171–74. I am inclined to concur in Michael McConnell's judgment that a state neither must, as a constitutional matter, nor should, as a policy matter, require of a school, as a condition of participation in a voucher program, that the school (1) permit voucher students to "opt out" of religious services or (2) forsake preferential admissions for co-religionists. See Michael W. McConnell, "The New Establishmentarianism," *Chicago-Kent Law Review* 75 (2000), pp. 453, 471–72. This is not to say that a state would be acting unconstitutionally were it to impose either of those two conditions.

20. In the sense in which I mean it here, to base a political choice on a belief—to make the choice "on the basis of" the belief—is to make a political choice that one would not make in the absence of the belief. To base a political choice partly, not solely, on a belief is still to make a political choice that one would not make in the absence of the belief.

21. In *Rosenberger*, the Supreme Court noted and then quickly dismissed such a possibility: "The governmental program here is neutral toward religion. There is no suggestion that the University created it to advance religion or adopted some ingenious device with the purpose of aiding a religious cause." *Rosenberger v. Rector and Visitors of University of Virginia*, 515 U.S. 819, 840 (1995).

22. The inquiry here—the inquiry into the possibility of a covert establishment of religion—is analogous to the inquiry into the possibility of covert racial discrimination. See *Village of Arlington Heights v. Metropolitan Housing Development Corp.*, 429 U.S. 252, 270 n. 21 (1977); Michael J. Perry, "Modern Equal

Protection: A Conceptualization and Appraisal," *Columbia Law Review* 79 (1979), pp. 1023, 1036–40.

According to the voucher program I sketched earlier in this essay, the amount of a voucher may not exceed, in any school year, the local school district's average per-pupil expenditure in the preceding school year. This feature responds to the concern that funding vouchers at too high a level would be constitutionally problematic. Would funding them at too low a level be constitutionally problematic? For an affirmative answer, see *Simmons-Harris v. Zelman*, 2000 FED App. 0411P (6th Cir.): "Practically speaking, the tuition restrictions mandated by the statute [\$2,250] limit the ability of nonsectarian schools to participate in the program, as religious schools often have lower overhead costs, supplemental income from private donations, and consequently lower tuition needs." The court then added this citation: "See Martha Minow, 'Reforming School Reform,' 68 Fordham L. Rev. 257, 262 (1999) (finding that voucher funding levels typically 'approximate[ing] the tuition level set by parochial schools [which] reflects subsidies from other sources')." The court erred, in my judgment. Funding vouchers at \$2,250 is not constitutionally fatal unless it can be shown that the funding level was chosen on the basis of the belief that the favored church(es) is, as such, better than one or more other churches or than no church at all.

In commenting on this essay, Fred Gedicks asks:

> Why not an establishment clause prophylactic as well? You endorse the Arlington Heights inquiry into legislative motivation, but given the general difficulty of establishing with any certainty whether a government actor established a facially neutral aid program in order to aid a church or religion generally because of a values-based belief in its superiority, why not reinforce the establishment clause norm with a rule providing that when the beneficiaries of a financial aid program are substantially/primarily/overwhelmingly—the precise line matters little—sectarian or religious, then the aid program should be understood as having as its principal purpose endorsement of the moral superiority of the aided religions in violation of the establishment clause. . . . This rule need not be understood as "religious discrimination"—which, I agree, should be prohibited, if we can only agree on what it is—but merely as a wise prophylactic even when the aid is distributed directly to students or their parents according to secularly defined benefit categories. This seems particularly appropriate if, as you suggest, we wish to avoid "judicial inquiry into the subterranean attitudes of legislators."

Letter from Frederick Gedicks to Michael Perry, December 13, 2000. The problem with this approach, I think, is that one can easily imagine a voucher program (indeed, many voucher programs) about which two things are true: (1) The beneficiaries of the program—that is, the secondary beneficiaries; the primary beneficiaries are the students and families who receive the vouchers— are, substantially, religiously affiliated schools; and (2) It is exceedingly unlikely that either those who lobbied for or those who enacted the voucher program had as their "principal purpose endorsement of the moral superiority of the aided religions." (I disagree that it is difficult to establish "with any certainty whether a government actor established a facially neutral aid program in order to aid a church or religion generally because of a values-based belief in its superiority.") In my judgment, therefore, the suggested prophylactic approach is draconian. Now, this is not to deny the possibility that a particular voucher program has as its "principal purpose endorsement of the moral superiority of the aided religions"—the possibility, that is, that the program is based on the belief that one or more churches are, as such, better than one or more churches or than no church at all. (Indeed, my second criterion is designed to defend against just that possibility.) If so, the voucher program violates the nonestablishment norm.

23. See Carl H. Esbeck, "A Constitutional Case for Government Cooperation With Faith-Based Social Service Providers," *Emory Law Journal* 46 (1997), p. 1; Douglas Laycock, "The Underlying Unity of Separation and Neutrality," *Emory Law Journal* 46 (1997), p. 43. The three most relevant recent cases are *Rosenberger v. Rector and Visitors of University of Virginia; Agostini v. Felton;* and *Mitchell v. Helms.* In *Rosenberger,* the Court stated:

> A central lesson of our decisions is that a significant factor in upholding governmental programs in the face of Establishment Clause attack is their neutrality toward religion. We have decided a series of cases addressing the receipt of government benefits where religion or religious views are implicated to some degree.... We have held that the guarantee of neutrality is respected, not offended, when the government, following neutral criteria and evenhanded policies, extends benefits to recipients whose ideologies and viewpoints, including religious ones, are broad and diverse.

Rosenberger v. Rector and Visitors of University of Virginia at 839. See also *Agostini v. Felton,* at 231 (1997) (arguing that it is constitutionally significant that the challenged aid "is allocated on the basis of neutral, secular criteria that neither favor nor disfavor religion and is made available to both religious and secular beneficiaries on a nondiscriminatory basis").

For the two most important state court decisions to date, see *Jackson v. Benson,* 578 N.W.2d 602 (Wisc. 1998) (holding, in part, that Milwaukee voucher program, which includes religiously affiliated schools, does not violate federal nonestablishment norm), cert. denied sub nom. *Gilbert v. Moore,* 119 S.Ct. 467 (1998); *Kotterman v. Killian,* 193 Ariz. 273, 972 P.2d 606 (Ariz. 1999) (holding, in part, that state law allowing state tax credit of up to $500 for donations to "school tuition organizations," including religiously affiliated school-tuition organizations, does not violate federal nonestablishment norm), cert. denied, 120 S.Ct. 42 (1999).

24. See *Mitchell v. Helms,* at 2536 (plurality opinion, written by Thomas, J., joined by Rehnquist, C.J., Scalia and Kennedy, JJ.).

25. As the three different opinions in *Mitchell v. Helms* disclose, the position of Justices Stevens, Souter, and Ginsburg is the most demanding; it is more demanding than the position of Justices O'Connor and Breyer, because the criteria that Justices Stevens, Souter, and Ginsburg apply include all the criteria that Justices O'Connor and Breyer apply and then some. See at 2556 (O'Connor, J., concurring in judgment, joined by Breyer, J.); at 2572 (Souter, J., dissenting, joined by Stevens and Ginsburg, JJ.). Justice Thomas, in his plurality

opinion, observed: "The dissent serves up a smorgasbord of eleven factors that, depending on the facts of each case 'in all its particularity,' could be relevant to the constitutionality of a school-aid program. And those eleven are a bare minimum. We are reassured that there are likely more. Presumably they will be revealed in future cases, as needed" (at 2550) (Thomas, J., joined by Rehnquist, C.J., Scalia & Kennedy, JJ.). For the dissenting justices' several criteria, see at 2577 (Souter, J., dissenting, joined by Stevens and Ginsburg, JJ.):

> At least three main lines of enquiry addressed particularly to school aid have emerged to complement evenhandedness neutrality. First, we have noted that two types of aid recipients heighten Establishment Clause concern: pervasively religious schools and primary and secondary religious schools. Second, we have identified two important characteristics of the method of distributing aid: directness or indirectness of distribution and distribution by genuinely independent choice. Third, we have found relevance in at least five characteristics of the aid itself: its religious content; its cash form; its divertibility or actual diversion to religious support; its supplantation of traditional items of religious school expense; and its substantiality.

Five years earlier, Justice Souter, in a dissenting opinion joined by Justices Stevens, Ginsburg, and Breyer, spoke of "the primacy of the no-direct-funding rule over the evenhandedness principle." *Rosenberger v. Rector and Visitors of University of Virginia,* 515 U.S. 819, 885 (1995).

26. See *Rosenberger v. Rector,* at 2559–60 (O'Connor, J., concurring in judgment, joined by Breyer, J.).

27. I am not persuaded by Justice O'Connor's defense, in *Mitchell,* of the direct/indirect distinction. See 2559–60 (O'Connor, J., concurring in judgment, joined by Breyer, J.). The plurality's position, rejecting the direct/indirect distinction as formalistic, seems to me quite sound. See 2544–46 (Thomas, J., joined by Rehnquist, C. J., Scalia and Kennedy, JJ.). As the plurality opinion put the point at the beginning of its critique of the distinction:

> If aid to schools, even "direct" aid, is neutrally available and, before reaching or benefitting any religious school, first passes through the hands (literally or figuratively) of numerous private citizens who are free to direct the aid elsewhere, the government has not provided any "support of religion." . . . Although the presence of private choice is easier to see when aid literally passes through the hands of individuals . . . , there is no reason why the Establishment Clause requires such a form. (2544–45)

28. For a thoughtful discussion of the matter, see Laura S. Underkuffler, "Vouchers and Beyond: The Individual Causative Agent in Establishment Clause Jurisprudence," *Indiana Law Journal* 75 (2000), p. 167.

29. According to the Ohio Pilot Project Scholarship Program, which was ruled unconstitutional in *Simmons-Harris v. Zelman,* "each scholarship for children attending a private school is payable to the parents of the student entitled to the scholarship. . . . Scholarship checks are mailed to the school selected by the parents, where the parents are required to endorse the checks over to the school in order to pay tuition." *Simmons-Harris v. Zelman,* 2000 FED App. 0411P (6th Cir.).

30. See John T. McGreevy, "Thinking on One's Own: Catholicism in the American Intellectual Imagination, 1928–1960," *Journal of American History* 84 (1997), pp. 97, 122–26.

31. Especially Justices Souter, Stevens, and Ginsburg. See *Mitchell v. Helms*, 120 S.Ct. 2530, 2572 (2000) (Souter, J., dissenting, joined by Stevens and Ginsburg, JJ.). See also *Agostini v. Felton*, 521 U.S. 203, 240 (1997) (Souter, J., dissenting, joined by Stevens, Ginsburg, and Breyer, JJ.).

32. For recent examples, see Steven K. Green, "Private School Vouchers and the Confusion over 'Direct' Aid," *George Mason University Civil Rights Law Journal* 10 (2000), p. 47; Marci A. Hamilton, "Power, the Establishment Clause, and Vouchers," *Connecticut Law Review* 31 (1999), p. 807; Marc D. Stern, "School Vouchers—The Church-State Debate That Really Isn't," *Connecticut Law Review* 31 (1999), p. 977. See also "Recent Cases": "Establishment Clause—School Vouchers—Wisconsin Supreme Court Upholds Milwaukee Parental Choice Program," *Harvard Law Review* 112 (1999), p. 737 (criticizing Wisconsin Supreme Court's decision in *Jackson v. Benson*, 578 N.W.2d 602 (Wisc. 1998), cert. denied sub nom. *Gilbert v. Moore*, 119 S.Ct. 467 (1998))1; Case Comment, "Government Aid to Religious Schools," *Harvard Law Review* 114 (2000), p. 239 (criticizing U.S. Supreme Court's decision in *Mitchell v. Helms*, 120 S.Ct. 2530 (2000)).

33. For example, the editorial board of the *New York Times*. See Editorial, "Breaching the Church-State Wall," *New York Times*, June 12, 1998 (criticizing Wisconsin Supreme Court's decision in *Jackson v. Benson*, 578 N.W.2d 602 [Wisc. 1998], which held, in part, that Milwaukee voucher program, which includes religiously affiliated schools, does not violate federal nonestablishment norm); Editorial, "Vouchers for Parochial Schools," *New York Times*, November 11, 1998 (criticizing U.S. Supreme Court's denial of certiorari in *Jackson v. Benson*, sub nom. *Gilbert v. Moore*, 119 S.Ct. 467 [1998]).

34. Commenting on the Supreme Court's most recent relevant decision, *Mitchell v. Helms*, 120 S.Ct. 2530 (2000), Akhil Amar has observed that according to Justice Souter and the two other justices (Stevens and Ginsburg), who joined his dissenting opinion in *Mitchell*, government aid may not go directly to religiously affiliated primary and secondary schools "even if this aid does not single out [such schools] for any preferential treatment." Amar, "Foreword," p. 119.

35. See John T. McGreevy, "Thinking on One's Own," pp. 97, 122–26; Laycock, "The Underlying Unity of Separation and Neutrality," pp. 50 ff. See also *Mitchell v. Helms*, 120 S.Ct. 2530, 2551–52 (2000) (plurality opinion). Laycock has emphasized that he is not a Catholic or even a religious believer. See Douglas Laycock, "Religious Liberty as Liberty," *Journal of Contemporary Legal Issues* 7 (1996), pp. 313, 352 ff.

36. Laycock, "The Underlying Unity of Separation and Neutrality," p. 58. (The tract Justice Douglas cited: Loraine Boettner, *Roman Catholicism* (Presbyterian and Reformed Publishing, 1962].) For a fuller account, see Brief of the Becket Fund for Religious Liberty as Amicus Curiae in Support of Petitioners, *Mitchell v. Helms*, 120 S.Ct. 2530 (2000).

37. Cf. Eugene Volokh, "Equal Treatment Is Not Establishment," *Notre Dame Journal of Law*, Ethics, and Public Policy 13 (1999), pp. 341:

Casting the matter in terms of discrimination frames the issue in a stark light, but such a characterization is accurate: Discrimination is indeed what it's all about. Fair-minded people may argue that the Constitution does require such discrimination; not all discrimination is bad. But there should be no denying that a constitutional rule excluding religious schools from generally available benefits rests on the theory that discrimination is constitutionally mandated.

38. See 120 S.Ct. 2530, 2572 (2000) (Souter, J., dissenting, joined by Stevens and Ginsburg, JJ.).

39. Amar, "Foreword," p. 119.

40. Amar, "Foreword," p. 119.

41. Justice O'Connor has noted that "the Religion Clauses prohibit the government from favoring religion, but they provide no warrant for discriminating against religion." *Board of Education of Kiryas Joel Village School District v. Grumet,* 512 U.S. 687, 717 (O'Connor, J., concurring in part and concurring in judgment).

42. Esbeck, "A Constitutional Case for Government Cooperation," p. 18.

43. Michael W. McConnell, "Political and Religious Disestablishment," *Brigham Young University Law Review* (1986), pp. 405, 413. Cf. *McDaniel v. Paty,* 435 U.S. 618, 640–41 (1978) (Brennan, J., concurring in judgment):

> That public debate of religious ideas, like any other, may arouse emotion, may incite, may foment religious divisiveness and strife does not rob it of constitutional protection. . . . The mere fact that a purpose of the Establishment Clause is to reduce or eliminate religious divisiveness or strife, does not place religious discussion, association, or political participation in a status less preferred than rights of discussion, association and political participation generally. . . . The State's goal of preventing sectarian bickering and strife may not be accomplished by regulating religious speech and political association. . . . Government may not as a goal promote "safe thinking" with respect to religion. . . . The Establishment Clause, properly understood, . . . may not be used as a sword to justify repression of religion or its adherents from any aspect of public life.

44. Cf. Esbeck, "A Constitutional Case for Government Cooperation," p. 18. "If the answer is that we are protecting a religiously informed conscientious right not to have one's taxes go toward the support of religion, the Supreme Court has already rejected such a claim [citing *Tilton v. Richardson,* 403 U.S. 672, 689 (1971)]."

45. Stephen G. Gilles, "Why Parents Should Choose," in Peterson and Hassel, eds., *Learning From School Choice,* pp. 395, 404.

46. Gilles, "Why Parents Should Choose."

47. See Kathleen M. Sullivan, "Religion and Liberal Democracy," *University of Chicago Law Review* 59 (1992), pp. 195, 208–14; Brief of Baptist Joint Committee on Public Affairs, National Council of Churches of Christ in the USA, American Jewish Congress, Union of American Hebrew Congregations, Hadassah, the Women's Zionist Organization of America, Inc., People for the American Way, and National Coalition for Public Education and Religious Lib-

erty as Amicus Curiae in Support of Respondents, *Rosenberger v. Rectors and Visitors of University of Virginia*, 515 U.S. 819 (1995).

In the words of Kathleen Sullivan, "the establishment clause necessarily requires that government 'disfavor' religion in relation to secular programs" because "government [may not] make us pay taxes to be used for religious indoctrination in faiths we may not share." Or, as the ACLU argued, the Wisconsin Supreme Court's upholding an evenhanded school choice program should be condemned because under it "Wisconsin taxpayers will be coerced into supporting religions, including sects and cults, with which they may not agree." Volokh, "Equal Treatment Is Not Establishment," p. 342.

48. *Rosenberger v. Rectors and Visitors of University of Virginia*, 515 U.S. 819, 856–57, 863 (Thomas, J., concurring). The majority opinion made the same point (840) (op'n of Court). See also Volokh, "Equal Treatment Is Not Establishment," p. 351; Steffen N. Johnson, "A Civil Libertarian Case for the Constitutionality of School Choice," *George Mason University Civil Rights Law Journal* 10 (1999/2000), pp. 1, 5–10. Akhil Amar recently rehearsed Justice Thomas's explanation: "In past church-state opinions, the Mitchell dissenters have tried to wrap themselves in the mantle of James Madison. But the kind of governmental aid to religion that Madison and his allies opposed was aid to religion as such, through laws that explicitly singled out some religious sects or institutions or practices ('Protestants' or 'Christians' or 'churches' or 'prayer,' for example)." Amar, "Foreword," p. 120.

49. For a discussion of this, see Joseph P. Viteritti, "School Choice and State Constitutional Law," in Peterson and Hassel, *Learning from School Choice*, p. 409. In *Jackson v. Benson*, the Wisconsin Supreme Court tamed such a state constitutional provision. See *Jackson v. Benson*, 578 N.W.2d 602 (Wisc. 1998), cert. denied sub nom. *Gilbert v. Moore*, 119 S.Ct. 467 (1998).

50. This, I think, is the deep meaning of certain "state action" cases. See, e.g., *Shelly v. Kramer*, 334 U.S. 1 (1948); *Burton v. Wilmington Parking Authority*, 365 U.S. 715 (1961).

51. On the idea of human rights, see Michael J. Perry, *The Idea of Human Rights: Four Inquiries*.

52. Thus, I disagree with Laura Underkuffler that "if we publicly fund parochial schools, Quaker schools, Jewish schools, and other mainstream institutions—actions which most citizens would, in all likelihood, find quite benign—then we must also fund the private religious schools that preach religious hatred, racial bigotry, the oppression of women, and other views." Laura S. Underkuffler, "The Price of Vouchers for Religious Freedom," *Detroit Mercy Law Review* 78 (2001), pp. 463, 475–76.

53. See Michael W. McConnell, "Governments, Families, and Power: A Defense of Educational Choice," *Connecticut Law Review* 31 (1999), pp. 847, 855, 858:

> The government may fund only government schools, or it may extend its funding neutrally, but it may not discriminate between students on the basis of the religious viewpoint or character of the schools. . . . If a legislature passed a bill forbidding

students to use their college grants at any institution where Marxism is espoused, it would be struck down in an instant. There is no more justification for forbidding students to use their educational grants at institutions where Christianity or Judaism is espoused.

See also Volokh, "Equal Treatment Is Not Establishment," pp. 365–67; Johnson, "A Civil Libertarian Case," pp. 31–36; Allan E. Parker, Jr., and R. Clayton Trotter, "Hostility or Neutrality? Faith-Based Schools and Tax-Funded Tuition: A GI Bill for Kids," *George Mason University Civil Rights Law Journal* 10 (1999/ 2000), pp. 83, 101–5. Cf. *Rosenberger v. Rector and Visitors of the University of Virginia*, 515 U.S. 819, 845 (1995): "The neutrality commanded of the State by the separate Clauses of the First Amendment was compromised by the University's action [denying financial support to an evangelical student organization]."

54. For several possible constitutional arguments, see Volokh, "Equal Treatment Is Not Establishment," pp. 365–73; Parker and Trotter, "Hostility or Neutrality?" pp. 83, 101–5.

55. *See Employment Division, Department of Human Resources of Oregon v. Smith*, 494 U.S. 872 (1990); *Church of the Lukumi Babalu Aye, Inc. v. City of Hialeah*, 508 U.S. 520 (1993).

56. For my understanding of (the Court's understanding of) the free-exercise norm, see Perry, "Freedom of Religion in the United States," pp. 297–302. I summarize as follows: What does it mean to say that government may not discriminate against religion—or, equivalently, that the free-exercise norm is an antidiscrimination norm? The answer is twofold. Government may not oppose one or another kind of conduct either because, or in part because, the conduct is, for some (*a*) a religious practice or (*b*) animated by a religious belief or beliefs thought to be false or otherwise objectionable, or because, or in part because, of hostility or indifference to the religious group (or groups) for whom the conduct is a religious practice—because of a failure to include the group within the circle of religious groups that government normally treats with active respect and concern (p. 302). In 1947, when it first applied the nonestablishment norm to the states, the Supreme Court wrote:

> [The First] Amendment requires the state to be neutral in its relationship with groups of religious believers and non-believers; it does not require the state to be their adversary. State power is no more to be used to handicap religions than it is to favor them. . . . [The state] cannot exclude individual Catholics, Lutherans, Mohammedans, Baptists, Jews, Methodists, Non-believers, Presbyterians, or the members of any other faith, because of their faith, or lack of it, from receiving the benefits of public welfare legislation. (*Everson v. Board of Education*, 330 U.S. 1, 16, 18 [1947], passages rearranged)

Given that the free-exercise norm is a religion-specific antidiscrimination norm, it is unnecessary to rely, in this context, on the equal-protection clause, which is a more general antidiscrimination norm. See Perry, "Modern Equal Protection."

57. See, e.g., Viteritti, "School Choice and State Constitutional Law," pp. 419–21. See also Johnson, "A Civil Libertarian Case," pp. 10–11.

58. In a recent decision by the Supreme Court of Maine, the court's ruling that Maine did not act unconstitutionally in discriminating against religiously affiliated schools was based on an inaccurate understanding of what the nonestablishment norm forbids. See *Bagley v. Raymond School Department*, 728 A.2d 127 (Maine 1999), *cert. denied*, 120 S.Ct. 364 (1999). (Accord, *Strout v. Albanese*, 178 F.3d 57 [1st Cir. 1999], *cert. denied*, 120 S.Ct. 329 [1999].) In the same year, the Supreme Court of Vermont made the same mistake. See *Chittenden Town School District v. Vermont Department of Education*, 738 A.2d 539 (Vermont 1999), cert. denied, 120 S.Ct. 626 (1999). Cf. *KDM ex rel. WJM v. Reedsport School District*, 196 F.3d 1046 (9th Cir. 1999), *cert. denied*, 69 USLW 3363 (November 27, 2000) (although challenged regulation "treats [students in religiously affiliated schools] differently by denying them state services on school grounds," no freeexercise violation existed because plaintiff did not prove any substantial "burden" on his religious conduct). For a critical comment on *KDM ex rel. WJM v. Reedsport School District*, see Recent Cases, "Constitutional Law—Free Exercise Clause—Ninth Circuit Upholds Oregon Regulation Limiting Special Education Services to Religiously Neutral Settings," *Harvard Law Review* 114 (2001), p. 954. "The Ninth Circuit's decision insulates a wide range of official state action targeting religion from meaningful judicial review, thereby weakening the guarantee of religious liberty at the heart of the Free Exercise Clause" (p. 954).

59. See Viteritti, "School Choice and State Constitutional Law," pp. 419–21. See also Johnson, "A Civil Libertarian Case," pp. 10–11.

60. See *Church of the Lukumi Babalu Aye, Inc. v. City of Hialeah*, 508 U.S. 520 (1993).

61. See Michael W. McConnell, "Governments, Families, and Power: A Defense of Educational Choice," *Connecticut Law Review* 31 (1999), pp. 847, 855, 858.

62. See Steven D. Smith, "Free Exercise Doctrine and the Discourse of Disrespect," *University of Colorado Law Review* 65 (1994), p. 519.

63. Joseph P. Viteritti, "A Truly Living Constitution: Why Educational Opportunity Trumps Strict Separation on the Voucher Question," *New York University Annual Survey of American Law* 57 (2000), pp. 89, 112. See also no. 127 (referring to Australia, Belgium, Canada, Denmark, England, France, Germany, Holland, Iceland, Israel, Scotland, Spain, Sweden, and New Zealand). "For years Catholics have pointed out to American lawmakers that Britain, France, Canada, Australia and other countries support church-related schools." Robert Drinan, S.J., "Mr. Bush Backs the Gospel on the Streets," *Tablet* (London), February 10, 2001, pp. 176, 177.

Chapter Twelve
Charting a Constitutional Course between Private Values and Public Commitments: The Case of School Vouchers

1. 268 U.S. 510 (1925). For a discussion of the background of the *Pierce* decision, *see* Barbara Bennett Woodhouse, "Who Owns the Child? *Meyer* and *Pierce* and the Child as Property," *William and Mary Law Review* 33 (1992), pp. 995–1122.

2. The Fourteenth Amendment to the U.S. Constitution states in part that "no ... state shall deprive any person of life, liberty, or property, without due process of law."

3. "Can the Supreme Court Guarantee Toleration?" *New Republic*, June 17, 1925, pp. 85–87.

4. David B. Tyack, "The Perils of Pluralism: The Background of the *Pierce* Case," *American Historical Review* 74 (1968), pp. 74–98, 79.

5. Phi Delta Kappa, *The 33rd Annual Phi Delta Kappa/Gallup Poll of the Public's Attitudes toward the Public Schools* (June 2001) (www.pdkintl.org/kappan).

6. Public Agenda, *On Thin Ice* (New York, 1999).

7. The First Amendment to the U.S. Constitution states in part that "Congress shall make no law respecting an establishment of religion, or prohibiting the free exercise thereof."

8. *Zelman v. Simmons-Harris*, 234 F.3d 945 (6th Cir. 2000), *cert. granted*, 122 S.Ct. 23 (2001).

9. For insightful discussions of the unsuccessful struggle by the Catholic clergy to obtain government aid for their schools in the late 1800s, *see* Diane Ravitch, *The Great School Wars: New York City, 1825–1925* (New York: Basic Books, 1974); Lloyd P. Jorgenson, *The State and the Non-Public School, 1825–1925* (Columbia: University of Missouri Press, 1987).

10. Ira C. Lupu, "The Lingering Death of Separationism," *George Washington Law Review* 62 (1994), pp. 230–79.

11. *Troxel v. Granville*, 120 S.Ct. 2054 (2000) (upholding parent rights to determine grandparent visitation); *Brown v. Hot, Sexy, and Safer Productions, Inc*, 69 F.3d 525 (1st Cir. 1995), *cert. denied*, 516 U.S. 1159 (1996)(rejecting parental objections to a sexually explicit AIDS-awareness assembly program for high school students); *Immediato v. Rye Neck School District*, 73 F.3d 454 (2d Cir. 1996) (rejecting parental objections to a mandatory community-service program as a requirement for high school graduation).

12. *See* Carl E. Esbeck, "A Constitutional Case for Governmental Cooperation with Faith-Based Social Service Providers," *Emory Law Journal* 46 (1997), pp. 1–41, 4; Douglas Laycock, "The Underlying Unity of Separation and Neutrality," *Emory Law Journal* 46 (1997), pp. 43–73, 45; Alan Brownstein, "A Decent Respect for Religious Liberty and Religious Equality: Justice O'Connor's Interpretation of the Religion Clauses of the First Amendment, *McGeorge Law Review* 32 (2001), pp. 837–75, 7.

13. *Board of Education, Island Trees Union Free School District No. 26 v. Pico*, 457 U.S. 853, 864 (1982), quoting *Ambach v. Norwick*, 441 U.S. 68, 76–77 (1979); *Bethel School District v. Fraser*, 478 U.S. 675, 681 (1986); *Edwards v. Aguillard*, 482 U.S. 578, 584 (1987), quoting *Illinois ex. rel. McCollum v. Board of Education*, 333 U.S. 203, 231 (1948).

14. *Fraser*, 478 U.S., p. 681.

15. Thomas Jefferson, "A Bill for the More General Diffusion of Knowledge," in Gordon C. Lee, ed. *Crusade against Ignorance: Thomas Jefferson on Education* (New York: Teachers College Press, 1961), pp. 85–92.

16. Robert M. Taylor, Jr., ed., *The Northwest Ordinance of 1787: A Bicentennial Handbook* (Bloomington: Indiana Historical Society, 1987), p. 81; David Tyack,

Thomas James, and Aaron Benavot, *Law and the Shaping of Public Education, 1785–1954* (Madison: University of Wisconsin Press, 1987), p. 81.

17. Charles Leslie Glenn, Jr., *The Myth of the Common School* (Amherst: University of Massachusetts Press, 1988), p. 151.

18. Lawrence A. Cremin, "Horace Mann's Legacy," in Lawrence A. Cremin, ed., *The Republic and the School: Horace Mann on the Education of Free Men* (New York: Teachers College Press, 1957), p. 19.

19. Ruth Miller Ellison, *Guardians of Tradition: American Schoolbooks of the Nineteenth Century* (Lincoln: University of Nebraska Press, 1964), pp. 338–39.

20. James Clarkson, "General Grant's Des Moines Speech," *Century Magazine* 55 (March 1898), 788, cited in David Tyack and Elizabeth Hansot, *Managers of Virtue: Public School Leadership in America* (New York: Basic Books, 1982), p. 77.

21. Joseph P. Viteritti, *Choosing Equality: School Choice, the Constitution, and Civil Society* (Washington, D.C.: Brookings Institution Press, 1999), p. 154.

22. Robert Michaelsen, *Piety in the Public School* (New York: Macmillan, 1970), pp. 89–90.

23. Susan Douglas Franzosa, "Authoring the Educated Self: Educational Autobiography and Resistance," *Educational Theory* 42 (fall 1992), pp. 395–412, 397–98.

24. G. Mark Yudof, *When Government Speaks* (Berkeley and Los Angeles: University of California Press, 1983), p. 213.

25. Michael W. McConnell, "The Problem of Singling Out Religion," *DePaul Law Review* 50 (2000), pp. 1–47, 28, quoting *West Virginia Board of Education v. Barnett*, 319 U.S. 624, 642 (1943). For a discussion of the history of the common school, see Rosemary C. Salomone, *Visions of Schooling: Conscience, Community, and Common Education* (New Haven: Yale University Press, 2000), pp. 10–34.

26. Rosemary C. Salomone, "Education for Democratic Citizenship," *Education Week*, March 22, 2000, pp. 48, 52.

27. *Everson v. Board of Education*, 330 U.S. 1, 15 (1947) (discussing the fight by Thomas Jefferson and James Madison against the imposition of a designated tax to support ministers' salaries and to build and maintain churches).

28. *Committee for Public Education and Religious Liberty v. Regan*, 444 U.S. 646, 662 (1980). Ira C. Lupu, "Government Messages and Government Money: Santa Fe, Mitchell v. Helms, and the Arc of the Establishment Clause," *William and Mary Law Review* 42 (2001), pp. 771–822, 815.

29. *Lemon v. Kurtzman*, 403 U.S. 602 (1971). In *Lemon*, the Court articulated a three-part test for addressing establishment clause challenges. First, "the statute must have a secular purpose"; second, "its principal or primary effect must be one that neither advances nor inhibits religion"; and third, "the statute must not foster 'an excessive government entanglement with religion," 612–13. In a series of opinions dating from 1984, Justice O'Connor has refined this test and transformed it into a two-part inquiry: "Whether government's purpose is to endorse religion and whether the statute [or action] actually conveys a message of endorsement." *Wallace v. Jaffree*, 472 U.S. 38, 69 (1985) (O'Connor, J., concurring). According to Justice O'Connor, "Endorsement sends a message to non-adherents that they are outsiders, not full members of the political com-

munity, and an accompanying message to adherents that they are insiders, favored members of the political community. Disapproval sends the opposite message." *Lynch v. Donnelly,* 465 U.S. 668, 688 (1984)(O'Connor, J., concurring).

30. *See e.g.,* Steven D. Smith, "Symbols, Perceptions, and Doctrinal Illusions: Establishment Neutrality and the 'No Endorsement' Test," *Michigan Law Review* 86 (1987); pp. 266–332.

31. See *Good News Club v. Milford Central School,* 533 U.S. 98 (2001).

32. *Mueller v. Allen,* 463 U.S. 388, 399 (1983); John Coons and Stephen Sugarman, "Family Choice in Education: A Model State System for Vouchers," *California Law Review* 59 (1971): 321–438. For a further development of the proposal see their *Education by Choice: The Case for Family Control* (Berkeley and Los Angeles: University of California Press, 1978).

33. *Witters v. Washington Department of Services for the Blind,* 474 U.S. 481 (1986); *Zobrest v. Catalina Foothills School District,* 509 U.S. 1 (1993); *Agostini v. Felton,* 521 U.S. 203 (1997).

34. Milton Friedman, "The Role of Government in Education," in Robert A. Solo, ed., *Economics and the Public Interest* (New Brunswick, N.J.: Rutgers University Press, 1955), 123, revised as Milton Friedman, *Capitalism and Freedom* (Chicago: University of Chicago Press, 1962), chap. 6.

35. Steven K. Green, "Private School Vouchers and the Confusion over 'Direct" Aid,'"*George Mason University Civil Rights Law Journal* 10 (winter 1999–Spring 2000), pp. 47–81, 78–79.

36. *Agostini* at 252 (Souter, J. dissenting, joined by Justices Breyer, Ginsburg, and Stevens).

37. Ira C. Lupu, "The Increasingly Anachronistic Case against School Vouchers," *Notre Dame Journal of Law, Ethics, and Public Policy* 13 (1999), pp. 375–96, 379.

38. *Mitchell v. Helms* 530 U.S. 793, 816 (2000) (Thomas, J., plurality, opinion joined by Justices Kennedy, Rehnquist, and Scalia); Ira C. Lupu, "Government Messages and Government and Government Money: Santa Fe, *Mitchell v. Helms,* and the Arc of the Establishment Clause," *William and Mary Law Review* 42 (2001), pp. 771–822, 815.

39. *Mitchell,* 819 n. 8 (Thomas, J., plurality opinion).

40. *Mitchell,* 842 (O'Connor, J., concurring, joined by Justice Breyer), quoting *Witters* at 493 (O'Connor, J., concurring in part and concurring in the judgment).

41. Lupu, "The Increasingly Anachronistic Case against School Vouchers," p. 378 n. 14.

42. Jesse H. Choper, *Securing Religious Liberty* (Chicago: University of Chicago Press, 1995), 181.

43. *See* Kathleen M. Sullivan, "Parades, Public Squares, and Voucher Payments: Problems of Government Neutrality," *Connecticut Law Review* 28 (1996), pp. 243–60, 252–53, discussing *Capitol Square Review and Advisory Board v. Pinette,* 515 U.S. 753 (1995).

44. *Good News Club v. Milford Central School,* 121 S.Ct. 2093, 2106 (2001), quoting *Capitol Square Review and Advisory Board v. Pinette,* at 779–80 (O'Connor, J., concurring in part).

45. *Good News Club,* at 2111 (Breyer, J., concurring in part), at 2119 (Souter, J., dissenting).

46. See William P. Marshall, "'We Know It When We See It,'": The Supreme Court Establishment," *Southern California Law Review* 59 (1986), pp. 495–550.

47. *Witters,* 474 U.S. 481 (1986).

48. David S. Petron, "Finding Direction in Indirection: The Direct/Indirect Aid Distinction in Establishment Clause Jurisprudence," *Notre Dame Law School* 75 (2000); pp. 1233–68, 1261–62.

49. For a discussion of the way in which law creates roles and relations and provides the materials and methods of a discourse, *see* James Boyd White, *When Words Lose Their Meaning* (Chicago: University of Chicago Press, 1984), p. 266.

50. *Church v. Bullock,* 109 S.W. 115, 118 (Texas 1908); *Billiard v. Board of Education,* 76 P. 422, 423 (Kansas 1904); *Hackett v. Brooksville Graded School District,* 87 S.W. 792, 793 (Kentucky 1905); *State v. Scheve,* 93 N.W. 169, 172 (Nebraska 1903).

51. *Tash v. Ludden,* 129 N.W. 417, 421 (Nebraska 1911).

52. For an interesting discussion, *see* Richard A. Baer, Jr., "The Supreme Court's Discretionary Use of the Term 'Sectarian,'" *Journal of Law and Politics* 6 (1990), pp. 449–68.

53. *Hunt v. McNair,* 413 U.S. 734, 743 (1973).

54. *Roemer v. Board of Public Works,* 426 U.S. 736, 755–59 (1976); *School District of the City of Grand Rapids v. Ball,* 473 U.S. 373, 384 n. 6 (1985); See Stephen V. Monsma, "The 'Pervasively Sectarian' Standard in Theory and Practice," *Notre Dame Journal of Law, Ethics, and Public Policy* 13 (1999), pp. 321–40, 322.

55. *Mitchell* at 886 (Souter, J., dissenting), quoting the *Catholic Code of Canon Law* 803, sec. 2, Text and Commentary 568 ("'It is necessary that the formation and education given in a Catholic school be based upon the principles of Catholic doctrine; teachers are to be outstanding for their correct doctrine and integrity of life' and that individual teachers will teach religiously.")

56. Donald L. Beschle, "The Conservative as Liberal: The Religion Clauses, Liberal Neutrality, and the Approach of Justice O'Connor," *Notre Dame Law Review* 62 (1987), pp. 151–91,184.

57. *Bowen v. Kendrick,* 487 U.S. 589, 621 (1988) (rejecting a facial challenge to a federal program that provided grants to religious and other institutions for counseling on teenage sexuality).

58. Caryle Murphy, "At Public Schools, Religion Thrives," *Washington Post,* May 7, 1998; Letter from Richard W. Riley, U.S. Secretary of Education, to Superintendents of Schools (August 10, 1995); *A Teacher's Guide to Religion in the Public Schools,* (Nashville, Tenn.: First Amendment Center, 1999); "Text of President Clinton's Memorandum on Religion in Schools," *New York Times,* July 13, 1995; the Equal Access Act of 1984, 20 U.S.C. §§4071–74 (1997) (providing that when a public secondary school receives federal funds, which essentially all public schools do, and permits student-led groups to meet on school grounds during noninstructional time, school officials cannot deny access to other students on the basis of religious, political, or other content of their speech); *Board of Education v. Mergens,* 496 U.S. 226 (1990); *Religion in the Public Schools: Guidelines for a Growing and Changing Phenomenon,* 2nd ed. (New York: Anti-Defama-

tion League, 1996); *Religion in the Public Schools: A Joint Statement of Current Law* (New York: American Jewish Congress, April 1995).

59. Neal Devins, "Social Meaning and School Vouchers," *William and Mary Law Review* 42 (2001), pp. 919–62, 945.

60. *Board of Education v. Mergens,* 496 U.S. 226 (1990); *Santa Fe Independent School District v. Doe,* 530 U.S. 290 (2000)(striking down prayer at public high school football games).

61. For a discussion of the concept of the parent as causative agent in relation to private choice, *see* Laura Underkuffler, "Vouchers and Beyond: The Individual as Causative Agent in Establishment Clause Jurisprudence," *Indiana Law Journal* 75 (2000), pp. 167–91.

62. *Lee v. Weisman,* 505 U.S. 577 (1992) (invalidating recitation of prayer at middle-school graduation ceremony); *Santa Fe Independent School District v. Doe,* 530 U.S. 290 (2000).

63. *Good News Club,* at 2104.

64. Abner S. Greene, "Why Vouchers Are Unconstitutional, and Why They're Not," *Notre Dame Journal of Legal Ethics and Public Policy* 13 (1999): 397–408, 400–401.

65. *Mitchell,* at 901 (Souter, J., dissenting).

66. *Mitchell,* at 857–59, (O'Connor, J., concurring, citing *Grand Rapids v. Ball,* 473 U.S. 373 [1985]).

67. Underkuffler, "Vouchers and Beyond," 189; Greene, "Why Vouchers Are Constitutional, and Why They're Not," 402; Sullivan, "Parades, Public Squares, and Voucher Payments," 256.

68. Michael W. McConnell, "Equal Treatment and Religious Discrimination," in Stephen V. Monsma and J. Christopher Soper, eds., *Equal Treatment of Religion in a Pluralistic Society* (Grand Rapids, Mich.: W. B. Eerdmans Publishing Co., 1998), pp. 30–54, 47.

69. *Mitchell* at 902 (Souter, J., dissenting).

70. Diane Gertler and Linda A. Barker, *Statistics of Nonpublic Elementary Schools, 1970–1971* (Washington, D.C.: U.S. Department of Health, Education, and Welfare, 1973), pp. 5–10; Stephen P. Broughman and Lenore A. Colaciello, *Private School Universe Survey, 1997–1998; Statistical Analysis Report* (Washington, D.C.: U.S. Department of Education, National Center for Educational Statistics, August 1999), p. 5, table 1.

71. Broughman and Colaciello, *Private School Universe Study,* p. 7, table 3.

72. Stephen L. Carter, *The Culture of Disbelief* (New York: Basic Books, 1993), p. 24.

73. John H. Garvey, "What's Next after Separationism?" *Emory Law Journal* 46 (1997), pp. 75–83, 80.

74. Andrew M. Greeley and Peter H. Rossi, *The Education of Catholic Americans* (Chicago: Aldine, 1966), pp. 152–54.

75. Anthony S. Bryk, Valerie E. Lee, and Peter B. Holland, *Catholic Schools and the Common Good* (Cambridge: Harvard University Press, 1993), p. 312, II.

76. Thomas D. Snyder, Charlene M. Hoffman, and Claire M. Geddes, *Digest of Education Statistics, 1998* (Washington, D.C.: U.S. Department of Education, Office of Educational Research and Improvement, May 1999), p. 156, table 146.

For a cogent argument as to the reasons behind increased participation, *see* Michael W. McConnell, "The New Establishmentarianism," *Chicago-Kent Law Review* 75 (2000), pp. 453–75, 473.

77. David E. Campbell, "Bowling Together: Private Schools, Serving Public Ends," *Education Next* (fall 2001), pp. 55–61.

78. *Convent of the Sacred Heart Elementary School Bulletin* (San Francisco).

79. *Mitchell* at 887 (Souter, J., dissenting), citing *Lemon v. Kurtzman*, at 616 (emphasis added).

80. Timothy Egan, "The Changing Face of Catholic Education," Education Life Supplement, *New York Times*, August 6, 2000 (noting that priests account for only 1 percent of the 157,000 teachers; nuns, 5.5 percent; and brothers fewer than 1 percent).

81. National Catholic Educational Association, correspondence from Sr. Dale McDonald, PBVM, February 26, 2001.

82. *Mitchell* at 886 (Souter, J. dissenting); see Devins, "Social Meaning and School Vouchers," pp. 940–45.

83. Laurie Goodstein, "Nudging Church-State Line, Bush Invites Religious Groups to Seek Federal Aid," *New York Times*, January 30, 2001; Laurie Goodstein, "Bush's Call to Church Groups to Get Untraditional Replies," *New York Times*, February 13, 2001; Steven Waldman, "Doubts among the Faithful," *New York Times*, March 7, 2001.

84. Jesse H. Choper, "Federal Constitutional Issues," in Stephen D. Sugarman and Frank R. Kemerer, eds., *School Choice and Social Controversy: Politics, Policy, and Law* (Washington, D.C.: Brookings Institution Press, 1999), pp. 235–65; Michael W. McConnell, "Unconstitutional Conditions: Unrecognized Implications for the Establishment Clause," *San Diego Law Review* 26 (1989) 255–75.

Response
Patrick McKinley Brennan

1. Mary Ann Glendon and Raul F. Yanes, "Structural Free Exercise," *Michigan Law Review* 90 (1991), pp. 477–550, 491–92.

2. See, e.g., Jesse Choper, "The Religious Clauses of the First Amendment: Reconciling the Conflict," *University of Pittsburgh Law Review* 41 (1981), pp. 673–701, 680 ("ad hoc judgments incapable of being reconciled"); Michael Stokes Paulsen, "Religion, Equality, and the Constitution: An Equal Protection Approach to Establishment Clause Adjudication," *Notre Dame Law Review* 61 (1986), pp. 311–71, 314 ("The Supreme Court's reading of the religion clauses is completely indefensible—historically, textually, and practically.").

3. John T. Noonan, Jr., *The Lustre of Our Country: The American Experience of Religious Liberty* (Berkeley and Los Angeles: University of California Press, 1998), p. 179.

4. Noonan, *The Lustre of Our Country*, pp. 209–10.

5. 120 S.Ct. 2530 (2000).

6. 268 U.S. 510 (1925).

7. 268 U.S. 510 (1925), 535.

8. Noonan, *The Lustre of Our Country*, pp. 88–89.

9. James Madison, "Memorial and Remonstrance against Religious Assessments," in Saul K. Padover, ed., *The Complete Madison: His Basic Writings* (New York: Harper and Brothers, 1951), pp. 299–300.

10. See *Mitchell v. Helms*, 2582 n. 6 (Souter, J., dissenting) (internal citation omitted). Cf. *Good News Club v. Milford Central School*, 533 U.S. 98 (2001) (Scalia, J., concurring); ("We have previously rejected the attempt to distinguish worship from other religious speech, saying that 'the distinction has [no] intelligible content' " (internal citation omitted).

11. See John Witte, Jr., *Religion and the American Constitutional Experiment: Essential Rights and Liberties* (Boulder, Colo.: Westview Press, 2000), p. 238 (noting the administrative state's tendency to absorb civil society). See generally Charles Glenn, *The Ambiguous Embrace: Government and Faith-Based Schools and Social Agencies* (Princeton: Princeton University Press, 2000).

12. Some of the analytic insufficiencies of "neutrality" are explored in Steven D. Smith, "Symbols, Perceptions, and Doctrinal Illusions: Establishment Neutrality and the 'No Endorsement' Test," *Michigan Law Review* 86 (1987), pp. 266–332.

13. Witte, *Religion and the American Constitutional Experiment*, p. 232.

14. See John H. Garvey, *What Are Freedoms For?* (Cambridge: Harvard University Press, 1996), p. 2 ("The law leaves us free to do x because it is a good thing to do x. This might seem pretty obvious. But it inverts the first principle of liberalism—it makes the good prior to the right.").

15. Witte, *Religion and the American Constitutional Experiment*, p. 232.

16. Bernard Lonergan, "The Human Good as Object: Differentials and Integration," in *Topics in Education*, vol. 10 of *The Collected Works of Bernard Lonergan* (Toronto: University of Toronto Press, 1993), pp. 48, 59.

17. General Assembly of the United Nations, "Declaration of the Rights of the Child" (1959), Principle 7, in *Human Rights: A Compilation of International Instruments* (New York: United Nations, 1994), vol. 1, part 1, p. 173.

18. Michael McConnell, "Governments, Families, and Power," *Connecticut Law Review* 31 (1999), pp. 847–59, 859.

19. John E. Coons, "School Choice as Simple Justice," *First Things* 22 (1992): 208–15, 212.

20. John E. Coons, "Intellectual Liberty and the Schools," *Journal of Law, Ethics, and Public Policy* 1 (1985), p. 511. See also John E. Coons and Stephen D. Sugarman, *Education by Choice* (Berkeley and Los Angeles: University of California Press, 1978).

21. John E. Coons, "The Religious Rights of Children," in John Witte, Jr., and Johan van der Vyver, eds., *Religious Human Rights in Global Perspective: Religious Perspectives* (The Hague: Martinus Nijhoff, 1996), pp. 157, 174.

Index